JORDAN CASTEEL

LEGACY RUSSELL
ASMA NAEEM
KATHERINE BRINSON

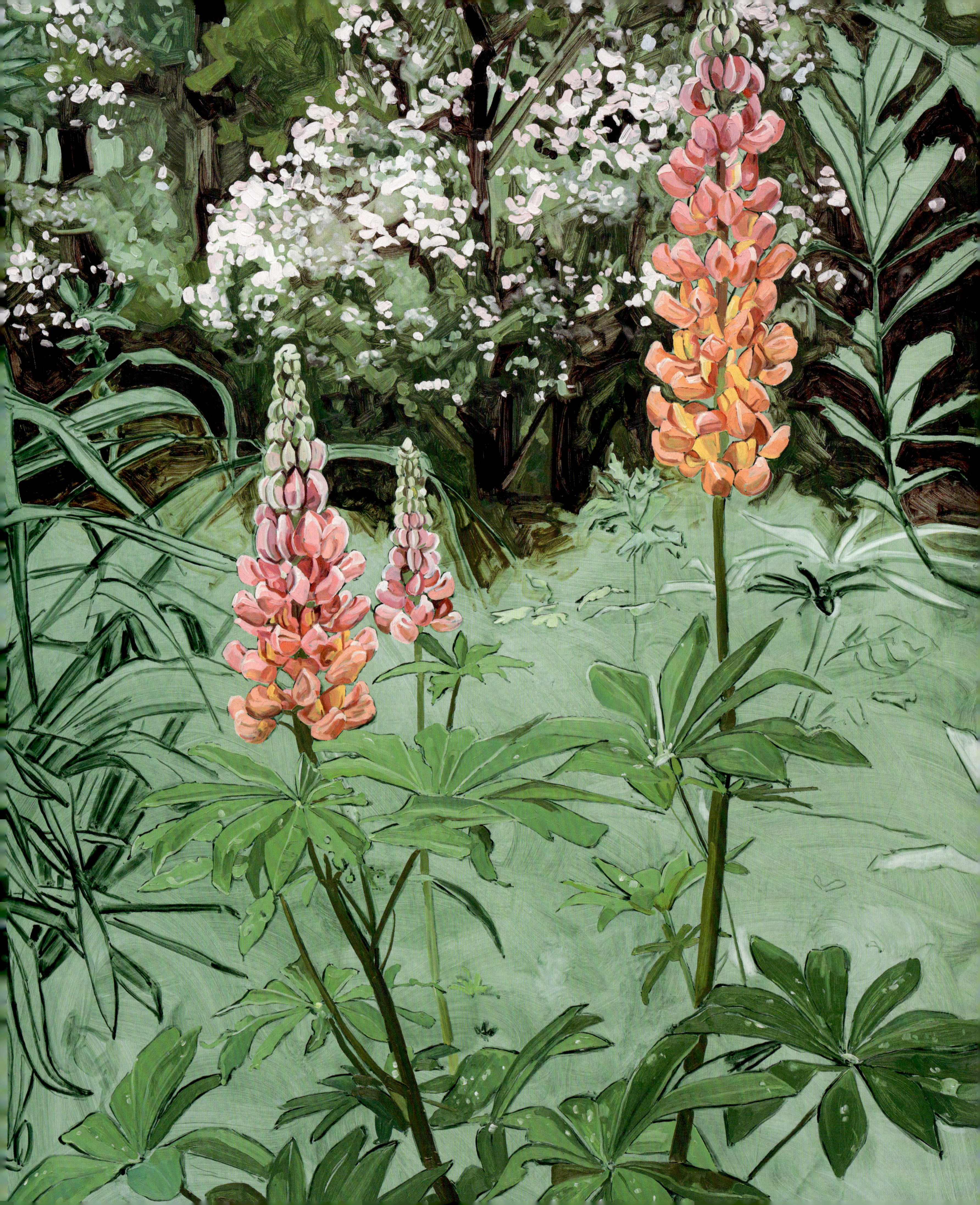

LUPINE, 2024
OIL ON CANVAS
127 X 102 CM

CONTENTS

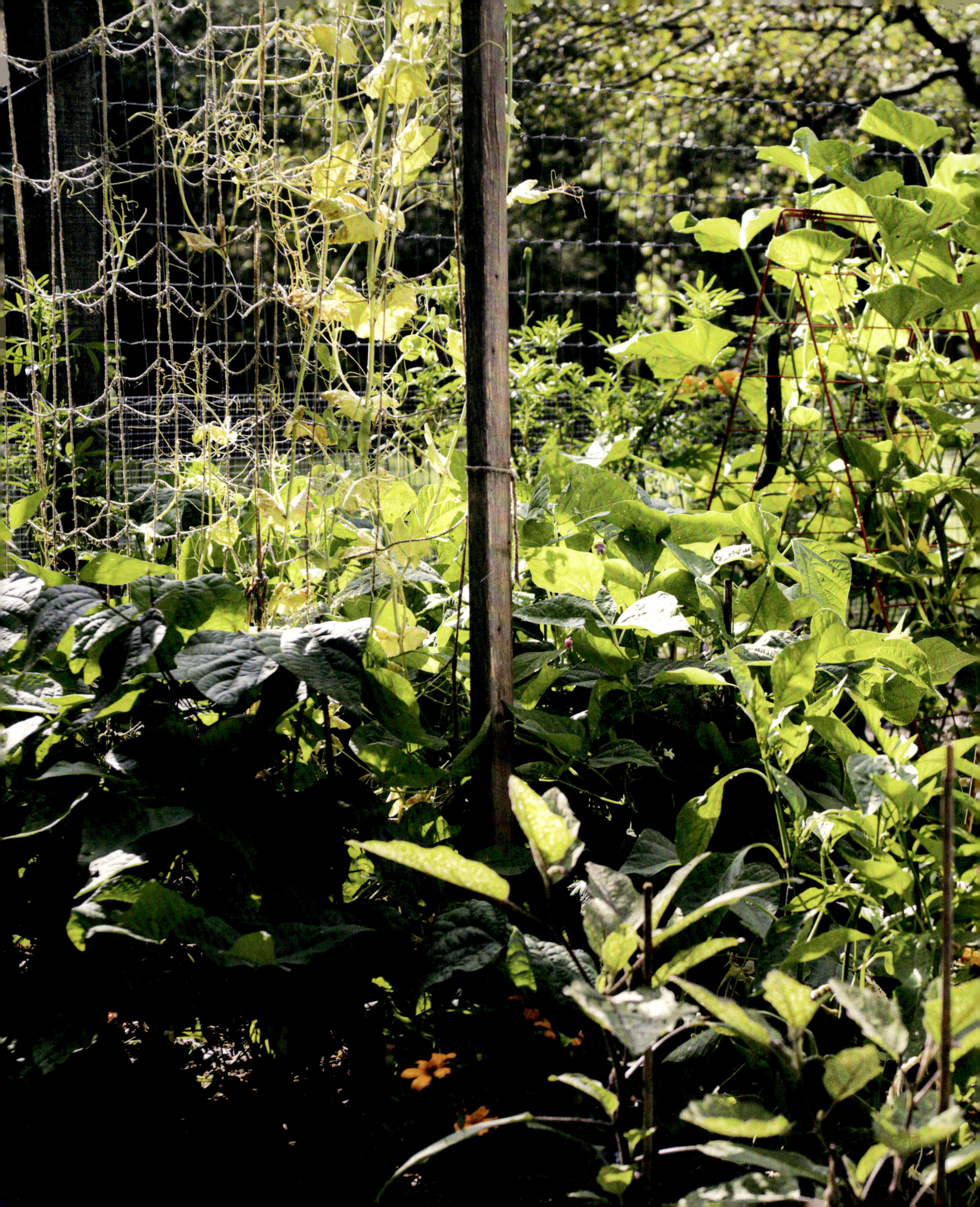

005 INTERVIEW

Legacy Russell in conversation with Jordan Casteel

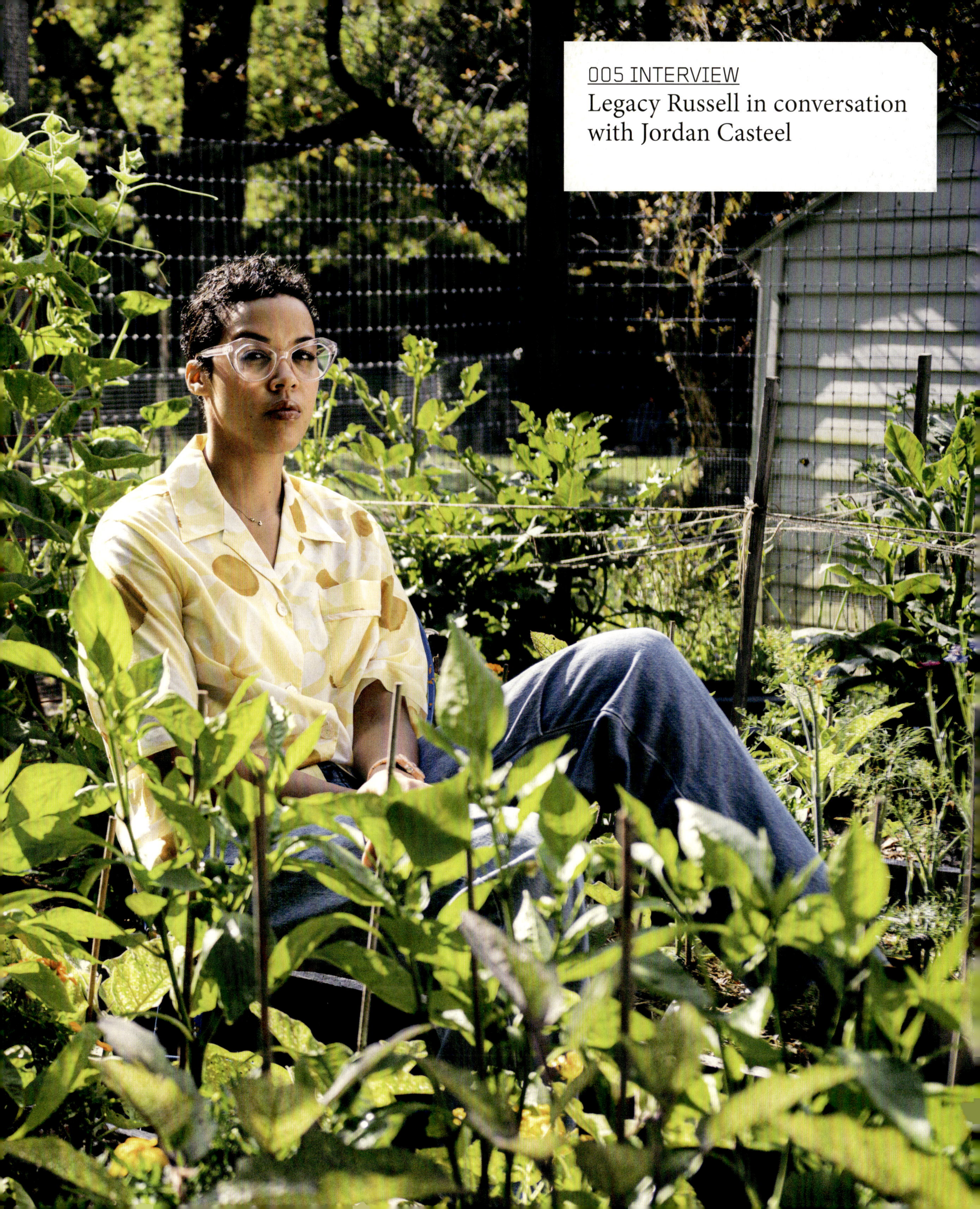

previous pages,
JORDAN CASTEEL, HUDSON
VALLEY, NEW YORK, 2024

LEGACY RUSSELL: *I want to start with your earlier history, in particular your family and your relationship to the arts. Do you have a first memory or an encounter that has been meaningful to you in relation to bringing you into an awareness of art?*

JORDAN CASTEEL: My upbringing was profoundly privileged in the sense that I had examples of Black creativity, thought and visual language very early on – it was everywhere. For example, I didn't know it at the time, but my maternal grandmother [Margaret Buckner Young] was significantly involved in supporting artists, particularly Black artists, in New York. It wasn't until recently that I found out she was the first Black woman board member at the Metropolitan Museum of Art, which explained why I grew up with examples of Black artists all around my home. I always knew she loved art; I just didn't realize the depths of her connection. I think I was enveloped in a sense that Black people were creative beyond measure and could represent themselves in very powerful ways – which is a unique experience.

RUSSELL: *I love this idea of you reflecting on this space of Black creativity, and that you were aware even of just the premise that it's possible for Black people to make art, and that that was something that you were inside of, and that was around you. Do you remember, as you grew in your trajectory as a thinker in the world, before you identified as being an artist, if there were first paintings that you saw that were interesting to you, or maybe piqued your desire for the medium?*

CASTEEL: I think that happened later in life for me. If I try to think of a specific artwork, that's more challenging. It's that feeling of being around art. There was Hale Woodruff, Faith Ringgold … In many ways, Ringgold's *Tar Beach* was the first time that I remember thinking, 'This is playful, fun and colourful'. It's a fantasy story of a Black girl, and what she imagines from a rooftop. That book played a significant role for me in recognizing that storytelling is a medium that I could use and see myself in. I didn't come to see and engage with painting as a medium until I was physically working with the material. So there wasn't a specific painting that I remember seeing, but rather it was about making something and feeling something within me that pushed me into understanding and becoming curious about how other people were making. I had to use my own hands and play for a while.

RUSSELL: *You've said in prior interviews or discussions that you took a trip to Italy at one point, and that that was immensely meaningful as a turning point. What was that experience like? You were in a different country, and you were learning actively through a wide breadth of art histories and thinking about that in relation to the representation of Blackness, or perhaps the absence of that. Can you talk about what that felt like at that point in time, given this immense space of art history in an Italian setting and that you, as an American Black person, were stepping into your own understanding of your identity as an artist and maker?*

CASTEEL: I found myself in Italy through a process of elimination. I was in my junior year at Agnes Scott College and I wanted to study abroad in Senegal. I had this deep desire to experience Africa for the first time, but my recent Lupus diagnosis dictated that if I was going to travel, I should consider a European country close to the extended family I have in Florence. I thought, 'Okay, well, if this is the case, I wonder if I could apply to the Lamar Dodd School of Art Study Abroad Program in Cortona, Italy?' I submitted a small portfolio with works I'd made in the few art classes I'd taken so far and was accepted, but I had no idea what I was getting into. My major at Agnes Scott up until that point

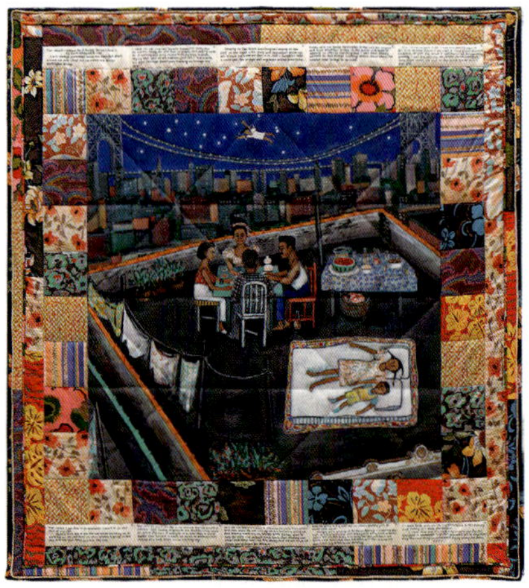

FAITH RINGGOLD
WOMAN ON A BRIDGE #1 OF 5: TAR BEACH, 1988
ACRYLIC ON CANVAS, PRINTED FABRIC, INK AND THREAD
190 X 174 CM

COTTAGE, 2013
OIL ON CANVAS
38 X 38 CM

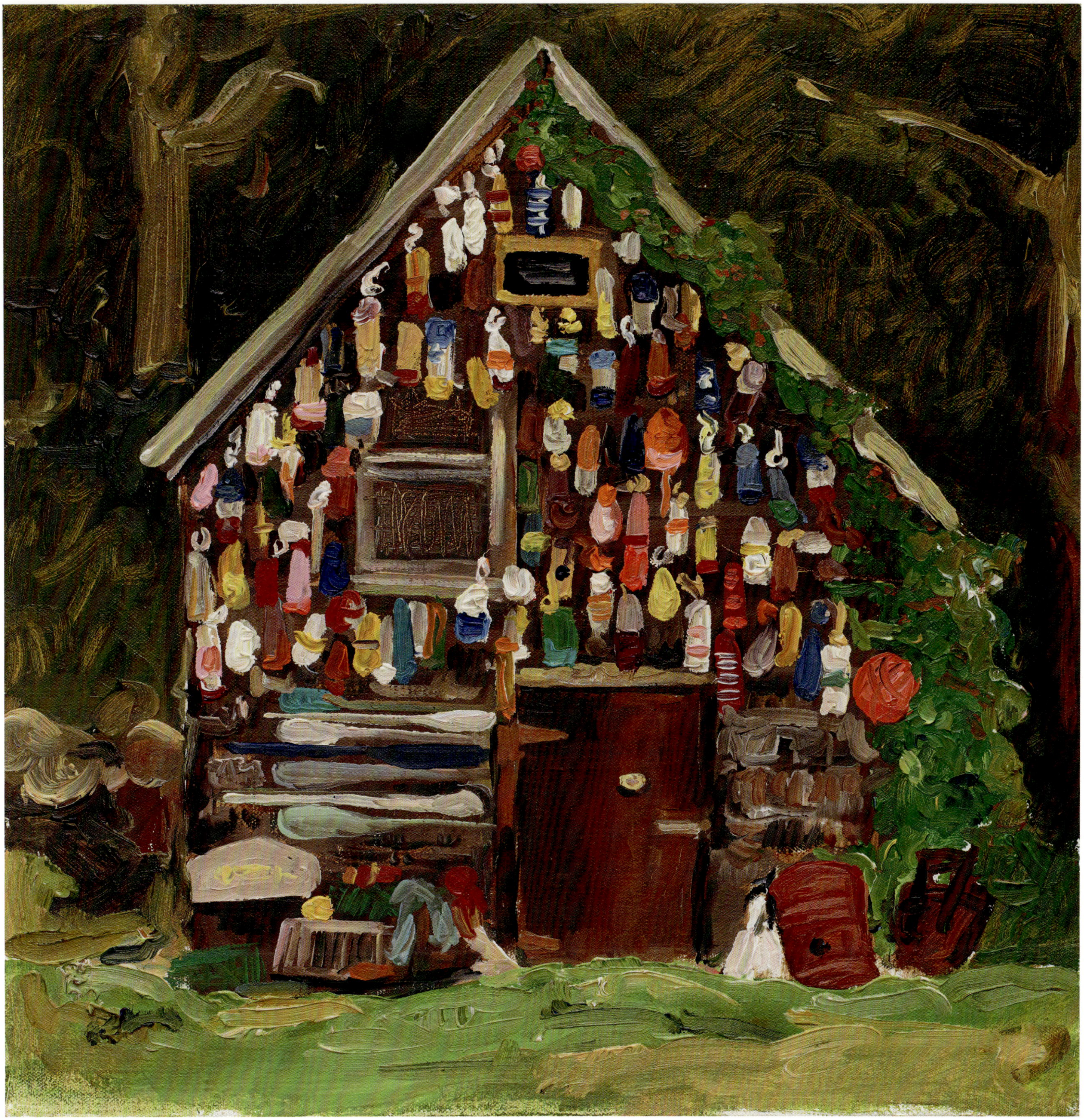

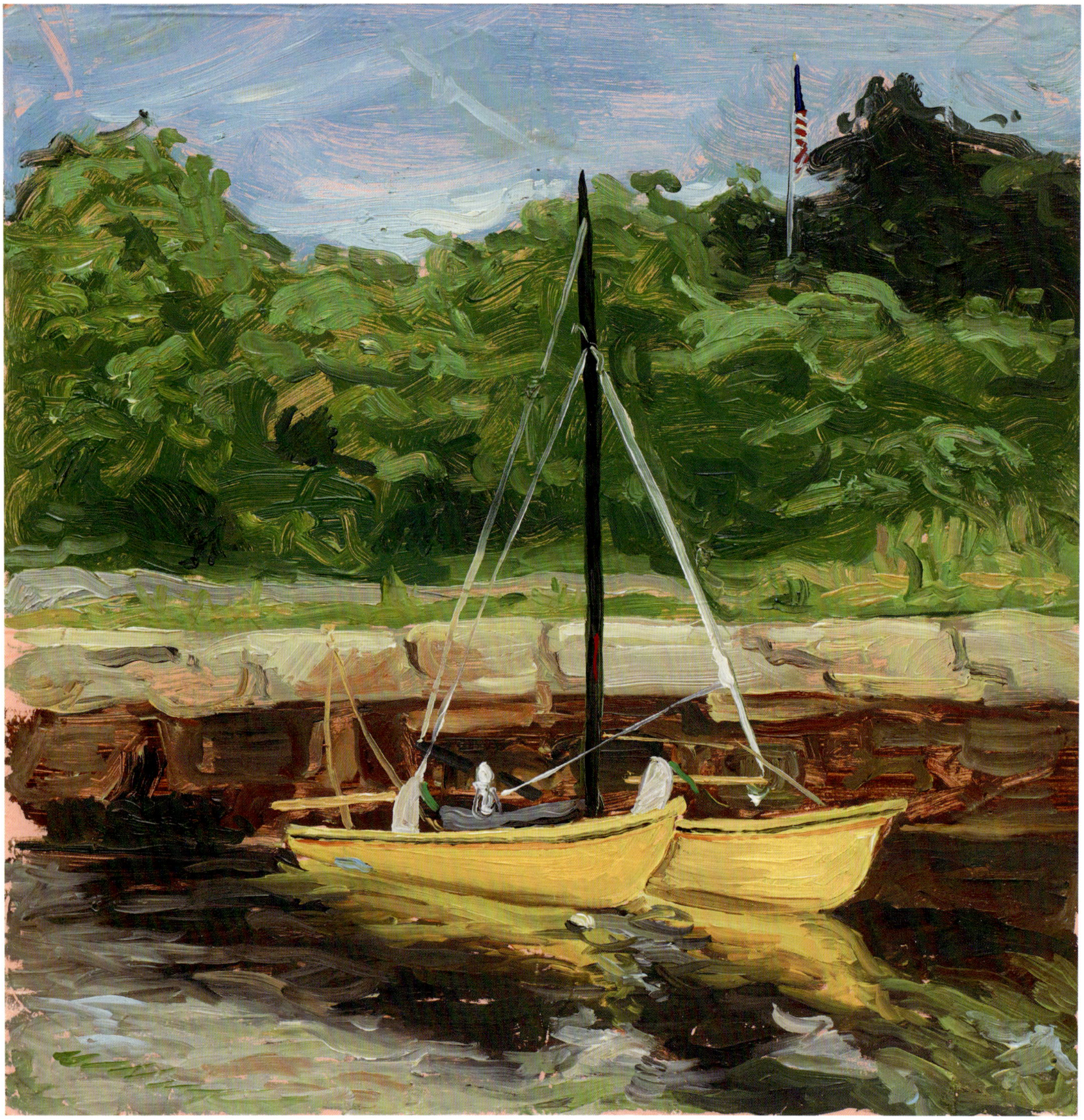

YELLOW BOAT, 2013
OIL ON CANVAS
31 X 31 CM

was Sociology and Anthropology. I had an oil painting class for the first time while in Italy. I also took a bookmaking class and an art history class. It was the first time that I felt like I was enveloped in a studio practice – I didn't know until then what that could feel like. There's no question I felt aware that I was a Black American woman in a foreign, mostly white context. I was one of two in the programme that semester – and I felt a sort of isolation. But I'd never been that far from home on my own, which inspired a certain curiosity about the world around me. It was a solitude-driven experience where I found comfort by building relationships with people who functioned a bit on the periphery of the programme. For example, Gino the groundskeeper and I became friends. He'd yell out of his small car if he saw me, 'Ciao, Jordan! Cappuccino?' and I'd hop in the car with him to go to town. We became quite close, actually. I found that I got closer with him than I did with my classmates. I did a portrait of him, and I remember just asking, 'Can I paint you?' I just had fun – it felt free. I keep a photo next to my desk that a classmate took of me and him during that experience. I deeply cherish that memory and am grateful

SEA 1, 2013
OIL ON CANVAS
28 X 36 CM

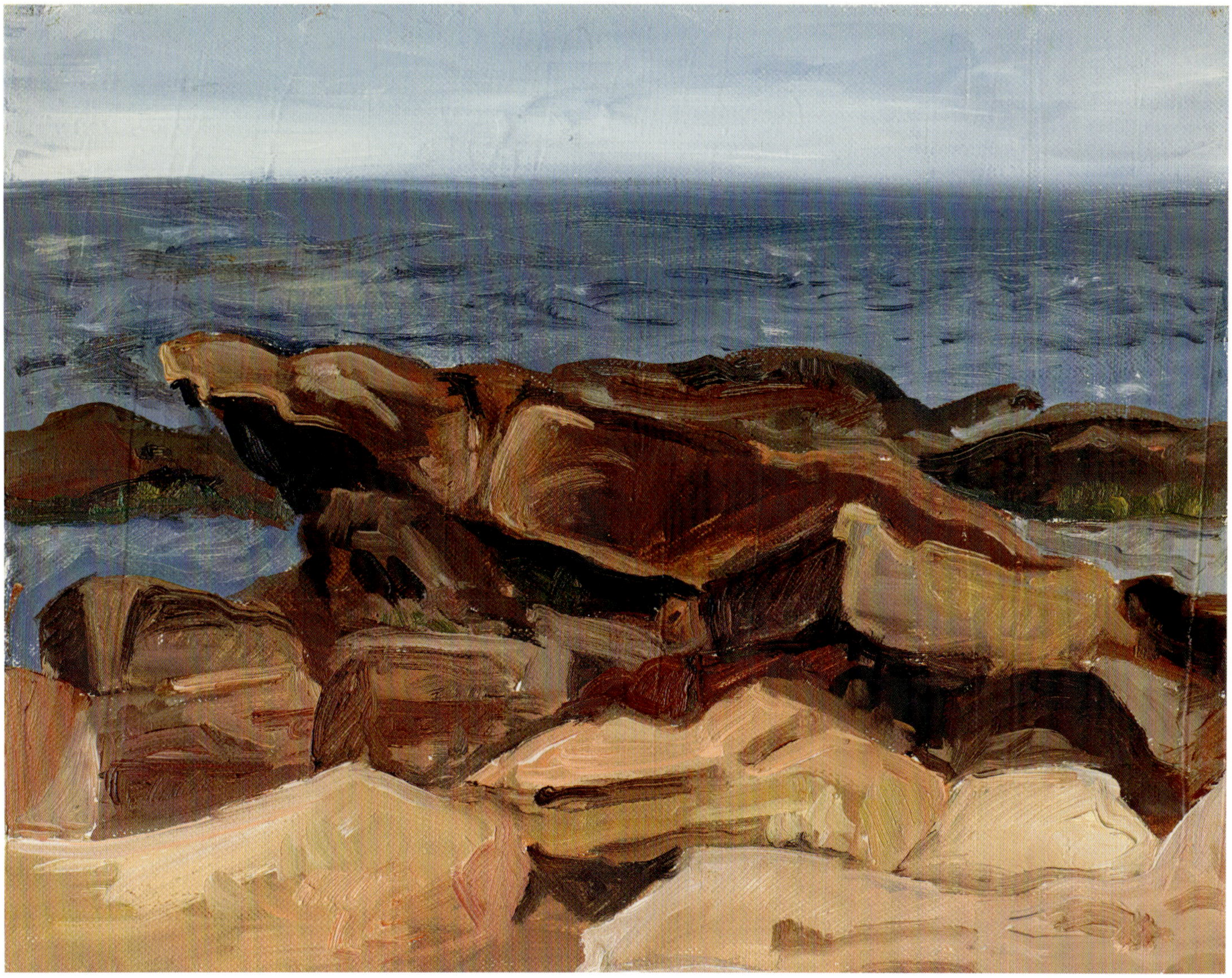

to have a document of it. I don't think I'd experienced freedom like that before. That's where being abroad in a studio-art-centred programme became the most transformative. And because I wanted to hold onto, with every ounce of my being, that sense of freedom, when I returned to the US, I brought that experience of painting and observing the people that I've come to love and admire with me.

RUSSELL: *There's so much mythology around this idea of being a painter right?*

CASTEEL: Yes.

RUSSELL: *Art history shows it's a very weighty identity, and of course, often people ask this question: 'When did you realize you were an artist?' But part of what I've found to be really profound in your journey is that there were many becomings. That's really important for folks who are seeking out this idea of what a creative belonging looks like to realize: it was multiple epiphanies across a long duration of time.*

CASTEEL: Yes.

RUSSELL: *But with that in mind, you said you had this experience of really feeling the joy of being in a studio space and able to work through what that meant and how that felt physically and creatively. Were there moments as you returned to the US, when you began to think differently about how to shape your identity as an artist? Was there a moment that was a key departure, where you began to claim that term more prominently and understanding that being an artist was your pathway?*

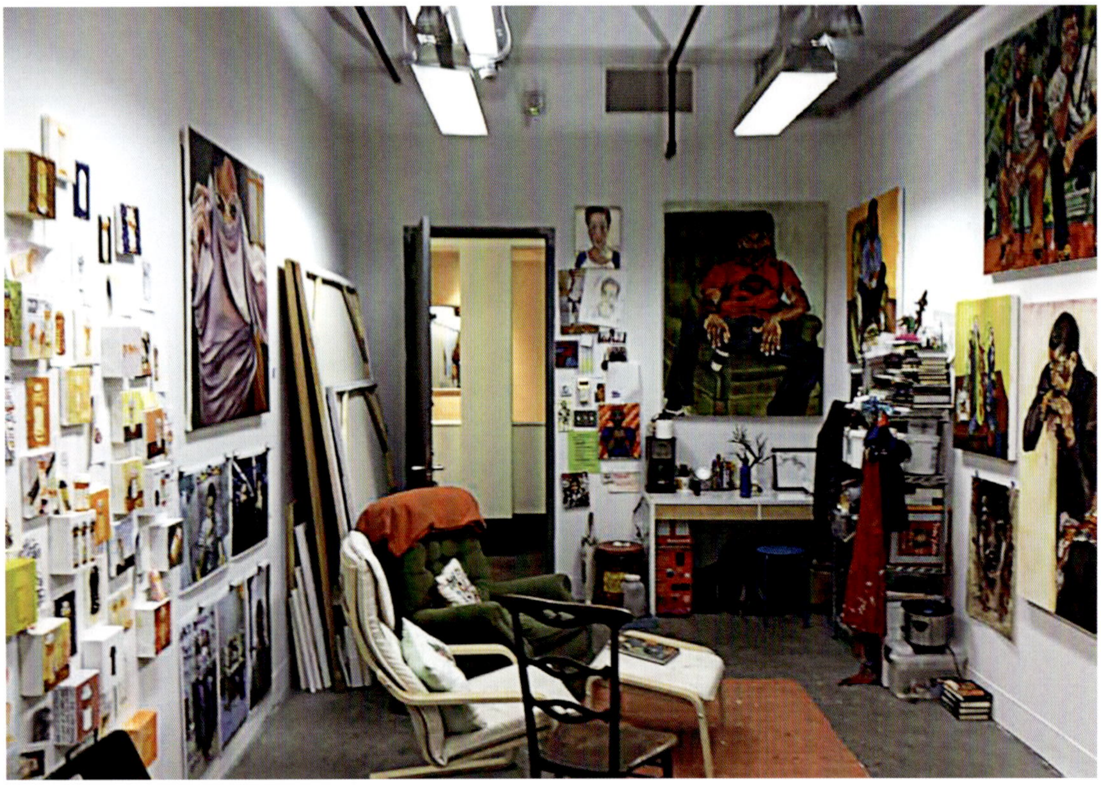

THE ARTIST'S STUDIO AT YALE SCHOOL OF ART, NEW HAVEN, 2013

opposite,
MOM, 2013
OIL ON CANVAS
122 X 92 CM

CASTEEL: I think that I came back inspired. There's no question that I wanted to find a way to continue that sense of confidence and freedom that I felt while solely focused on making things abroad. But I was returning to Agnes Scott's campus, which had a very small studio-art programme that wasn't set up to support oil painting. I had advisors, Anne Beidler and Nell Ruby, professors who just wanted to find a way for me to continue to do the thing I was inspired by. They were committed to me and my desire to continue to push the medium of oil painting. I didn't know what it meant, but they really gave me the space to continue to play. They helped me find a space in the building where I could make a body of work for my senior thesis. This encouragement gave me the confidence to switch my major to studio art. I'd been taking art classes, painting, drawing, kind of doing the baseline classes while I was there, but when I came back from Italy, I decided that I wanted to put all of my energy into building a portfolio and being in the studio.

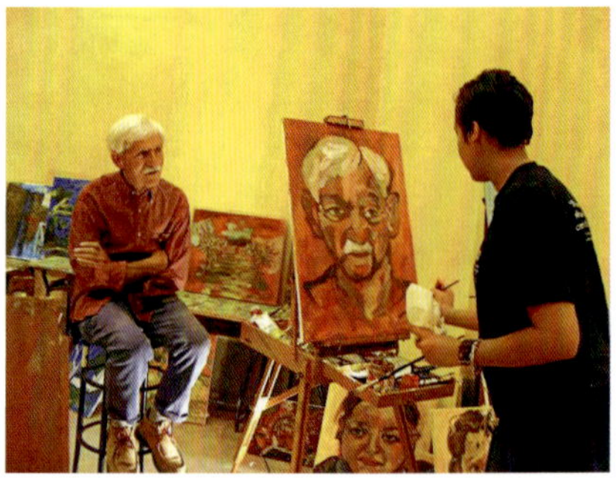

THE ARTIST PAINTING A PORTRAIT OF GINO SCHIPPA, LAMAR DODD SCHOOL OF ART, UNIVERSITY OF GEORGIA, CORTONA, ITALY, 2010

One of the first paintings I made was of Betty Hart, who worked as the baker in the cafeteria and was literally the first person I met when I got on campus. I remember the day I met her so clearly. My mother marched me into the cafeteria and said, 'You met the president today, you've met the deans, but the people who are really gonna become your family on this campus are the people who are the real backbone of this campus. They're going to be your family.' And so she took me into the cafeteria, and at the time I was like, 'Oh, no, mom, I'm an adult, let me be', but she was totally right. I love to bake and she walked me over to Betty and said, 'Will you look after my daughter? She also loves to bake, and I want her to know the people who will really have her back while she's here.' And Betty did. Very quickly she began to feed me. Sometimes she'd invite me to her home, or bring me Sunday dinner on campus. She was one of the first people when I returned, having been inspired by painting Gino, who I wanted to paint. I remember trying to do her portrait in acrylic, and it was very unsatisfying. That's when I went to the Professor and asked, 'Can I please find a way to continue to work with oil?', because I was accustomed to working wet on wet. I felt the way that the material was drying with acrylic wasn't going to allow me to achieve instant engagement with Betty while she sat in my studio for the portrait. But I remember when she showed up, I'd never seen her outside of her uniform. She was usually in leisurewear, but she showed up in this white, cloud-like ruffled shirt, and I remember

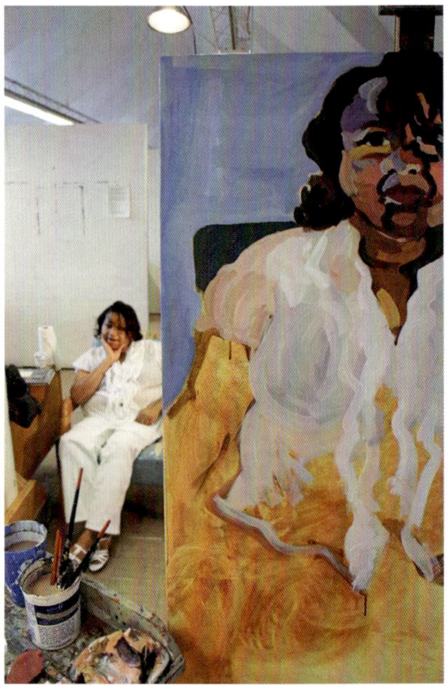

THE ARTIST PAINTING A PORTRAIT OF BETTY HART, AGNES SCOTT COLLEGE, DECATUR, GEORGIA, 2011

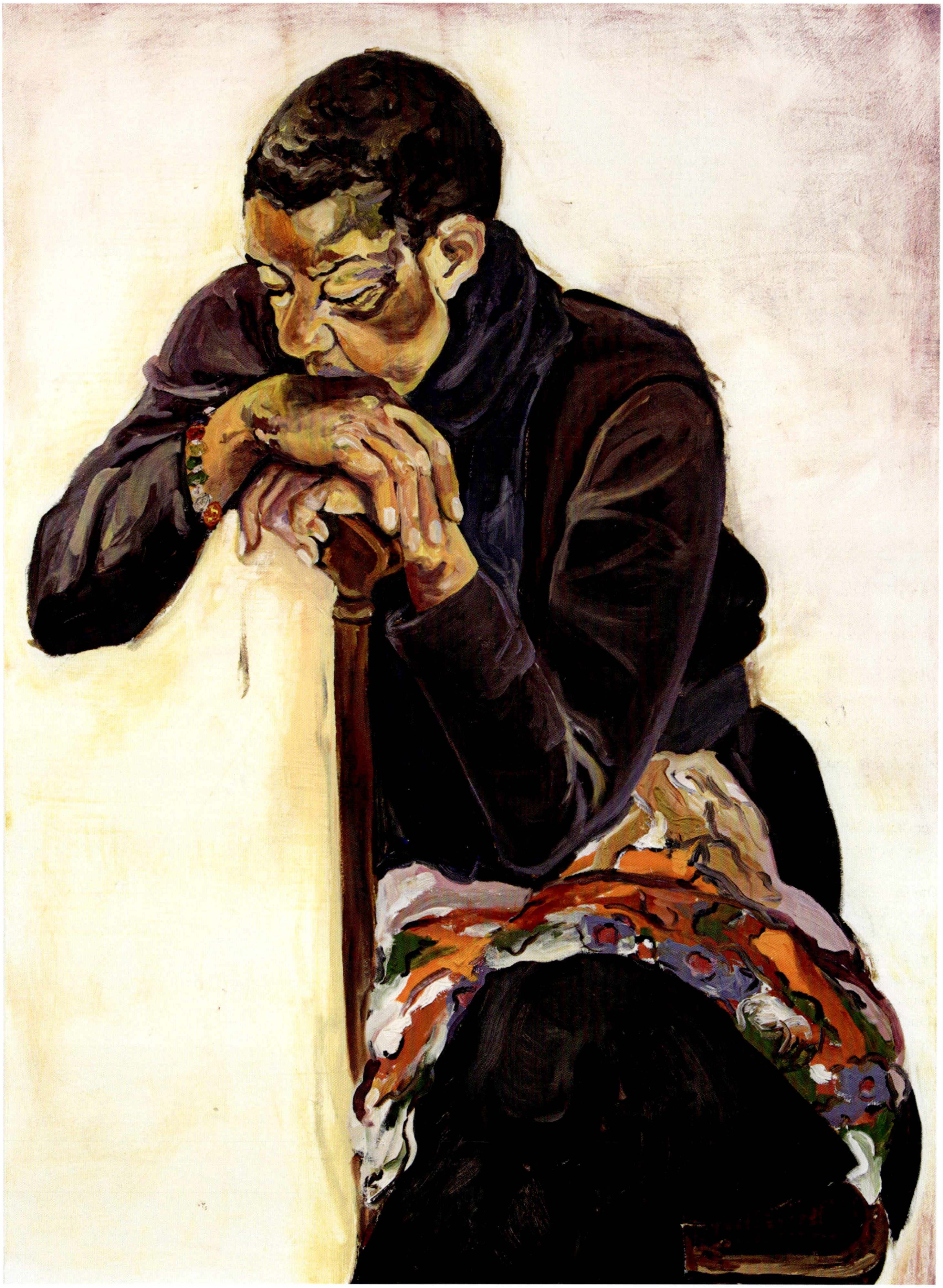

CLIENT, 2015
OIL ON CANVAS
51 X 41 CM

thinking she looked a little like an angel. She just looked heavenly and was so proud to be seen by me. It was this moment that, I think, set me on the trajectory of all the work that I've gone on to create in the last ten years. That moment was so inspiring to me, alongside the moment with Gino. I knew I had the ability to build those relationships in meaningful ways, and painting became a tool for me to do that. Did I think I was an artist at that moment? No, I didn't necessarily claim that for myself, or give myself the permission to be an artist. I'm a very practical person. I needed a job, and I felt that being an artist wasn't a practical career pursuit. I've always loved teaching as well – so as I prepared to graduate, I actually pursued teaching, and I taught special education for a year before health circumstances caused me to change course and I began to consider going back to art.

RUSSELL: *You've said that sociology is an interest of yours as part of the root of your studies, as well as your love for people, and understanding how to connect with folks across many different lines of geography, place, space, association, profession. This is something that continues to be a profound part of your figurative work. Maybe it helps people see themselves in the way that they want to be seen, which is really important. But I want to think about that moment when you're in the basement, with your beginnings of a studio, working on your early paintings. What was the experience of beginning to form a studio practice? And are there things that are traditions from that period of time – things that you began to do as part of the ritual of setting that space into being? What do you like to have around? What are the ways in which, if you're working on something durationally, you plan for that, and what are some of the core practices that you've learned in the last ten years?*

CASTEEL: There's been a really beautiful evolution. I started in Italy, where I was overlooking a Tuscan town called Cortona. It was stunning – there was a valley that I could see from the top. So I started at the top quite literally, and then I went into the basement at Agnes Scott, where there was very little light, and I was surrounded by the storage items of the building. But in that space, I think that the thing that has stayed the most consistent, that I've loved, is the solitude that I feel while making. I find great peace and stillness when I get to be in front of the canvas for long periods of time. The actual process of making the paintings hasn't changed much over time. I paint for long sessions, sometimes three to five hours at a time, working wet on wet. Then I step away to do something else, and then maybe the next day, I do it all over again. But even from the beginning, working with immediacy is one of the paramount ways of engaging with the material that I'm interested in. I've never been a revisionist painter in the sense that I've never finished a certain section of a painting and then gone in and revised it later.

RUSSELL: *What's on the canvas, stays there.*

CASTEEL: Yes. When I'm doing a portrait, I usually start with the face. But no matter where on the canvas I start my painting session that day, I'll work all day until I finish that entire section. For example, I finish the face all in one sitting, and then I finish an arm or a shirt all in one sitting – utilizing and working with wet paint only. In order to keep things from getting 'muddy', I'm wiping my brush consistently with a rag in one hand, brushes in another, cleaning the brushes when I need them in Gamsol. I'm just ripping the paint off the brush and then mixing a new colour and going back and building the highlights and the shadows all at once, until I have a form that I feel comfortable with. There have been very few times that I've gone into a canvas and wiped something away. Once it's dry, it's done. I think that's been one of the most consistent parts of how my paintings are made. I've always thought of myself as someone who's attuned to other people's needs, and I'm really conscious of the things and expectations around me. I'm a rule follower, to my own demise, but when it comes to painting,

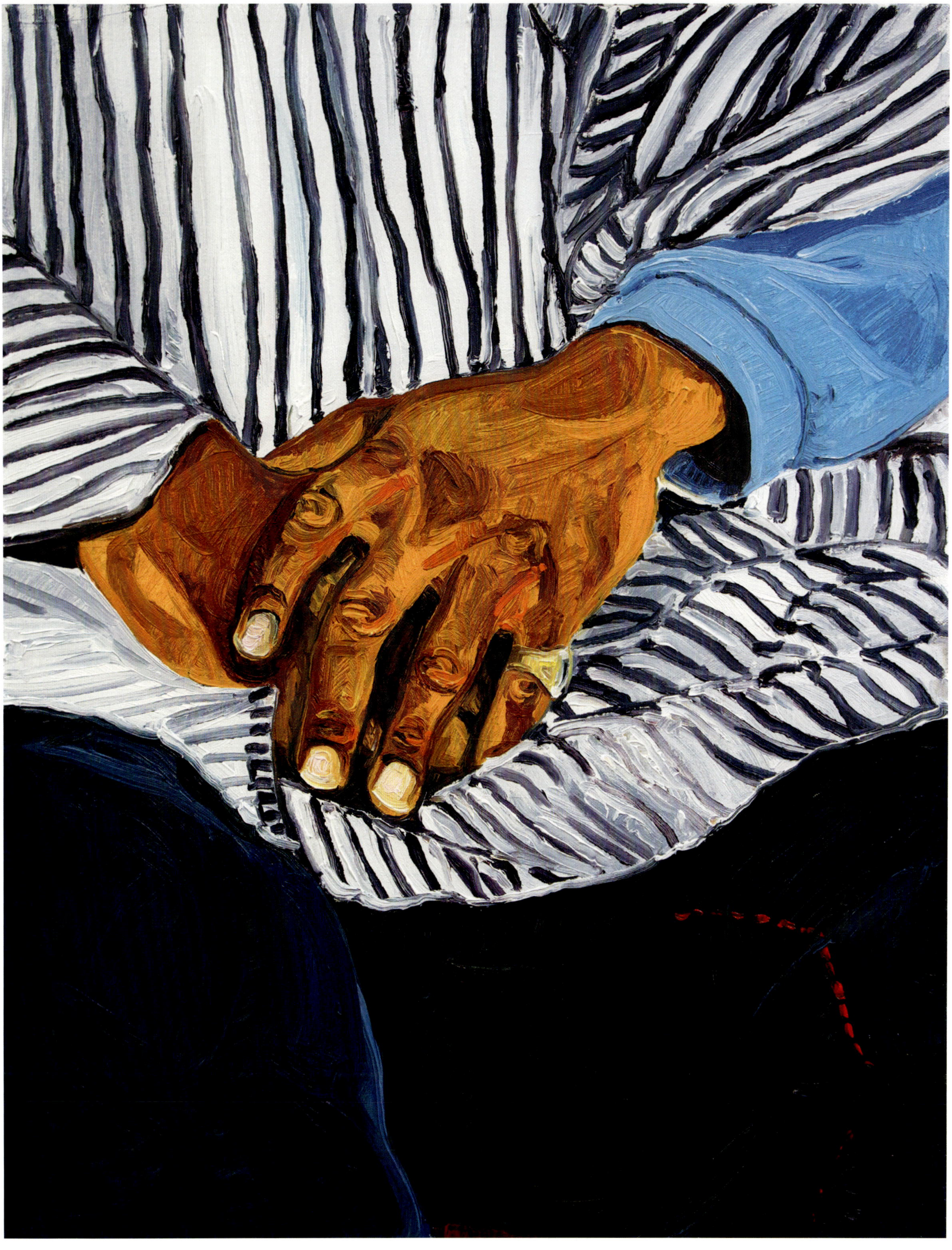

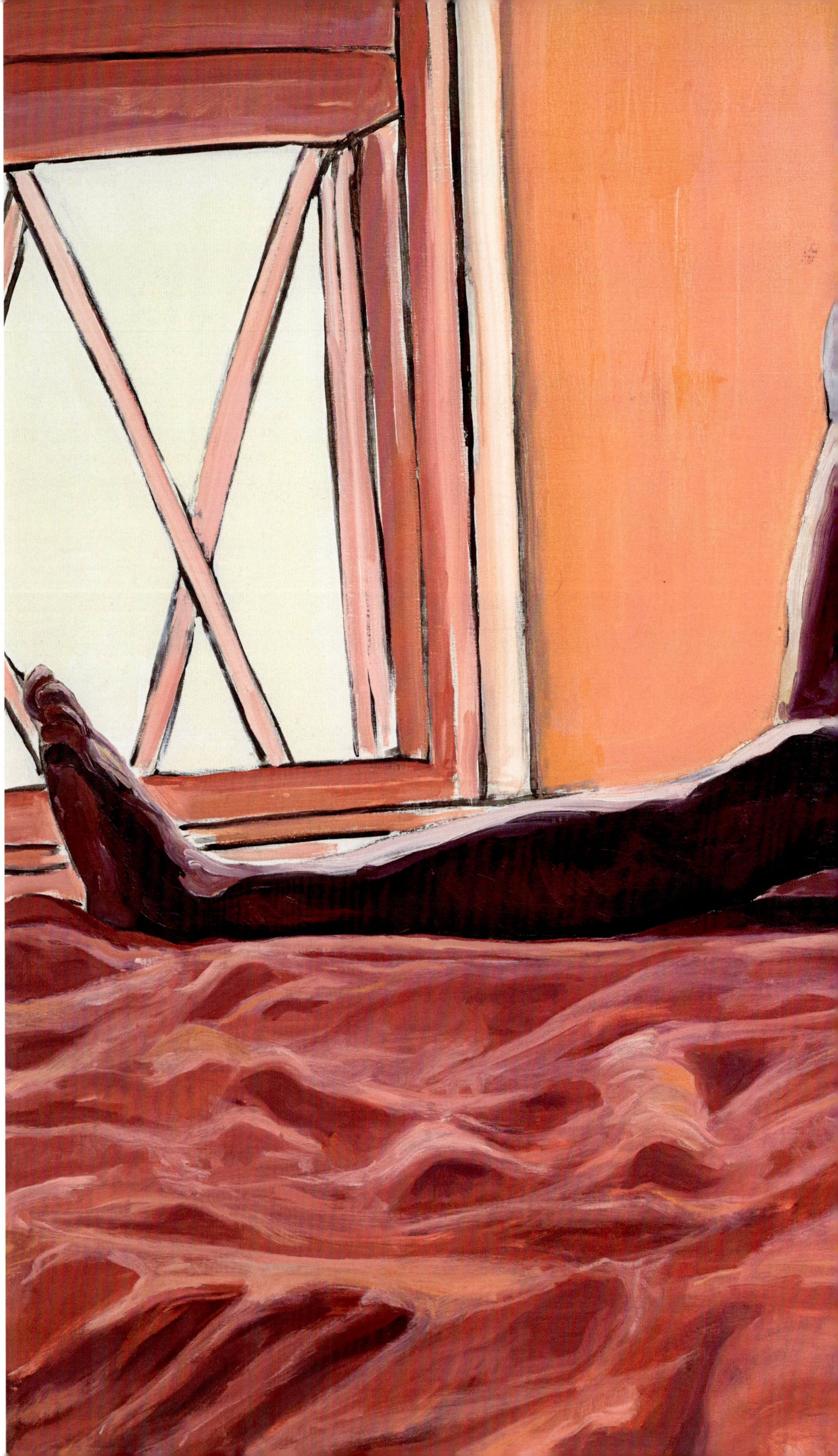

AARON, 2013
OIL ON CANVAS
133 X 211 CM

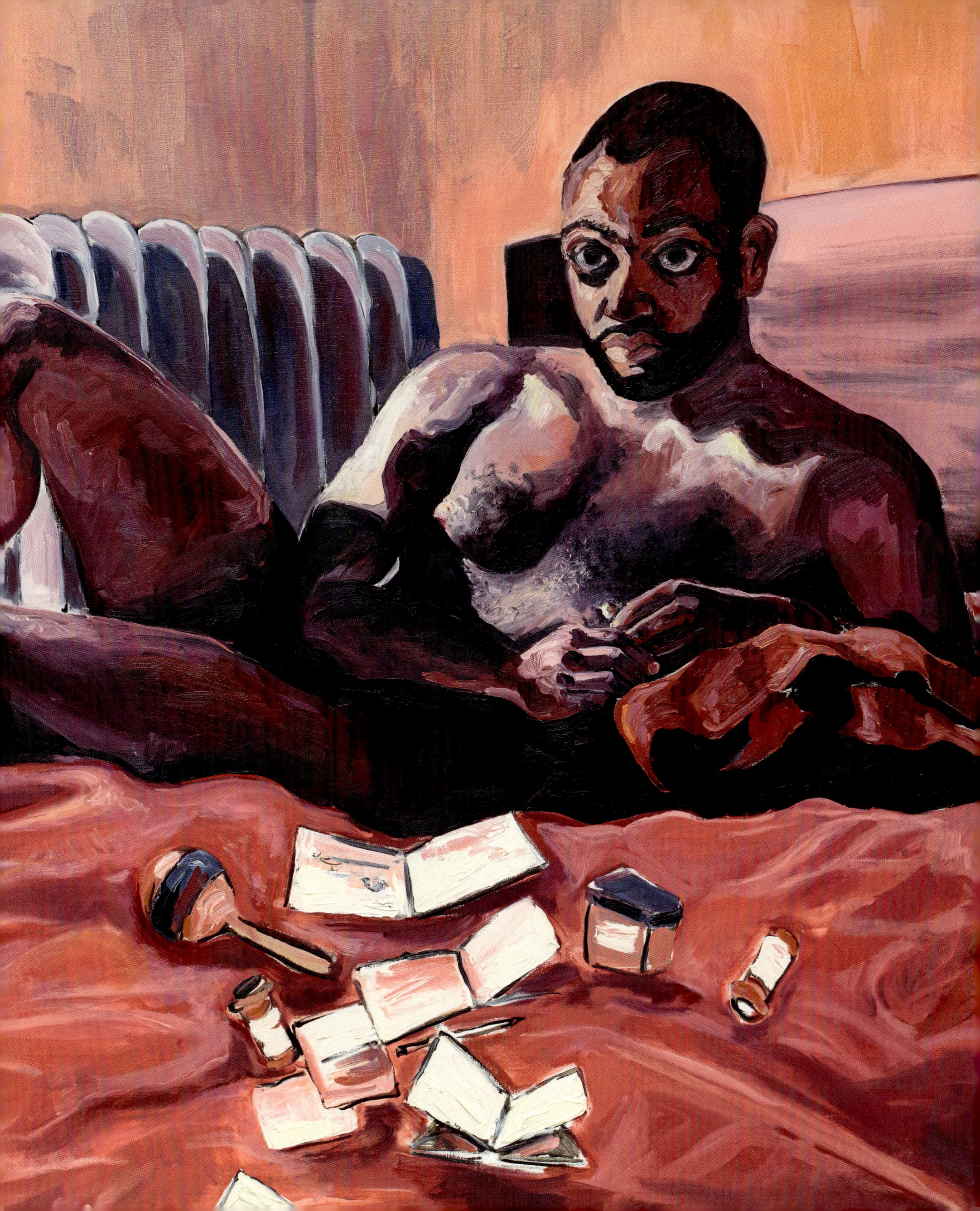

ATO, 2014
OIL ON CANVAS
183 X 137 CM

it's the one place of true freedom. I don't revise myself when I'm making; overthinking is bad, and that started from the very, very beginning. I think the freedom I feel is really rooted in making marks confidently, quickly and without judgment. It's a genuine desire to express myself in the most authentic way possible, and to have enough trust to let it exist as it is.

RUSSELL: *And to have the honesty of that as well.*

CASTEEL: Totally.

RUSSELL: *That may also be in relationship to representing others. It puts into the frame a different level of responsibility about what that initial brushstroke might be, where you decide to begin and really seeing it through, holding yourself accountable for making it whole. But inside of your studio space, what do you like to have around you? Are there, for example, certain oils, linseeds or washes, and how do you relate your initial building of the image to your colour practice? What has that looked like over time? Have you found that certain things always have to be at your fingertips to make sure that you're able to have that sincere and fully focused process?*

CASTEEL: I have had times where I've tried different media. I used an equal mixture of stand oil and Liquin for a certain period of time to give volume to the paint and a kind of sheen, so that it wouldn't feel too dry. The quality changes depending on how much you're able to spend. The pigment and viscosity of paint can vary significantly. I've gradually made my way from store-brand oil paints to Williamsburg handmade oil paint. I'm now just so familiar with Williamsburg and the viscosity and transparency of certain colours, I can't imagine changing it. In the beginning phases of my discovery, it was so important that I tried everything – every medium, brush and brand. The honest truth is that I knew so little before I got to Yale School of Art for my graduate degree. I showed up there asking, 'What are mediums?' I'd never stretched a canvas before. I didn't know what different kinds of brushes were out there. I was mostly getting things at Michaels, and having a great time with whatever said 'canvas' and whatever said 'brush' and whatever said 'oil paint' that I could afford.

I've always had a very pared-down colour palette. It's a Burnt Umber. It's a Titanium White. It's a Quinacridone Magenta. It's a Cadmium Yellow Light. It's a Phthalo Blue. Really those five colours is the spectrum. During my earliest phases, I was always making my own colours from that very pared-down palette. Now there are a few other colours that have entered that I just enjoy. There's an Ultramarine Blue or Sèvres Blue, which has different undertones from Phthalo. I also love Persian Rose and recently added a Cadmium Green along with Provence Violet Bluish. I thoroughly enjoy that act of mixing colours and trying to match colours to the colour-aids or references I have in the studio. Colour-aids in particular are something that pretty early on in my practice became a tool for me to see colour and then try to challenge colour relationships. I really enjoy building a palette before I even begin painting; it's my own *mise en place*. I think now my understanding of colour has deepened, and I trust myself to mix colours that I see in the natural world without the explicit help of a colour-aid. A piece of glass on a rolling cart with drawers functions as my palette, a few paintbrushes, oil paint and some Gamsol are all I really need. Oh, and a lot of rags.

RUSSELL: *I love what you're saying about matching colours that you see in the natural world. Your application of colour, and how you've chosen to approach the figure have changed. I'm wondering if you could talk a little bit about what it's meant to go from the primary colours that were your go-to, to this notion of what's real when shaping a vision of skin or body?*

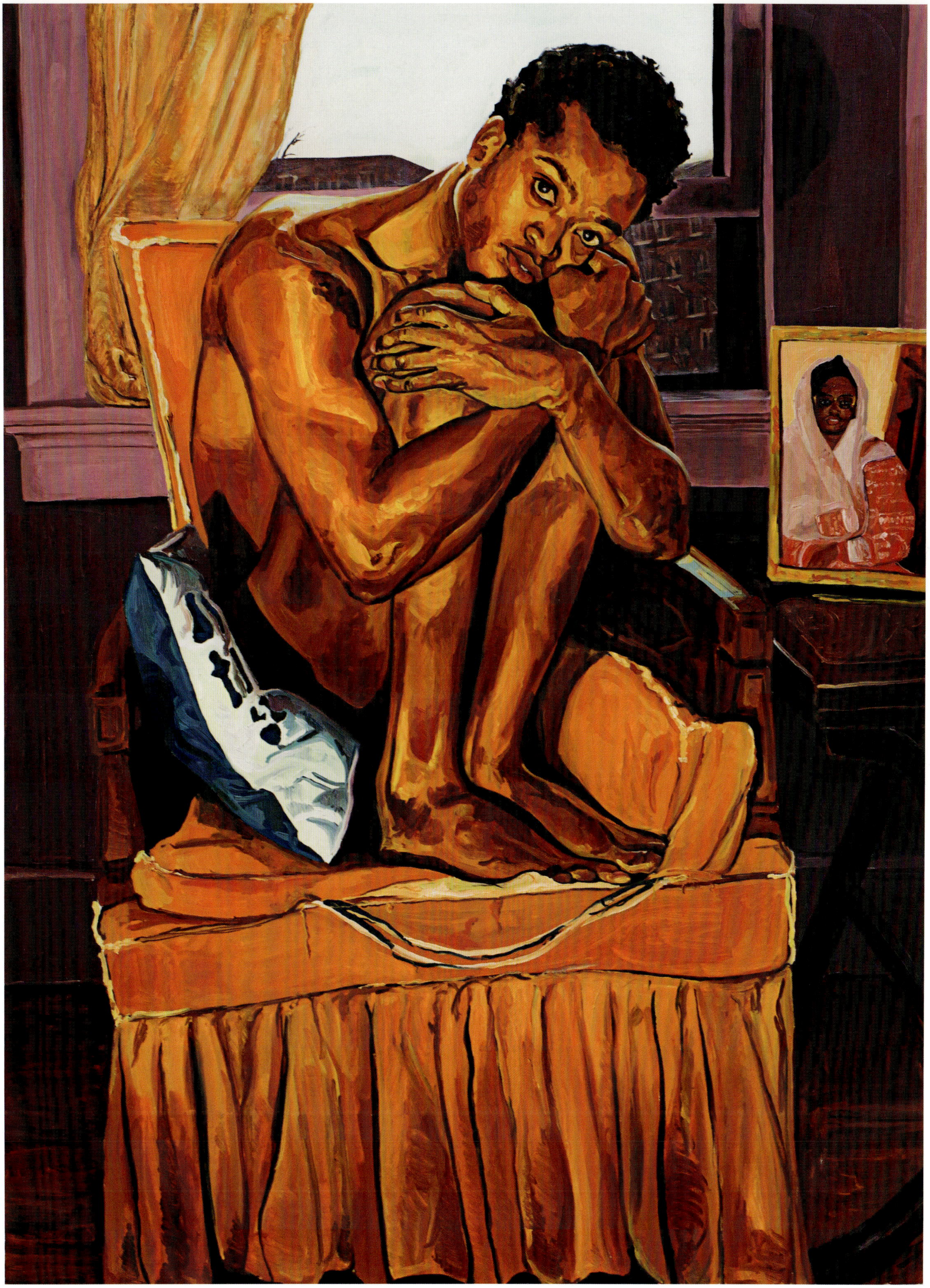

ALBERT AND MALENDA (TOP TASTE), 2023
OIL ON CANVAS
239 X 203 CM

CASTEEL: If I look back at the first painting that I made of Betty, the colours that were in her face at that time were an entire rainbow. I mean, I was literally building her face with planes of colour. They were just flat spaces used to create form, and that confidence around colour has carried through the practice. I can build form within it, and not be limited by 'skin', but rather see skin as an opportunity to play with colour and challenge the viewers' relationship to colour along the way. Skin is a space in which colour can be applied in a multitude of ways and, I think, in our natural world, also exists in a multitude of ways. I remember thinking very explicitly that in my family, none of our Black skin is the same. We represent Blackness in all the ways possible. So I wanted to treat colour in a very similar way. And the first body of work in which colour was so profoundly recognized within the practice was my 'Visible Man' series. I was painting nudes of Black men, intentionally choosing expansive colours to challenge the viewers' assumptions about these Black male bodies in general. I liked the idea that, with these paintings, the viewer can be asked to interrogate their own subconscious or conscious assumptions or biases. My hope was that they would be challenged while engaging with these paintings I'd make, and so colour became one way I would push against people's assumptions. I was having conversations in the studio where people would say, 'Oh, you're painting Black men', and then quickly shift to 'Oh, well, actually, he's green', or 'That person's pink or purple', because, quite literally, the figures were those hues in the most exaggerated forms. I like bearing witness to people coming to terms with their own biases or assumptions or understanding. Not only that, but also the assumptions they made about how I, a Black woman, was approaching the making of a painting of a brown or Black body.

RUSSELL: *Thinking about the spectrum of many different colours that Blackness embraces, why would we assume it to be monochrome? So that in itself is its own exercise.*

CASTEEL: Exactly. I think that's the sociologist in me. Before I started making those paintings, I spent almost a month – which is a long time in grad school – reading and researching. I was studying all the ways that Black bodies have historically been represented, and thinking about how I was going to use the frame of the canvas with intention down to the inch. I wanted the figures to literally feel like they were pushing up against the boundaries of the canvas. That's when the canvases became bigger. I wanted these Black men to feel lifelike, to hold a certain agency wherever they went, as if they could step out of the canvas and enter into the viewer's immediate space. I wanted their gaze to be direct – asking them to look at me – because I didn't want any opportunity for a viewer to deny their existence. I became very intentional about their genitalia, aware of the hypersexualization that can occur of the Black male body. So my decision to refocus the gaze elsewhere became a subtle aspect of the paintings. As I said, I liked the idea that people would make assumptions that they were all Black men, even though their skin was green, pink or purple and their genitalia were not present.

Another layer was that people would assume, because my name is Jordan, that it was a Black man making these paintings. For the first two or three years that I was in New York, I'd overhear people say, 'Where is he?' or I'd get an email addressed to 'Mr. Casteel'. This misgendering was also something that I found interesting, in that it was kind of messy, and correcting people challenged the assumptions placed on me and my work. Colour just continues to be another form of me expressing my relationship to the world to the fullest extent, and also my autonomy to make choices that are outside of the bounds of people's expectations. My perspective was, 'Whatever you think, I'm gonna just push it.' I don't know; my mother would probably say that it's a stubbornness. I like to say it's a sense of humour.

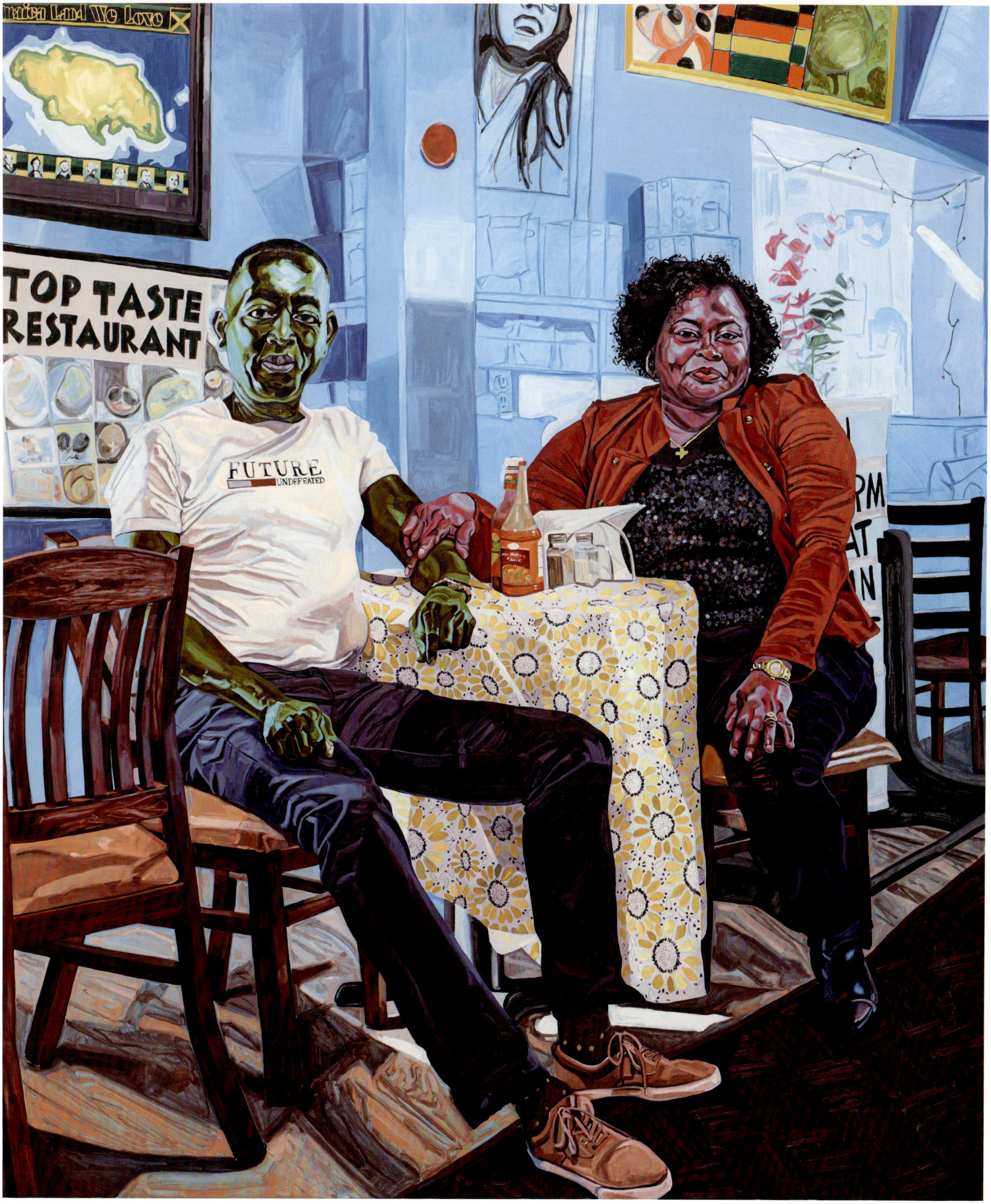
maica Land We Love
TOP TASTE
RESTAURANT
FUTURE
UNDEFEATED

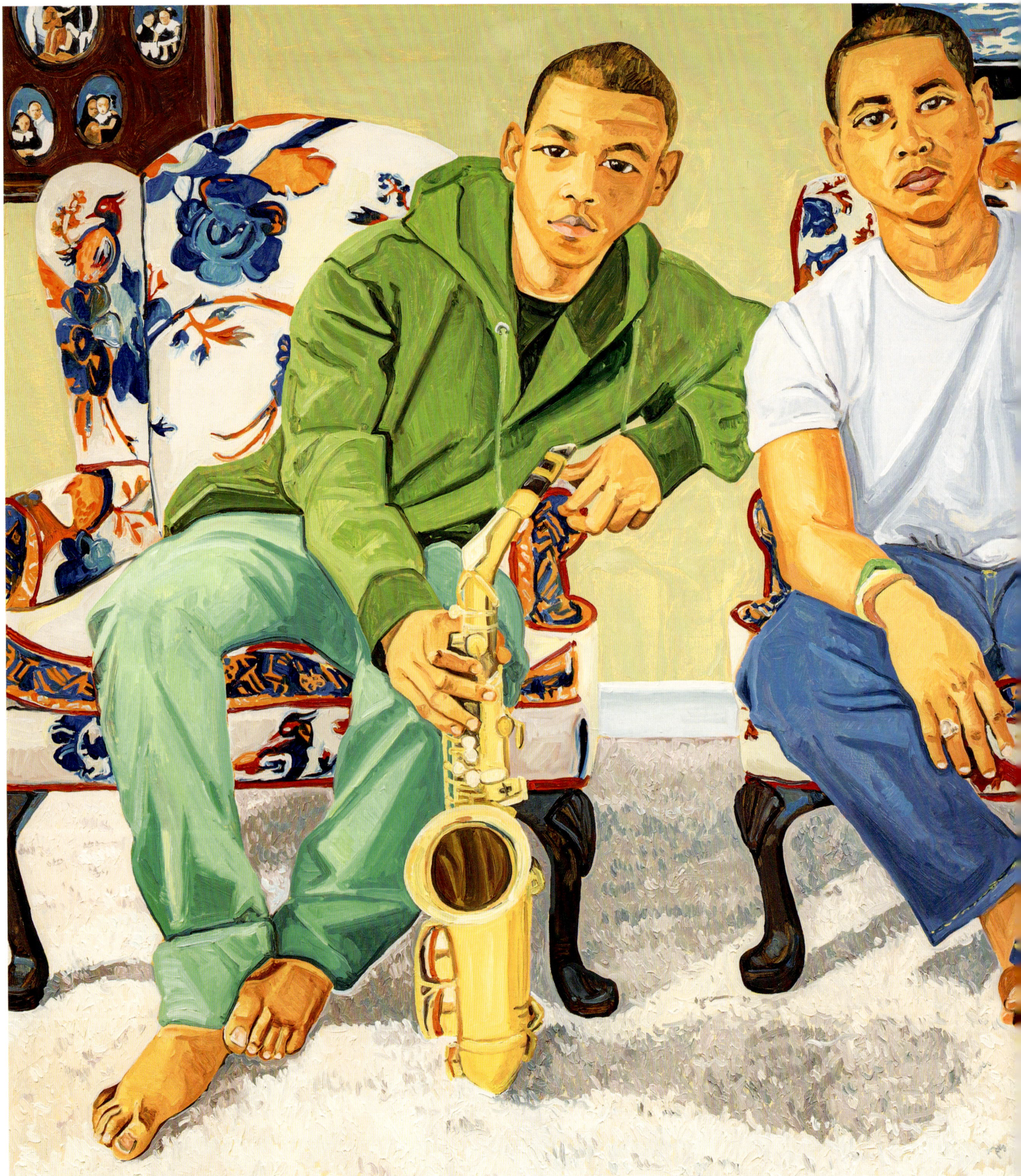

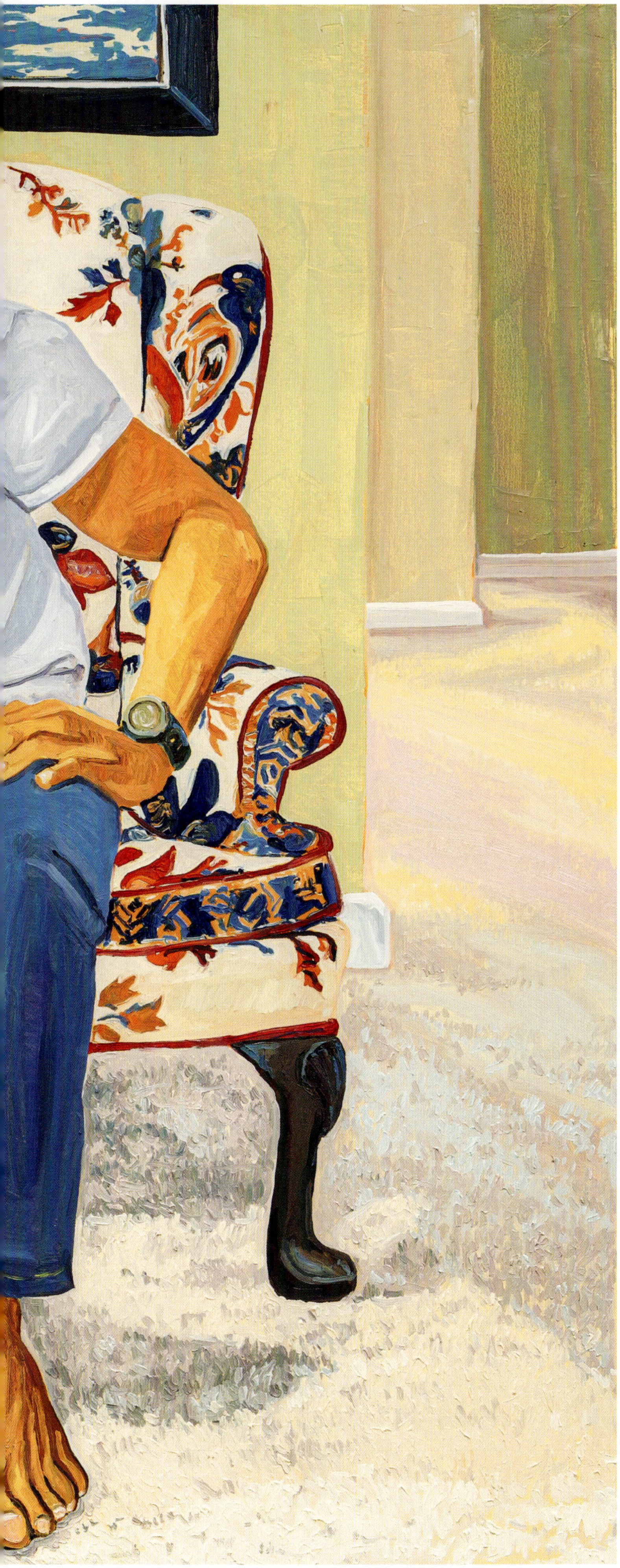

CROCKETT BROTHERS, 2015
OIL ON CANVAS
137 X 183 CM

RUSSELL: *It's both.*

CASTEEL: Yes, I think ultimately both things are true. I can be a little stubborn, but I can also plant seeds for people to consider and reconsider how they're engaging with my practice and the world around them. Then there's also just the plain fact that I love colour. I was always really good at making rainbows as a young child. I remember in preschool, I'd arrange everyone's crayons in a rainbow. So my desire to push the realms of possibility around relationships between colours, and how colour functions and supports a visual narrative, is central to my work and has been my whole life. In tandem, the composition of each painting is something that I'm deeply interested in. So you're starting to see there's all these layers at play.

RUSSELL: *I want to talk about some of the binary assumptions in relationship to gender and how this has piqued your curiosity and humour. Thelma Golden wrote in an essay for the 1994 exhibition 'Black Male' that 'One of the greatest inventions of the twentieth century is the African-American male'* [1] *and I think this is an interesting place to break open some of the questions and themes around this ongoing inquiry into the invention of Blackness you're talking about – the invention of how we perceive and engage with colour. There's this huge and very dense set of questions about why even do it in the first place? What does it mean to be in stewardship of carrying forward this layered representation of a Black male? What does that mean to you? As you said, it involves many very weighty notions of subjecthood, of empowerment, of sexuality and many very weighty histories of extraction, as well as maybe even questions of consent.*

CASTEEL: Yes, it's really interesting, because the decision to paint very explicitly, and to seek out Black men was a very deliberate exploration for me at that time. For about two years, starting with my graduate thesis work, I sought out Black men to paint. Exhibiting those paintings in New York during my first show 'Visible Man', was really the last time I did a series of that kind. I haven't made nudes of Black men since then, but that series set me on a trajectory of curiosity. I started to wonder: what does it mean for Black men to be in relationship to one another? This throughline became the exhibition 'Brothers'.

By that time, I was a resident at the Studio Museum in Harlem, bringing questions of Black masculinity and my relationship to it as a Black woman with me. I started to make paintings of Black men in Harlem. Now, nearly ten years later, as the years have gone on, and in retrospect, I've tried to understand my own decision-making and my sense of self when I first started making work in New York. I realize how much my painting practice as a whole has been almost a surrogate for questions of my own identity, on a very intimate level. In the absence of being able to ask some of the questions of those closest to me, the people that I was painting and was seeking out became proxies for the answers that I was looking for. In many ways, I was making paintings about wanting to have more intimate conversations with those I loved – about their safety, about their vulnerability, about their preciousness and humanity in its purest form. For a myriad of reasons, it was hard for me to be able to have those conversations directly. I still had this desire to protect the people I loved, and so the painting practice became an opportunity for me to express those intimacies and questions. If I couldn't protect the real humans in my life, then I was going to do everything I could to protect their representations – the surrogates of their bodies – in my paintings. That really became a catalyst for understanding how invisible I, as a Black woman, would become in relation to making these works of Black men.

When I was misgendered or confused for someone else in those spaces, it made me confront how society perceives who can make what work, and when, and at what scale. I think the practice as a whole has now become consistent with what I'm constantly battling: how I want to be seen in relation to all of the people and places

MINNESOTA, 2020
OIL ON CANVAS
198 X 152 CM

that I represent. Phrases like, 'You only paint Black men' somehow continue to follow me – and I find that to be almost violent – since it isn't representative of me, nor the entirety of the practice. I remember feeling, and sometimes continue to feel, so explicitly invisible through the shorthands created to define me or my work. It's weird to sometimes feel completely invisible, even as I'm trying to make people visible.

For me, it's always about the relationship. It's about me and the way that I see those people and want others to see them. It's not just about how they need to exist in the world. It's about me as a Black woman, seeing the world around me. It's about me as a Black woman being in Harlem or in the Hudson Valley and introducing myself to a population of people. I'm building a family and community for myself in a very explicit way.

Ultimately, the work is very much about me in relation to the people that I love, and the things that I see that help to frame my sense of self.

RUSSELL: *And also maybe help you slow down as well, because painting is different from many other media – it requires a different type of speed. It takes a certain amount of speed to do the work, and then for the material to dry, and then for it to go into the world; there are many different stages of its liveness.*

CASTEEL: Totally.

RUSSELL: *With your representation of the figure, one of the goals is to have the figure stay: it's not intended to exist in a format that renders the figure as something that exists in the past, or no longer walks this earth. Many of these individuals that you've collaborated with and represented are in this world right now. It's this living legacy that's really powerful. You often start your process with photographs. I know that you've spoken about folks coming and sitting for you in different ways, but photography has been a big part of the process. Can you talk about what the camera does for you? When you're thinking through how you're able to sustain different types of attention, or even to go back to something after you've seen it, and to look at it further with a different perspective, does a camera help you do that? Maybe a brush doesn't. I'm going to just say this to be provocative, but is there failure in that? That's a real question. Or are there ways in which these two media are mutually supportive of one another?*

CASTEEL: Photography first entered the practice as a means to an end. It was when I first started making the 'Visible Man' series. Up until that point, I'd been painting people from life. I had this $1, second-hand green chair that I put in my studio, and I'd invite classmates over to sit and I painted them. And when I started to conceptualize my thesis work and had done all the research, I wanted the figures to be life-size, and I wanted to enter the homes of the people. I wanted to put myself in a vulnerable position, to a degree, by entering the vulnerable spaces of others. Asking someone to come to my studio, into my space, and to sit for me was dictating the environment they had to enter, and I didn't want that. In New Haven, to get a large canvas in someone's home would have required navigating everybody's crazy hallways and the numerous flights of stairs. So I recognized the best way to capture someone in the intimacy of their home was to photograph them. Using a camera was an opportunity for me to capture quickly and take pictures as reference material of someone in their space. I'd then bring those images back into the studio and begin to paint. I'm not a photographer – so much so that even yesterday I was photographing someone and I had to call my partner in order to figure out how to adjust the ISO. I don't even really understand what ISO is, which is insane given that I've been taking pictures for ten years now. I'm so uninterested in the camera in comparison to how interested I am in being present in the moment – focusing on building a relationship with somebody. I want them to feel comfortable,

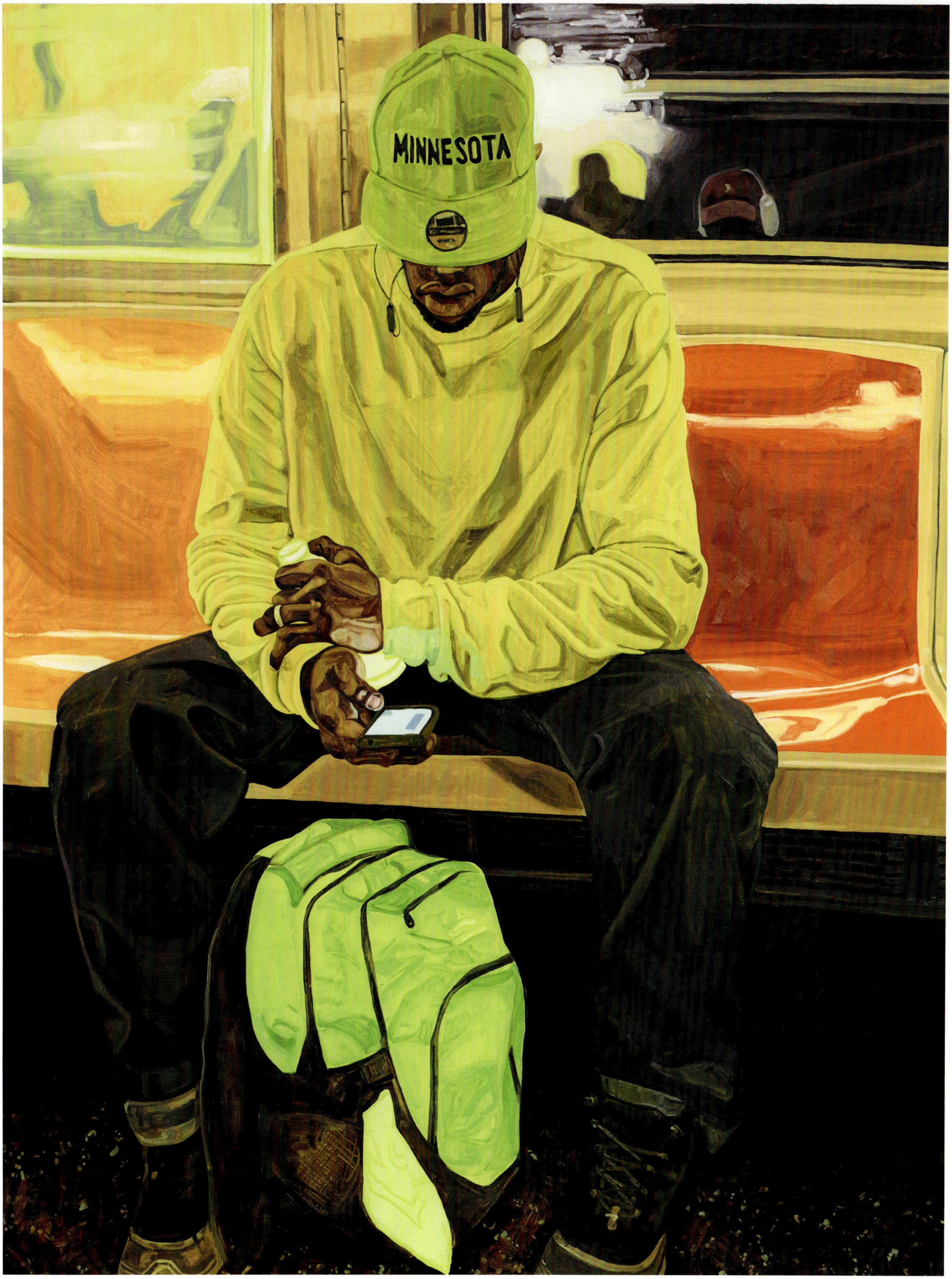
MINNESOTA

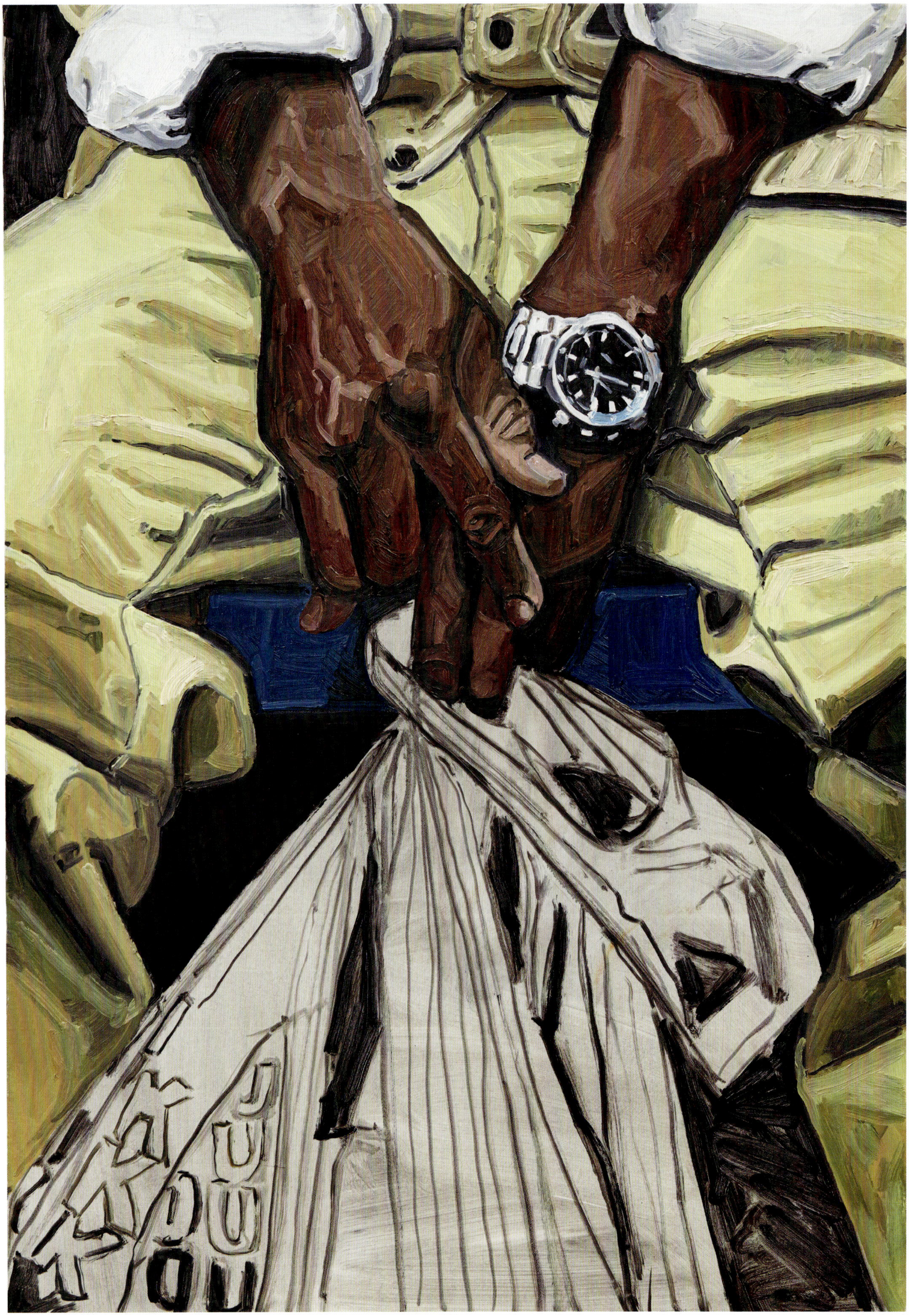

left,
SUBWAY HANDS 2, 2017
OIL ON CANVAS
86 X 61 CM

opposite,
WOVEN, 2022
OIL ON CANVAS
91 X 76 CM

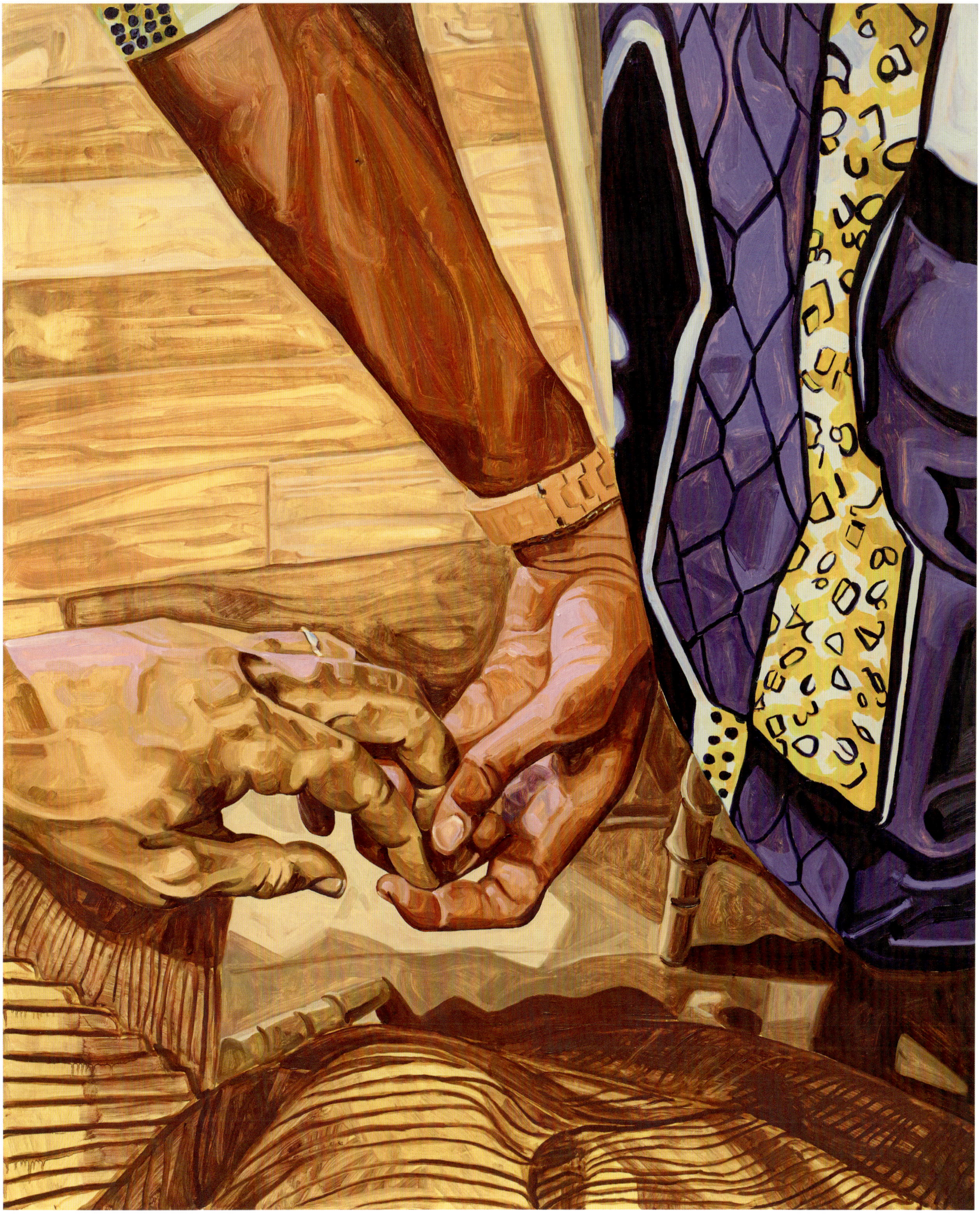

SUBWAY BOUQUET, 2025
OIL ON CANVAS
127 X 102 CM

and ensure they feel safe in their environment in whatever ways they need. Thus, the photograph becomes secondary – it's a chronicle of me with someone in a specific place. It's history – a capturing of the landscape of a life. The photograph is simply the mechanism that allows me the opportunity to get to know someone and to capture the essence of their being, all in order for me to try to recreate that feeling. I think that's where the immediacy of the painting becomes important, because then it brings me back into the paint.

RUSSELL: *Each one can have their space.*

CASTEEL: Yes. There have been many times throughout my career when people have asked if I'd ever show my reference photographs. They exist in my studio, plastered all over the wall until I complete a body of work. I have the photographs I take of people readily accessible. But once the work is done, then they get filed away.

RUSSELL: *You keep that as an archive of the work.*

CASTEEL: Yes. The printouts that I use that are covered in paint and have the tape on them, rips, et cetera, those get archived and set aside for me to reference later. The paintings, unlike the photographs, become my impressions of life. The camera is important because it allows me to stay present. It's similar to working with a brush – the more time you spend with the material, the better you understand what you need from it. The camera is just another material that I use and it just needs to be a brainless tool that will give me the highest quality image possible, so that I have it as reference. For the longest time I was just printing on copy paper. A picture could be out of focus, and I didn't even care. It was my job, as the painter, to bring that moment to life.

RUSSELL: *The quality isn't the priority, right? Because it's not about the preciousness of the photograph, it's about what happens afterwards.*

CASTEEL: Totally.

RUSSELL: *You've spoken at various points about stepping outside the studio and being in a space where you're convening with the elements, in nature, and having that as part of your process, to perhaps create a point of connectivity between these different models of liveness. I'm curious to hear you reflect on what that meant for you in thinking about the figure. Plant life has been something that you've begun to explore further. What has that looked like as a model of ongoing work and research in recognition of different ideas of representation, and the expectations about what painters and 'Black painters' should be doing? As you've said, in certain parts of your practice you've had to step back and almost render yourself invisible as part of the exercise of uplifting and upholding others. But with a practice that goes into a different realm of engaging nature, are those things still priorities?*

CASTEEL: I think that they're definitely still priorities. They're in my thought process. It's interesting when you say, 'convene with nature'. I think that I've always, in many ways, been curious about convening with my environment. That environment has varied from a cityscape to a more natural setting. I'm literally in a green space now, but if I think very explicitly about convening with nature, that curiosity has always been at the crux of my practice.

Over time, the semiology has evolved, without question, as the canvases became bigger. I remember very explicitly the moment that I became interested in the environment as a whole. It was when I was at the Studio Museum and thinking about Harlem as the landscape. I was really interested in the way that this seminal space and place existed

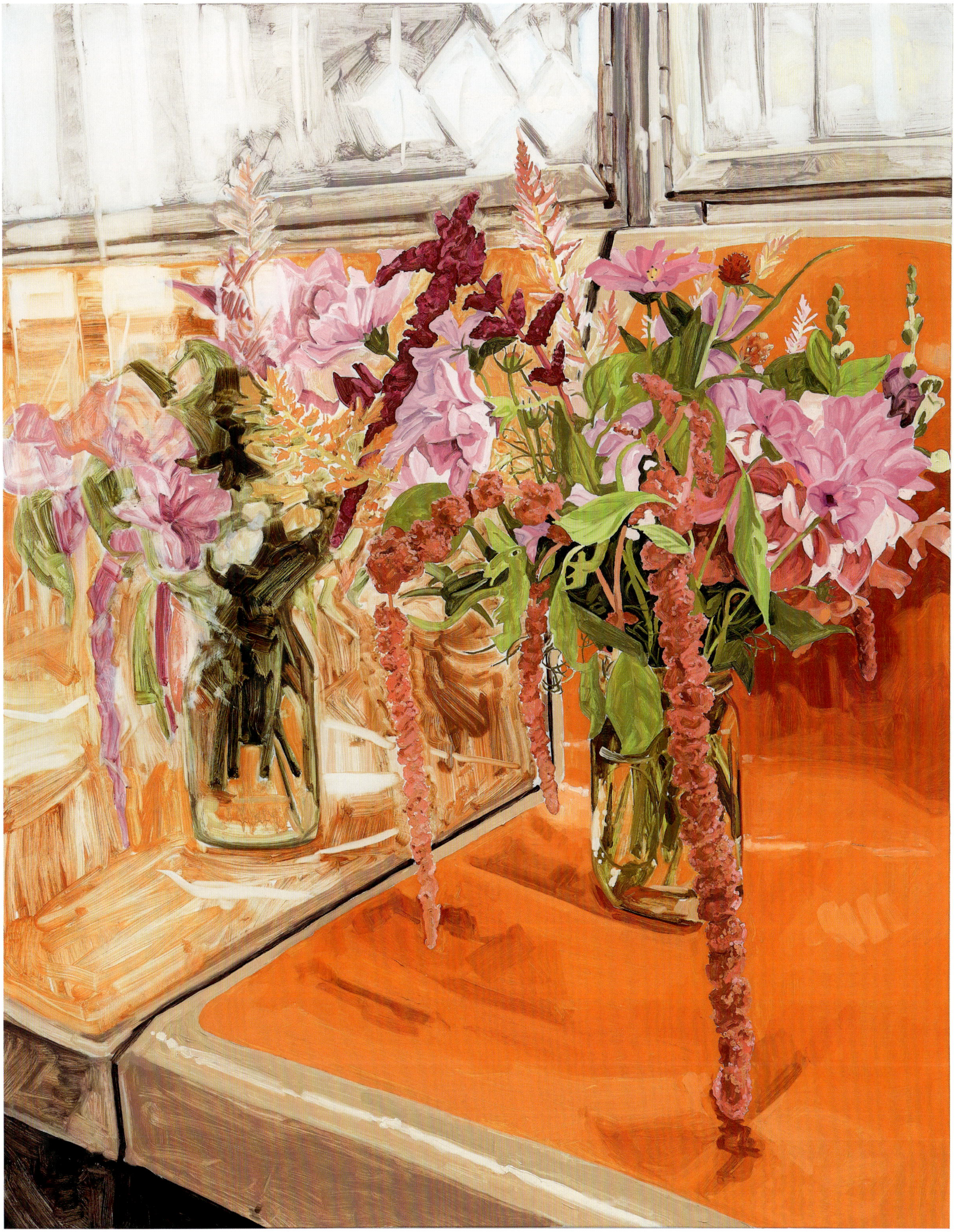

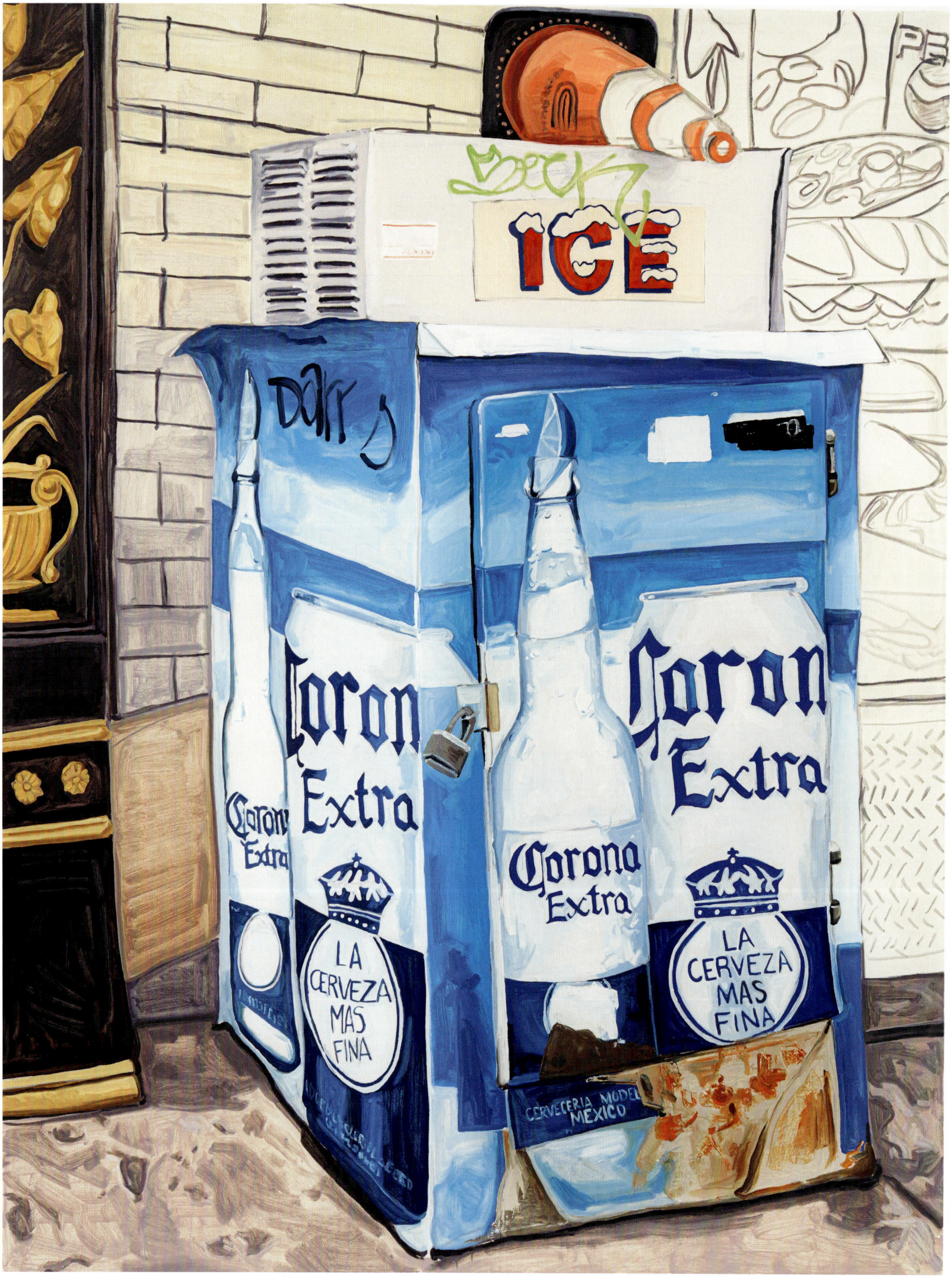
ICE
Corona Extra
LA CERVEZA MAS FINA
CERVECERIA MODEL
MEXICO

<u>ICE</u>, 2018
OIL ON CANVAS
198 X 152 CM

around the frame of the figure, and so the canvases became wider to include more of the cityscape – signage for Lenox Avenue or Sapphire Lounge. These are things that existed in that real time, in that specific moment. Some of those things are no longer there, but similar to the figures, they all existed in this moment together. It was about contextualizing the person in the space that they existed in, and I became very interested in those environments.

During a studio visit with Thelma Golden – and she might tell me she didn't say this – but I've created this memory of her saying to me that she felt that I was actually a landscape painter. And I remember thinking, 'That doesn't make any sense.' Yet she's brilliant like that. There's no doubt that whatever she's saying is with intention. I didn't fully understand at the time, but as the years have gone on, I've absorbed that more and more, and it's really stuck with me. I have been, and continue to be, very interested in the landscape, or the environments, that people exist within. It's about the person within their context – at home, on the street, and the street itself. I started making paintings like *Memorial* (2017), which is of a discarded floral arrangement sitting on the corner of Lenox Avenue and 128th Street. The absence of the figure was so present, and that was the power of that painting for me. Or *ICE* (2018) and *Amina* (2017): these paintings were representative of that place at the time that I was there. I think the evolution of the practice mirrors my personal evolution – seeking different kinds of spaces to create within, and finding a sense of peace and belonging. Harlem has always been a place where I feel deeply engaged and belong. It was the first place I felt at home in New York.

Ultimately, it's the figure and the landscape together that tell the whole story. These elements meet like sentences in a journal, or scrapbook of my life, capturing the people within places that inspire me, that I don't want to forget and want others to see and know. Recently, I've come to love gardening and being in my garden, which has become more explicitly represented in my work as a part of what my life is now, along with the people I'm meeting. I'm still very much focused on painting people of colour. Women entered the narrative long ago, and it became more than just Black people explicitly. Back in 2018, I made a painting of Fatima, a Muslim woman. She would sell coffee and bagels right outside of the Studio Museum in Harlem. That painting of her was a very significant representational moment for me and I've tried to continue to feel free to represent a broad range of people of colour. That intention still feels really important to me – capturing the people of colour in my landscape.

RUSSELL: *This idea of being a landscape painter is powerful because what landscape shows us is often a study of interiority that is set out in the natural world. It's geopolitical. It's radical. Even the very idea of people of colour feeling safe to move freely in a space is in and of itself a question. We're seeing examples of how that's failed. I think that it's a really wonderful and also ecstatic proposition you're putting forward, which is about this idea of context, not having a figure exist in a vacuum, but having a figure exist with a rich interiority and an exteriority, and a right to roam.*

THE NEW BLACK VIEW (STILL LIFE WITH JAMES AND YVONNE), 2021
OIL ON CANVAS
127 X 102 CM

CASTEEL: Totally!

RUSSELL: *And you know, when you talk about the relationship to not only Black men, not only Black people, but people of colour and women, I have to note we're in a unique moment right now. It's August 8 in 2024, and Kamala Harris is running for the next presidential seat in this wild country. So with that in mind, I want to take time to reflect on questions of Black womanhood. Given that you've also continued to unpack this idea of landscape, I'm wondering if this is a moment when your visibility could function differently? Have you thought about what the new works that you've been producing look like in terms of what I'm going to say provocatively is a very gendered history of representing landscape and green life, to be a Black woman in this moment? Is this a different moment to think about being seen, and about how that viewership is represented?*

CASTEEL: I think the paradoxes of society are on full display at the moment, especially in terms of what it means to embody all the possibilities that we're told we have at our fingertips, and of what it means to be a Black woman in American society. Kamala Harris can secure the Democratic presidential nomination, while literally at the same time, Sonya Massey was killed in her own kitchen by the cops she called for help because they were threatened by a pot of boiling water on her stove. When I witnessed those two realities side by side, it was disorienting. It was an intense experience for me to see on social media, within a span of 24 hours, a Black woman being slain, lynched, in her kitchen, and a Black woman standing on a podium vying for the presidential seat. I couldn't reckon with these truths juxtaposed back-to-back. And I grapple profoundly with what it means to be a Black woman today. I find myself sceptical that a Black woman president is, in fact, possible. Because the real world for me feels more akin to the lynching of somebody in their kitchen.

There's a poem called 'Hottentot Venus' that you read at the Loophole retreat in Venice, which I took some time to research and read again. There's the line: 'Business is booming and I am not loved the way I want to be.'[2] That really stood out to me.

RUSSELL: *Right.*

CASTEEL: I think there's something really accurate in that poem, particularly considering the context in which you read it. The intention was to share and hold space, to dive into conversations about Black womanhood, specifically in relation to the arts. That sentence in particular, in this moment of Kamala Harris and Sonya Massey, felt so true and relevant in terms of my experience within the context of the art world. I often feel the risk of not being loved, constantly questioning the love that I receive, and not knowing whether that love is real or not.

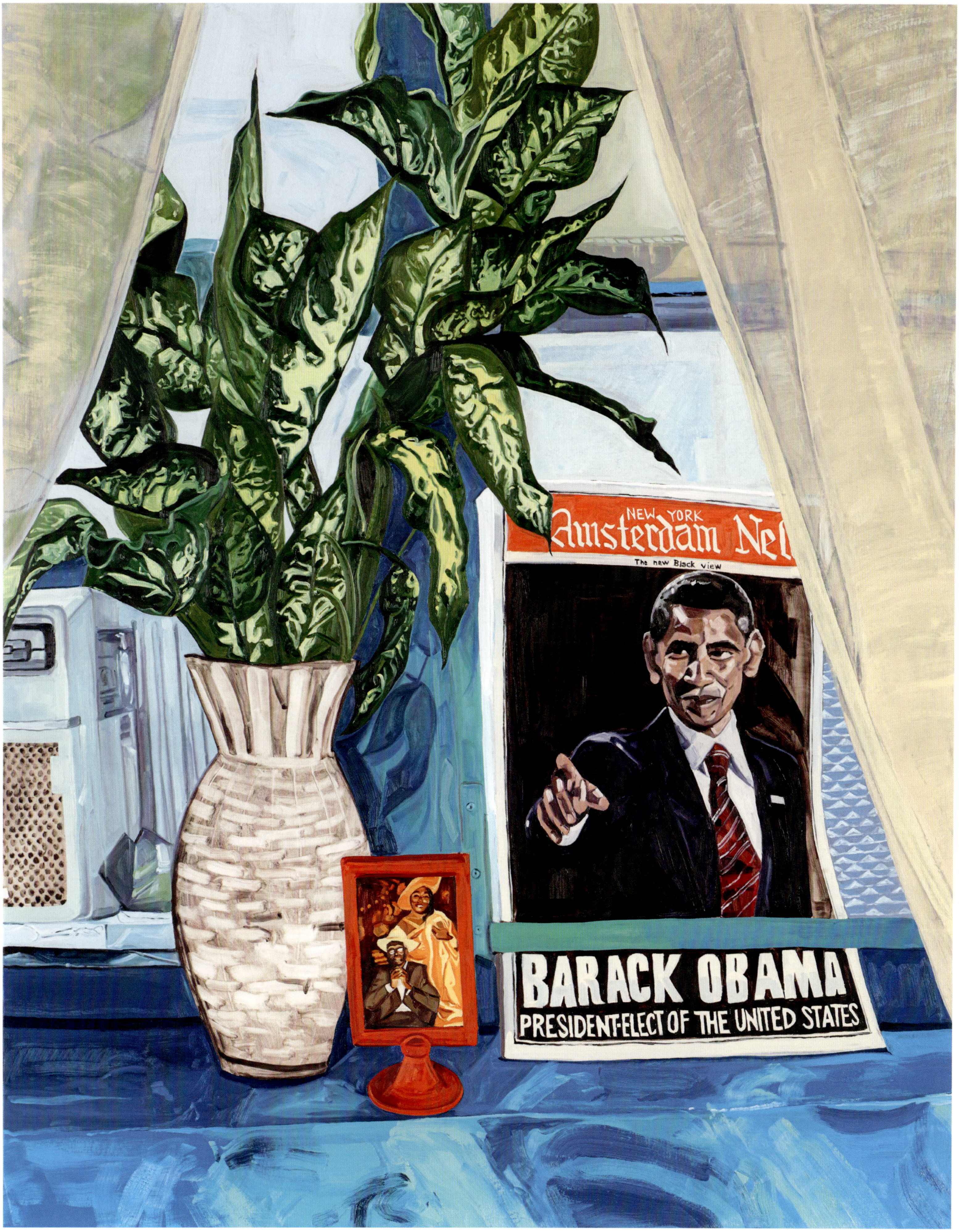
NEW YORK
Amsterdam
The new Black view
BARACK OBAMA
PRESIDENT-ELECT OF THE UNITED STATES

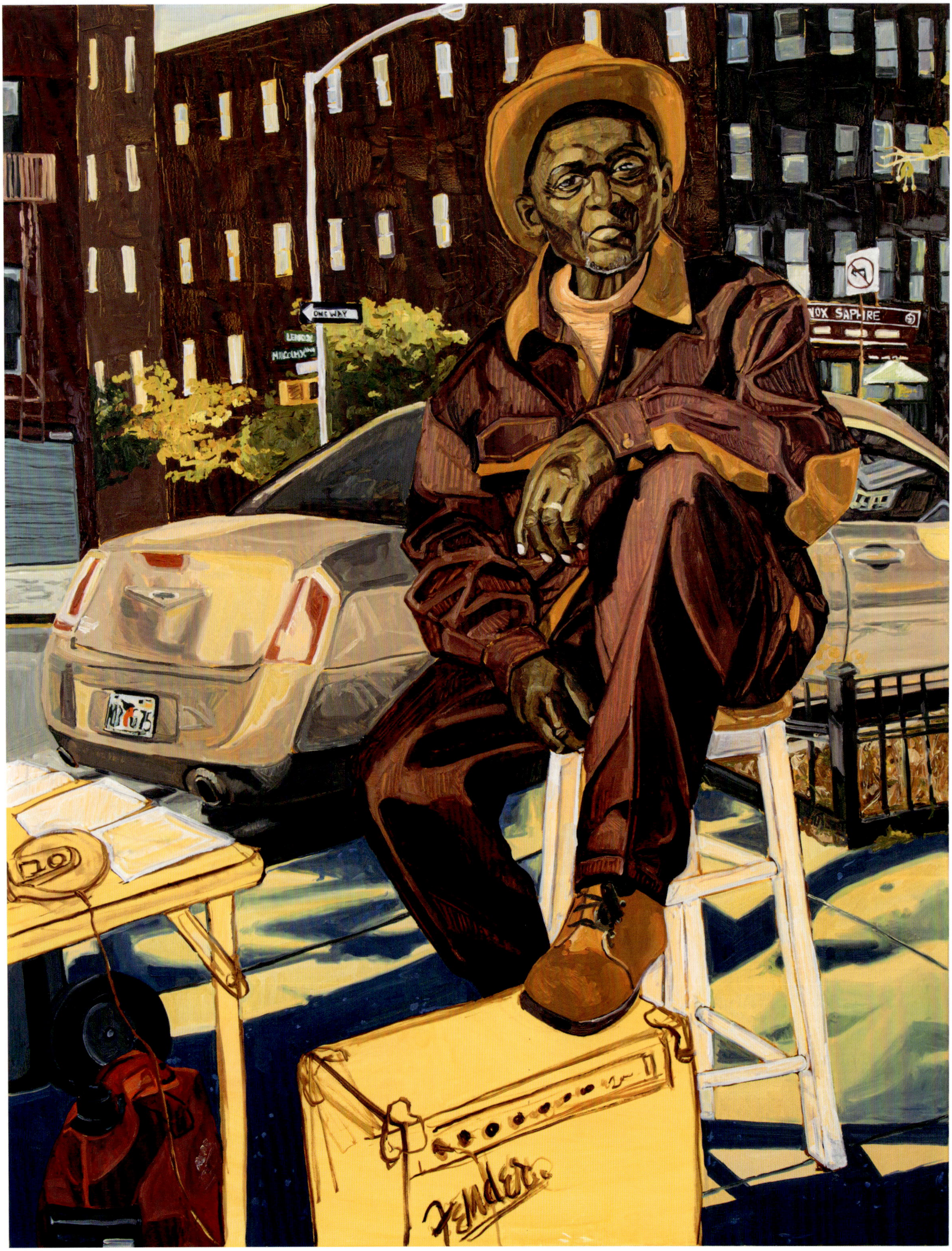
ONE WAY
Fender

JAMES, 2015
OIL ON CANVAS
183 X 142 CM

I think this is the challenge of a Black woman in this moment, even with you, as the two of us have this conversation. What does it mean for us, as two Black women, to be having this conversation now? To be represented within a historical context and valued, yet still vying for love? That's what I'm trying to communicate within the broader practice as a whole, in my own anxieties about invisibility. That's where the people that I paint, my love for my garden, and the relationships I'm building on a daily basis come in. When I began walking down Lenox Avenue as a newly minted resident at the Studio Museum in Harlem, I'd made the journey from Denver to Atlanta, back to Denver, to New Haven, to New York City. Harlem became the place that I first began to seek love and feel love. That came from people who I believe, like me, were vying to be loved, and to not be rendered invisible.

RUSSELL: *Hilton Als once said, in a conversation – I'm going to paraphrase – 'Don't go to institutions with the expectation of being loved'. Right? You've got to find those things elsewhere. I've always reflected on that as a statement, because of the fact that what it shows us is that the art is kind of empty architecture, so we have to carry out the sustained work of doing the loving and having that take on different forms in a wide variety of representations to embed itself fully inside of some of these empty architectures – socially, culturally, politically. And so when we ask the question about the work, as in these incredible legacies that you've shaped and created and held and preserve so tenderly, what has it meant for you to think about this idea of placemaking in relation to home? You've said that Harlem in some way has been a home to you, a grounding force for you. What does that look like in relationship to the very many people that you've continued to meet and steward along the way as part of growing as an artist?*

CASTEEL: I think home is so directly tied to all of them. I may be spending most of my time now in Hudson Valley, New York, but James [The sitter in *James,* 2015 (opposite), *Yvonne and James,* 2017 (p. 34), and *Yvonne and James II,* 2021 (p. 35)], who's in Harlem, is somebody I still talk to on a regular basis. Betty, the sitter I mentioned earlier, is also somebody I still talk to on a regular basis. Making those paintings brought a closeness, and I believe that the act of seeing and loving somebody else in an authentic way produces a sense of home – with my sitters and within their environment. In my experience, if you're approaching someone with the hope of seeing them where they are, and wanting them to see you, home is always possible, and I've found that even in this transition. Without a doubt, when we first got this place in Upstate New York I didn't imagine that it would become a full-time residence. It was hard for me to imagine leaving Harlem and the people I love there. But what has been most encouraging and surprising is that home can be created with intentionality anywhere. Moving up here has led to a real intentional effort to create community. I've co-founded a community organization, Upstate Color, that only exists because of everybody else's engagement with one another. Being here has reminded me of how the practice started out from the very beginning, saying, 'Hi! My name is …' and learning that home is created anywhere that I go, and that I have

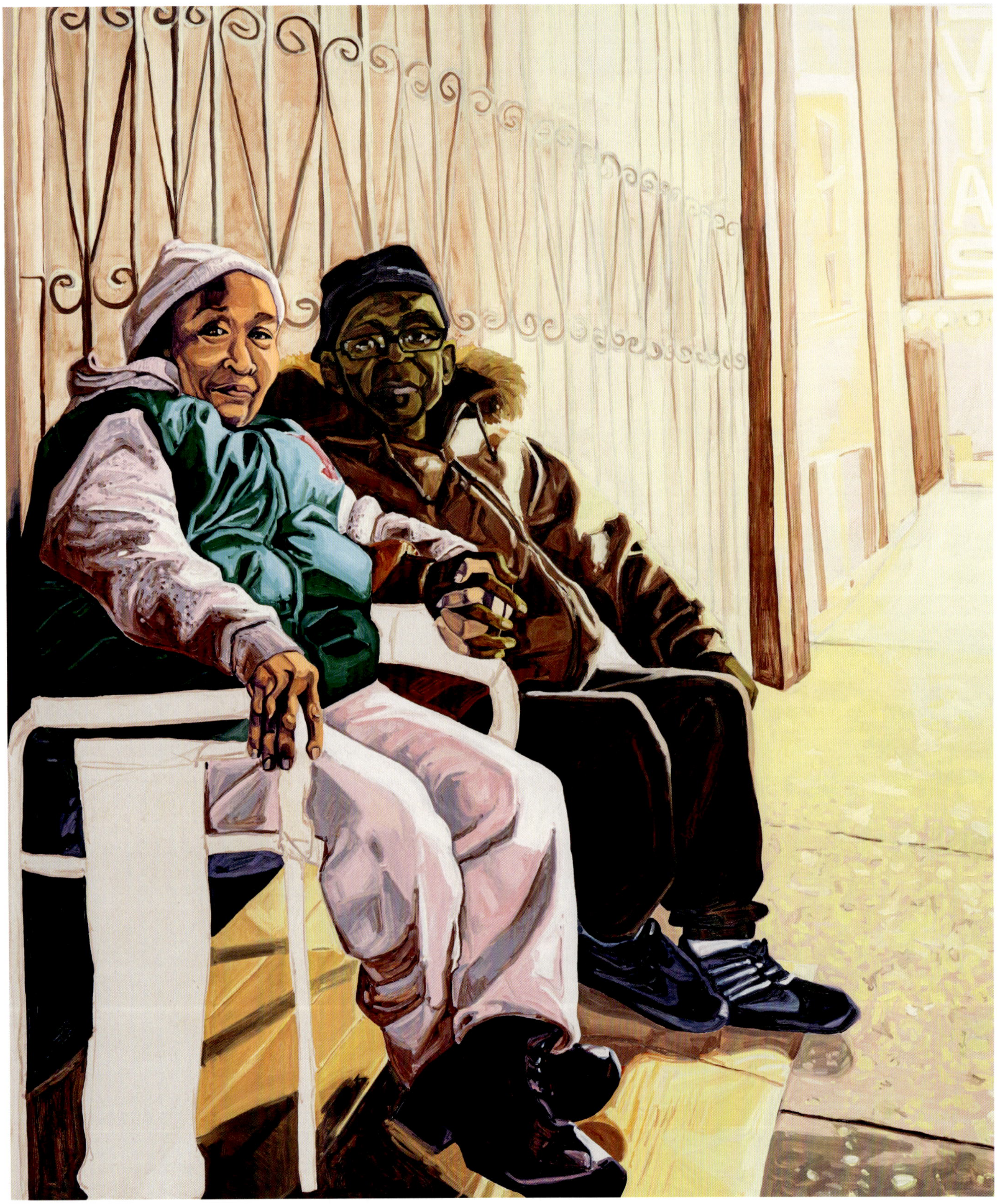

left,
YVONNE AND JAMES, 2017
OIL ON CANVAS
229 X 198 CM

opposite,
YVONNE AND JAMES II, 2021
OIL ON CANVAS
229 X 198 CM

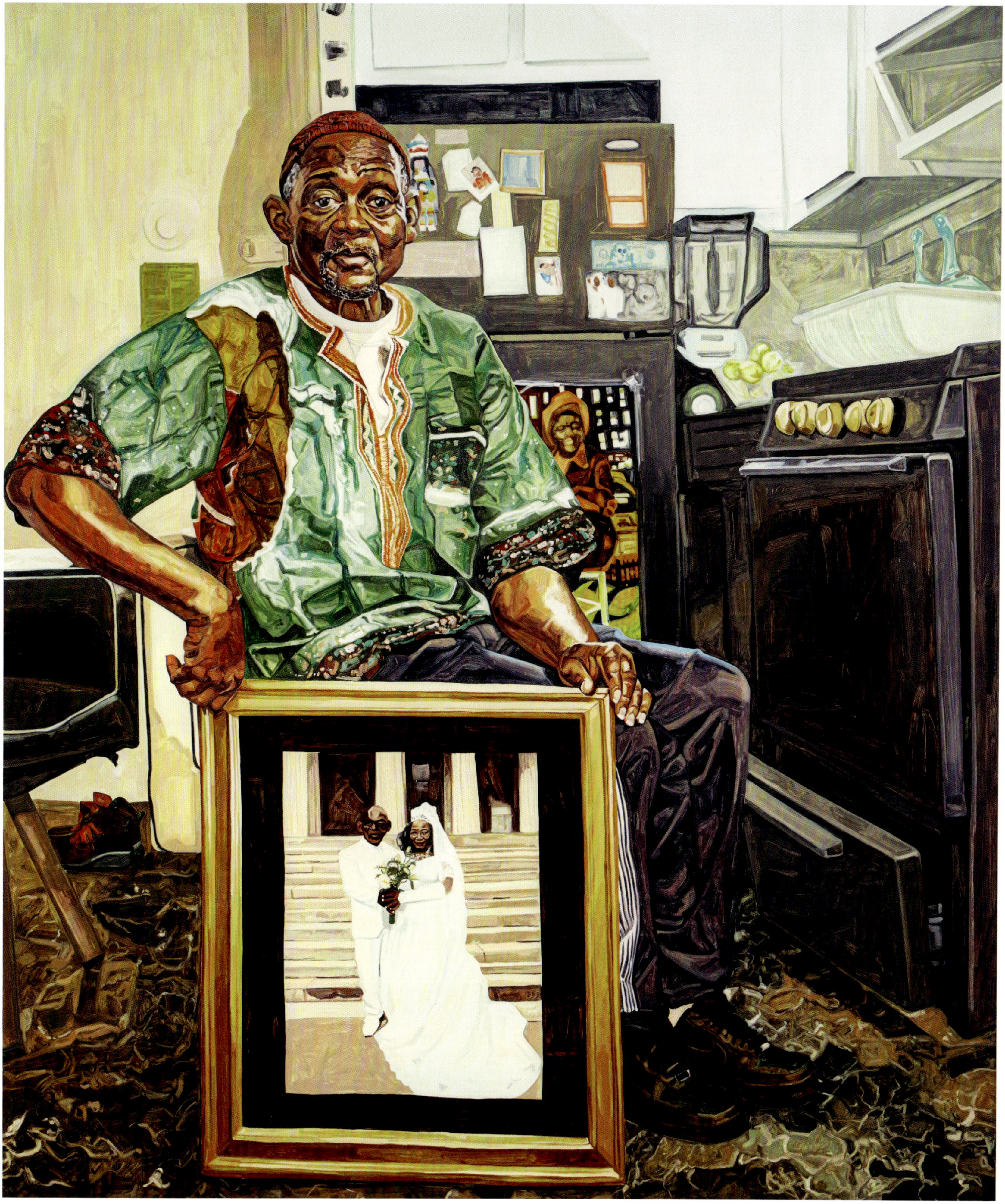

JENNA, 2019
OIL ON CANVAS
198 X 152 CM

the capacity, even in isolation, to create a community that feels like home, no matter how spread out or rural it is. That inspires the practice. I've found that home is not only the physical space that I'm in, but finding balance in myself. I'm way more introverted than my practice might suggest. My practice is a way to encourage myself to step out of my own head and into the world, but I still need solitude. I return to the studio in isolation, to sit with the experience of being in the world and of the world, to engage and reflect. So yes, home is ever-evolving and home for me is in a multitude of places. It's in Harlem, it's in Denver, it's in Upstate New York. It's still in Atlanta in many ways, too.

RUSSELL: *Of course. Have you found that through this process, some of your understandings of the audience or the publics that are receiving your work have changed?*

CASTEEL: I think the first audience, especially if it's a figurative painting, is the person or people I've painted. That's usually the audience I care about the most. What are they going to think or feel when they see themselves represented so explicitly through my gaze? It's realistic, but not hyper-real by any means. I think that I have to attach myself solely to that audience's opinion because the audience that exists beyond that is very complicated, and approaches the work from very nuanced perspectives. It starts with the people seated in the frame. Then it expands into those who see themselves within it – those who see themselves represented, myself included. And then there's everybody else – those who want to understand. I think the direct gaze is a way for me to try to circumvent the commodification or the objectification of the paintings and the people represented in them as they move into the world.

RUSSELL: *I think it's actually a profound thing, because it's an invitation that shifts entirely what the act of looking and these complicated histories of voyeurism and extraction in relation to black subjecthood can be. Can you talk a little bit about influences that exist outside of the realm of visual art? You've been in your garden Upstate and that has been meaningful to you. Are there sounds? Are there texts? Is there music?*

CASTEEL: I think that for me, there's actually more of a stillness wherever I am than there is noise – not noise per se, but sound. Whether it's in Harlem or in the Hudson Valley, I consistently wear headphones even if I have a space entirely to myself. I very rarely play music out loud. There's something about becoming wholly internal that feels essential to the act of making. I'm inspiring, soothing and preparing myself for making work. It's where I want to find that freedom that I was describing earlier, of not thinking, not overdoing, not overworking, not self-correcting. I almost have to, in a meditative way, leave my body to allow it to do what it naturally wants to do, letting my hand and my brain move with a certain kind of fluidity, without interruption.

For this stillness, there's a set-up involved; I need a lot of order around me. Gardening and baking provide a similar headspace of meditation, allowing my brain to quiet in order to just do and make and be. Having things clean and put away while painting allows me to have a certain freedom when making the work, and I think the garden provides that too. There's a lot of order in my garden at first glance, but then it's also a place where I get to put my hands in the dirt. The thing that I enjoy the most is digging for potatoes. I always start by thinking 'I'll just grab a potato or two', then next thing I know, I have a whole mound of potatoes with my nails full of compacted dirt. The action of letting my hands dig and search and find, and then provide, is the same act and the same steps, for me, as making a painting. It's freedom.

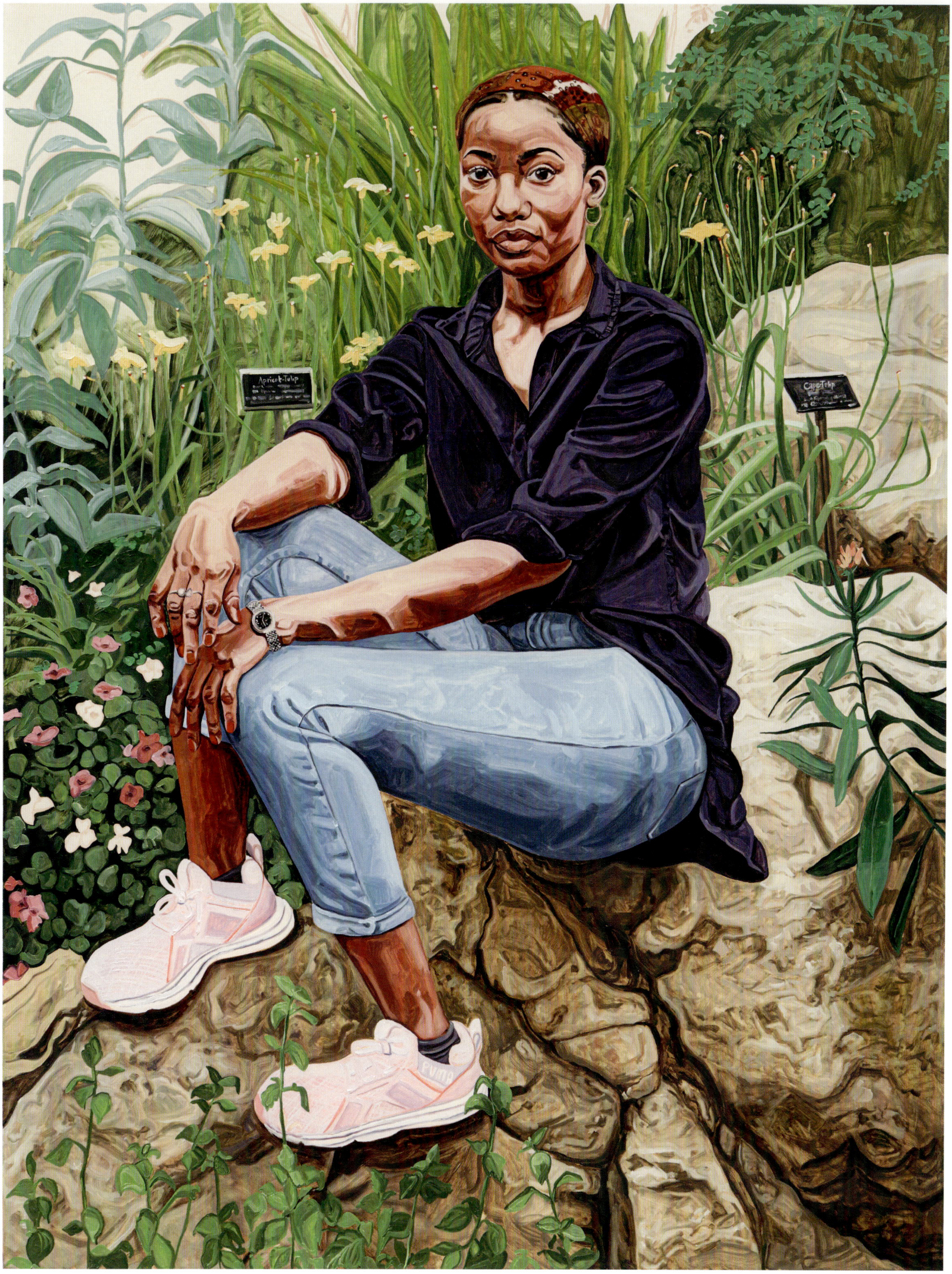
Apricot-Tulip
Cape-Tulip

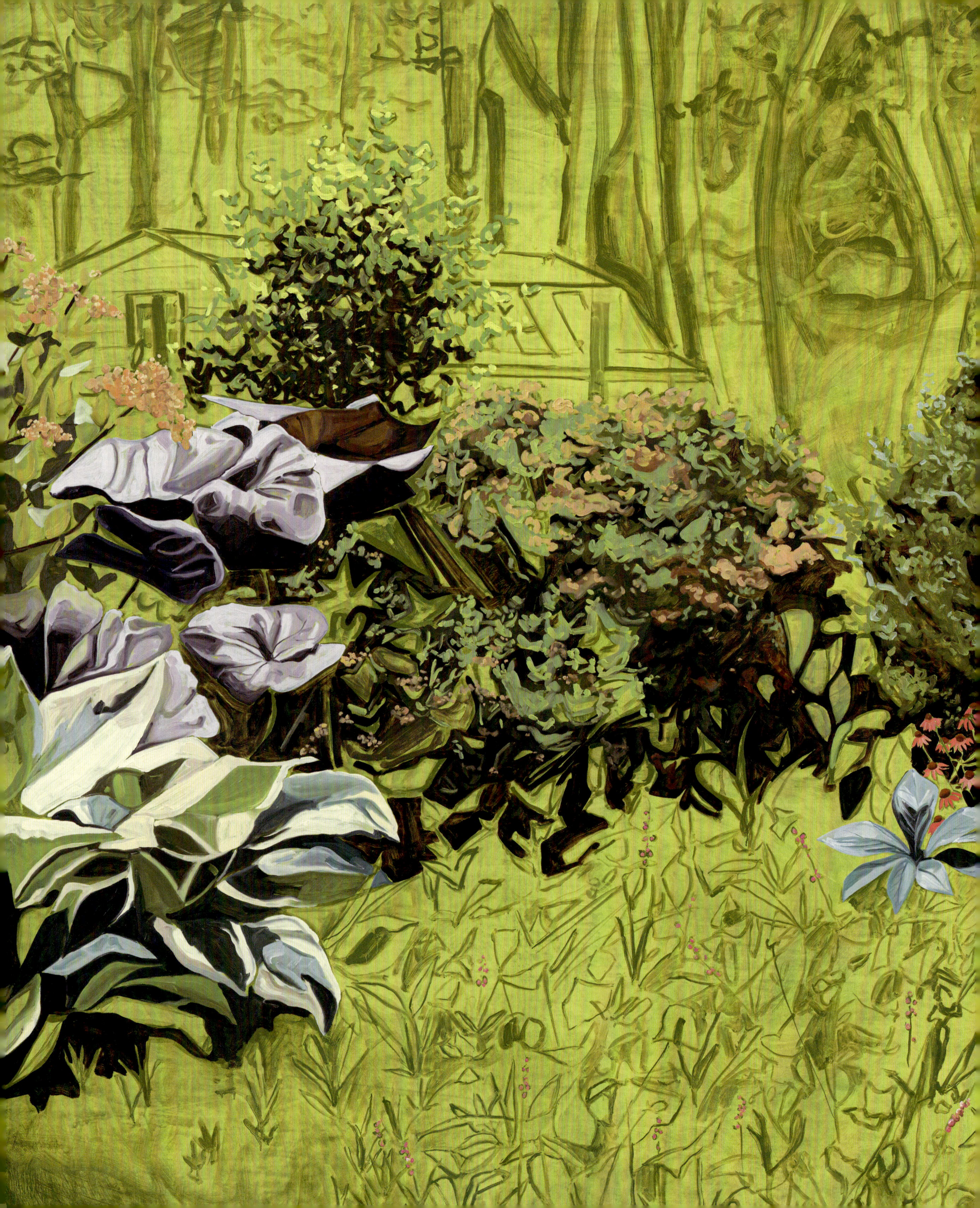

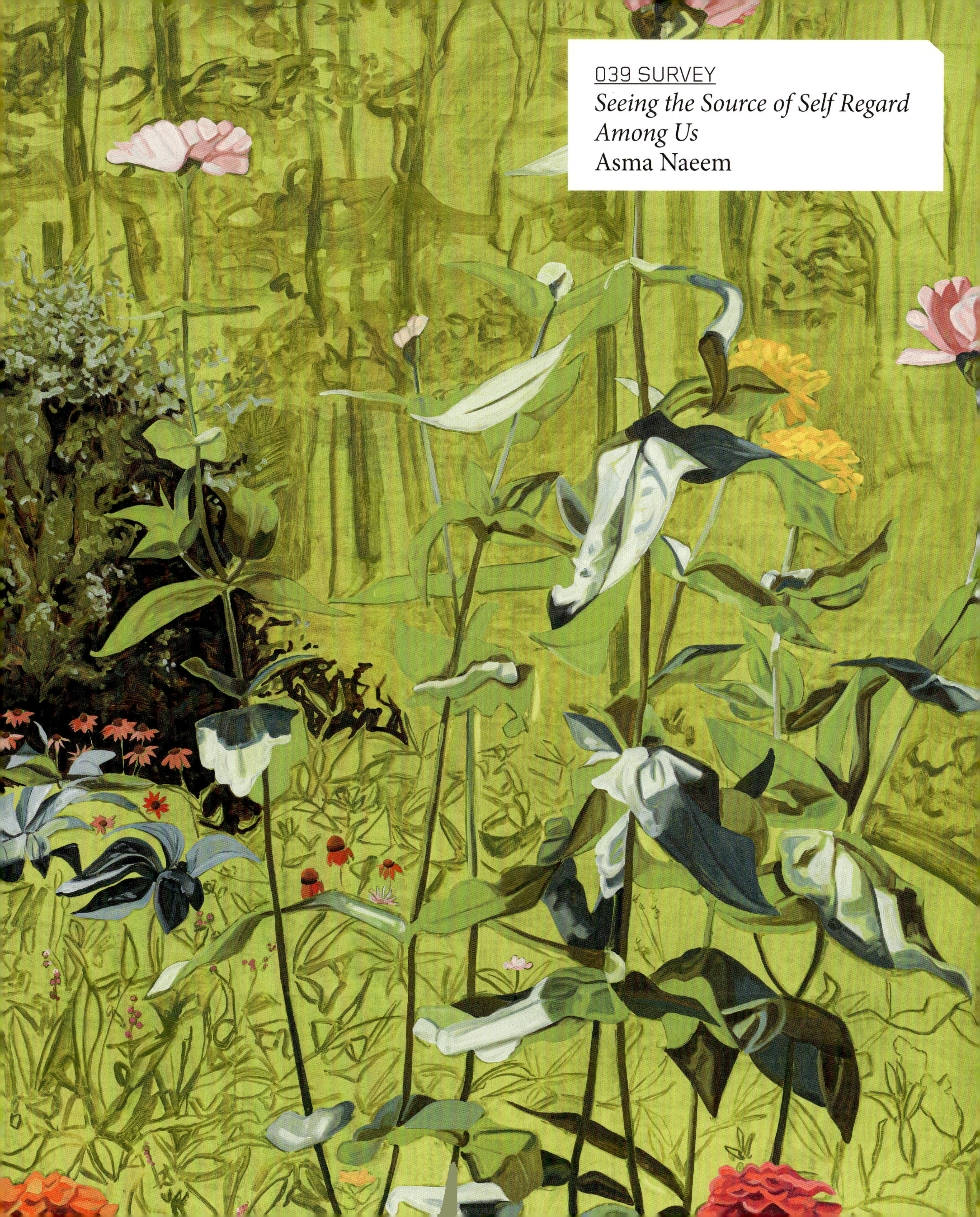

Seeing the Source of Self Regard Among Us

Asma Naeem

previous pages,
IN BLOOM, 2022
OIL ON CANVAS
198 X 229 CM

right,
NINA, 2024
OIL ON CANVAS
229 X 198 CM

The genre of portraiture – the stuff of history, fame, gilt-and-cobwebbed places of grandeur – inevitably frames Jordan Casteel's painting practice. In the history of art, portraiture has been used as a tool wielded as an assertion of power and privilege. So many examples bubble up, but for starters, think of Roman emperors on coins from antiquity, the fifteenth-century couple in Jan van Eyck's *The Arnolfini Portrait* (1434), Renaissance nobility kneeling at altars, or the Anglo-European chest-thumping tradition of the 'hall of worthies': a parade of portraits touting imperial lineage and colonial conquests of the 'noble savage'. And as far as portraits in the valorized medium of oil painting go, depictions of Blackness are typically relegated in a binary to whiteness, unnamed and marginalized.

Then in 1839 came the invention of photography, a quick form of portraiture, and another tool for self-empowerment. No one understood the potential of this mimetic technology better than renowned orator and abolitionist Frederick Douglass, who had escaped from slavery to become one of the most photographed persons of the nineteenth century. Douglass realized that his words alone could not counter the dehumanizing and violent tropes around Blackness in America's brutal horror of slavery – a carefully crafted public image as a powerful statesman and scholar could be just as potent.

Some fifty years later, in the Jim Crow era, Harlem Renaissance portraitist James Van Der Zee opened his photography studio, replete with Victorian props and furniture, to help represent an emerging Black middle-class in New York, dressed in their finest. In significant ways, new understandings of beauty and nostalgia across race began to flourish. As Black men fighting against objecthood and surveillance, Douglass and Van Der Zee were pioneers in approaching the critical enterprise of representation in visual culture on their own terms. Whether as sitter or artist, both understood agency and reception, the potency of crafting the image, how it is created and circulated among an intended audience. Decades later, 'representation' for the literary giant Toni Morrison meant 'lifting the veil' to reveal an interiority otherwise unshared. She explained, 'I'm looking to find and expose a truth about the interior life of people who didn't write it (which doesn't mean that they didn't have it) … I'm trying to fill in the blanks that the slave narratives left – to part the veil that was so frequently drawn, to implement the stories that I heard…'[1]

This unveiling was perhaps less easily achieved in oil painting. What do we know, for example, about the lives of the two unnamed Black women in *Untitled* by Lois Mailou Jones (p. 43), a leading light of the Harlem Renaissance and pillar of the Howard University Art department? Her 1945 portrait is an intervention for American modernist painting at the time: the portrait evokes unequivocal beauty through difference, but if this was a portrait of two real individuals, their names and their stories are lost to history.

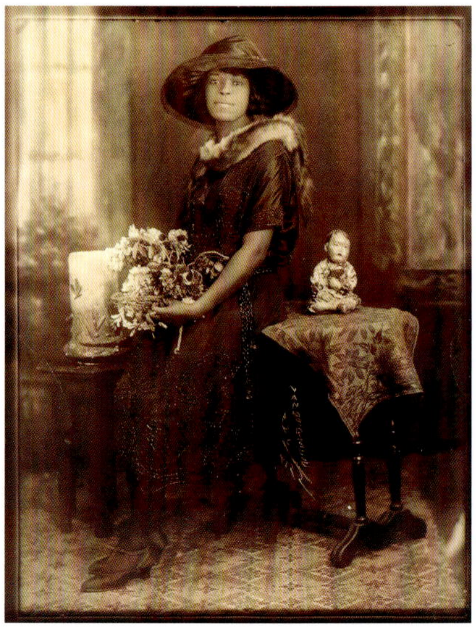

JAMES VAN DER ZEE
EVENING ATTIRE, 1922
GELATIN SILVER PRINT
25 X 20 CM

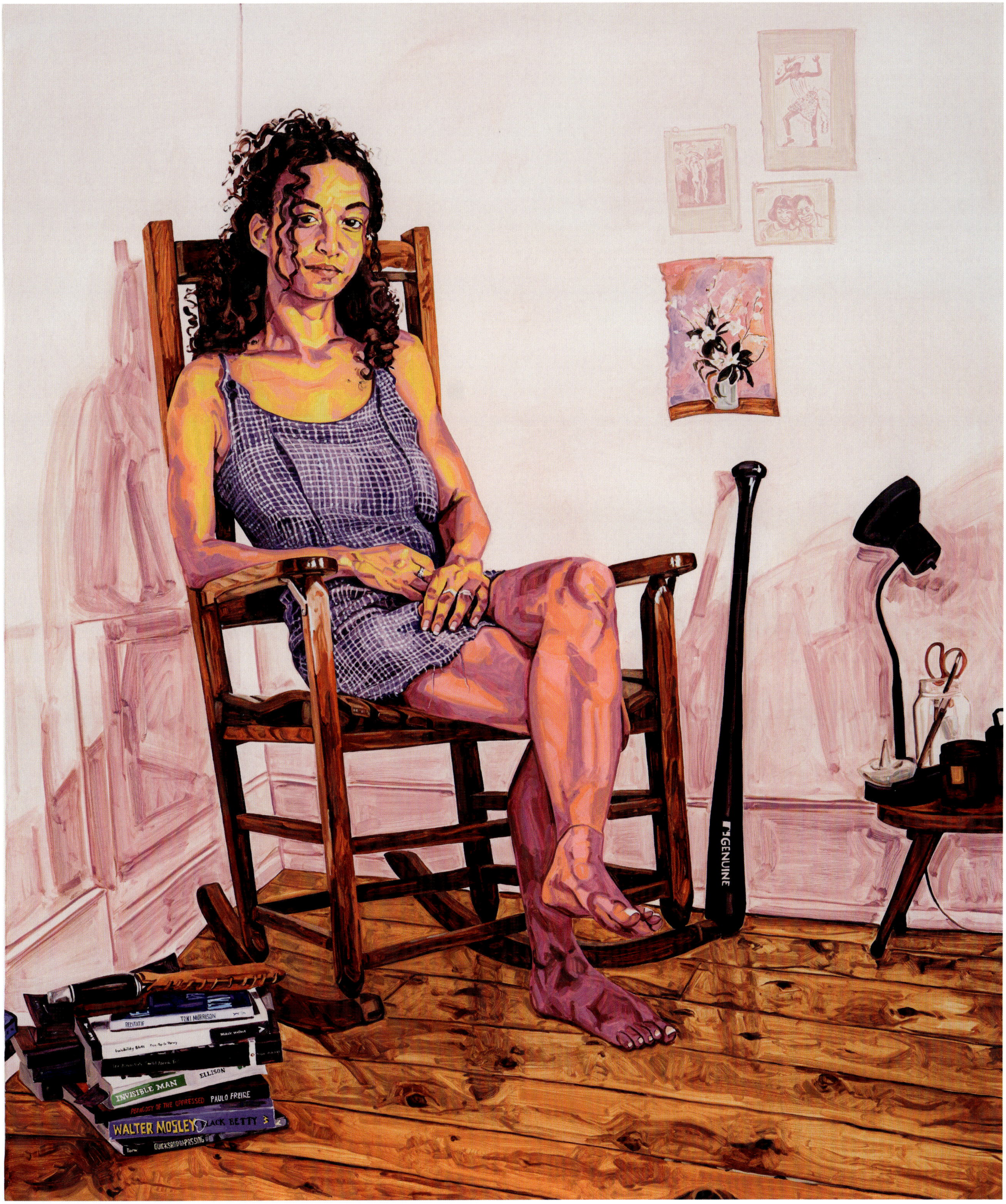
TONI MORRISON
INVISIBLE MAN
ELLISON
PAULO FREIRE
WALTER MOSLEY
BLACK BETTY
GENUINE

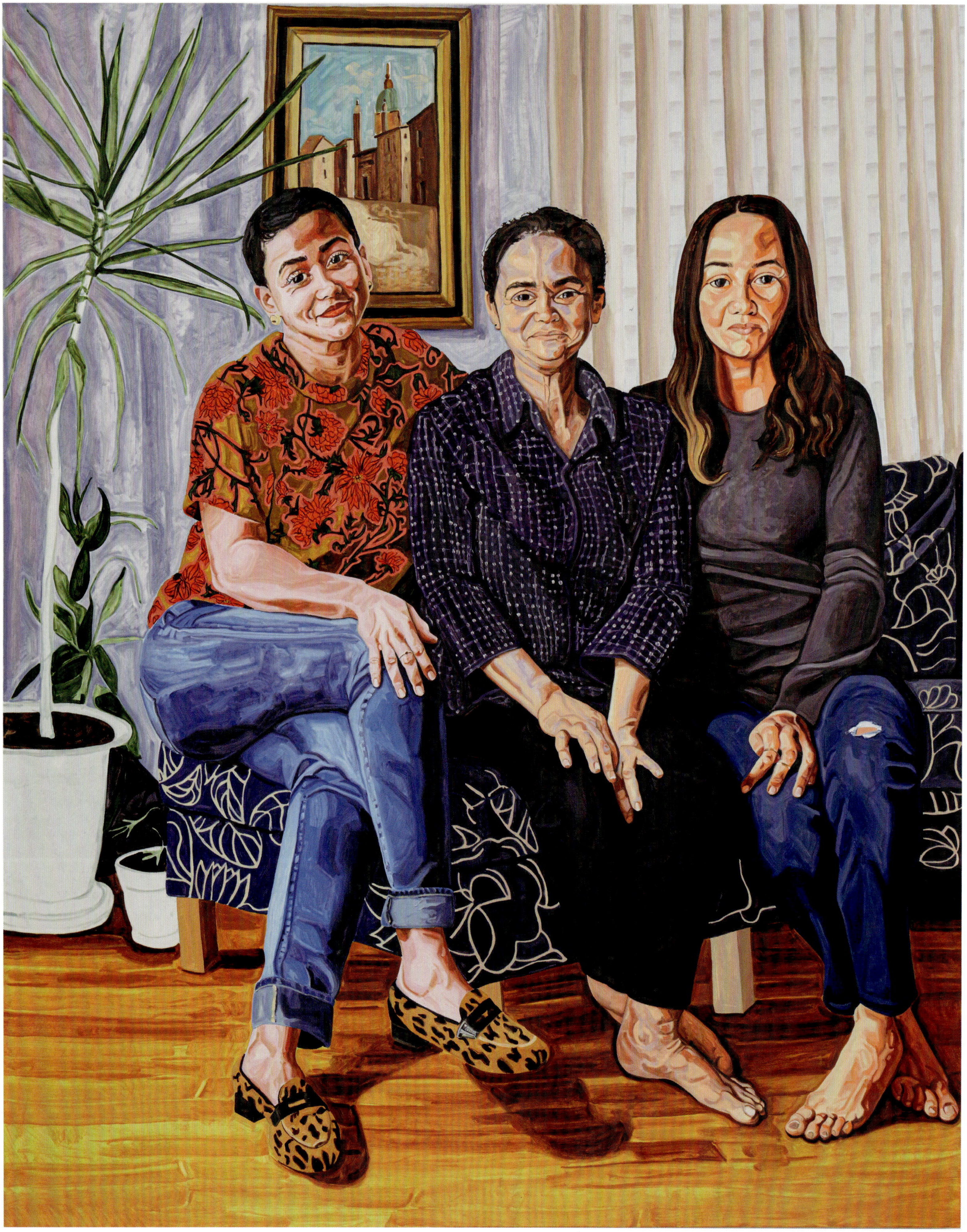

MEDINILLA, WANDA AND ANNELISE, 2019
OIL ON CANVAS
244 X 198 CM

Jordan Casteel's work flows from and builds on these radical thinkers and artists. Being able to capture her sitters and environments quickly and cumulatively through a camera became an access point in her painterly investigations of *representation*. Here's what she said in 2020 about her early perspective: 'I wanted to contribute very humanized, vulnerable representations of the Black male, and of Black bodies in general. I think I needed it. I needed more representations of that in my life, as the world was completely inundated with other images and narratives. [And if painting was going to be a reprieve for me], maybe it could also work for those people who are feeling unseen in the world … intimate, vulnerable people trying to navigate the world just like the rest of us.'[2] Casteel was referencing her prescient 'Visible Man' series, a poetics emerging from her considerations of her relationships with Black men in terms of her positionality as a Black woman. The work continues to be relevant, even as Casteel's dialectical gaze radiates in numerous directions today.

Guided by an unyielding emotional intelligence and passion for painting, Casteel's practice has tracked the various landscapes of her life, drawing Black and brown individuals into the foreground. Recently, the autobiographical element that has always been present in her paintings has become less easy to glimpse, not unlike peering through the twines in *Peak Summer* (2024, p. 46). And, as we see in *Peak Summer*, nowadays, her paintings of flowers attempt to reconcile seeming oppositions, like the moribundity of everyday beauty and timelessness, or the jolt of the nearly fluorescent orange with the deep greens and purples. As we shall see, this move to depictions of nature is less discordant than it might seem, since these works track the artist as she moves through the world, assessing, contemplating and shaking the shoulders of what she sees around her. When something or someone catches her eye, she begins to engage the subject both relationally and observationally with her camera, taking dozens of photographs. When depicting people, a narrative of personhood begins to accrue from which her paintings are constructed. Looking at the printed photographs in her studio and recalling the emotional valence of the encounter with her subject generates a prospective colour palette for her work.

Rifling through rectangular cards of saturated sample hues helps her hone in on the subject's psychic state, the flashes of expressions, maybe even the energy she felt, to visualize the personality of her subject.

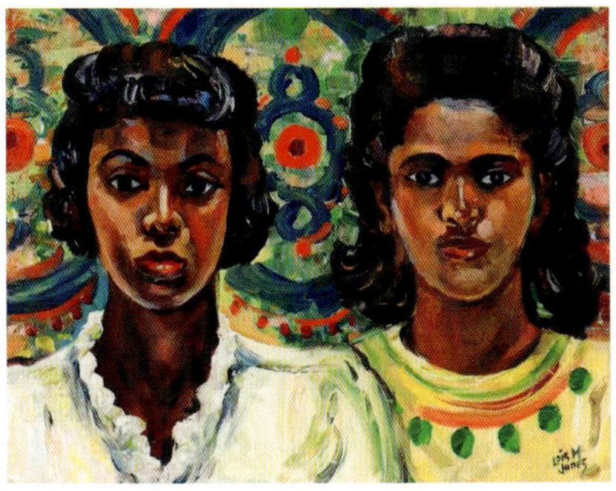

LOIS MAILOU JONES
UNTITLED, C. 1945
OIL ON LINEN
39 X 52 CM

THREE LIONS, 2015
OIL ON CANVAS
137 X 183 CM

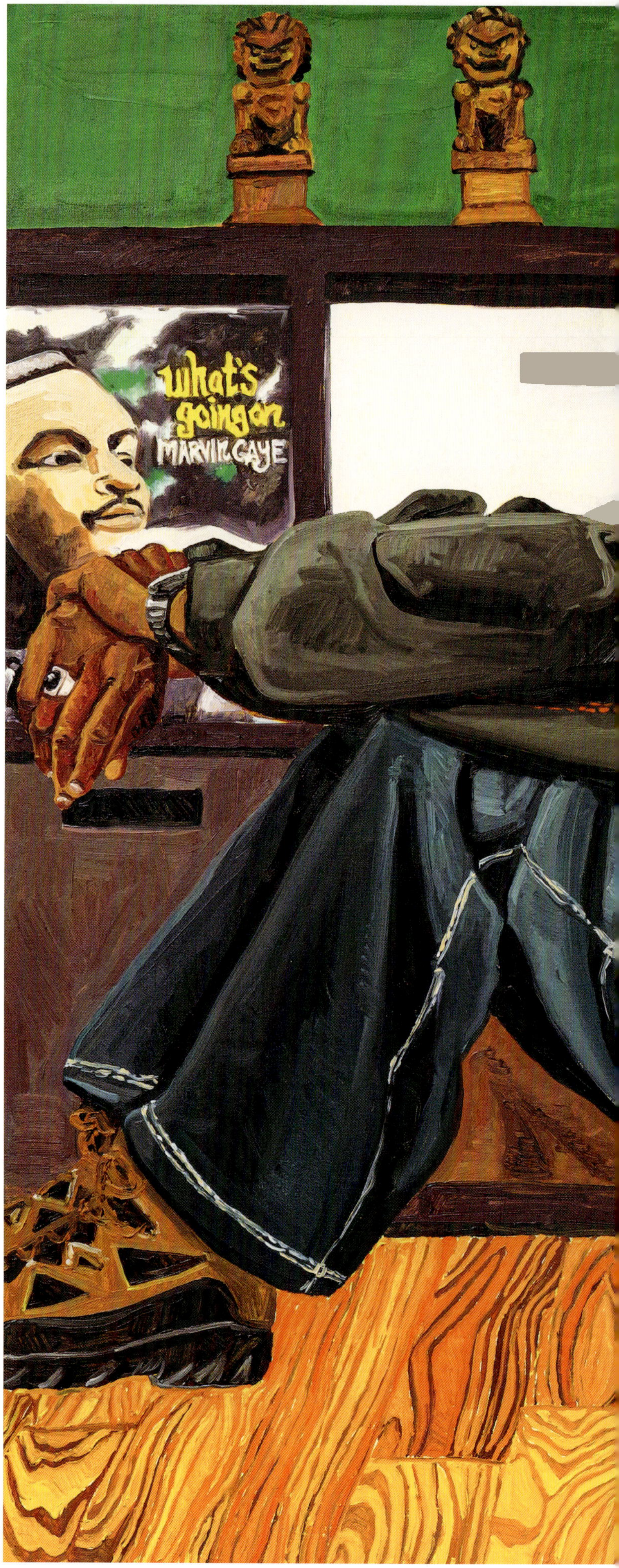

Colour seems to be the eye of the storm for each canvas, the nexus of energy from which the swirls of brushstrokes and particulate matter of her compositions emanate. In front of her canvas, she paints a base colour wash to set the tone for all that is to follow. Sketching with turpentine and paint, she draws the composition on canvas, and then works wet-on-wet to see what the colours from her preselected palette do and how they react to one another. With a rag in one hand, she is able to prevent colours from muddying through a constant wiping of her brush. Often she begins with the subject – for a figurative painting, she generally starts with the eyes – anchoring the composition with an aspect of the painting that she wants the viewer to experience, creating hierarchies of perceived importance throughout the frame. In contrast to her predilection to plan everything in advance, she leans into a deeply intuitive mode of creating. Abundant spontaneity can be detected when brush is applied, and each gesture of her brush is allowed to remain: she never edits or changes a painterly decision. Her process is not unlike the improvisational passions that electrify the jazz music of John Coltrane or Ornette Coleman, which as Fred Moten notes in *In the Break: The Aesthetics of the Black Radical Tradition* (2003), is grounded in structure but then overwhelmed by the musician's emotional and intuitive responses in real time as the instrument is played – resulting in an unfettered freedom that is unavailable for editing. The theoretical unboundedness of jazz and

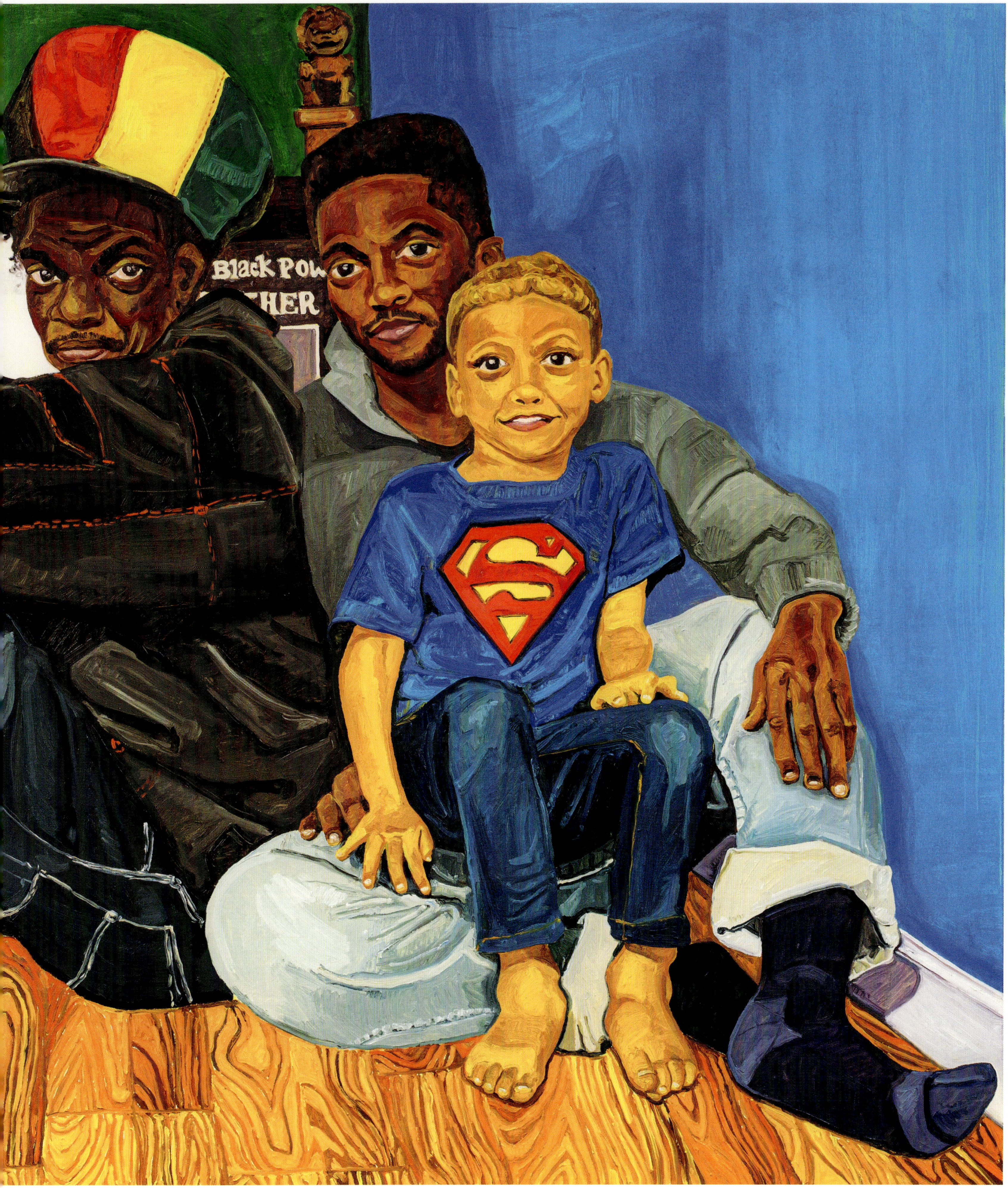

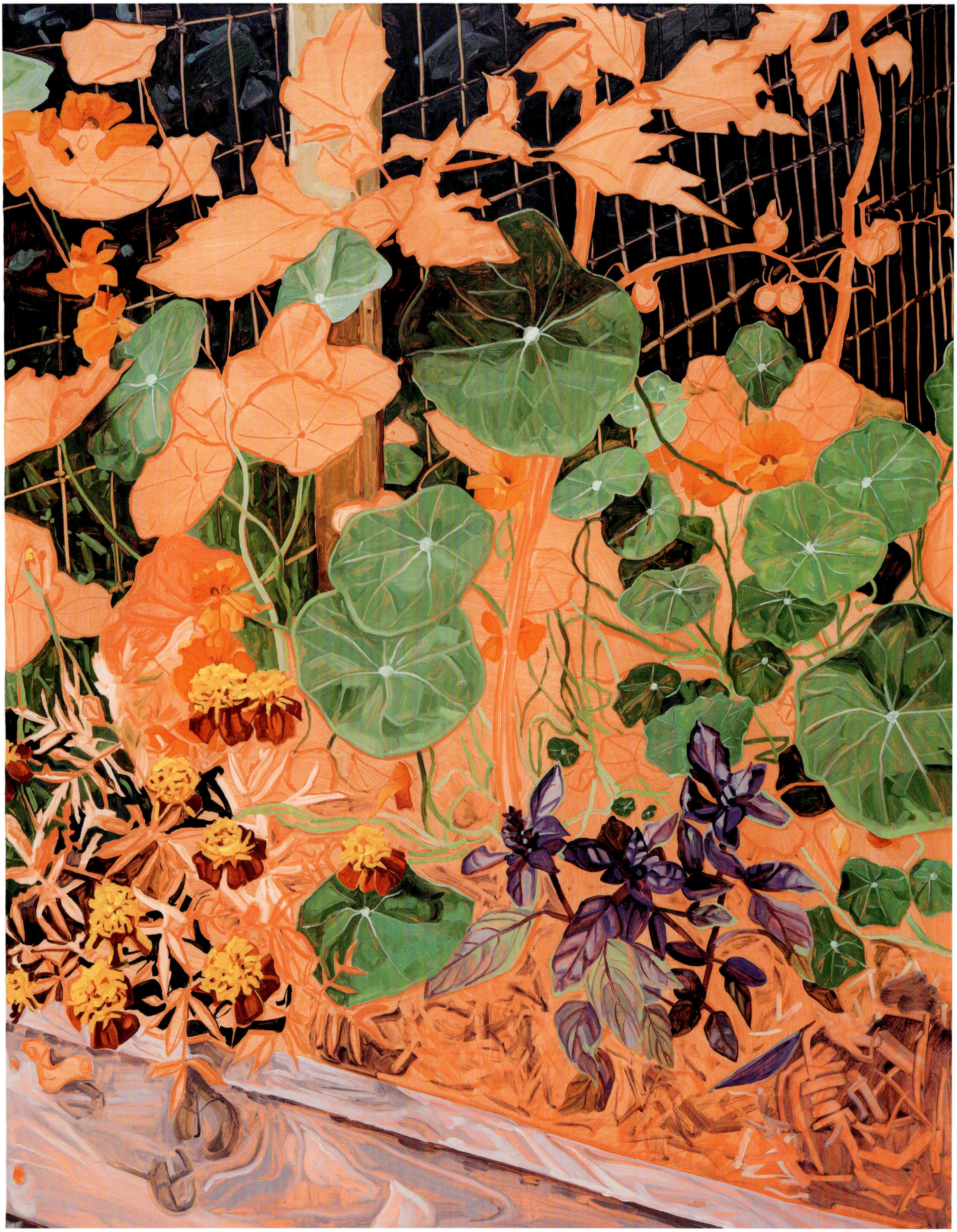

PEAK SUMMER, 2024
OIL ON CANVAS
127 X 102 CM

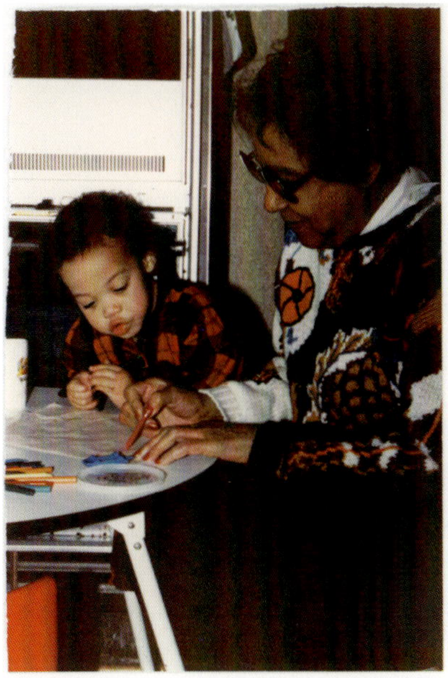

MARGARET BUCKNER YOUNG AND THE ARTIST, DENVER, 1992

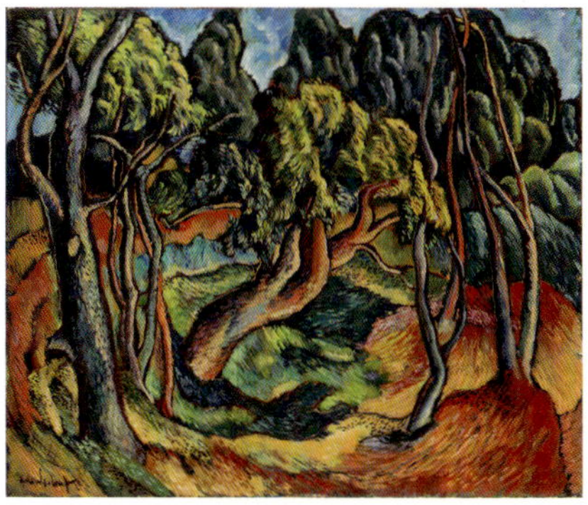

HALE WOODRUFF
GEORGIA LANDSCAPE, C. 1934–35
OIL ON CANVAS
54 X 65 CM

what it inspired in visual artists has a solid footing in the mid-1960s. Sam Gilliam, for example, was deeply influenced by Coltrane's trademark 'sheets of sound' melodic construction, his ecstatic canvases exemplifying the unstructured process and in-the-moment responsiveness and trust of instinct. Gilliam and his peers – not unlike Piet Mondrian two decades earlier when he created the iconic *Broadway Boogie-Woogie* (1942–43) – saw fit to translate the transcending qualities of the new genre by embracing abstraction, itself a breakaway from historical painting canons. Casteel, conversely, imports the pioneering ethos of jazz into figurative painting, somehow repositioning the liberated Black sounds within an immediately recognizable African-American cultural aesthetic.

Such bold updating of a rooted visual and musical tradition can effectively be traced back to Casteel's affinity with the first generation of 'Post-Black' artists, and their embracing of 'the dichotomies of high and low, inside and outside, tradition and innovation, with a great ease and facility'.[3] Originally coined by Robert Farris Thompson in 1991, and later popularized by Thelma Golden and Glenn Ligon, the term 'Post-Black' is now widely used to describe the work of Rashid Johnson, Julie Mehretu, Kara Walker, Kehinde Wiley and the other artists included in 'Freestyle' at the Studio Museum in Harlem in 2001 – an exhibition propelled in equal measure by the energy generated by the turn of the Millennium and the great multi-cultural rhetoric of the 1980s. Well-educated and influenced by different experiences, the participants in 'Freestyle' displayed a desire to explore Blackness in a more nuanced and individualized way. They also had very few qualms about deploying references across a remarkably broad spectrum – an unmistakable sign that something a lot more crucial than a simple generational turnover was taking place. Golden herself was taken aback by how comfortably the participants would mention artists like Robert Colescott and Sigmar Polke in the same sentence. 'It wasn't about one being better than the other or the need for one more than the other – like I need to cite Polke so you'll know I'm a serious artist working in the Western tradition or I need to cite Colescott so you'll know I'm down. No, it was Polke Colescott.'[4]

Born in Denver, Colorado in 1989, Casteel has long been exposed to the power of a vast and actively engaged community through her familial ties. Her maternal grandfather, Whitney Moore Young, Jr. (1921–71), was the fourth president of The National Urban League (NUL) during one of its most impactful periods, at the height of the Civil Rights era in the 1960s. In fact, Casteel was named after the subsequent president of The National Urban League, close family friend, lawyer and presidential advisor Vernon Jordan. Similarly, her maternal grandmother, Margaret Buckner Young (1921–2009), a Spelman College professor of educational psychology and children's book author, was a tireless advocate for empowering Black communities. While in New York, Buckner Young sat on the board of the Metropolitan Museum of Art, Lincoln Center and Dance Theatre of Harlem. Perhaps due to her influence, Casteel's childhood home was filled with art and books by such Black masters as Romare Bearden, Elizabeth Catlett, Hale Woodruff, Faith Ringgold and Charles White.

In 2011, Casteel left Denver to attend Agnes Scott College, a small liberal arts women's college in Decatur, GA. She initially majored in Sociology and Anthropology, but found herself changing her major to Studio Art after studying abroad for a semester in Cortona, Italy. It was here that she took her first oil-painting class.

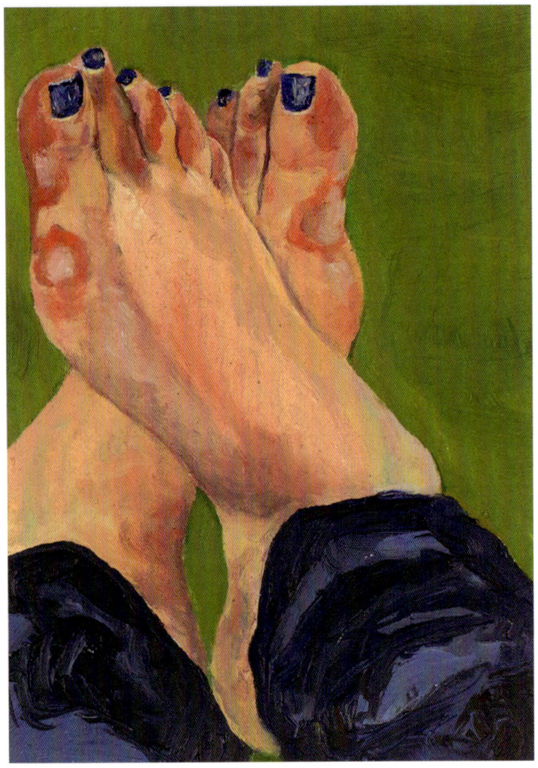

left,
LUPUS FEET, 2012
OIL ON CANVAS
18 X 13 CM

opposite, clockwise from top left,
SELF PORTRAIT (CLOSED EYES), 2013
OIL ON CANVAS
23 X 18 CM

SELF PORTRAIT (PASTEL), 2013
OIL ON CANVAS
75 X 61 CM

SELF PORTRAIT, 2013
OIL ON CANVAS
81 X 66 CM

SELF PORTRAIT (GREEN FACE), 2013
OIL ON CANVAS
46 X 36 CM

Drawn immediately to the possibilities offered by art as an outlet to express complex ideas through images, she soon made a conscious decision to elevate craft as her primary mode of communication, and began to represent the environment surrounding her in a way that remains in much of her practice today. The objects, landscapes and people who enriched her experience became muses for the work she would go on to make. Casteel's portraits, in particular, while compositionally different from those she would create later (in most cases, only the head of the sitter is visible), displayed from the outset an intensity that made them powerful and thought-provoking. The emotional investment in her subjects is expressed through a mature use of form and colour, the latter arranged on the faces in a mosaic-style that reflects the complexity of an individual's identity and layers of existence. The expressiveness of Casteel's work did not escape her hometown press, who hailed her as one of the twelve artists from Colorado under thirty-five to watch after seeing her work in a group exhibition at the now defunct Sellars Project Space in Denver. 'This recent graduate from Agnes Scott College in Decatur, GA., is bounding with potential' wrote Kyle Macmillan from *The Denver Post*.[5] Casteel's list of influences in the article, spanning from Egon Schiele to Alice Neel, supports what Golden had said a decade earlier about the wide references made by the artists involved in her 'Freestyle' exhibition. Casteel adds a note of social engagement in her statement: 'Artists of my generation can engage in societal dialogue and question our identities in more vulnerable ways. My generation is choosing to think critically and interact with the world around us with a more intentional social change consciousness. We are no longer just dealing with local communities; we have tapped into the world through new media forms.'[6]

After graduating from Agnes Scott College in 2011, Casteel spent a year teaching primary and secondary school before she sought her Master's in Fine Arts to combine her love of art and education. Accepted by the esteemed Yale School of Art, Casteel stepped into her first formalized art-educational space. The Yale years, from 2012–14, sowed the seeds for some of the most fruitful aspects of Casteel's practice. They provided the high-calibre faculty and foundational training that would ultimately round out her natural talent, propelling her artmaking and defining who she wanted to be as an artist. It is likely that her decision to explore self-portraiture during this time was borne out of accessibility, but we also know from looking at centuries of history of art that self-portraits almost invariably signal a moment of recalibration and introspection in the careers of artists.

Indeed, by seeking challenges and new approaches that would push her beyond her comfort zone and support her voice and vision, Casteel was searching for her own language. She found that painting herself offered a way to build a painterly confidence and vocabulary. She realized how much she had to learn about artmaking, but that pushing herself to grow also meant retaining aspects

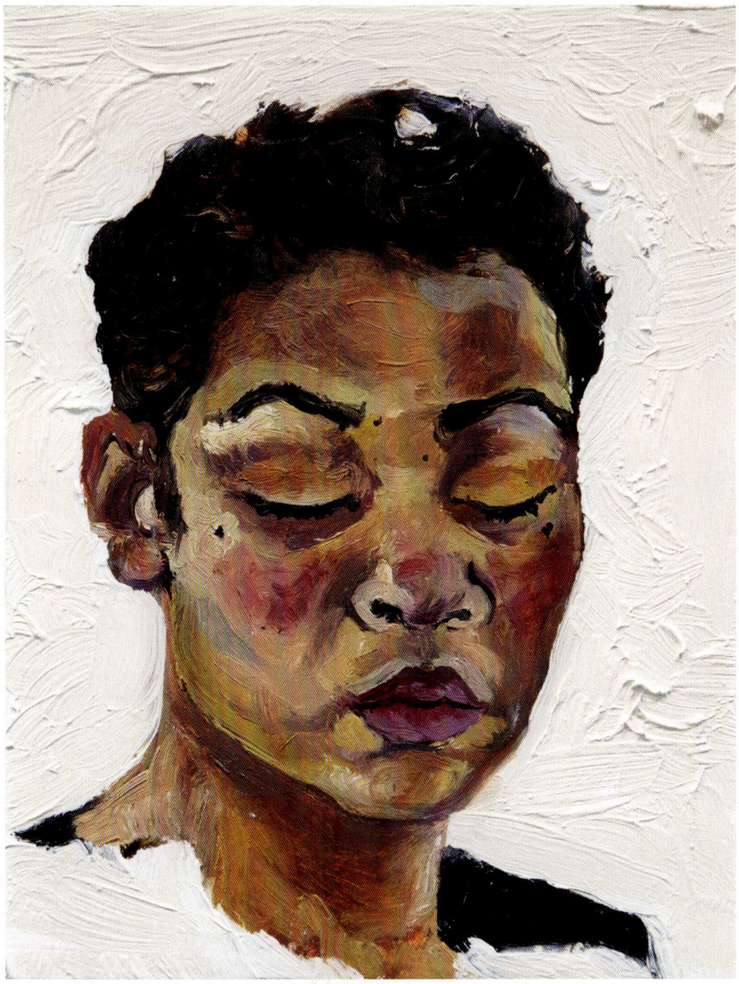
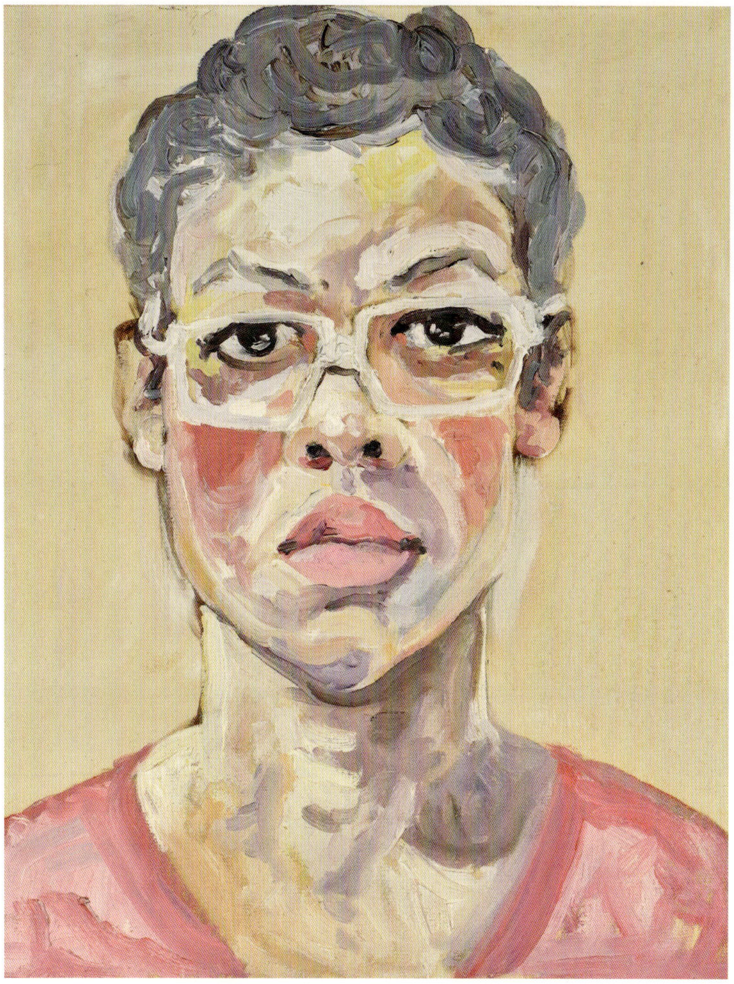
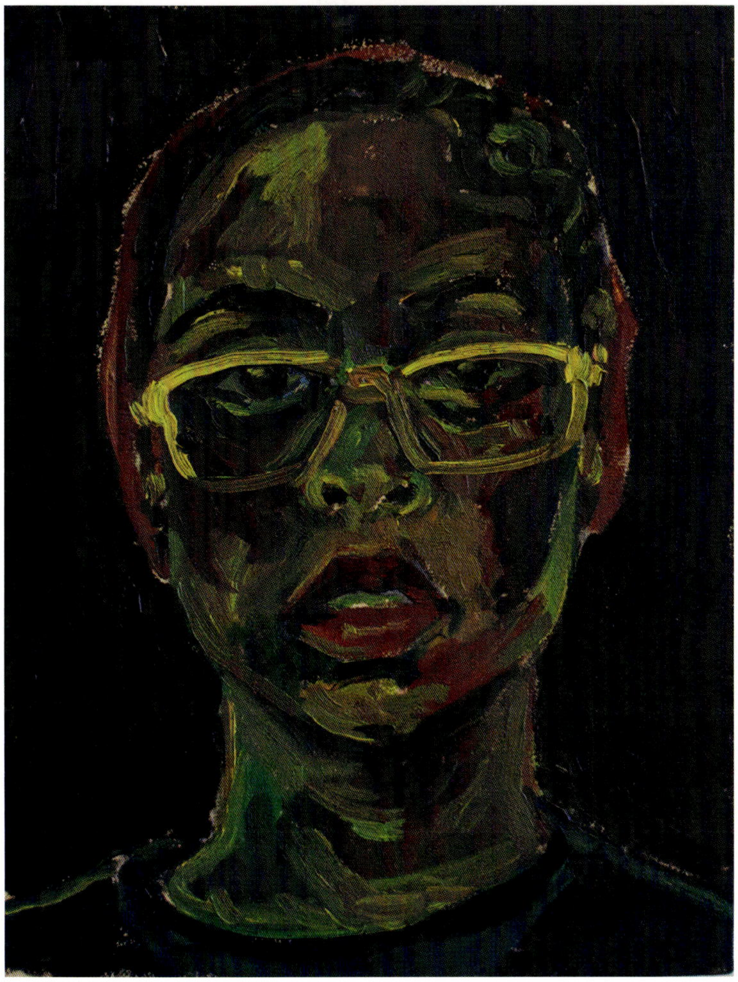
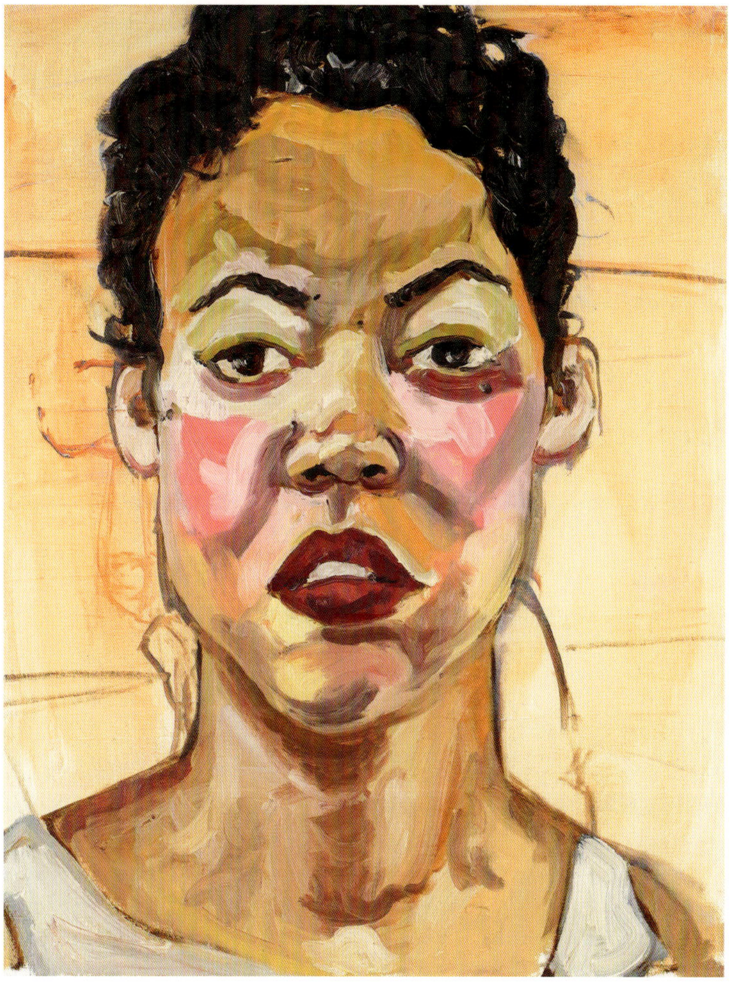

JIRÉH, 2013
OIL ON CANVAS
183 X 132 CM

of herself and her authenticity. Between her first and second years, she spent time in Gloucester, MA, creating *plein-air* paintings and contemplating the learnings of the year before in order to return to campus for her final year with a strong sense of purpose.

It was also during this time that Casteel deepened her knowledge of a series of artists and exhibitions that would eventually help her to solidify her status as 'a painter's painter', seduced by the medium's depth and traceability. She was, as she would acknowledge later, 'drawn to the way painting holds my translation and allows me to see through the eyes of all the painters who have come before.'[7] Apart from the aforementioned 'Freestyle' show, there was the Charles Gaines-curated 'The Theater of Refusal: Black Art and Mainstream Criticism' (University of California Fine Arts Gallery, Irvine, 1993), a ground-breaking exhibition that further pried open the assumptions and contradictions about Black creativity and the existence of multiple art histories; Thelma Golden's 'Black Male: Representations of Masculinity in Contemporary American Art' (Whitney Museum of American Art, New York, 1994), a survey featuring the work of about thirty artists that would permanently rewrite the way Black masculinity is represented in art, film and television. Then there was Kara Walker's investigation of race, gender, sexuality and violence through a group of iconic silhouetted figure-based works that would position her as the bridge between the old and new generation; and of course Kerry James Marshall's quest for restoring the balance of Black representation within the mainstream canon by reactivating and subsequently updating the Renaissance tradition of art as a conduit for scientific knowledge and social change.

One of Marshall's early efforts – the arresting self-portrait *Portrait of the Artist as a Shadow of his Former Self* (1980), would end up playing a foundational role in Casteel's first New York solo exhibition. Inspired by Ralph Ellison's seminal novel *Invisible Man* (1952), *Portrait of the Artist as a Shadow of his Former Self* makes a damning critique of Western painting where Marshall flips the script on its formal aspects – colour, light, shadow – to craft an image that is both stereotype and truth at its rawest. Taking as her starting point Ellison's statement 'I was looking for myself and asking everyone except myself questions which I, and only I, could answer',[8] as well as Toni Morrison's famously pungent response to Ellison: 'Invisible to whom? Not to me',[9] and Marshall's visual rendition on the dilemma of being present and absent at the same time, Casteel embarked on a series of paintings borne from a desire to create sensitive depictions of the Black men who were a part of her world. There were, of course, other considerations of a historical, contemporary and

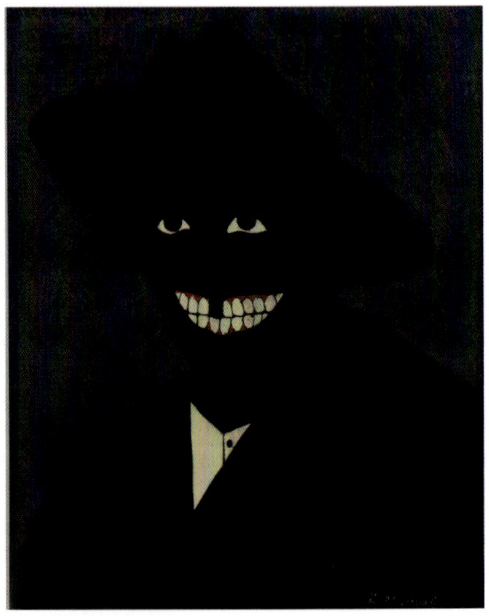

KERRY JAMES MARSHALL
PORTRAIT OF THE ARTIST AS A SHADOW OF HIS FORMER SELF, 1980
EGG TEMPERA ON PAPER
20 X 17 CM

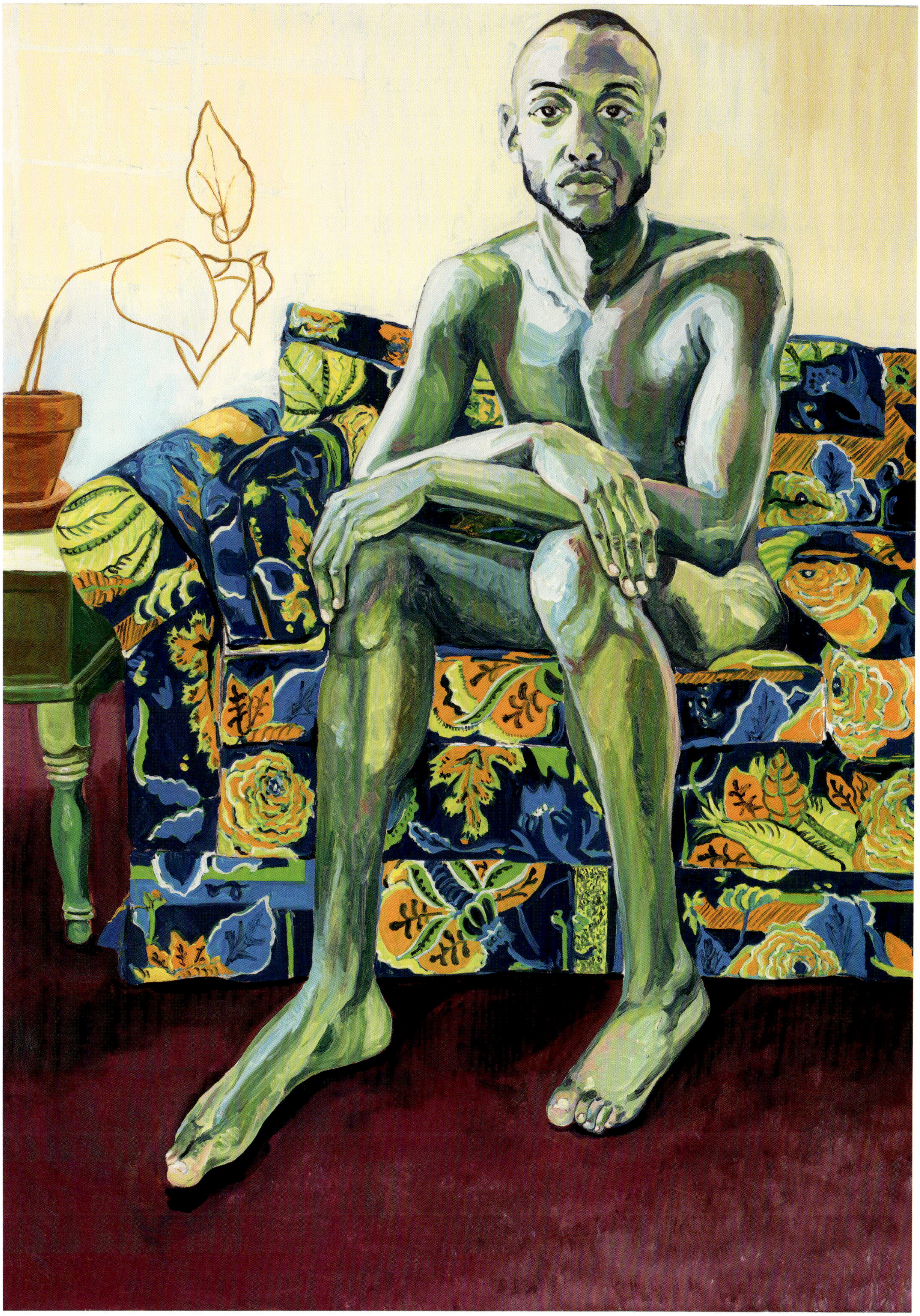

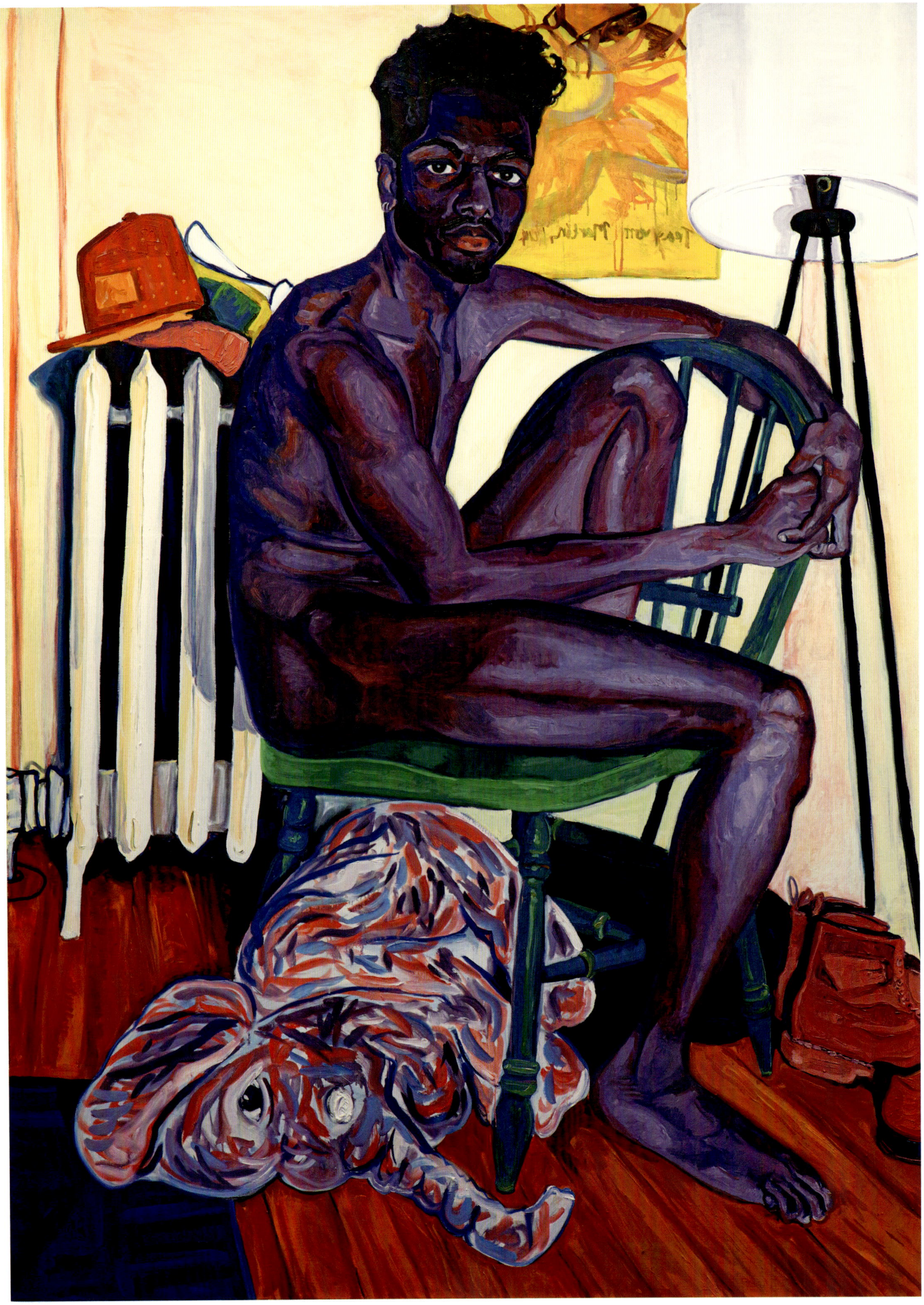

DEVAN, 2014
OIL ON CANVAS
188 X 137 CM

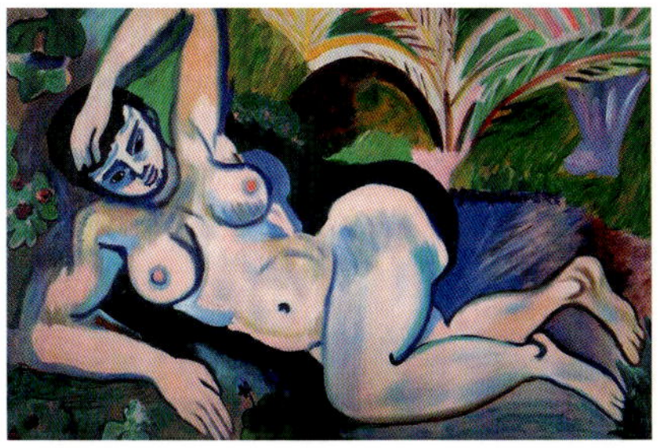

HENRI MATISSE
NU BLEU, SOUVENIR DE BISKRA (BLUE NUDE: SOUVENIR OF BISKRA), 1907
OIL ON CANVAS
92 X 140 CM

procedural nature. The series re-introduced bell hooks' writings as a significant companion in Casteel's thinking. As articulated by hooks in *Black Looks: Race and Representation*, 'For those of us who dare to desire differently, who seek to look away from the conventional ways of seeing blackness and ourselves, the issue of race and representation is not just a question of critiquing the status quo. It is also about transforming the image, creating alternatives, asking ourselves questions about what types of images subvert, pose critical alternatives, and transform our worldviews and move us away from dualistic thinking about good and bad.'[10]

Casteel's question became, 'How do I create a painting of these men who have been in my life as their truest selves? You know, as the loving, intimate, caring fathers, sons, brothers, friends, men I've dated, kissed. The ones that I've had a very real history with.'[11] Her first foray, a portrait of a family friend, incited reactions that stereotyped the sitter based on his clothing and footwear. Clothing on a Black male body, Casteel discovered, can create distractions for viewers, since it carries a number of assumptions about race, class and culture. To wrest her subjects from what could be seen as racializing presentations or typical signifiers of Blackness, Casteel shifted the approach to paint her subjects nude, a self-fashioning without the fashioning if you will, highlighting them as human beings who are both vulnerable and comfortable in their own skin.

Casteel's engagement with her sitters in their own space and comfort zone coincided with a significant increase of scale in her paintings. This can be attributed to a boost of confidence in what the ever-self-questioning artist perceived, and correctly so as it turned out, as the beginning of a cycle where all the elements she had been looking for were finally coming together. But there is more. To better capture their environment as well as their complex psychological and physical nuances, a more detailed methodology designed to collect as much information as possible over a limited amount of time was now required. That's when photography entered the picture. Equipped with a camera – a tool she would later come to define on multiple occasions as exclusively a research device – Casteel would take multitudes of shots of her subjects, enriching her compositions with constructed composites driven by the desire to see the familiar as well as the unknown in a different light. The fact that within the space of one month during the summer of 2014 – the very same summer Casteel debuted 'Visible Man' in New York – Eric Garner and Michael Brown lost their lives to unaccounted brutality, added to the poignancy.

When Casteel shared work from the series with faculty, a few questioned how her depictions of nude Black men would be interpreted. One school member dismissed the absence of visible genitalia – a deliberate decision on the artist's part to steer away from distraction and

ELIJAH, 2014
OIL ON CANVAS
132 X 183 CM

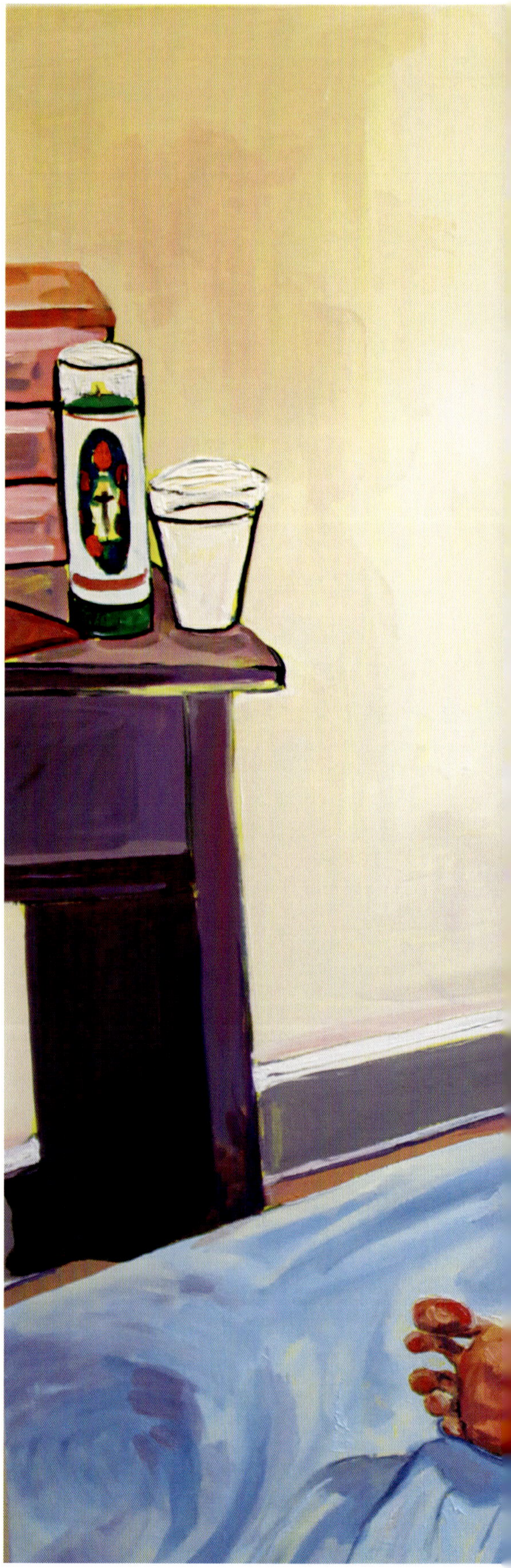

give the male Black body the respect it historically deserves – as an 'act of castration'. The resources of support might have felt thin, but Casteel was not deterred, encouraged by the few mentors who saw merit in what she was doing, and in particular by the words of art historian Sarah Lewis, an ardent supporter who made the core of her studies the concept of failure as a cornerstone of innovation and creativity. 'Jordan, I have so much respect for you, because you do not and will not. I urge you to continue to fight that fight.'[12] Fortified by Lewis's encouragement, Casteel went back to her work with a renewed sense of resolve. This is particularly evident in *Devan* (2014, p. 52), where we find one of Casteel's former classmates, nude, and looking directly at us, sitting with his long lean limbs arching around the back of a green-painted Windsor chair. On the floor are boots and a stuffed elephant painted in zipping strokes of red, purple and blue. The sitter's skin is interpreted with deep violaceous tones that evoke an inner force. It was during this time that Casteel began to use a spectrum of colours to represent skin tone as one of her 'critical alternatives'. Like Bob Thompson or Beauford Delaney, who each in their own strokes and style rendered their figures in bold, expressive colours, Casteel is interested in pushing the viewer's experience of Blackness through colour. The grand scale of the work, over six feet high, is aggrandizing and yet intimacy is registered by the gentle regard and openness of the sitter. It is hard to imagine what Casteel said or did to achieve such a level of comfort, hard to imagine the trust-building that must have had to occur for such deeply personal looking and exchange. Meeting people in their homes, sometimes for the first time, Casteel's intention was to capture them where they felt most at ease, in a by no means pre-determined or preconceived but rather collaborative manner. What Casteel describes as the 'call and response' dynamic of portraiture is generative for the artist – you sense that the subject's extended glance is first towards her, and then for us all. Casteel has commented on how this series galvanized her artistic trajectory. The project may have been driven by a powerful desire to image a *relationality* or humanity, not to mention a counteracting of the reductive and essentializing depictions of Black men rampant in popular culture, but it also emboldened the artist to come into her own.

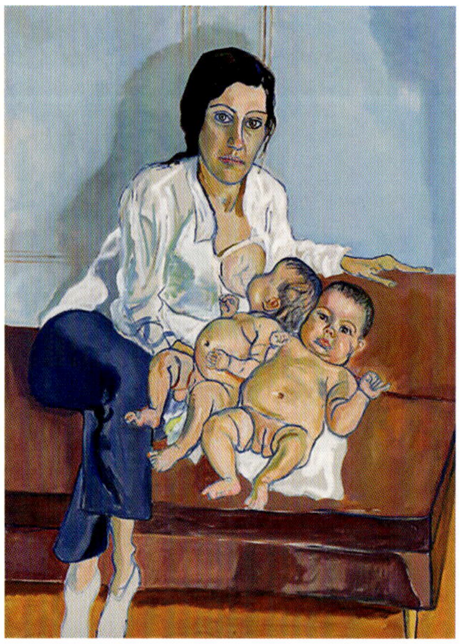

ALICE NEEL
NANCY AND THE TWINS, 1971
OIL ON CANVAS
137 X 102 CM

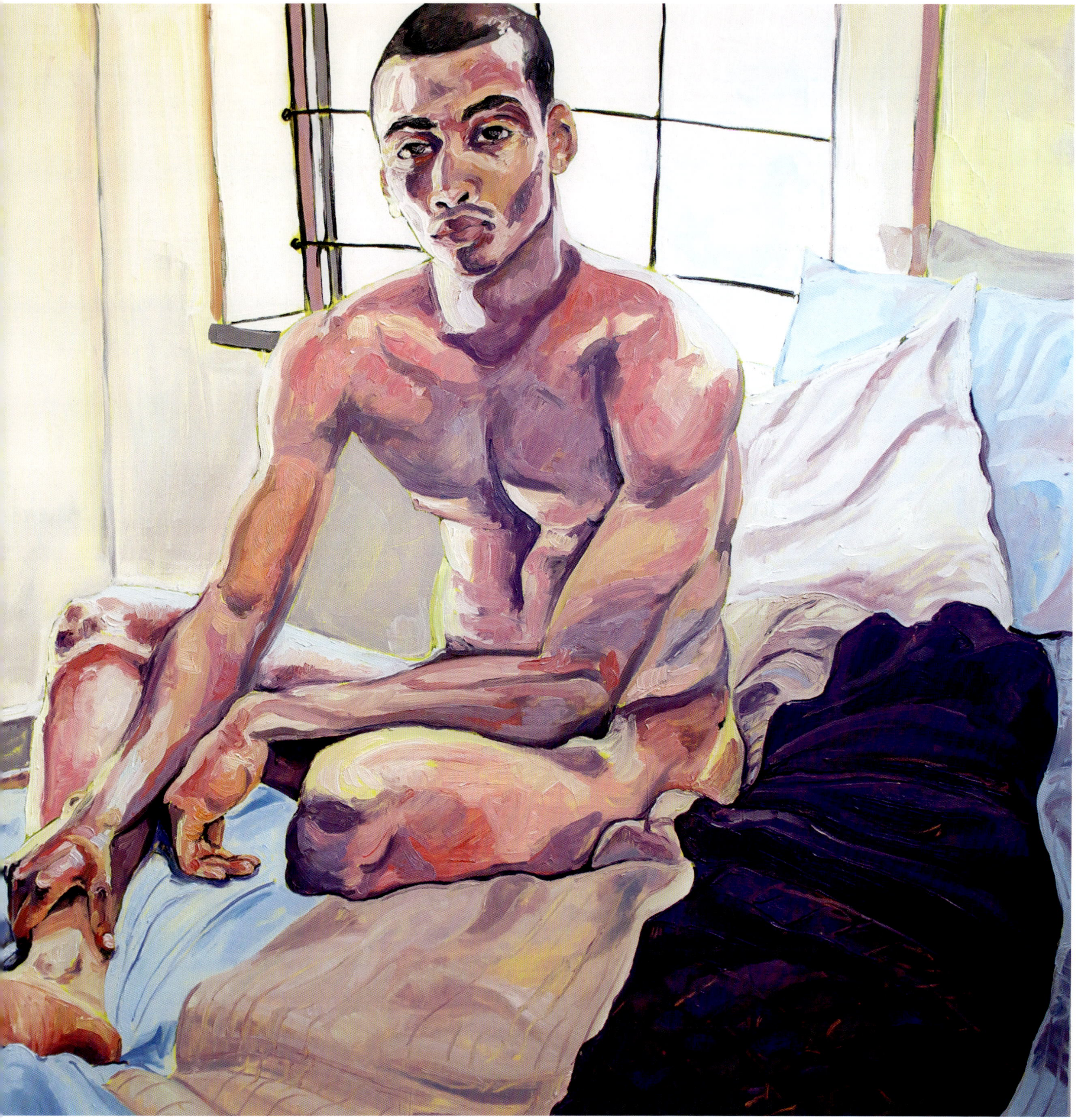

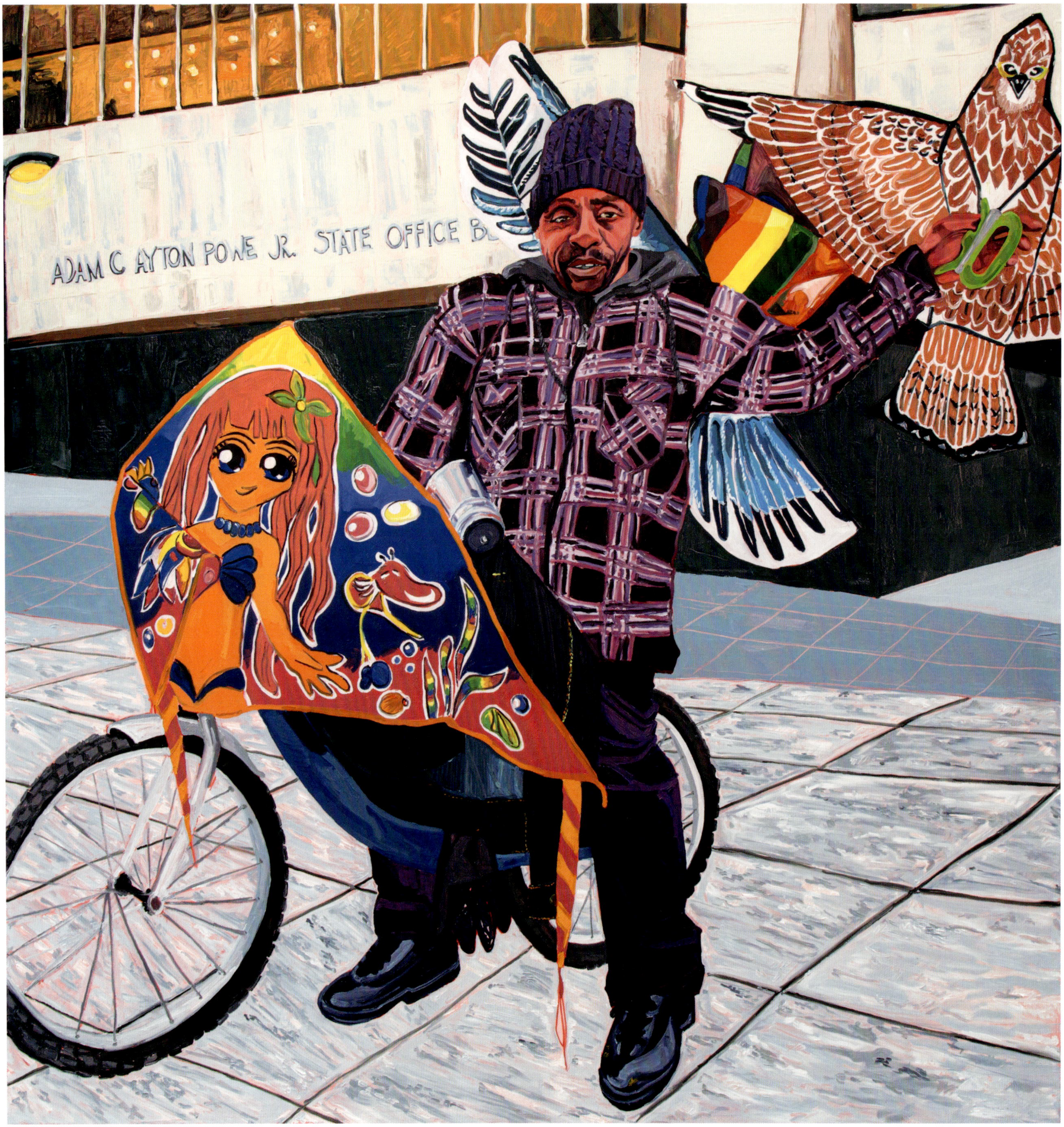
STATE OFFICE

opposite,
KEVIN THE KITEMAN, 2016
OIL ON CANVAS
198 X 198 CM

Aaron (2013, see pp. 14-15), another painting from the series, shows a nude man lying on a bed in his home, a still life of objects falling out of the frame, and a bright window balancing the composition. With its wild, fulminating palette and twisting form, the work specifically recalls the iconic painting *Blue Nude* by Henri Matisse (p. 53). Like the *Blue Nude*, which was a grenade in the post-Enlightenment project that spurred protests and burning effigies for its unnaturalness, Casteel's work is a contravention of the cultural imagination. And like the *Blue Nude*, this naked Black man in oil on canvas dares us not to stare at him, moody, with almond-shaped eyes, a chest seemingly glowing with embers. At the same time, the bands of colour pull the eye across the composition, with the undulating crimson blanket and assorted objects (bottles, Vaseline, cards) arranged on it, creating a cocooning effect for the richly painted body of dark purples and passages of palette knife creating a thick impasto. The work is an experiment in striking colour (that unexpected light apricot wall), levels of finish, and different mark-making.

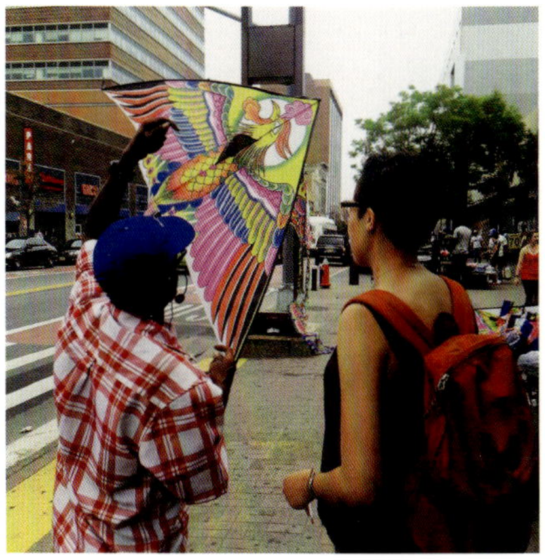

THE ARTIST WITH KEVIN HINES, HARLEM, NEW YORK, 2016

It was the work of Alice Neel that inspired Casteel to find the language she was looking for, where colour could become line and line could become colour, and equally important, where a charged dynamic with her sitters, singed with compassion could be established. In works like *Aaron* and *Elijah* (2014, see pp. 54-55), for example, the body is contained in the space, with a dramatic widening of the frame. Time and time again, her figures can barely be accommodated by the canvas, with their heads cropped or their toes touching the bottom. These choices by Casteel seem to mimic social borders or constraints of misrepresentation, and enhance anxieties around what we might be missing or cannot understand. Similarly, the direct gazes of her subjects are cemented during this time as an explicit decision by Casteel to both exhibit the subjects' confidence and protect them as the paintings leave the care of the author, never allowing the subject or artist to be rendered invisible.

As another of Casteel's subjects, playwright Mansa Ra (formerly known as Jiréh Breon Holder) articulated it, 'Jordan's paintings "saw" something in us, and we were able to see something in each other that was and remains deeply meaningful.'[13] By portraying her fellow Black students at Yale, Casteel had documented, and in a way created, a community through a strong visual language made up of powerful strokes and a sapient construction of space. Such a community, it has to be noted, was not built around characters conspicuous for their being 'people of interest'. The men portrayed by Casteel are not heroes, villains or victims. They reflect instead a group of 'ordinary people' with ordinary lives and aspirations, and are elevated to the status of subjects in a painting precisely because of their being inextricably bound up with the historical context in which they are represented.

The acclaim received by her exhibitions 'Visible Man' in 2014 and 'Brothers' in 2015 had established Casteel as an extraordinary, upcoming talent in New York. Being then selected for the prestigious residency at the Studio Museum in Harlem from 2015–16 had the twofold effect of giving Casteel a chance to shift her focus while further strengthening her connection to the city. In the most storied neighbourhood for Black creativity

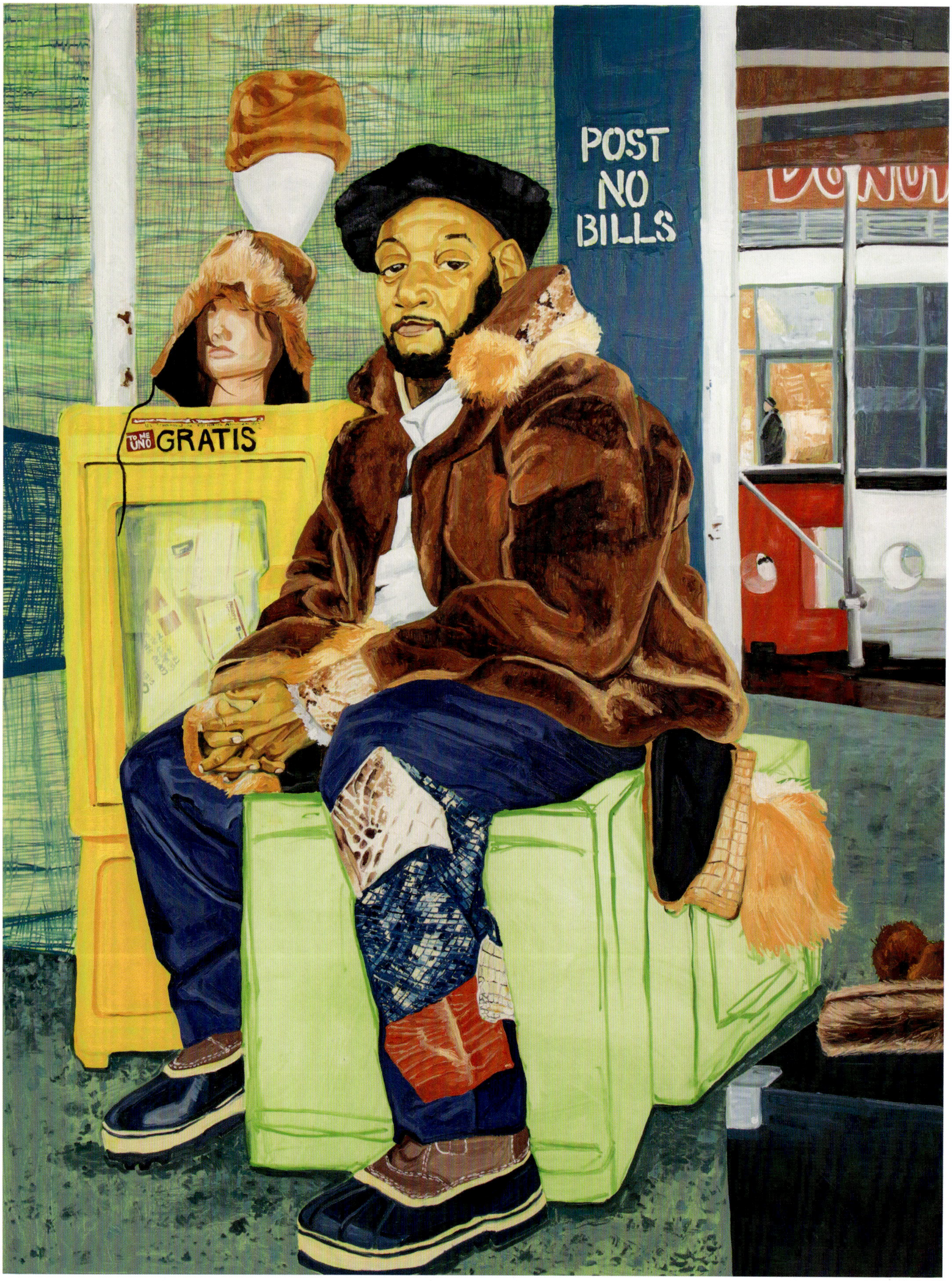

left,
CHARLES, 2016
OIL ON CANVAS
198 X 152 CM

opposite,
JARED, 2016
OIL ON CANVAS
183 X 137 CM

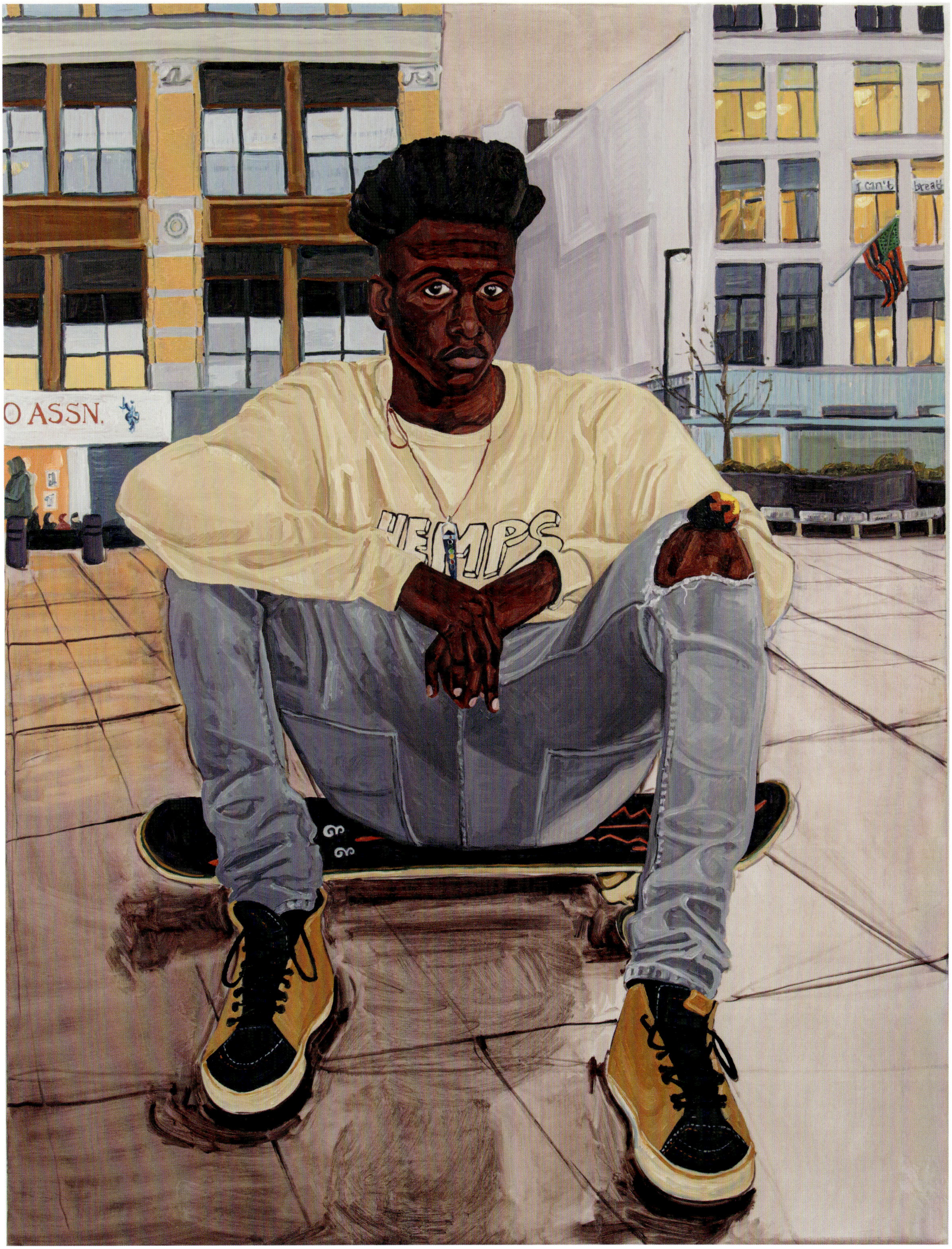
O ASSN.
HEMPS

GLASS MAN MICHAEL, 2016
OIL ON CANVAS
142 X 183 CM

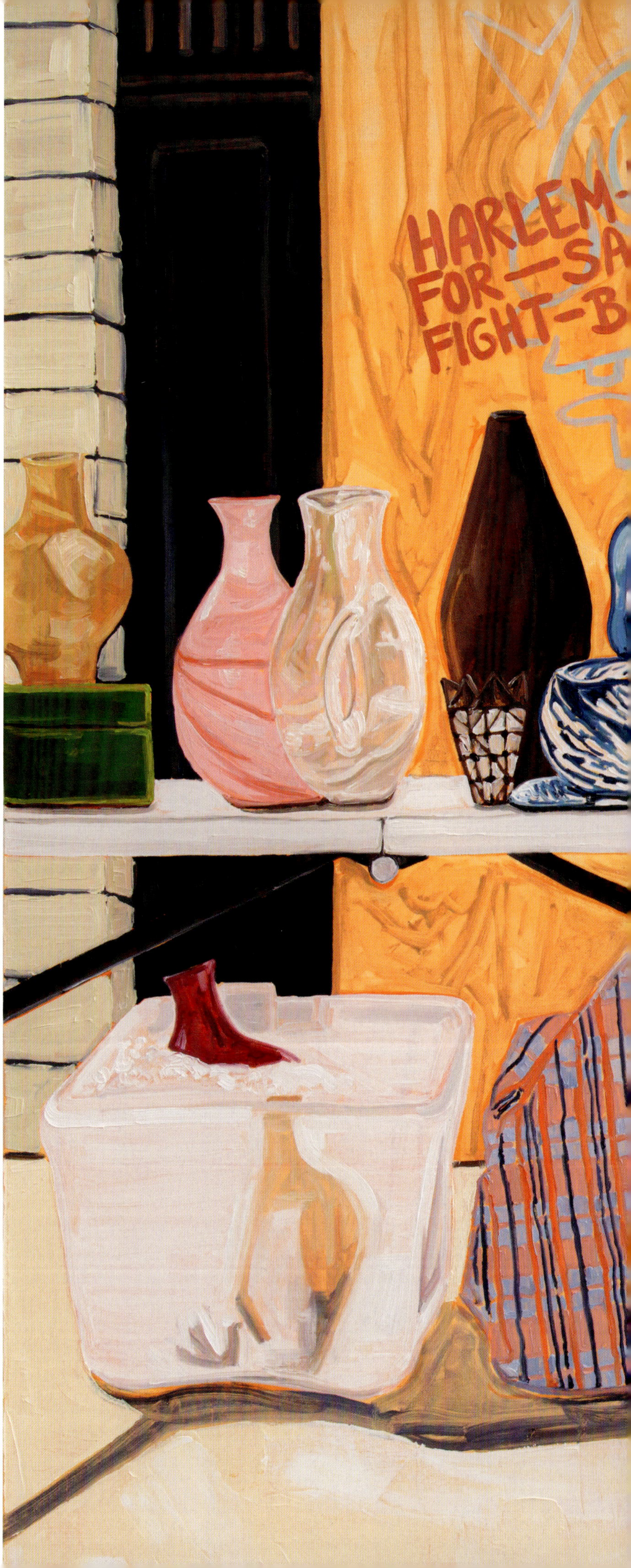

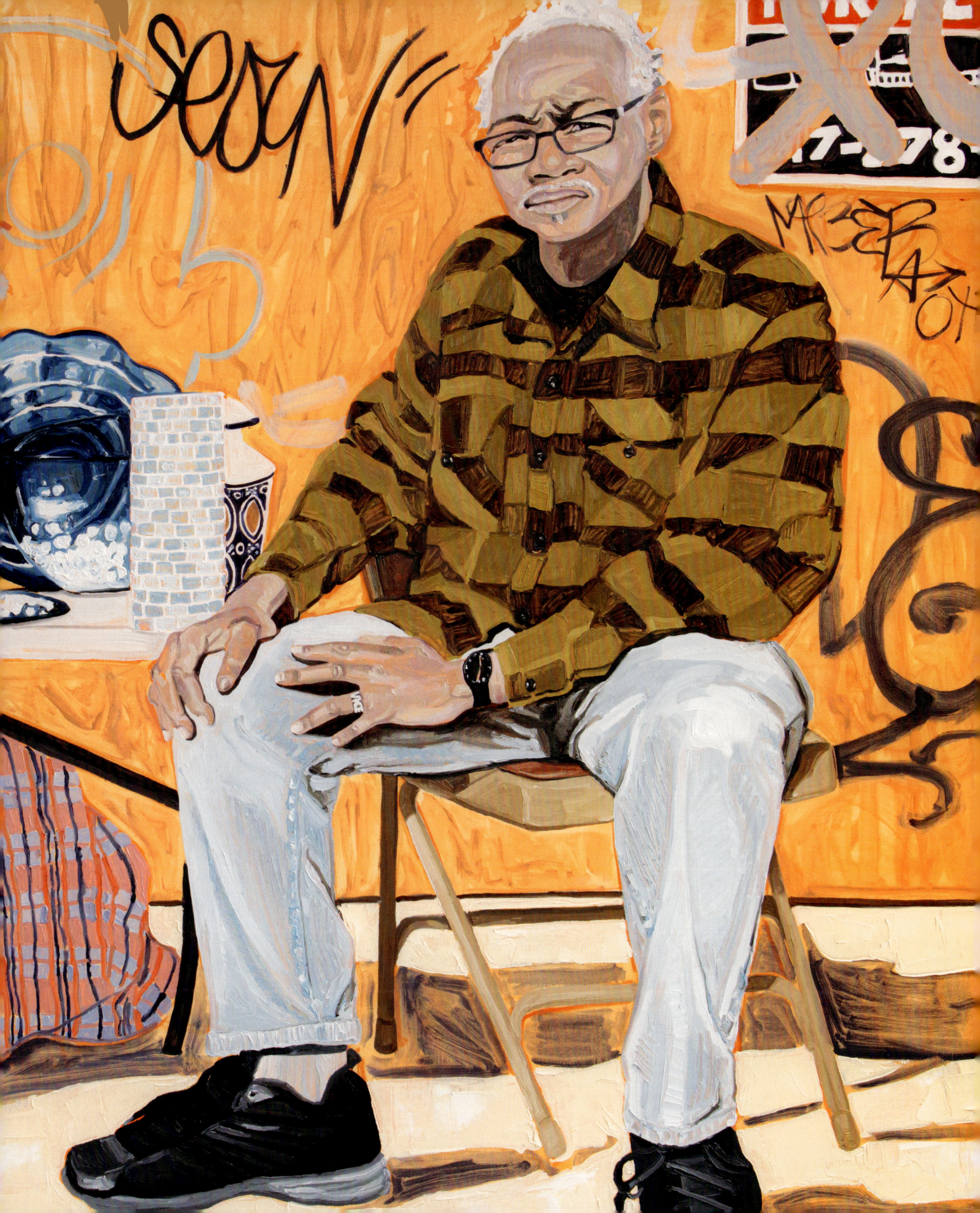
seen

BENYAM, 2018
OIL ON CANVAS
229 X 198 CM

and excellence, Casteel and her burgeoning artistic practice found a sense of belonging. The physical environment of the streets also contributed to opening her ideas about painting. As Casteel puts it, the work 'moved as I have moved'.[14] Like the artists and residents who also shared the rich history of 125th Street, Casteel was drawn to and marvelled at the intersections of activity. Predecessors like Julie Mehretu, Willie Cole and Abigail Deville, artists whose practices are deeply rooted in a sense of place, set the stage as Casteel began to deploy the notational language of landscape, becoming more aware of the public sphere and the space around bodies. A centuries-old genre also grounded in ideas of dominion and control, landscape painting traditionally worked in opposition to portraiture. If artists depicted bodies in the outdoors, those bodies were minimized by a nature that Edmund Burke and John Ruskin theorized as the sublime, picturesque or pastoral. Casteel's work of this time both invokes and flouts this orthodoxy, not only with the contemporary vocabulary of the Harlem streets as domestic interiors began to encompass street scenes, but also with the blurring of the sitters in the fulsomeness of their out-of-doors environment, one in which Blackness was the dominant culture, block by block, building on how Harlem was seen through the camera lens and imagination of famed artist and photographer Roy DeCarava.

The residency resulted in six paintings and a cosmos of meaningful relationships, concretizing an artistic and social practice built from layers of daily encounters in the neighbourhood. Casteel's street casting was often ignited with the simplest approach: 'Hi, I'm Jordan. Can I take your picture to make a painting?' One of the most commanding works from her residency is the portrait of *Charles* (2016, p. 58), clad in duck boots, patchwork jeans, black hat and brown jacket. He sits atop a humble throne of turned-over newspaper boxes, minimally modelled and amidst the panoply of disparate things one encounters in a cityscape – mannequin heads, signs about posting no bills, donuts and a weathered kiosk of free newspapers. Despite the surroundings, we are compelled by Charles's majestic bearing to reassess the fur trim on his coat and hat as akin to monarchical ermine. The composition, almost extravagant, includes colour-blocking in hues both acidic and warm, unfinished areas to counterbalance, and an arrangement of overlapping geometries in a push-pull effect. A similar juxtaposition can be seen in *Jared* (2016, p. 59) and the tangerine-inflected *Glass Man Michael* (2016, pp. 60-61). In all these paintings, the real draw is the protagonist, and the spell that Casteel has cast over us in wanting to know more about them, and to care about them.

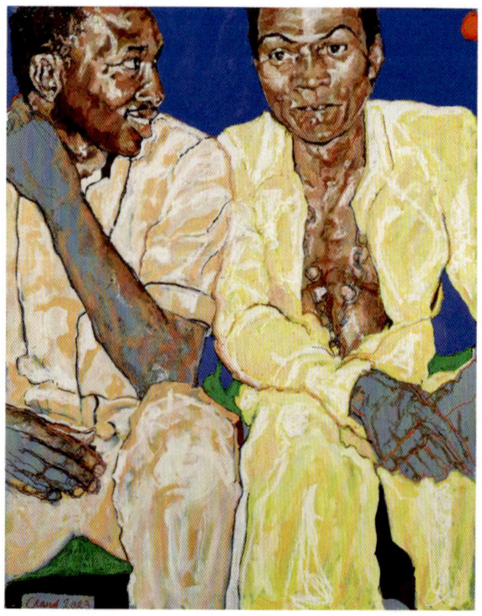

CLAUDETTE JOHNSON
FRIENDS IN PINK + YELLOW ON COBALT, 2023
OIL AND PASTEL ON PAPER
154 X 122 CM

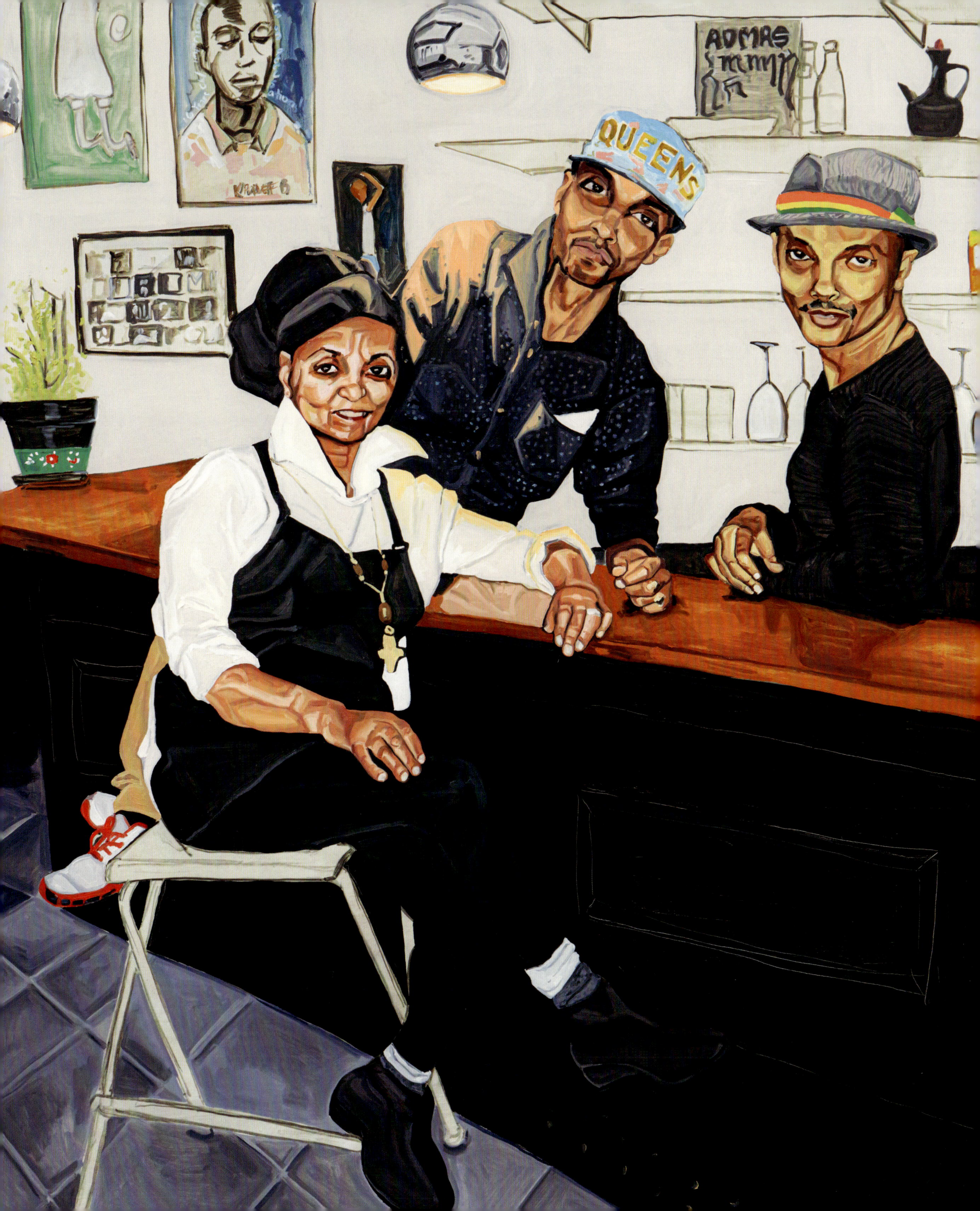
QUEENS
ADMAS

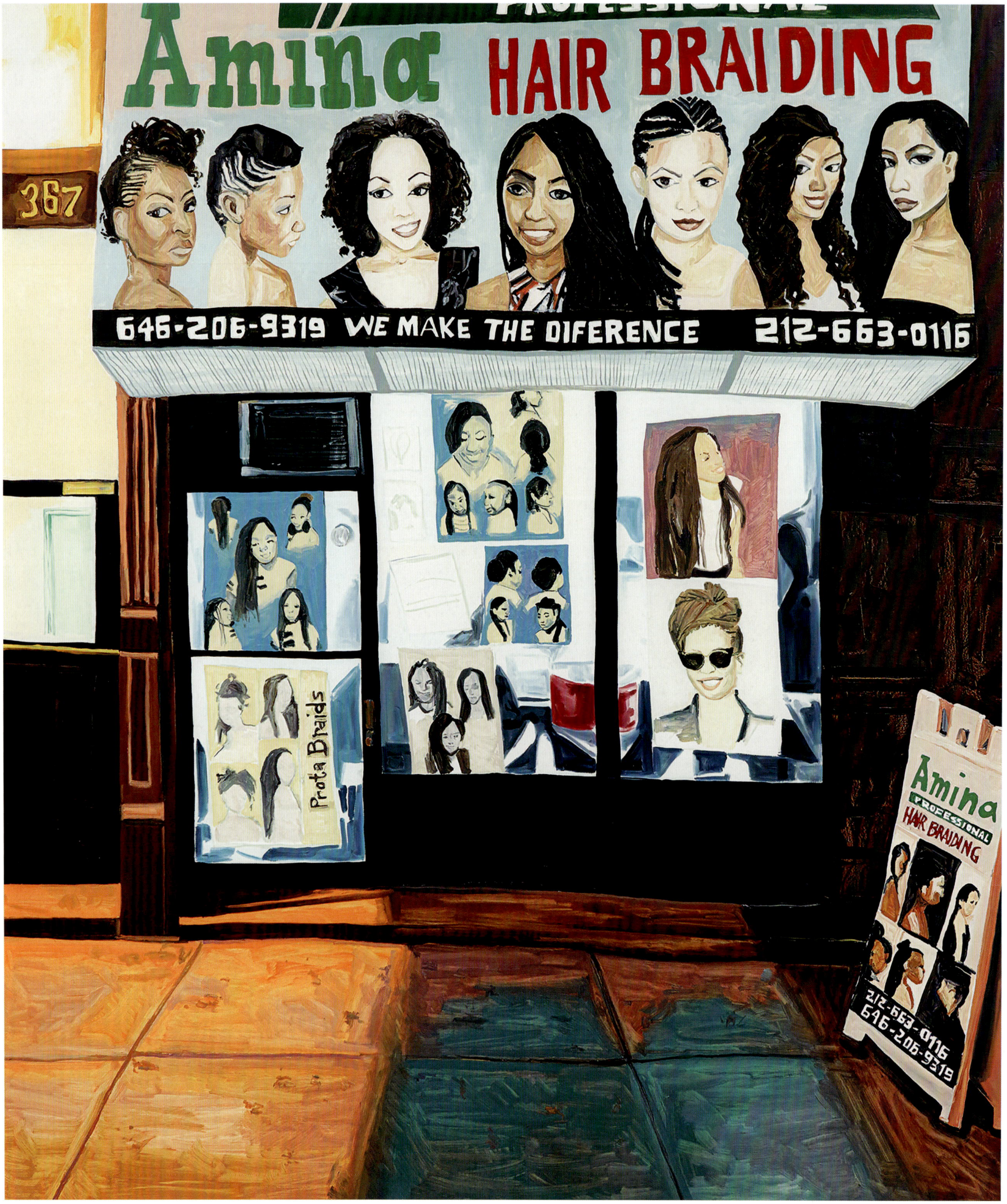
Amina
HAIR BRAIDING
646-206-9319 WE MAKE THE DIFERENCE 212-663-0116
367
Amina
PROFESSIONAL
HAIR BRAIDING
212-663-0116
646-206-9319

left,
AMINA, 2017
OIL ON CANVAS
229 X 198 CM

following pages, from left,
COWBOY E, SEAN CROSS, AND OG JABAR, 2017
OIL ON CANVAS
229 X 198 CM

HAROLD, 2017
OIL ON CANVAS
198 X 152 CM

British artist Claudette Johnson (p. 62) also divines a magic or charisma from her sitters, and indeed Casteel and Johnson have similar perspectives. But whereas Johnson's sitters vibrate through energetic line, negative space and colour palette, Casteel's approach of infusing landscape with the specificity of her subjects elicits the viewer's personal experiences and attendant emotions. We have all walked past a Charles or Jared, we all know those shoes, but how many of us have noticed them with such acuity as Casteel? Her portraits operate with an *aesthetics of attention*, not the sit-up-and-notice or rubber-necking kinds of attention, but the relational kind: the artist is paying attention to, or taking special care of, someone who in turn conjures, somewhat unexpectedly, the same reaction out of us. During her time in Harlem, Casteel's paintings explored the relationship between figure and ground, bodies and space, and how each works against and with the other, resulting in this *aesthetics of attention* to captivating effect.

In *Stanley* (2016, p. 69), the juxtaposition yields a very different narrative and includes a more spatially complex and culturally loaded landscape. It should be noted that these are direct transpositions of the sitters and their environments in that moment. Here, underneath a poster of victims of police terror asking, 'which side are you on?' Stanley, painted in a similar black and white palette as the poster victims, is enveloped in an almost spiritual hue of blue. Next to him we see another surface papered with an advertisement that was dotting the city – the slogan for Arizona's Iced Tea drink, 'Feel the Buzz', repeating over and over again with a somewhat ominous echo. The work reminds me of Ming Smith's photograph *America Seen through Stars and Stripes* (p. 68) taken fifty years earlier. A Black man stands in front of a store window hung with American flags celebrating the nation's bicentennial, but the work is complicated by a reflection of the city street in the window and the man's mirrored sunglasses. In both images, city storefront windows that depict the here and now offer a sobering backdrop to the plight of people of colour within the long tale of national history. Threading through this work, and so many others by Casteel, is a more subtle timestamp, an entangling between the individuals and their surroundings through which the specific moment of time in which these individuals lived is discerned.

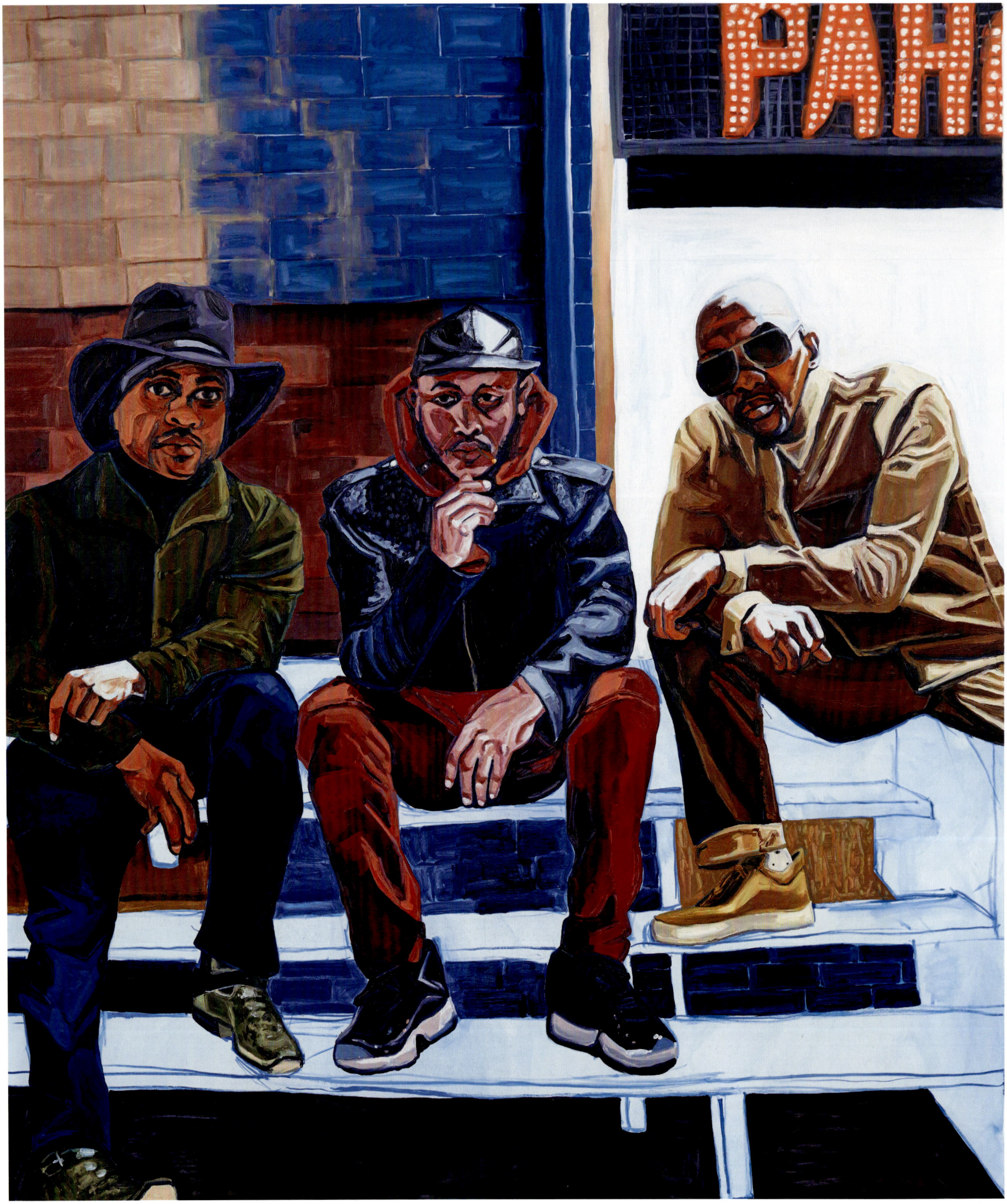
PAR

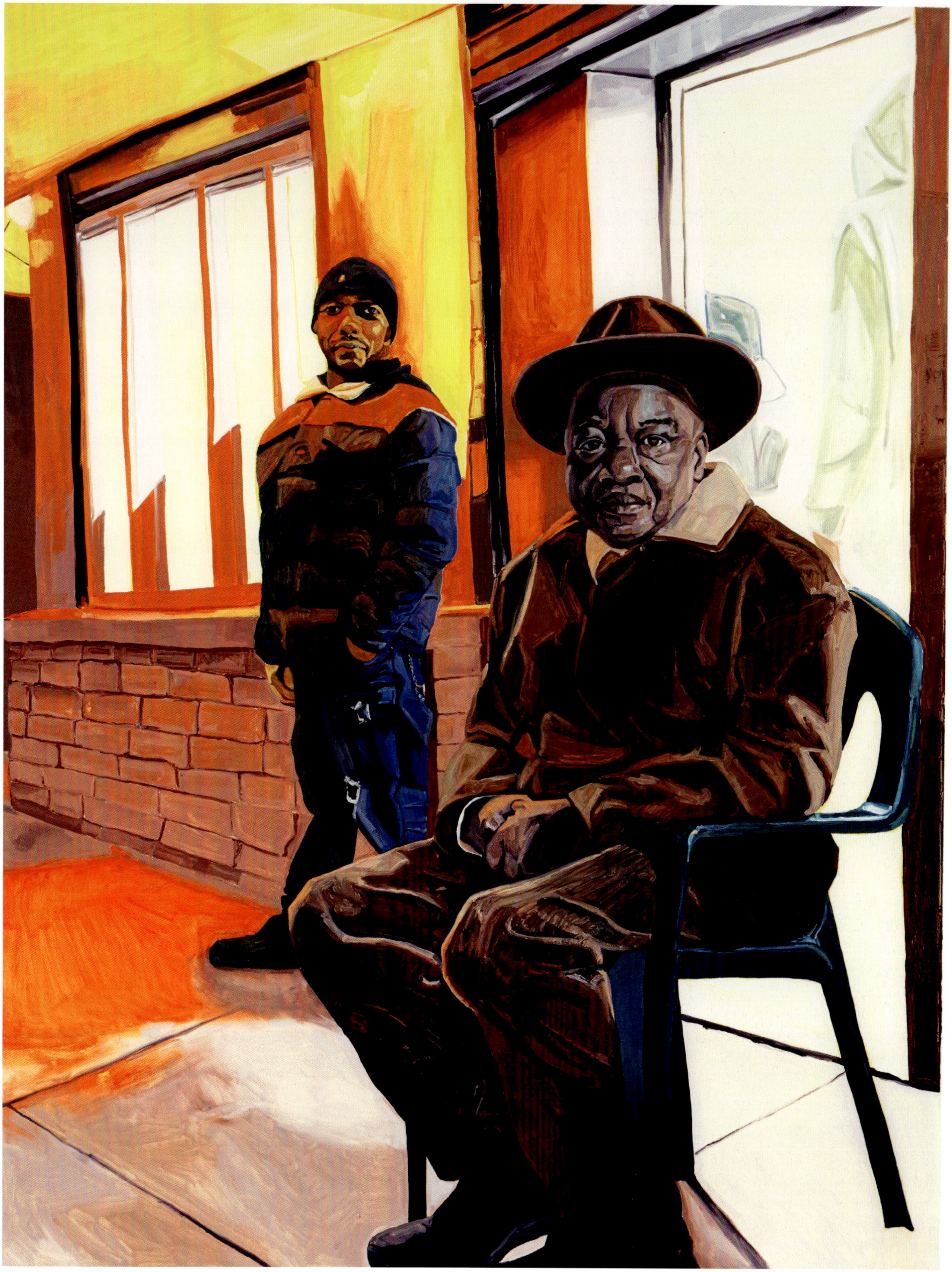

opposite,
STANLEY, 2016
OIL ON CANVAS
198 X 152 CM

next pages,
WITHIN REACH, 2019
OIL ON CANVAS
89 X 152 CM

In the years following the Studio Museum residency, Casteel's practice evolved as she found her footing within her Harlem surroundings, further integrating herself into the landscape. In *Amina* (2017, p. 64) Casteel depicts a hair-braiding salon, one of the most intimate spaces for Black women to connect and bond. Choosing to show the salon from the exterior, she emphasizes a feeling of longing for what we might find inside. Instead of a directly engaged subject, thirty-seven headshots of Black women with an array of different skin tones and hairstyles from weaves to cornrows become, somewhat tongue in cheek, portraits for us to consume throughout the image. Patches of light blue suggest glass and the hollow interior, and an empty sidewalk reflecting the gloaming light of the streetlamps takes up much of the foreground. The text in the image, 'We make the diference' is a real-life misspelling that Casteel purposefully repeats. The tenor of Casteel's interpretation of an unremarkable storefront captures the atmosphere of the neighbourhood with a knowability that materializes within us. It is a thoughtful meta-representation, indeed a representation of representation, and the power of self-presentation.

Amina and other works like *Cowboy E, Sean Cross, and Og Jabar* (2017, p. 66) and *Harold* (2017, p. 67) testify to how Casteel's surveying of the history and rapid transformation of Harlem streets, combined with her move to nighttime scenes and multi-figure portraits, resulted in the 'Nights in Harlem' series. The artist ventured on a mission to find different kinds of subjects, scales and compositional decisions, assembling an anthropology of Harlem and its inhabitants. *Harold* (2017) represents a man holding his position with clear recognition of the viewer. Perched on his chair out on the sidewalk, while another man in a puff jacket, baggy jeans and beanie hat looks on, Harold is brilliantly backlit by the bright fluorescence of the bodega and a wash of fiery oranges and yellows. His interiority is also suggested, a world of watching passersby on the street – a world, too, that perhaps the younger man over his shoulder will inhabit, when the generational difference between the fedora-clad gentleman and the onlooker collapses.

As time and place conflate within the narratives of her sitters, Casteel introduces us to James. One of the few subjects whom Casteel has painted more than once, James was first represented in 2015 seated with his foot upon a Fender amp on Lenox Avenue (once aptly described by Langston Hughes as 'Harlem's heartbeat' in his poem *Juke Box Love Song*). The resulting painting, *James* (2015, p. 32), was first displayed at Open Studios during the Studio Museum in Harlem residency, where James' wife, Yvonne, was struck by Casteel's portrayal and her ability to convey the man she loved with such personhood. Two years later, Casteel painted *Yvonne and James* (2017, p. 34) capturing the couple as the sun set while they were selling goods in front of the famed Sylvia's Restaurant. Their bodies at ease, holding hands, bring the artist into the fold as they look knowingly towards her and those of us just beyond the canvas. The bond between painter and subject is evidenced within this tender Harlem landscape, drawing us into a heightened sense of security and connection. In the third painting depicting James of what can be seen as an expanded triptych, *Yvonne and James II* (2021, p. 35), Yvonne is palpably absent. Holding a framed portrait of the couple on their wedding day, James pays tribute to their union in the wake of Yvonne's passing. The enduring companionship between James, Yvonne and Casteel is highlighted through the insertion of the artist's presence (her shoes placed by the door) and a reproduction of Casteel's 2015 portrait is tacked to the refrigerator.

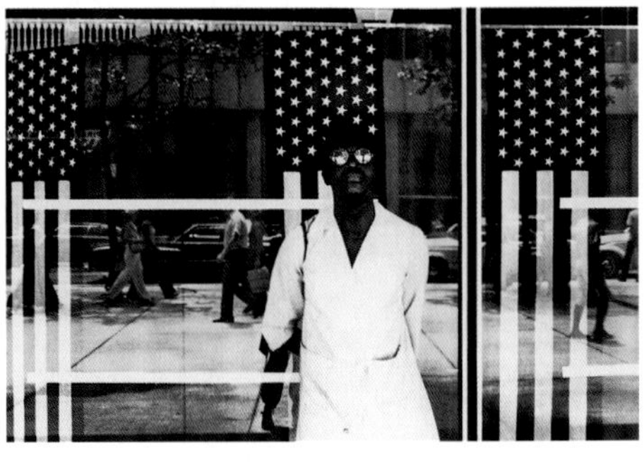

MING SMITH
AMERICA SEEN THROUGH STARS AND STRIPES, 1976
INKJET PRINT
61 X 91 CM

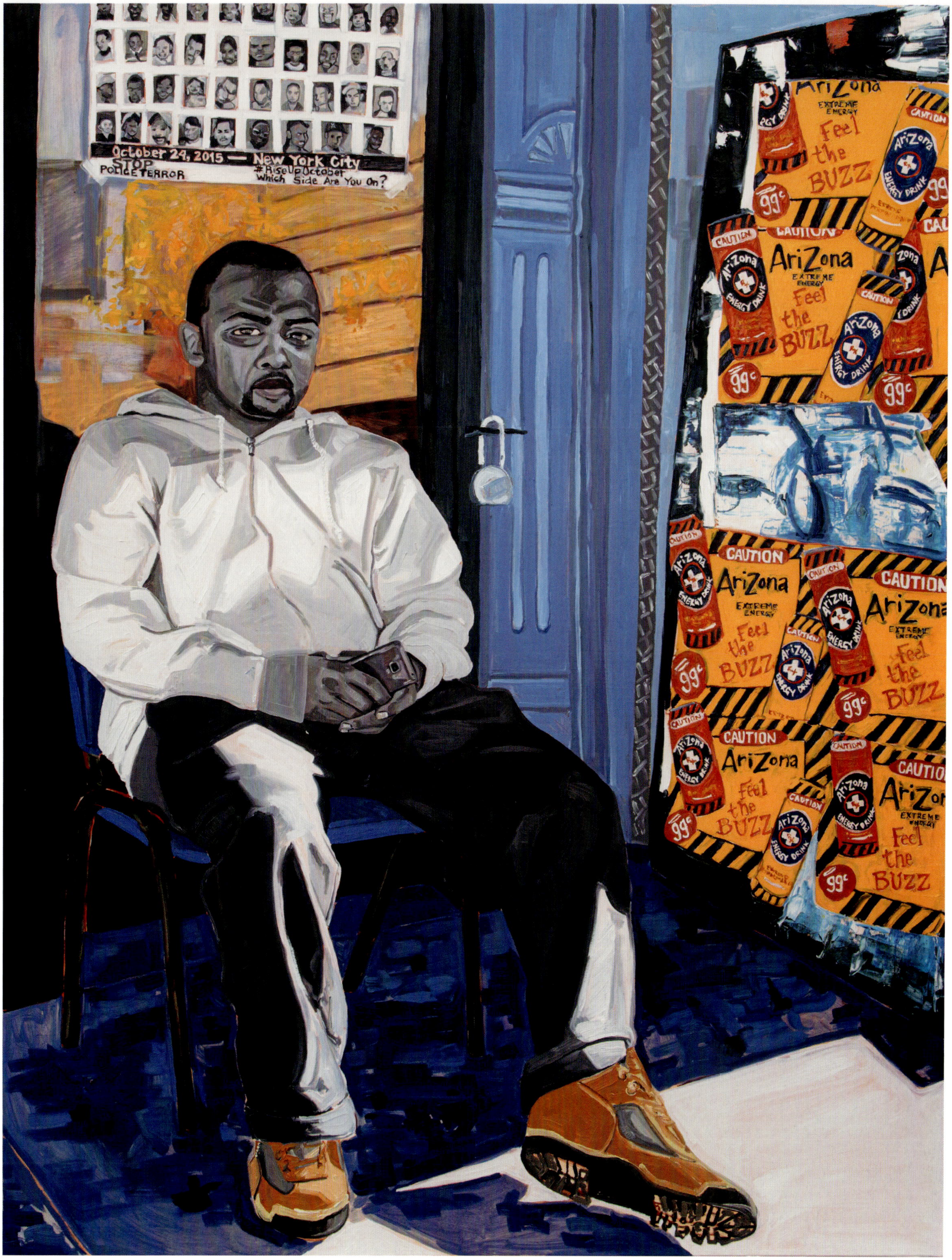
October 24, 2015 — New York City
STOP POLICE TERROR
#RiseUpOctober
Which Side Are You On?
CAUTION
AriZona
EXTREME ENERGY
Feel the BUZZ
ENERGY DRINK
99¢

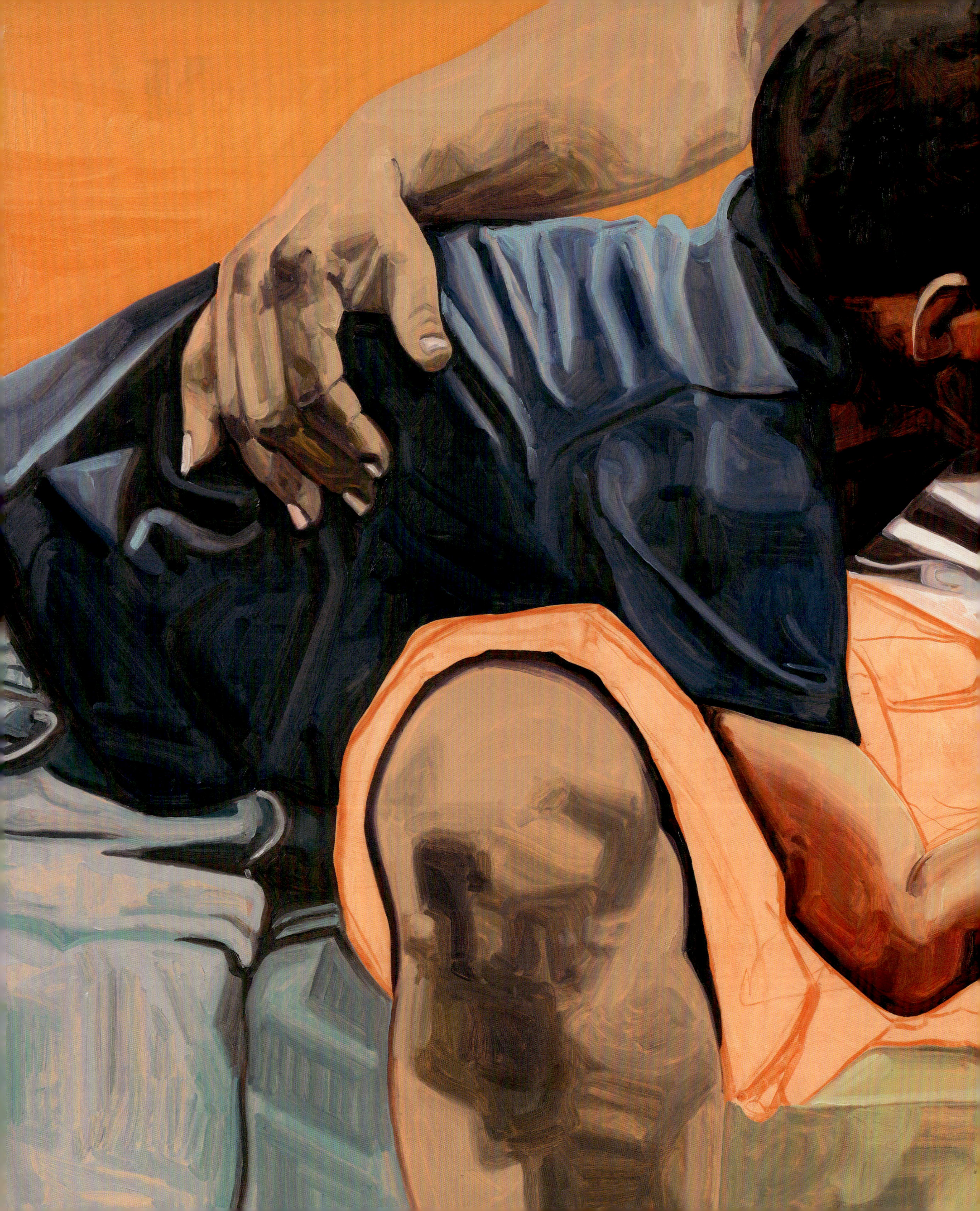

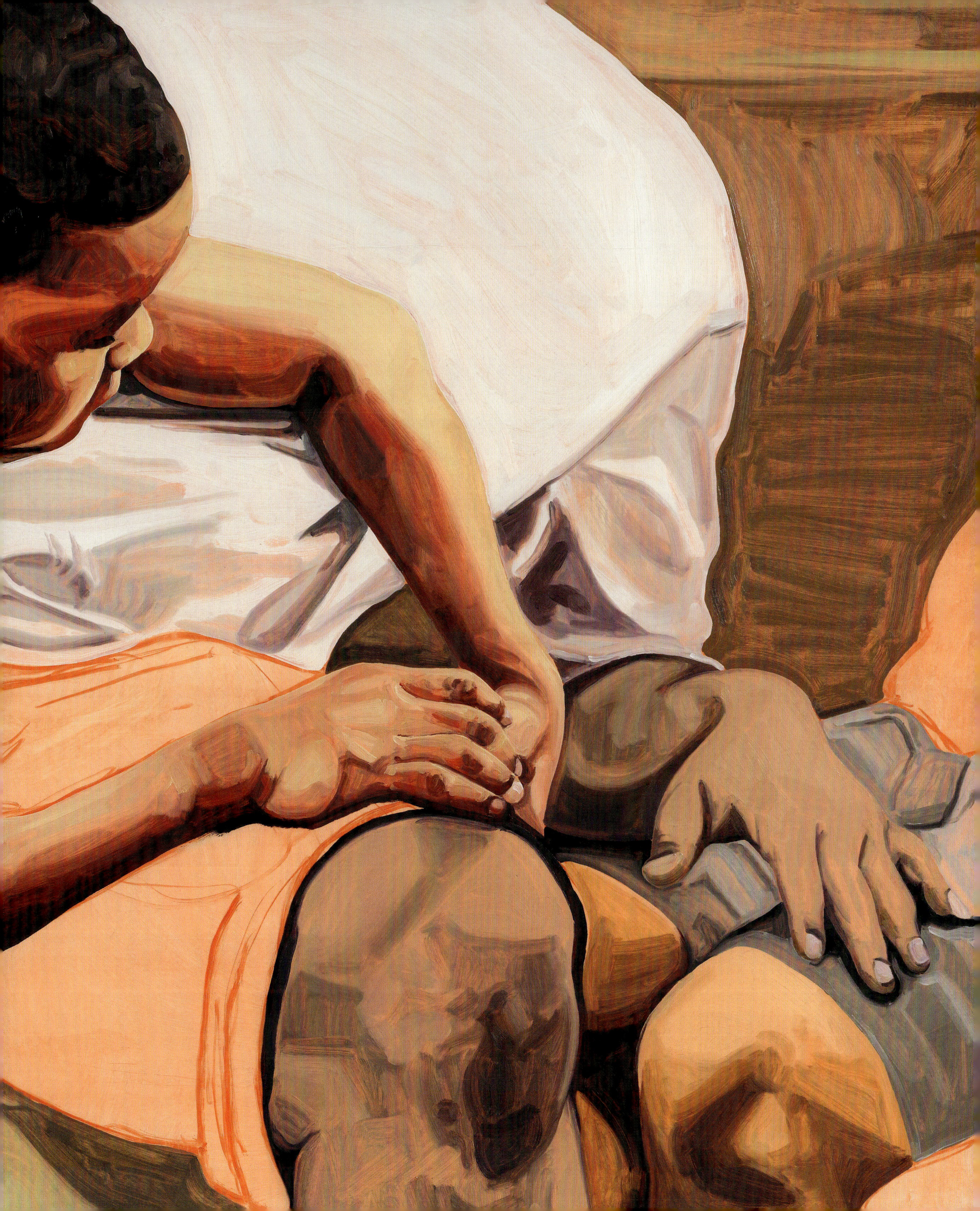

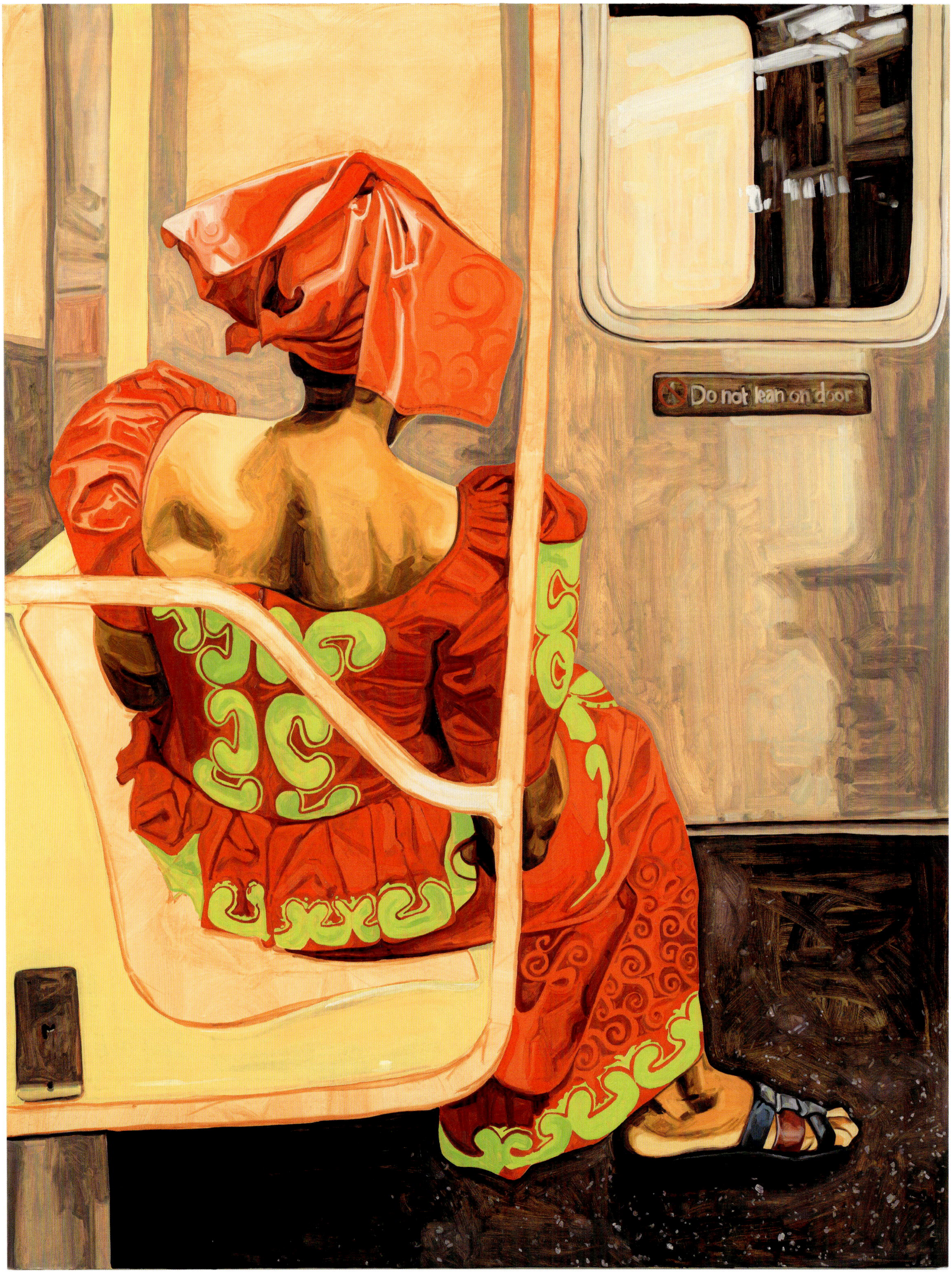
Do not lean on door

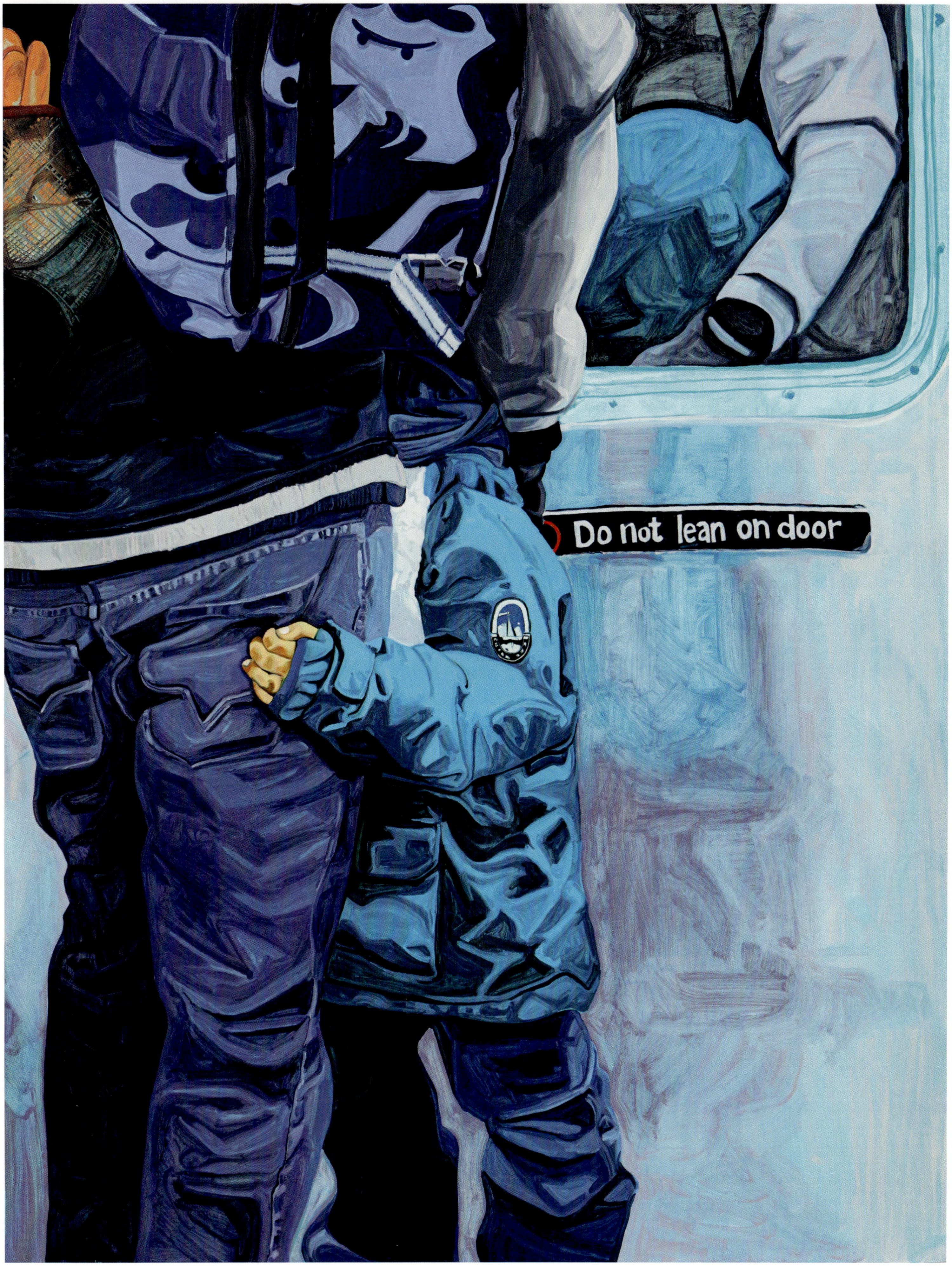
Do not lean on door

previous pages, from left,
HER TURN, 2018
OIL ON CANVAS
198 X 152 CM

LEAN, 2018
OIL ON CANVAS
183 X 142 CM

right,
KIMMAH, 2019
OIL ON CANVAS
229 X 198 CM

Casteel was interested in offering another kind of community building and relationality by engaging her students at Rutgers University-Newark, where she worked as an Associate Professor in the Department of Arts, Culture and Media from 2016 to 2021 – the year she was tenured. She taught them about the empowerment that comes from using painting as an investigative tool, an opportunity to pose a question and seek an answer, while also realizing the inspiration and guidance her students shared with her. Returning to bell hooks' writings on reciprocity between teacher and pupil within an age of multiculturalism, Casteel invited her students to take part in her practice. With the students sitting within settings of their own choosing – from childhood bedrooms to botanical gardens – the sincere portrayals convey a mutual engagement and in turn, a more levelled power dynamic. In *Serwaa and Amoakohene* (2019, p. 112), we see the intertwining of respect for tradition of an immigrant family in their home. Perching on the arm of a floral couch that reminded the artist of her early nudes, landscapes and still-lifes, the mother cradles her son, and behind her, proudly displayed, is her portrait made as a gift by her son.

Firsthand exchanges and lasting relationships turn to anonymous encounters in Casteel's series of 'subway' or 'cropped' paintings. Tapping into the communal experience of riding the New York City subway, Casteel continues to find beauty in the ordinary. Time and time again, we are confronted with the seemingly uninspiring, the banal or the mundane, but with captivating aesthetic effect. With tightly cropped compositions, candid figures fill the frame. We often feel movement within each work as we are carried towards a pair of clasped hands, the mindless tapping of a cell phone or tired limbs at rest. Her subjects' lines of sight are cast downwards or off to the side, keeping the viewer at arm's length while eliciting a collective familiarity. The sophistication of Casteel's visual journaling also pokes at the lumbering giants of art history, with musings that riff on portraiture, still life and even abstraction. *Her Turn* (2018, p. 72) could almost be an abstract work, with lime green zipping through swaths of red, lemon yellow, tans and caramels. In these subway works, some depicting only hands, the artist began to experiment with colour, form, subject and a concentrated composition. The work produced is of a different emotional register, a tenderness perhaps achieved through the removal of the sitter's gaze. Along these lines, consider *Lean* (2018, p. 73), where a loving embrace is cropped, seen from the perspective of a fellow subway rider, and the subway door and window, coats, jeans and backpack gleam in a symphonic arrangement of blues (see also, in the same vein, *Elizabeth and Roman* from 2024, p. 98). In *Bounty* (2020, p. 114), we see a scene so ordinary that many of us would have simply ignored it, but through Casteel's painterly transcription it becomes so much more. Out of the inharmonious patterns and colours – floral, patterned wallpaper, orange seats, blue jeans and green packaging – we take in this woman with her groceries, and a feeling of earnestness and respect seeps in. The subway is a vessel of the quotidian, but as we look at other fellow riders, we vacillate between an outwardness and inwardness. If Baudelaire described modernity – life in bustling nineteenth-century Paris with its blur of sensorial experiences and psychic states – as 'the transitory, the fleeting, the contingent', then Casteel's project is not just to bring visibility to those normally in the shadows, but an *aesthetics of attention* that pictures modern life – a twenty-first

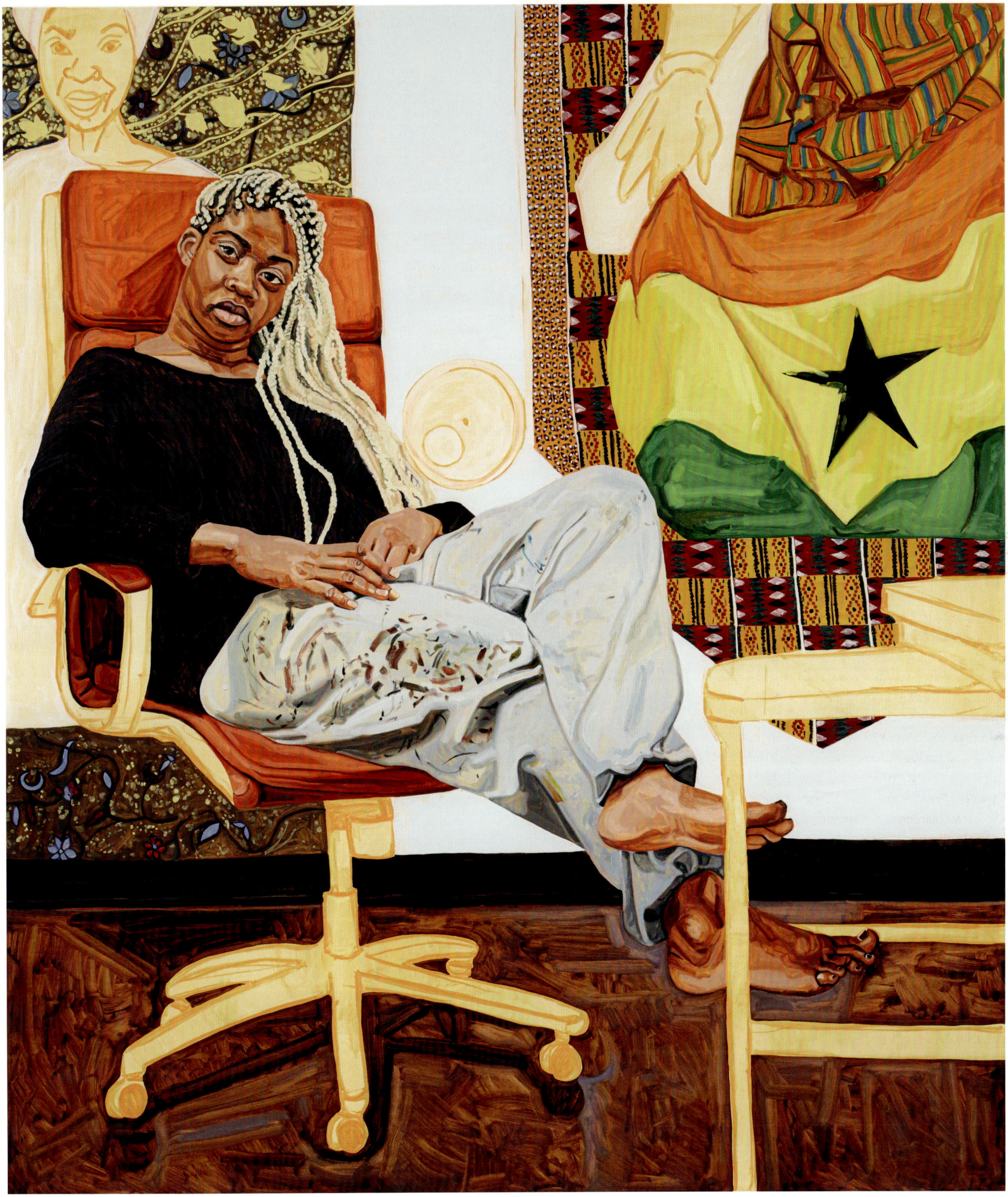

THE BAAYFALLS, 2017
OIL ON CANVAS
198 X 229 CM

next pages,
THE BAAYFALLS, 2019
MURAL PAINTING
130 SQ M

INSTALLATION VIEW AT THE
HIGH LINE, NEW YORK, 2020

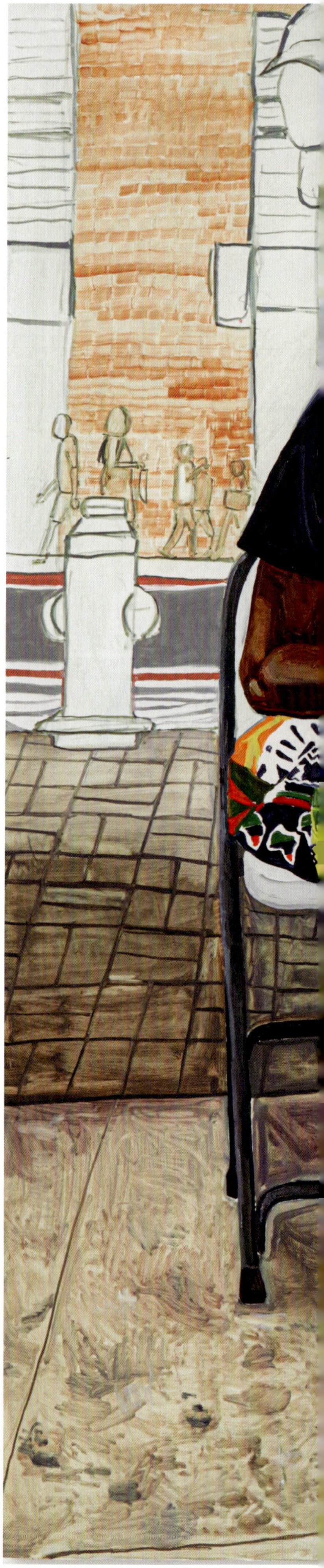

century Manet if you will. The transitional space of the subway, one of the most democratizing in contemporary life, permits a capturing of the fleeting encounters and moments that typically recede for so many of us in the onslaught of social media and a twenty-four-hour news cycle. And in Casteel's worldview, it is precisely those seemingly peripheral encounters and moments that make our day all the more meaningful.

In 2019, Casteel bridged her portraits of the New York City landscape and her later body of work with the topography of the city itself, when asked to participate in the High Line Art programme. A recreation of the 2017 painting *The Baayfalls,* the High Line mural version (2019, pp. 78-79) enlarges the work to a monumental 130 square metres. Created during the fertile time when Casteel was living in Harlem, the portrait depicts Fallou, a Senegalese immigrant who is selling hats and jewellery of her own design, and her brother, Baaye Demba Sow, a member of Baye Fall, part of the Sufi brotherhood Mouride, visiting from Senegal. The resulting work from that encounter shows Fallou wearing a hat, pants comprising a panoply of traditional and contemporary African textiles and a t-shirt in which the words, 'I am not interested in competing with anyone. I hope we all make it.' can easily be read. The civic optimism was not lost on Casteel, for she was drawn to 'the way that the communities around us use language to honour and protect themselves'.[15] Fallou's brother is similarly clad in traditional dress, jewellery and refinery. Both the brother's blue skin tone and the transformation of the graffiti on the wall into a hieroglyphic-like underdrawing bestow a mystical aura on the double portrait, a leitmotif heightened further when one learns that Fallou's hand gesture represents Allah among members of Baye Fall. Make no mistake, the portrait of Fallou and Baaye Demba Sow was a canny choice on the part of the artist to be emblazoned at such a breathtaking scale. At this point in her career, her problematizing of scale and spatiality for Black and brown sitters and its attendant effects on the beholder were universally celebrated, but the High Line version of the *Baayfalls* – and its siting in one of the most visited New York City parks – achieved something different altogether. Hand-painted by Colossal Media on a 22nd Street wall, the mural and its commanding presence offer an unprecedented take on Toni Morrison's aforementioned idea of representation and the sharing of interiorities and worlds previously occluded. And in a more geographical sense, the mural knits the downtown West side park not only to the uptown neighbourhood of Harlem but also to Senegal and the continent of Africa. From street to canvas, back to street, Casteel's High Line public project became a jubilant heralding of Black and brown communities, seen far and wide, another rousing affirmation of the possibilities of public art.

When the COVID-19 pandemic brought the entire world to a screeching halt in mid-March 2020, a lot of things were happening or about to happen in Casteel's life.

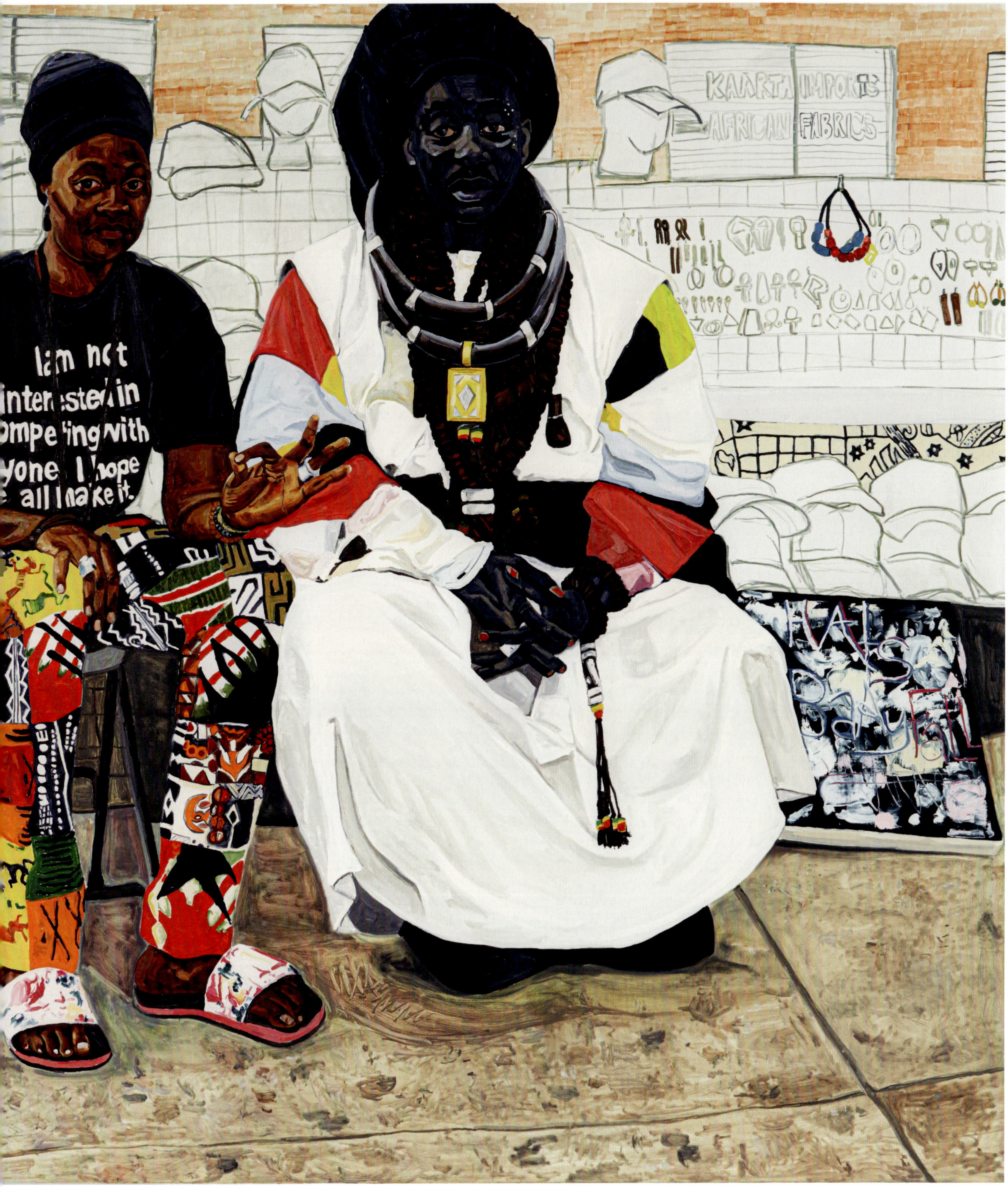
KAARTA IMPORTS
AFRICAN FABRICS
I am not
interested in
ompeting with
yone I hope
all make it.

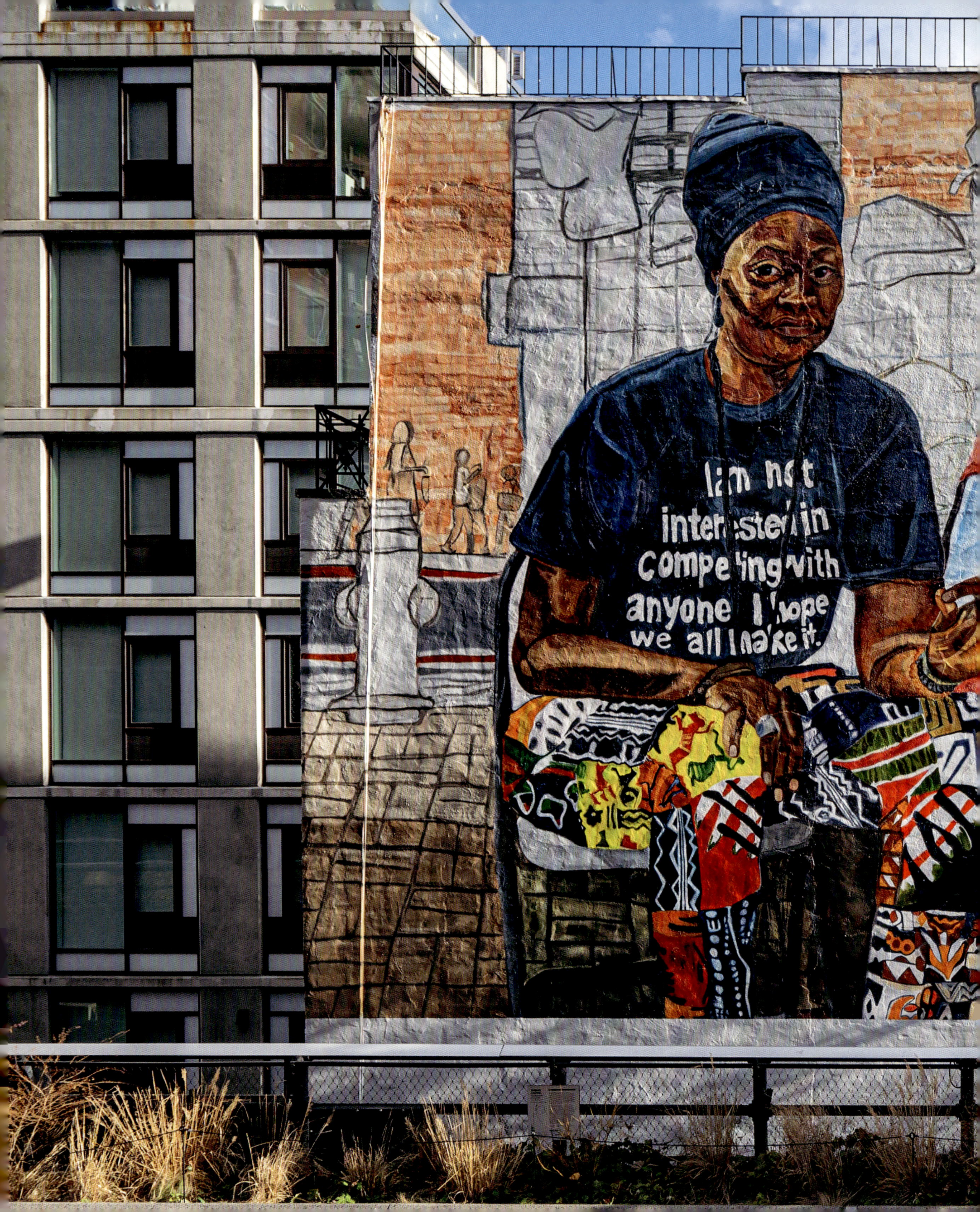
I am not
interested in
competing with
anyone I hope
we all make it.

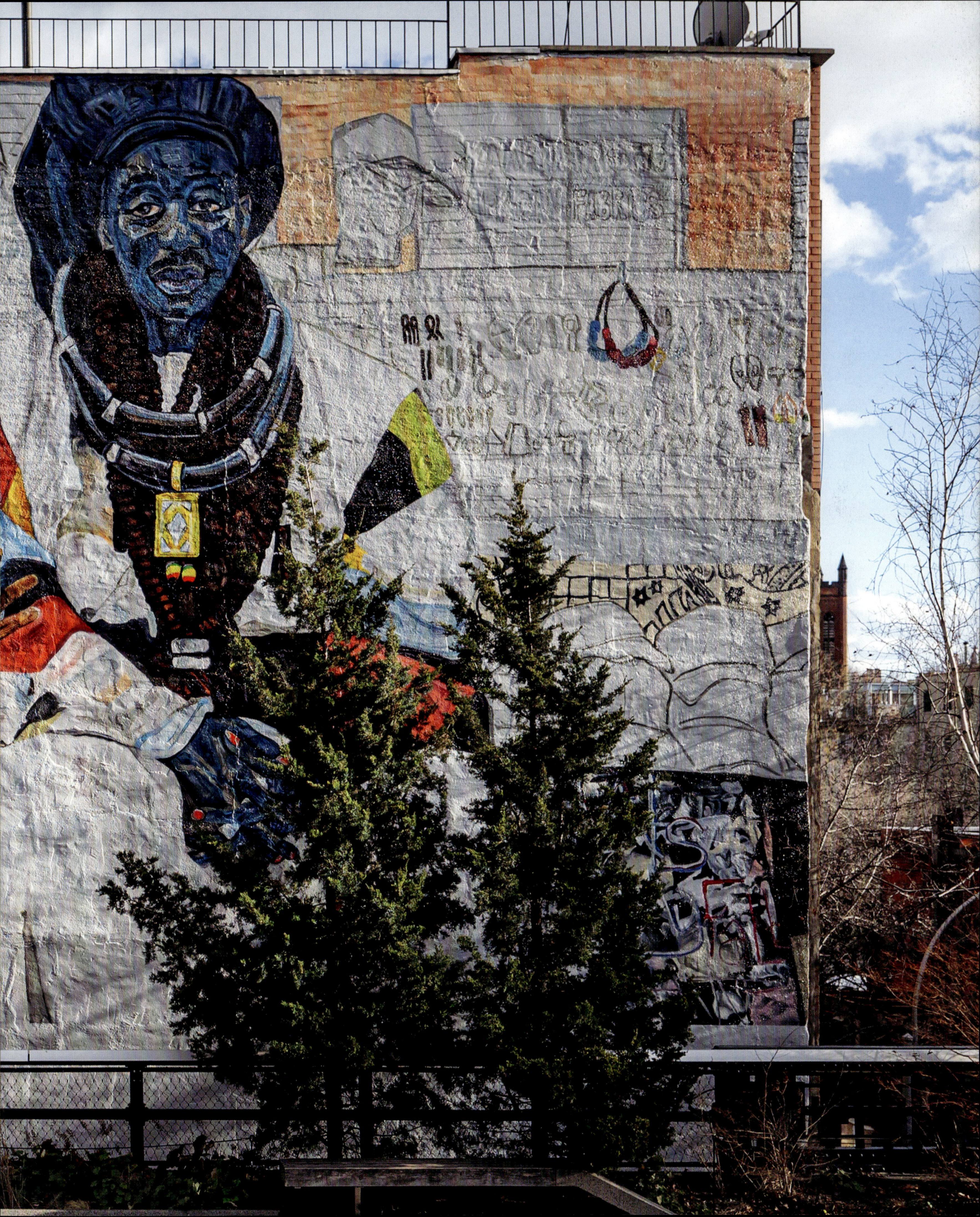

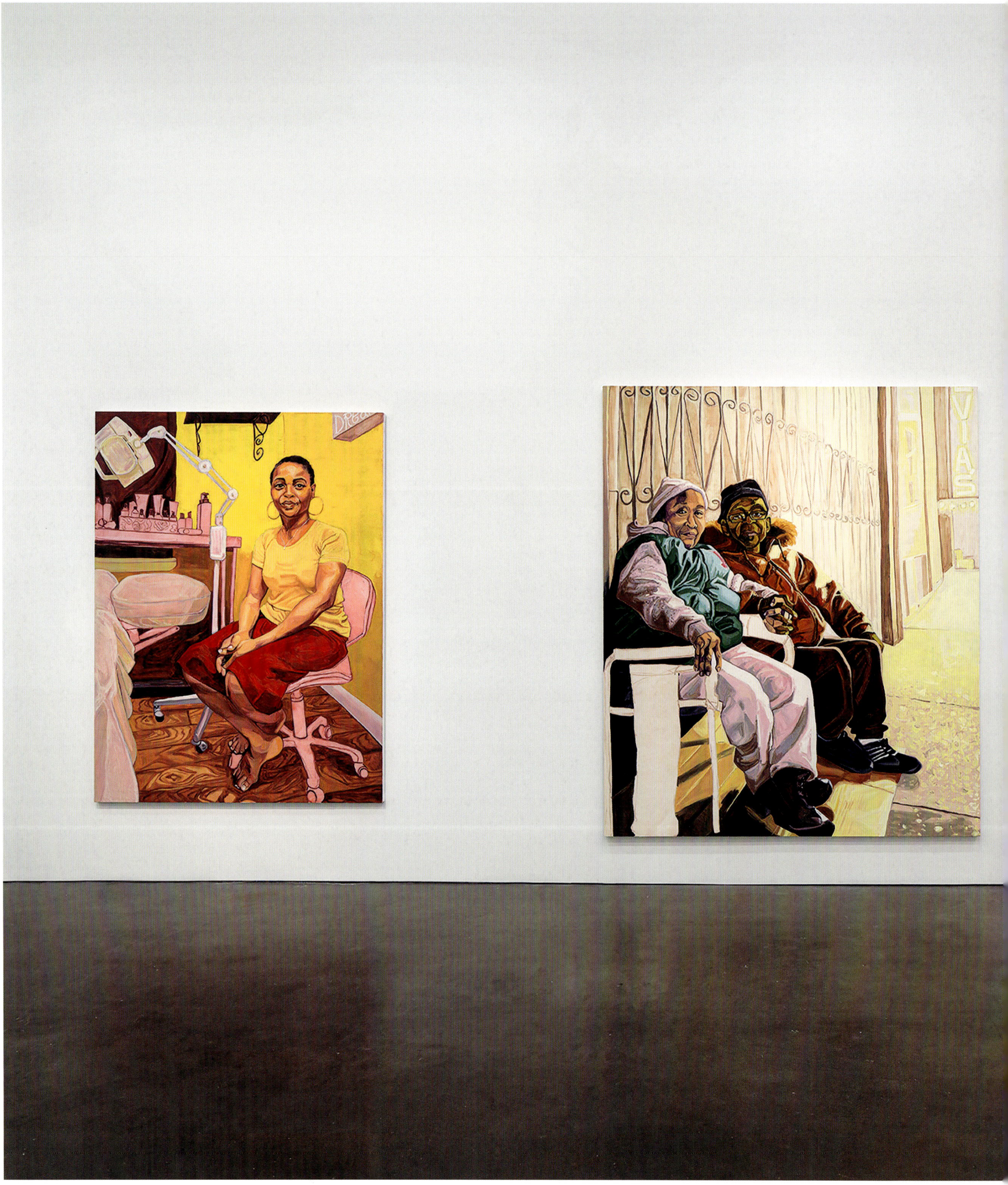

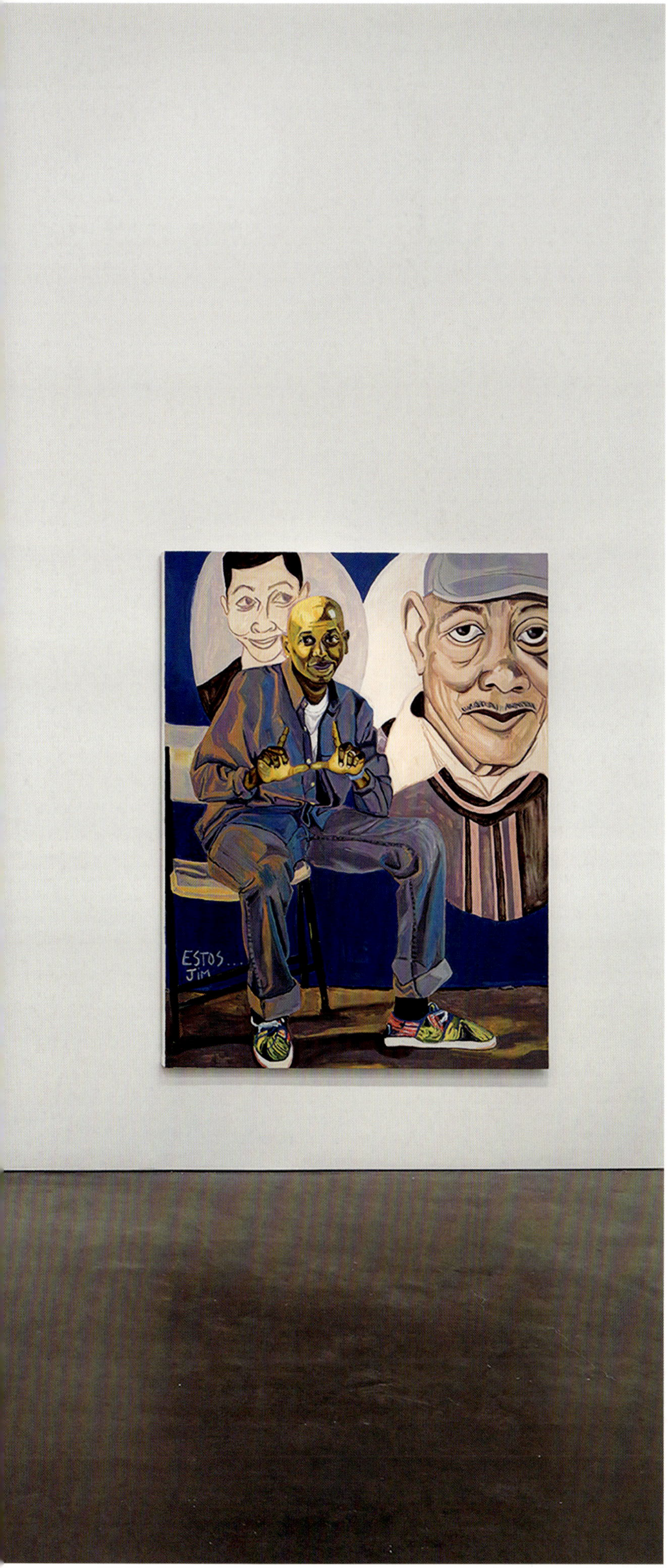

from left,
SHIRLEY (SPA BOUTIQUE2GO),
2018
OIL ON CANVAS
198 X 152 CM

YVONNE AND JAMES, 2017
OIL ON CANVAS
229 X 198 CM

TITO, 2017
OIL ON CANVAS
198 X 152 CM

INSTALLATION VIEW AT
THE NEW MUSEUM OF
CONTEMPORARY ART,
NEW YORK, 2020

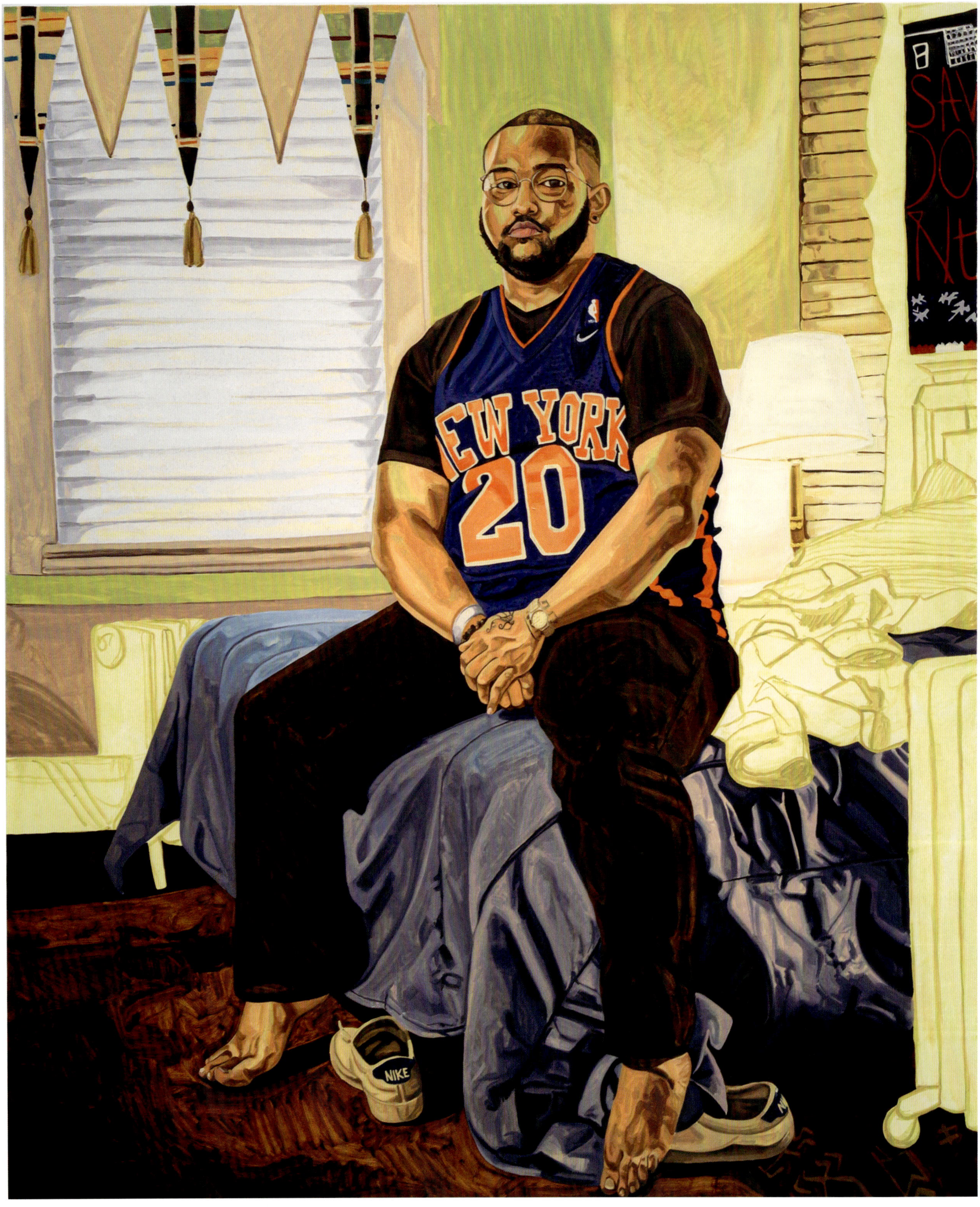

right,
<u>LOURDES AND KARINA</u>, 2019
OIL ON CANVAS
229 X 198 CM

opposite,
<u>JAHI</u>, 2019
OIL ON CANVAS
229 X 198 CM

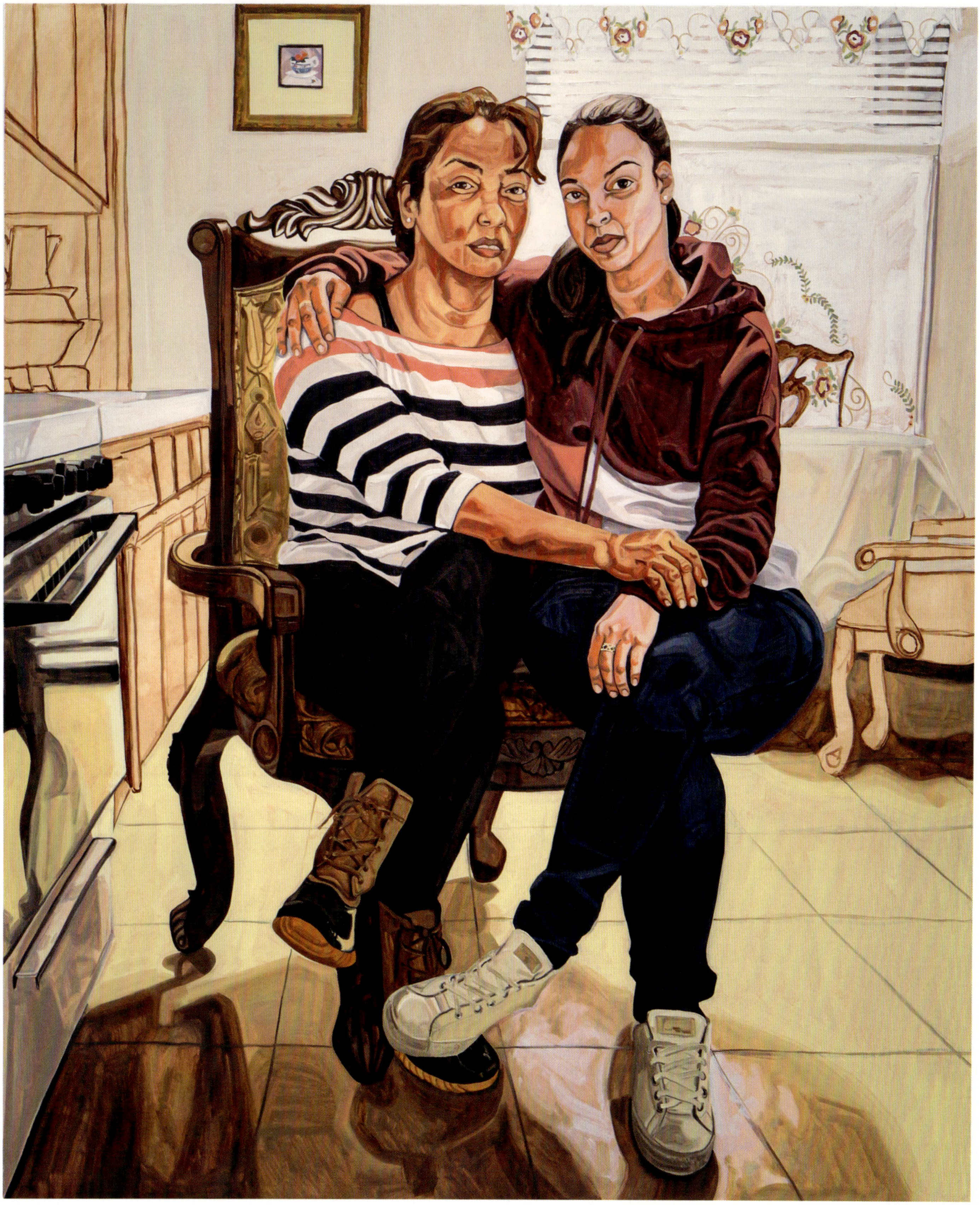

JORDAN, 2020
OIL ON CANVAS
229 X 198 CM

On February 19, following institutional presentations at the Harvey B. Gantt Center in Charlotte, NC (2017), and in her hometown at the Denver Art Museum (2019), her first sweeping mid-career retrospective, 'Within Reach', opened at the New Museum of Contemporary Art in New York. The forty works made over seven years, when viewed all together, revealed the breadth and depth of Casteel's sustained effort to bring to the fore her ever-growing community and their environments. If the timing was unfortunate, it is also true that the restrictions dictated by the first lockdown – a moment marked by extreme uncertainty and isolation, social distancing and heightened awareness of racial and social inequality – resulted in the museum initiating a series of virtual public engagements that serendipitously resonated with a practice rooted in the concept of visibility and care.

Perhaps out of necessity, Casteel also moved back into the centre of the frame. In *Jordan* (2020) she pictures herself wearing sweatpants and a t-shirt emblazoned with the word 'Black' (a creamy concoction of pinks, greys and tans), curled on a couch, with an enviable library (Whitney M. Young, Jr., Toni Morrison, Hilton Als, Dr. Seuss, Hanya Yanagihara, Thelma Golden, Gordon Parks) and several lively pastel-tinged plants close by. Her eyes meet our own with a commanding serenity and intensity. Whereas in her self-portraits Faith Ringgold centres herself almost like a mystical Byzantine icon against a geometric background, her skin an alchemy of teal, caramel and chocolate, Casteel depicts herself both as a fully relatable person and the painter she has become. We seem to hover above her, and the centre of the painting showcases her elongated hands. Her limbs encircle her, not unlike the plants that surround her, foreshadowing what is to come.

The other big innovation in *Jordan,* however, resides in the background, where Casteel's Harlem apartment is distinctly recognizable – the crystallization of the end of another cycle ahead of her move to a new home in Upstate New York. Having been born and raised in Colorado, it is little surprise that Casteel would enjoy spending more time in the mountains and the pastoral setting of the Hudson Valley. The New Museum show had already highlighted the background landscapes present in many of her works created from 2015 and 2020 and how her pictorial syntax of bodies and space has been filtered through a self-reflective lens. This spirit of landscape, in the following years became less and less about the geometry of concrete and glass and centred more on the curvature of grass, dirt and flowers. In *Field Balm* (2022, p. 117), we find a more playful and opaque self-portrait: we only see a bird's-eye view of Casteel's feet in her Crocs, dotted with various personal trinkets. The translucency of Casteel's purple legs highlight the tension between the hypervisibility or invisibility of a subject. In this case, it feels as if the artist is acknowledging how inextricably linked she is to her work. As discussed in Roland Barthes' essay 'The Death of the Author',

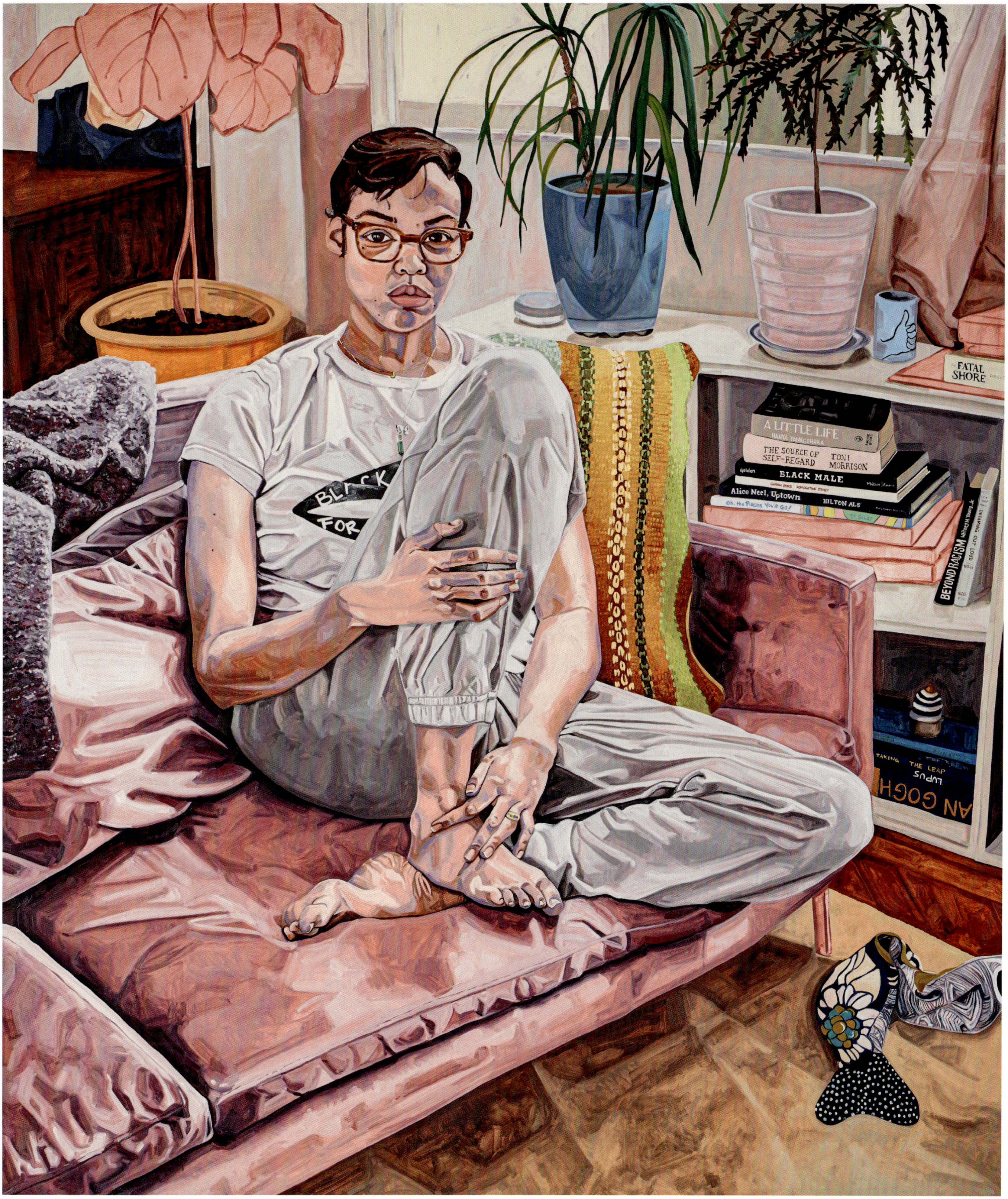
FATAL SHORE
A LITTLE LIFE
HANYA YANAGIHARA
THE SOURCE OF SELF-REGARD
TONI MORRISON
BLACK MALE
Alice Neel, Uptown
HILTON ALS
Oh, the Places You'll Go!
BEYOND RACISM
TAKING THE LEAP
LUPUS
AN GOGH

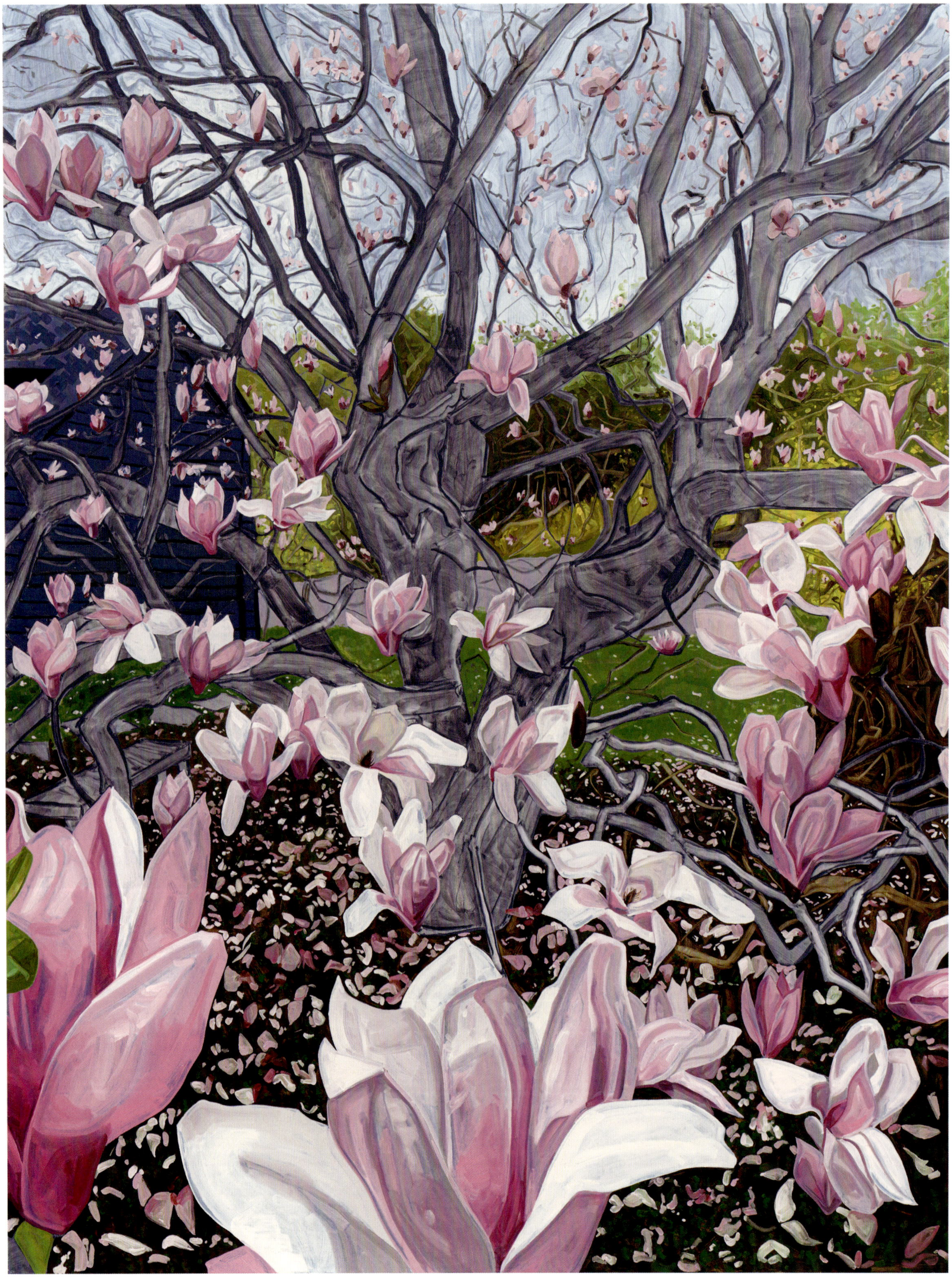

MAGNOLIA, 2022
OIL ON CANVAS
198 X 152 CM

authorship in this post-modern era emphasizes the 'prestige of the individual'. But what does it mean when the artist's identity supersedes the recognition of their craft? Even in this moment where the 'The Author's empire is still very powerful',[16] Casteel's disappearing legs suggest a tension between the presence of her subjecthood as 'Author' and a conceivably deepening desire to overturn the societal implications of this.

Casteel's paintings act as records. Recently, the artist has been naturally drawn to the canvas of her backyard. Time spent in the garden has fuelled her creative production, becoming a panacea and retreat. Her gardens are a space both like and unlike painting, where colours, textures and light collide to reveal varying kinds of beauty, where she takes a seed and turns it into a luscious scene. 'I put everything into this garden. I nourished it. I was spending an immense amount of time there and I just felt free and calm in a way that I haven't for a very long time.'[17]

Plein air painting offers the artist a profoundly different kind of engagement with her subject, a *relationality* and *aesthetics of attention* that portraiture can't afford, an inventiveness with space, depth and focus impossible to achieve in portraiture's fixity and formula of figure and ground. Nonetheless, the probity of the social contract, the approaching of all life with considered observation that Casteel has always applied to her subjects is applied with equal rigour to her depictions of nature in her small-scaled garden series. Casteel's cultivated flowers, started from seeds in her studio, are like self-portraits too – emblems of time passed and the universal sentiment of impermanence. *Garden (Nasturtium)* (2023, p.88), with its flattening of the picture plane, captivating use of line and a carefully edited palette of brilliant fuchsia, lavender and yellow, offers an emphatic frontality. The refusal of depth in conjunction with the decentred moments of energetic colour, at once confound and lure the viewer. Spatiality seems to become less material and more philosophical in this avoidance of single-point perspective and illusion of three dimensionality. *Magnolia* (2022), larger in scale, throws us into the dizzying branches of a magnolia tree, where plush blossoms open right under our noses, scattering across the image without a readily apparent logic of depth, reminiscent of how a Joan Semmel painting makes you feel: our eyes adjust and we discern, receding from our view but still looming, thickened lines cutting across each other further in the picture plane. In between the branches, we can make out the glorious tapestry of petals blanketing the ground. Landscapes such as *In bloom* (2022, pp. 38-39) broaden our vantage point. The lush ground of Casteel's backyard, and the receding barn shrouded by bushes and leaves, are largely left undone. The underpainting, or drawing for what is to come, anchors the composition in shades of green and loosely applied brushwork. Vibrantly coloured zinnias foreground the viewer as if we are peeking at the expanse behind a bushel of flowers. The spirit of this landscape holds the same depth of disposition as a figurative portrait. Mirroring the rhythmic patterns inherent to the flow of the seasons with the cycles of life that tether body and

GARDEN (ZINNIA), 2023
OIL ON CANVAS
30 X 23 CM

GARDEN (NASTURTIUM), 2023
OIL ON CANVAS
18 X 13 CM

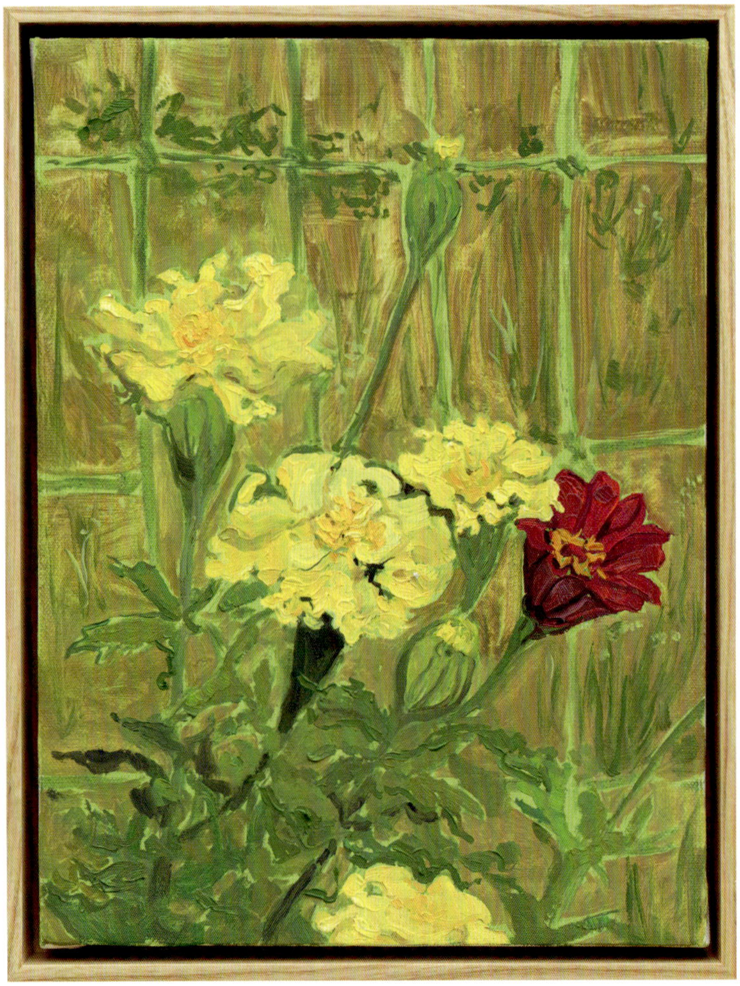

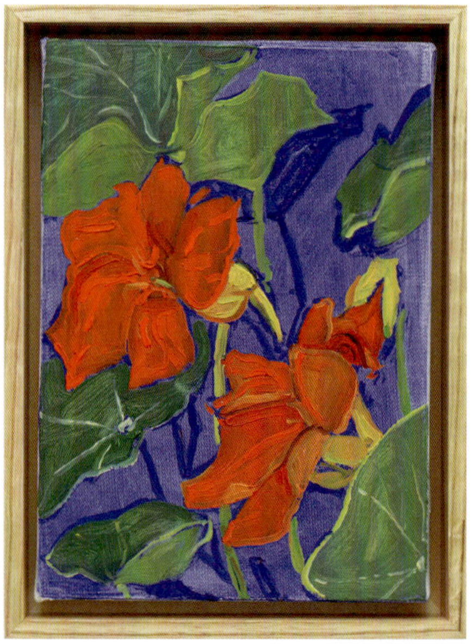

GARDEN (THAI HOT), 2023
OIL ON CANVAS
30 X 23 CM

GARDEN (PANSY), 2023
OIL ON CANVAS
36 X 28 CM

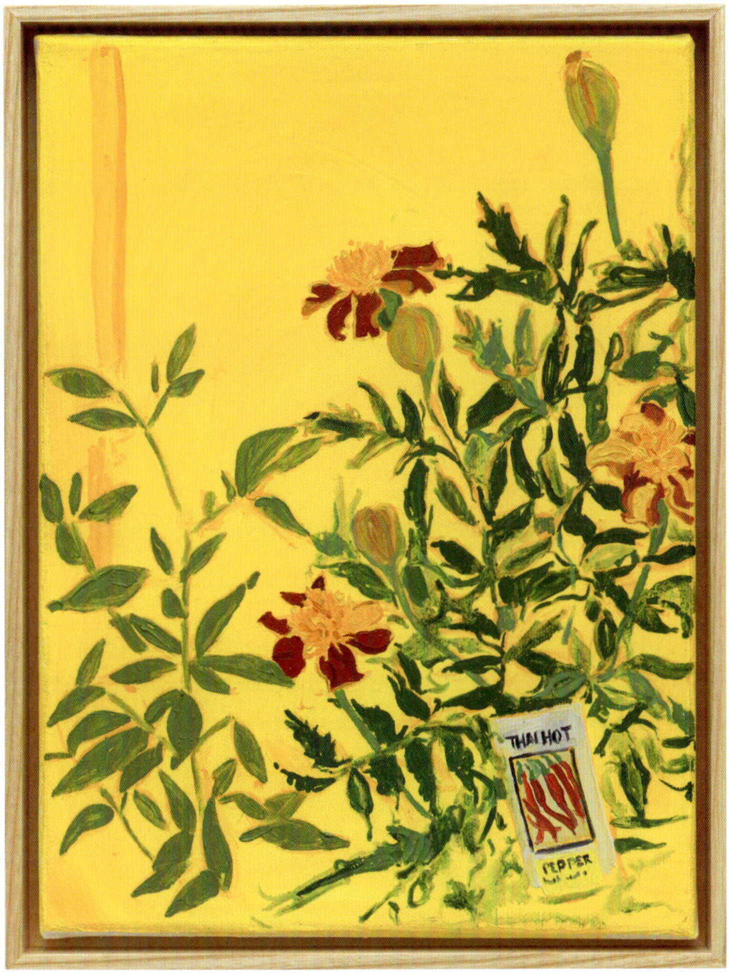

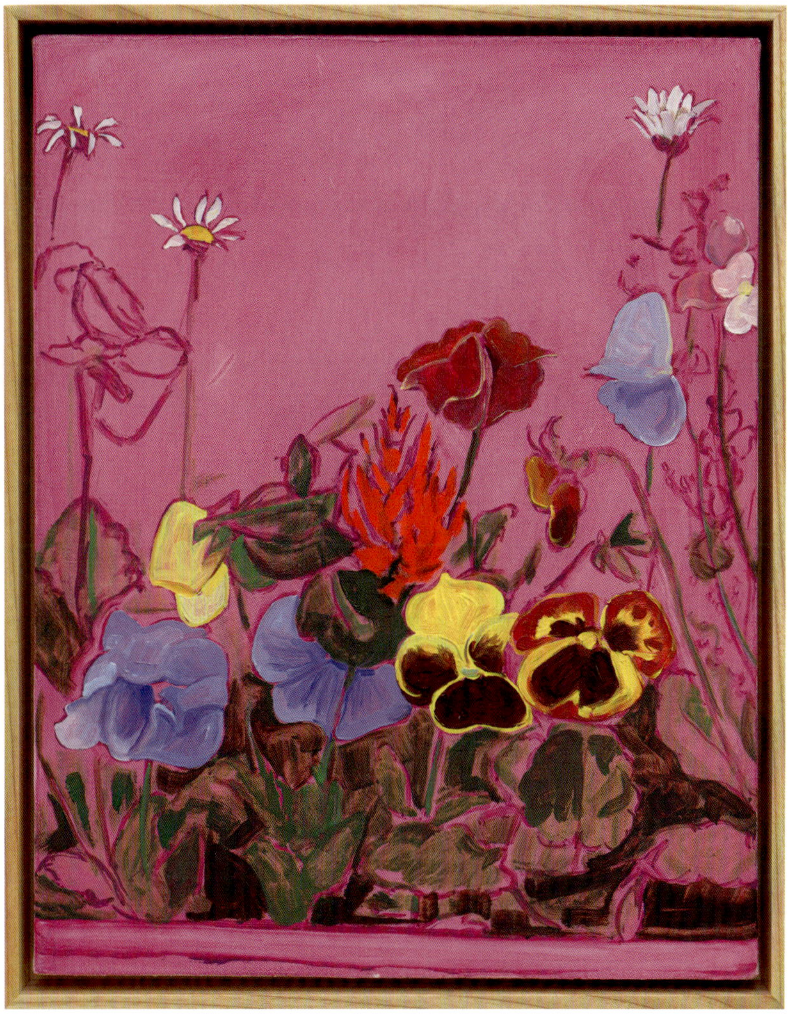

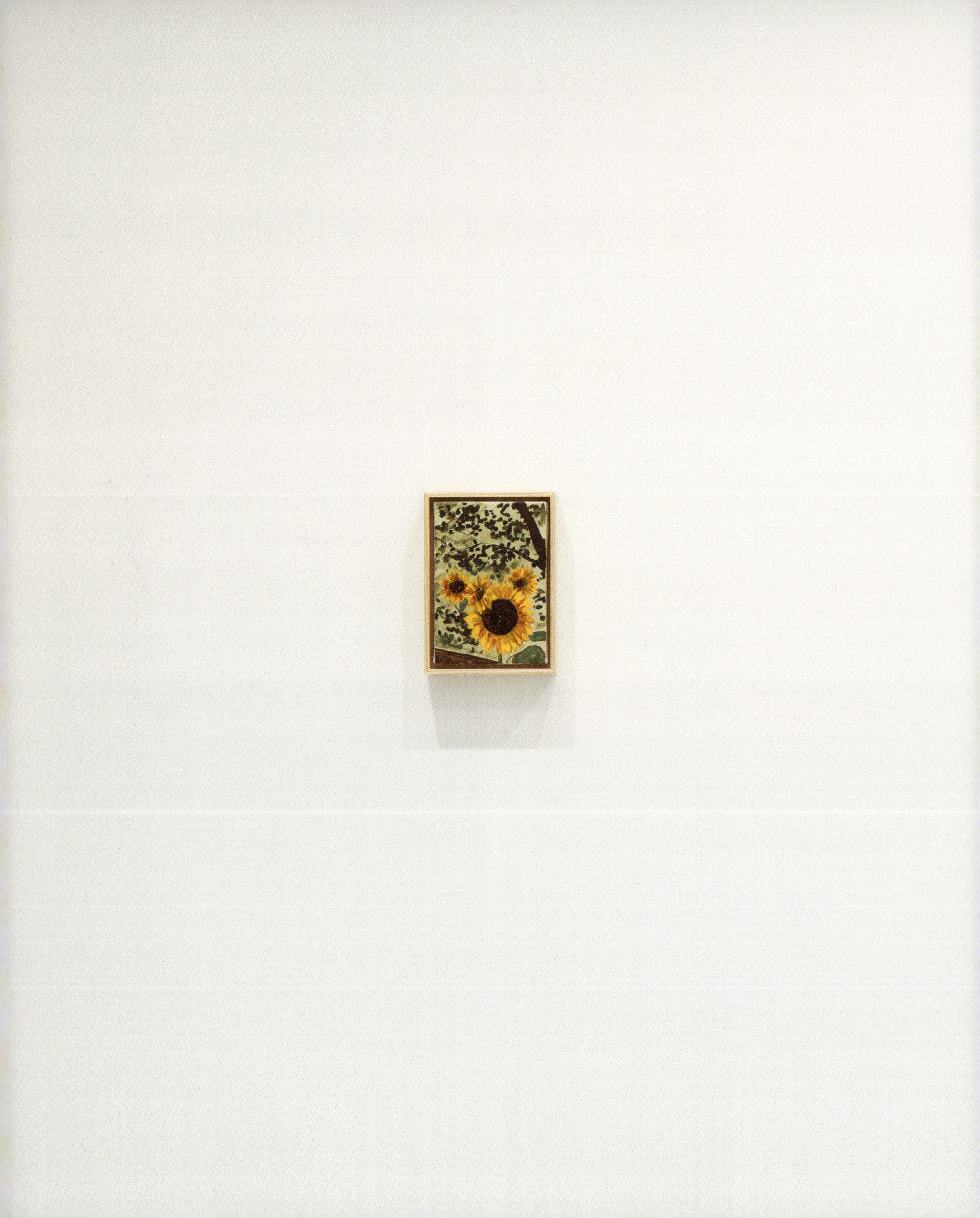

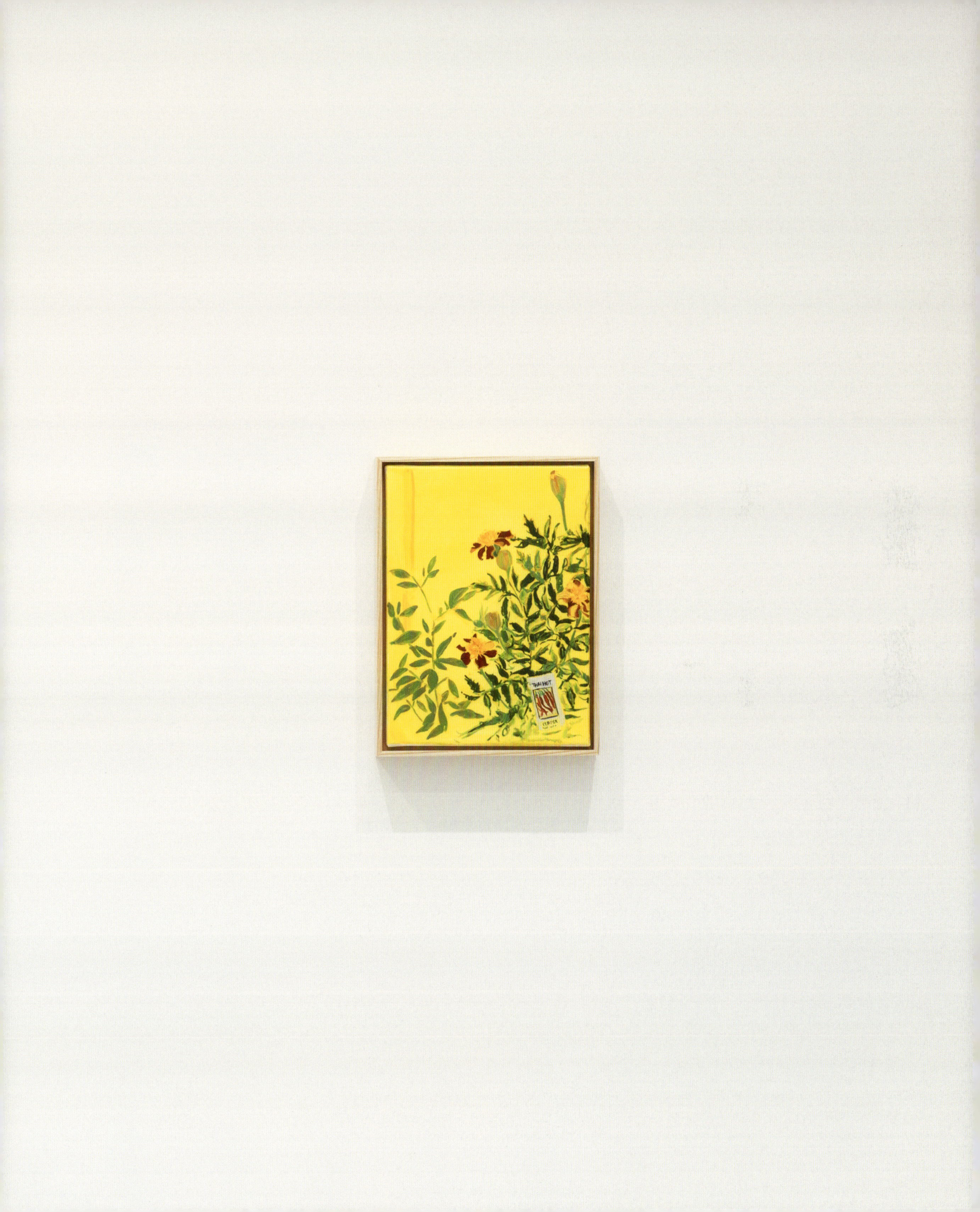
THAI HOT

previous pages, from left,
GARDEN (SUNFLOWERS), 2023
OIL ON CANVAS
18 X 13 CM

GARDEN (THAI HOT), 2023
OIL ON CANVAS
30 X 23 CM

INSTALLATION VIEW AT CASEY KAPLAN, NEW YORK, 2023

following pages, from left,
NOOR AND ADAM, 2021
OIL ON CANVAS
229 X 198 CM

MARISA, ISABEL AND SAGE, 2022
OIL ON CANVAS
239 X 203 CM

opposite,
NAIMA'S GIFT (DEON, KYM AND NOAH), 2023
OIL ON CANVAS
239 X 203 CM

nature, Casteel contemplates those who shape an environment. In her sylvan haven, her proximity to community required a rethink.

The absence of a highly visible Black community like that of Harlem soon set in motion an online discourse that bridged connections between people of colour in the Hudson Valley and Upstate New York, later known as Upstate Color (UPCO). Through the formation of the group, Casteel has developed relationships that are now present within her painting practice, combining people with the natural landscape in a more organic way. This is the case with *Morgan* (2022, cover), where the artist registers the sun's light through shadows that submerge the scene in reflections of plant life. Morgan's silhouette, perching next to a garden bed in front of her home, lit by a setting sun, merges the human form with the natural world, making further allusion to the artist's forever-presence in the work. As the seasons changed, Casteel photographed Damani, another UPCO community member, in his home with his daughter: *Damani and Shola* (2022, p. 96). A distilled light bouncing off the snowy ground outside is cast across the room, cocooning a leisurely household on a quiet winter morning. The representation of multigenerational ties – from mother and child or mentor and mentee to unlikely friendships – recurs throughout the practice in a monument to acts of nurturing, in all its forms. *Naima's Gift (Deon, Kym and Noah)* (2023, p. 93) is a brio of handling, and perhaps most gleefully an integration of figure and ground through colour and maturity of vision. Among the blooms and billowing stalks in a garden they harvested and grew themselves, this sun-kissed couple holding their baby blend into one compositional unit in a portrait that demonstrates the bounties of care and cultivation. When viewed next to a painting from the 'Visible Man' series like *Aaron*, *Naima's Gift (Deon, Kym and Noah)* makes the evolution of Casteel's practice spectacularly visible. Created during a period marked by heightened political urgency

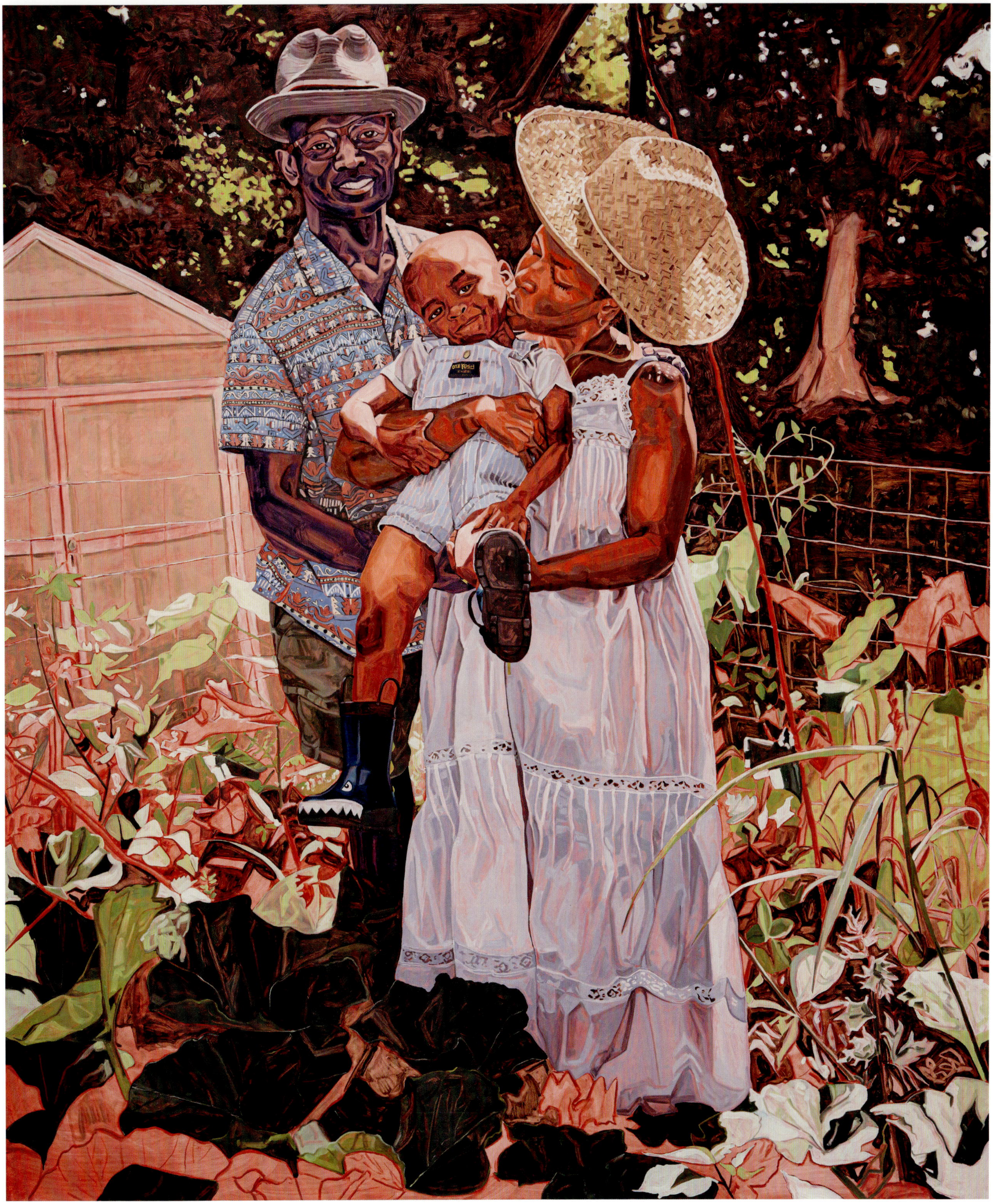

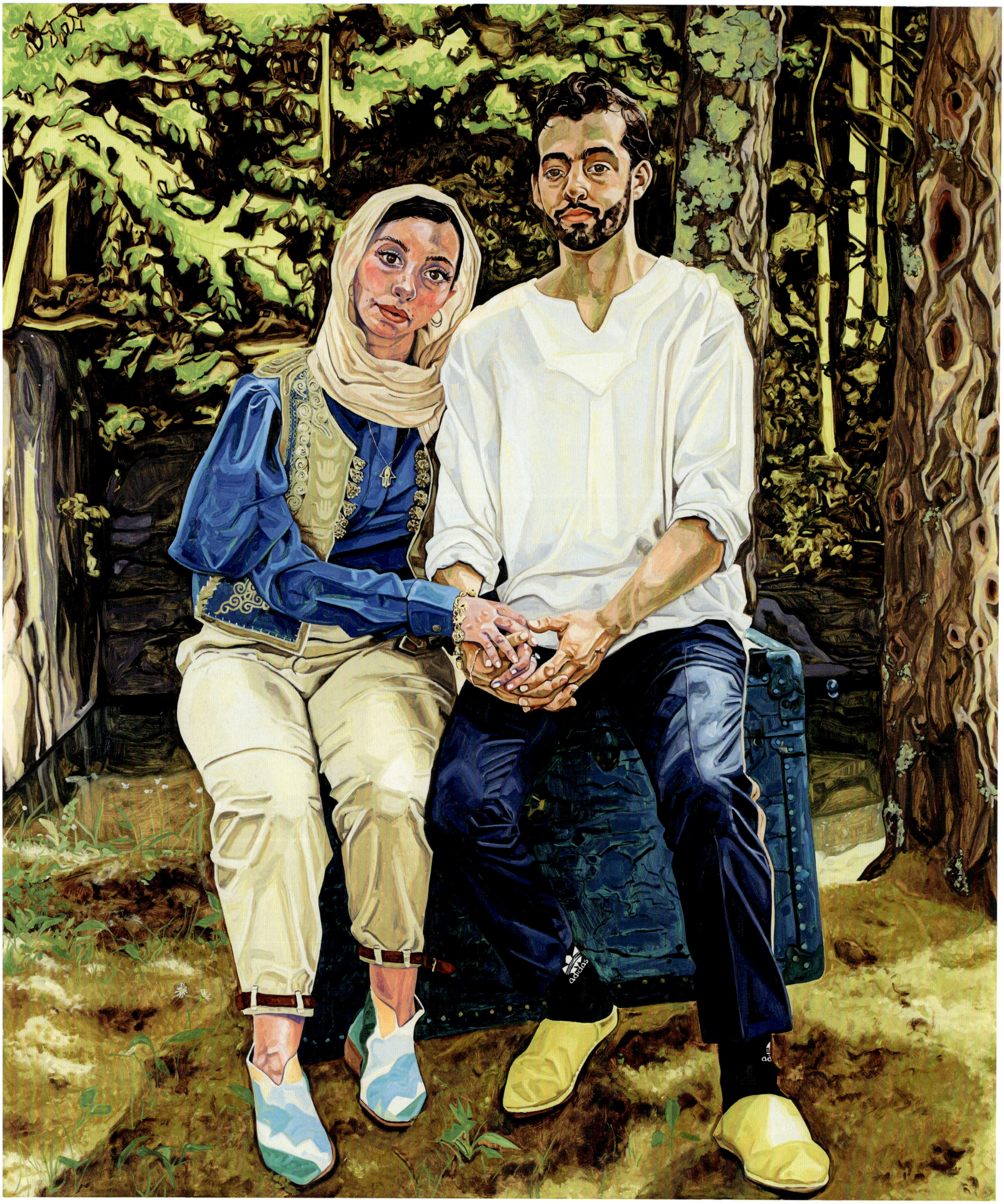
adidas

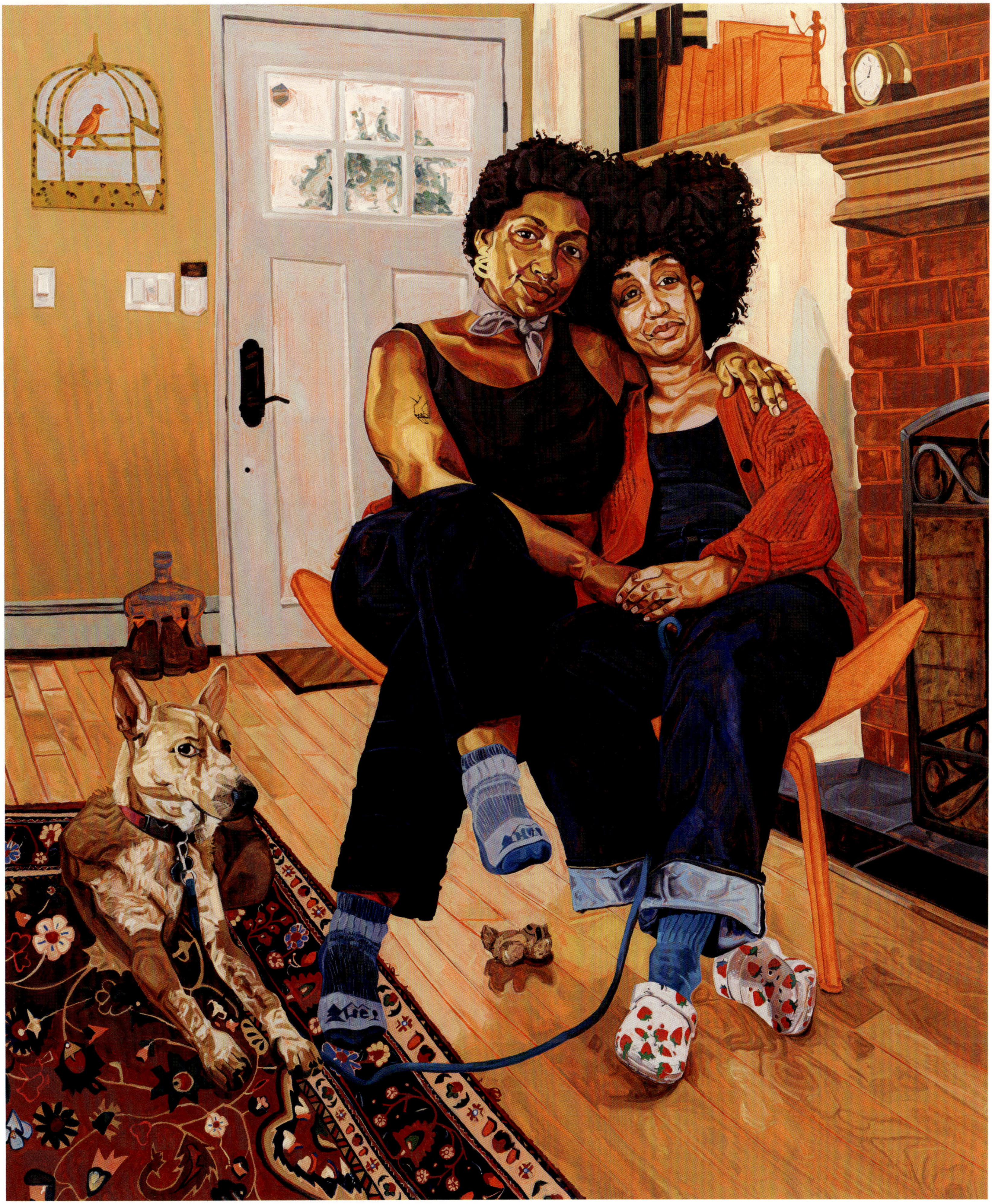

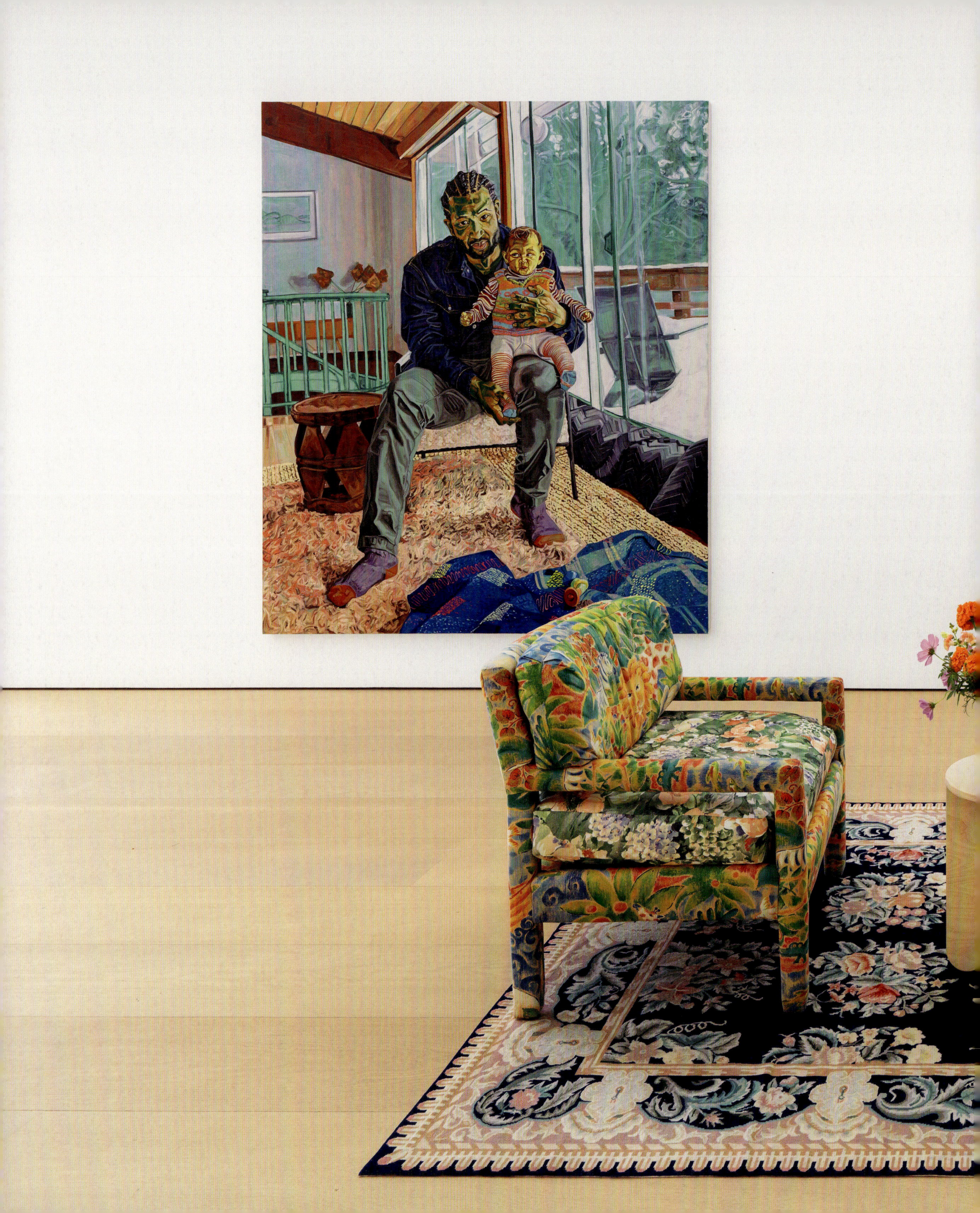

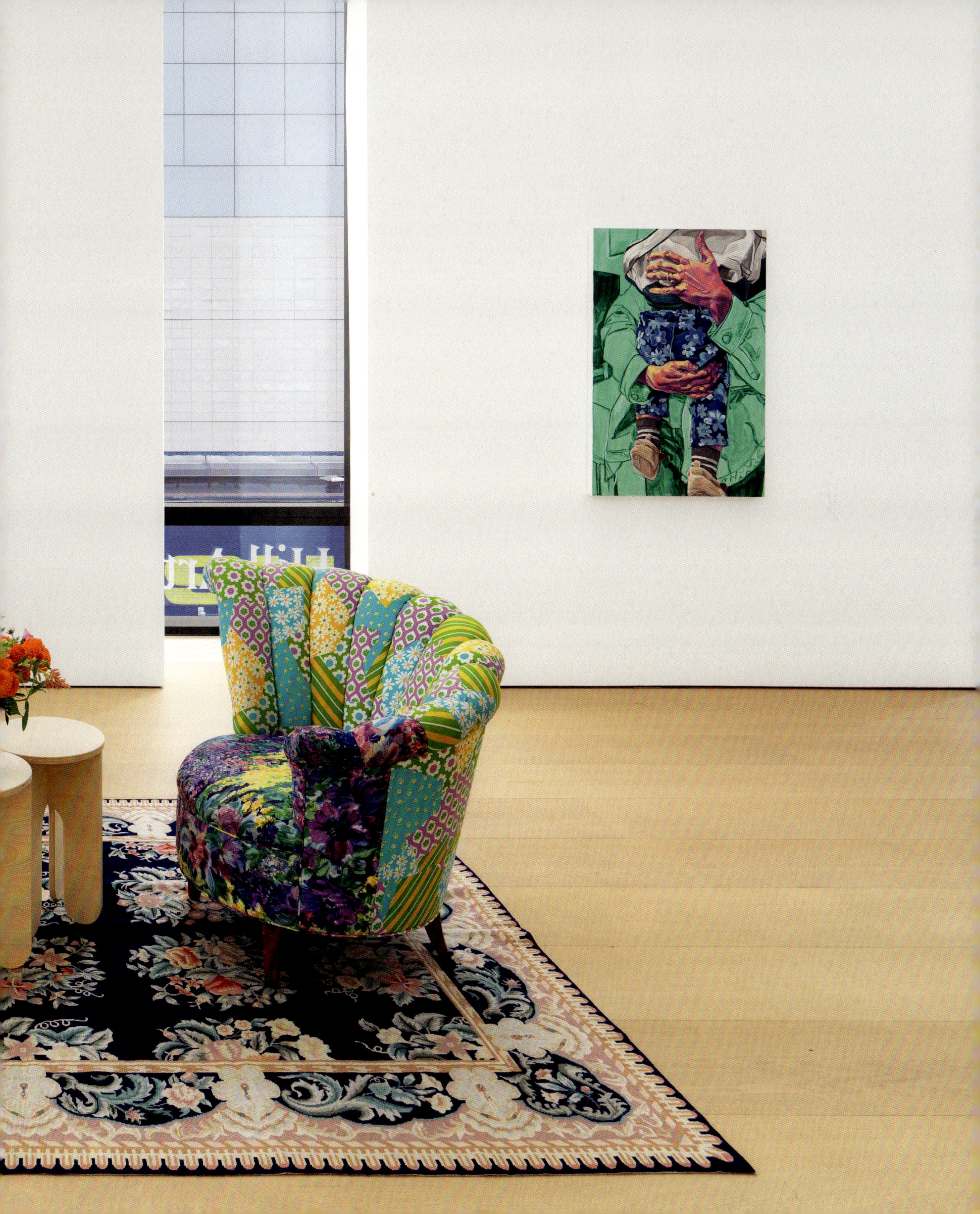

left,
ELIZABETH AND ROMAN, 2024
OIL ON CANVAS
114 X 76 CM

opposite,
CRASPEDIA, 2024
OIL ON CANVAS
127 X 102 CM

previous pages, from left,
DAMANI AND SHOLA, 2022
OIL ON CANVAS
229 X 198 CM

ELIZABETH AND ROMAN, 2024
OIL ON CANVAS
114 X 76 CM

CHAIRS DESIGNED BY
BATSHEVA HAY

INSTALLATION VIEW AT THE
HILL ART FOUNDATION, NEW
YORK, 2024

and self-exploration, *Aaron* confronts the viewer with a direct gaze and unambiguous presence, demanding recognition in an ignorant cultural landscape. A decade later, *Naima's Gift (Deon, Kym and Noah)* reflects Casteel's deepened trust in both her practice and her audience. The work no longer relies on confrontation to assert significance; instead, it invites the viewer into an intimate atmosphere where presence is communicated through emotional texture, environmental detail and a softened gaze that radiates care and safety.

One of the latest works made by Casteel is *Craspedia* (2024). Decisive cropping and diagonality order the composition, with wire fencing on one side, and the wild, errant, tall stalks of spherical craspedia bending and a few vivid zinnias turning to the other. The leaves create a mesmerizing effect, and overall there is more restraint than usual in the visual information that Casteel has given us. Whereas we have always understood Casteel's inherent presence in her work and her relationality to the subject, *Craspedia* adumbrates a future in which the artist's position or a rational space are not so readily suggested, a future in which the delineation of a totalizing environment is no longer necessary, where beyond the fencing that protects and fosters beauty is nothing but a formless, vast expanse.

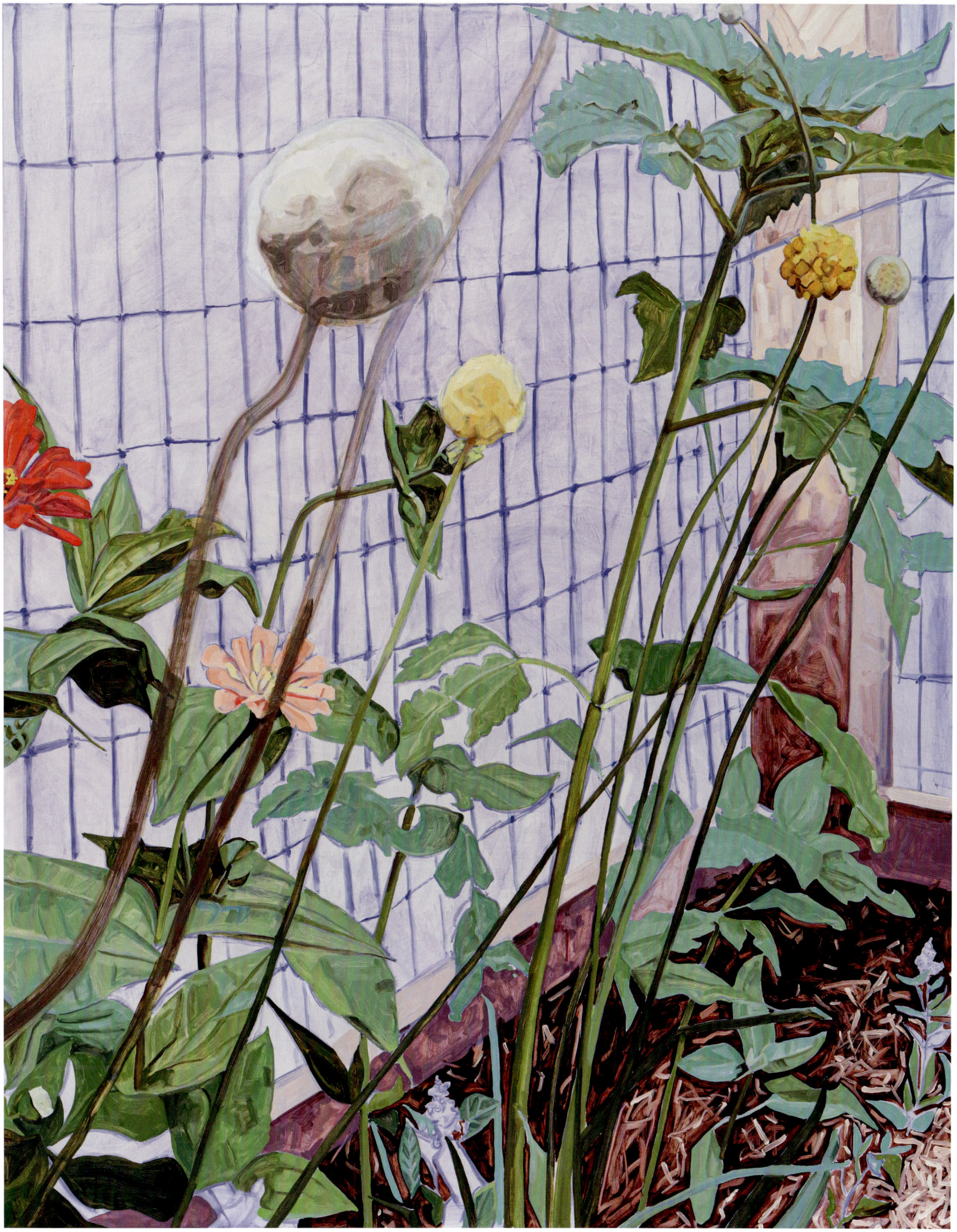

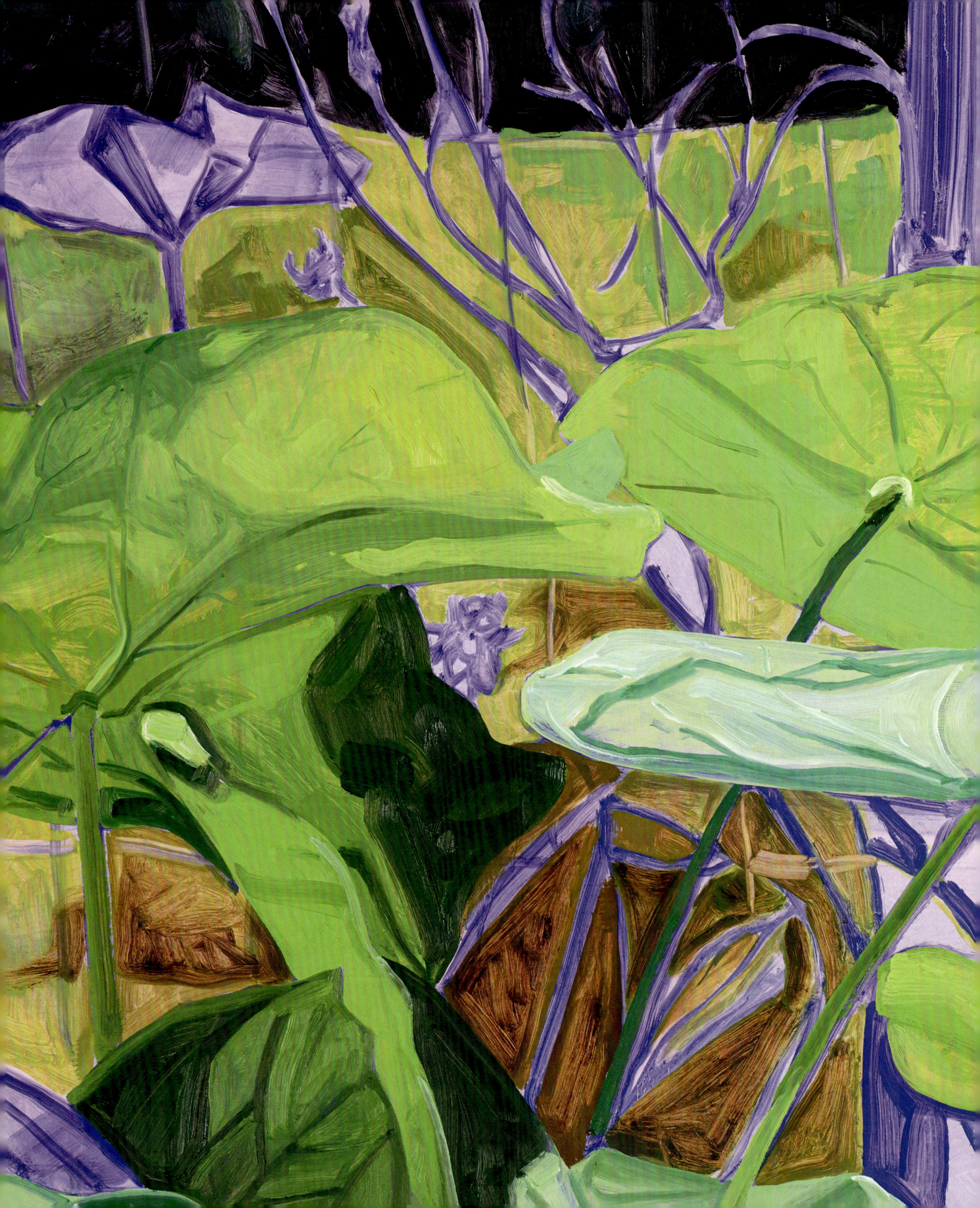

101 FOCUS

Nasturtium

Katherine Brinson

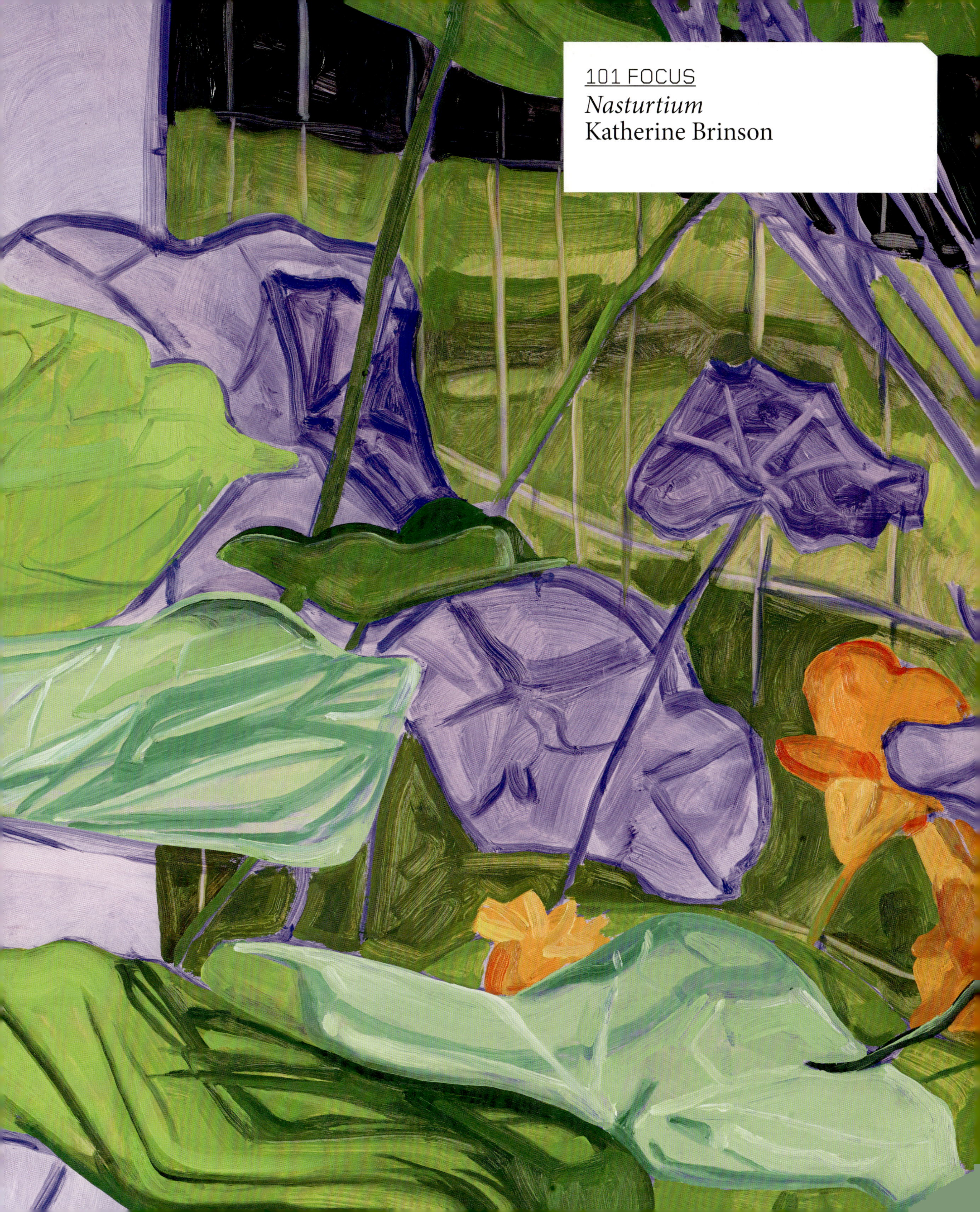

previous pages,
Nasturtium (DETAIL), 2021
OIL ON CANVAS
183 X 142 CM

opposite,
Nasturtium, 2021
OIL ON CANVAS
183 X 142 CM

On an October visit to Jordan Casteel's home in the Hudson Valley, our first stop was not the airy studio building where she paints daily, but a tour of her densely planted garden. Casteel had spent the morning hard at work amidst the raised beds, meticulously harvesting seeds for storage over the winter. Within the studio, neat rows of brightly hued sachets labelled as yellow marigolds, double click cosmos or bachelor buttons lay drying out on tables, a dormant riot of colour and form that would be coaxed into life by the artist in the coming spring.

Seeing this carefully tended plot and Casteel's ritual of salvage and regeneration recalled a statement that she made in a 2022 conversation with fellow artist EJ Hill, in which she discussed a painting titled Nasturtium as her most vulnerable work to date. 'Nasturtium felt like a more honest depiction as a self-portrait than the one I did in 2020',[1] she mused, referring to an earlier canvas, Jordan, in which she addresses the viewer with an incisive gaze, surrounded by the rosy-hued domestic clutter of the Harlem studio apartment that circumscribed her daily life during the pandemic.

For a viewer familiar with the charismatic renderings of the human figure that brought Casteel to wide acclaim in the first decade of her career, Nasturtium might appear a surprising choice to describe as a portrait, let alone a work of special self-revelation. Eschewing any human presence, it lavishes painterly attention on a verdant corner of fenced garden. The eponymous plant crowds the picture plane, while a vista of meadow and forest recedes behind the geometry of a climbing wire and post. Casteel begins every painting with a brushed monochromatic colour upon which she sketches out her imagery, working decisively and intuitively from an amalgam of photographic sources and recalled sensation. In this canvas, the astringent violet ground and slightly darker purple underdrawing are left exposed in certain sections, while other passages of leaves, nasturtium blooms and the bucolic backdrop are rendered in their natural hues. The result is an exhilarating dance between veristic representation and compositional liberties that jolt us into an awareness of the temporal and material vicissitudes of making a painting.

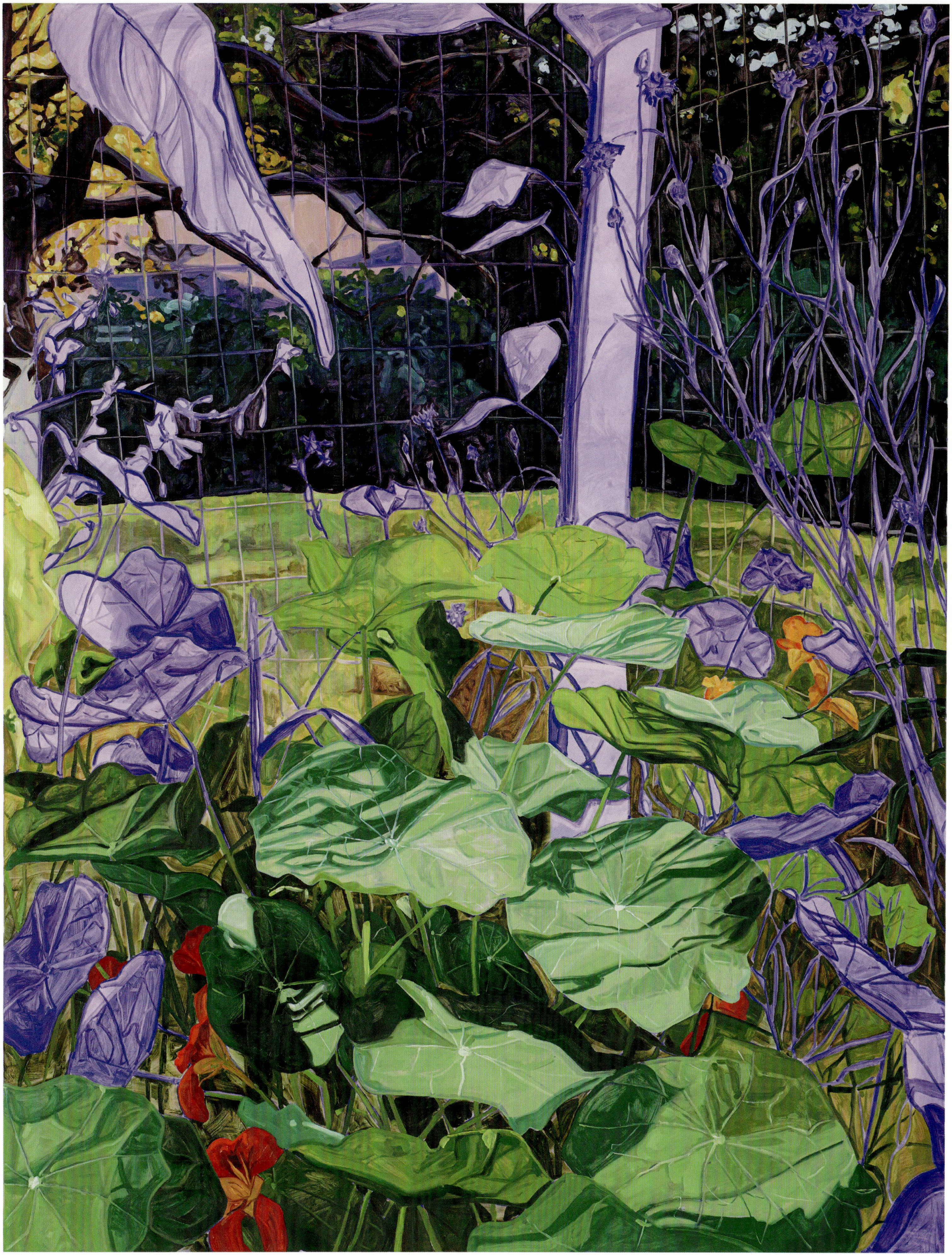

ELIZABETH AND ROMAN II,
2025
OIL ON CANVAS
239 X 203 CM

While an intense interest in environmental surroundings has suffused Casteel's practice from the beginning, her earlier works were characteristically grounded in the vividly realized subjecthood of her sitters. Any portrait of significance evokes a nuanced imbrication of artist and subject, but Casteel's canvases emerge from an unusually collaborative process that begins when the artist is drawn to an individual encountered over the course of her daily life. Drawing on what she terms 'the deeply emotional and personal levels of engagement that are required to make the work',[2] she forges warm relationships of mutual trust that result in the depiction of people at ease and in their element, whether their homes, their workplace or the streets of their neighbourhood.

Certainly, these are works that engage the aristocratic tradition of the formally posed sitter rather than the anonymous bustle of the genre scene, but Casteel's penetrating focus on the way an individual or family group inhabits space allows her works to accrue social as well as psychological meaning. Instead of isolating her subjects against a monochrome background in the tradition of Alex Katz or Barkley L. Hendricks, her works render the ambient details of ordinary but precious lives lived – usually the lives of people of colour whose likenesses have not historically been inserted into the privileged space of the museum or gallery: 'I've always had an inclination towards seeing people who might easily be unseen', as she puts it.[3] The artist Dawoud Bey has elaborated on Casteel's 'commitment to ordinary black people as both subject and source of her social and aesthetic investigations', situating her in 'a long line of artists intent on pushing their practice forward by crafting complex objects while conspicuously foregrounding common people as the conceptual center of that work'.[4]

What then, did it mean for Casteel to initiate a body of work that removed this conceptual centre entirely? In part, the creative pivot was circumstantial. In 2021, pressured by the vulnerability of a long-term medical condition amid the ongoing reverberations of the pandemic, the artist and her partner acquired a modest farmhouse in a rural area of Upstate New York, and with it inherited an overgrown patch of flower and vegetable beds. Casteel had never gardened before, but immediately set about

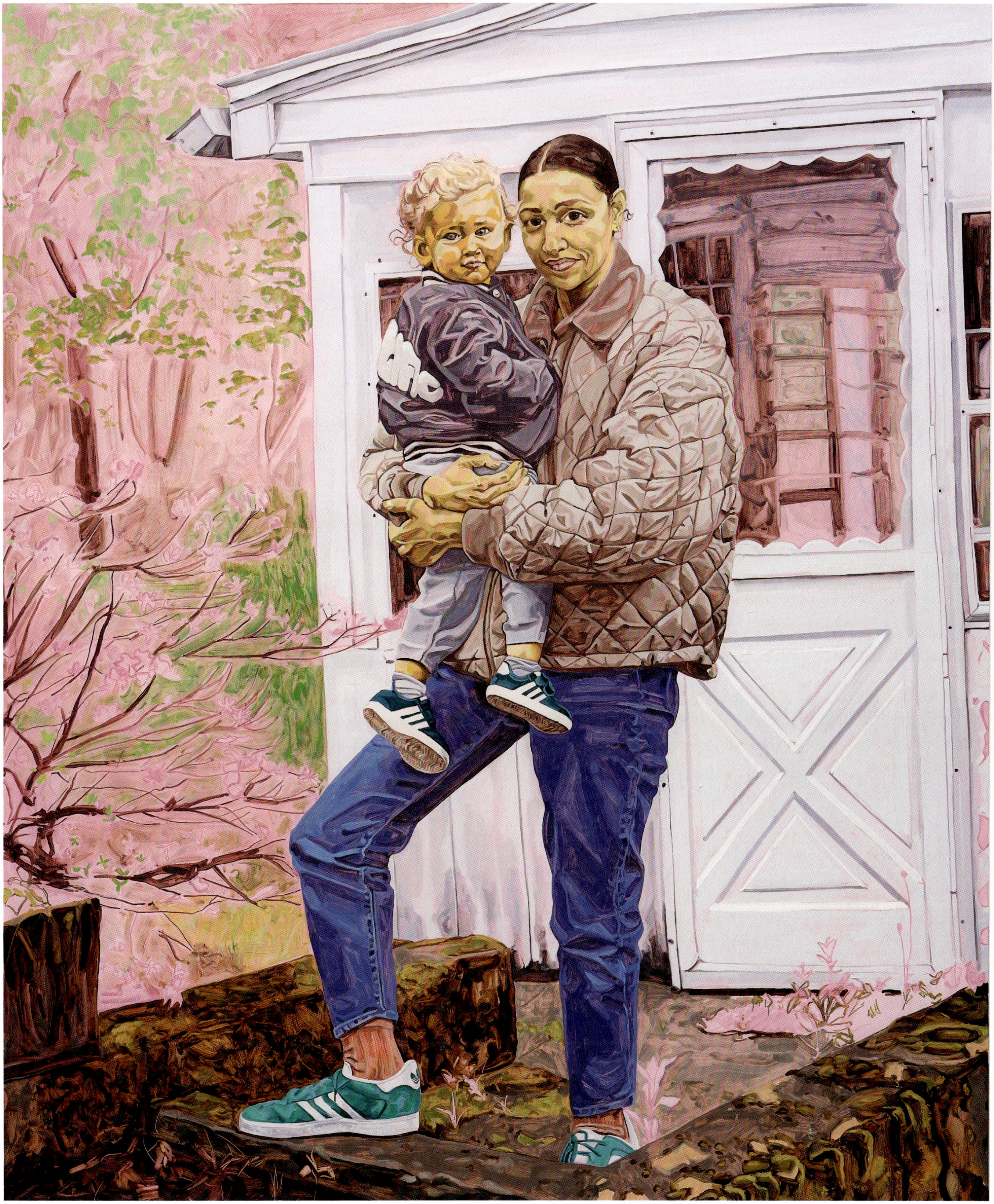

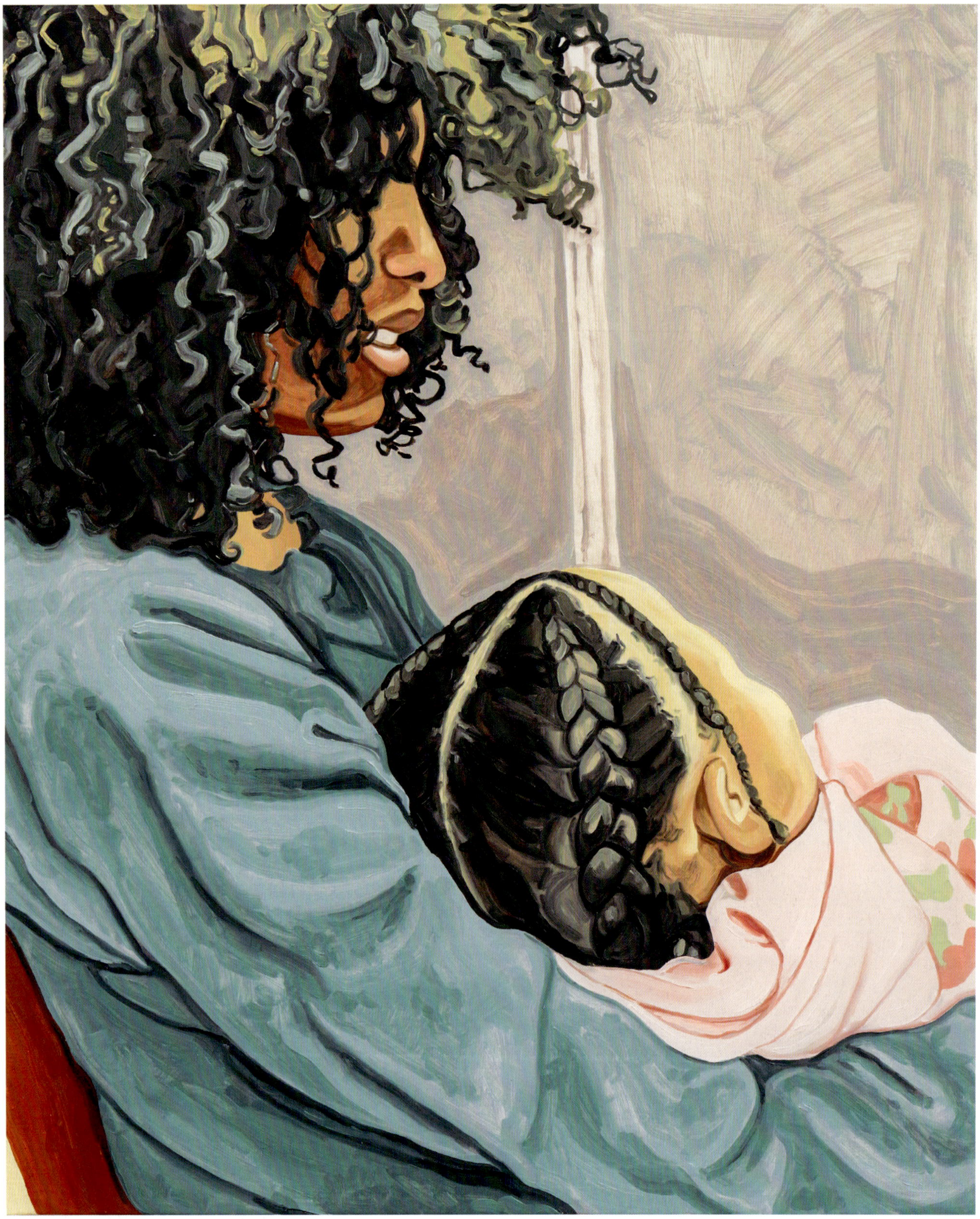

left,
GOD BLESS THE CHILD, 2019
OIL ON CANVAS
91 X 76 CM

opposite,
THE CAROLINAS, 2021
OIL ON CANVAS
239 X 203 CM

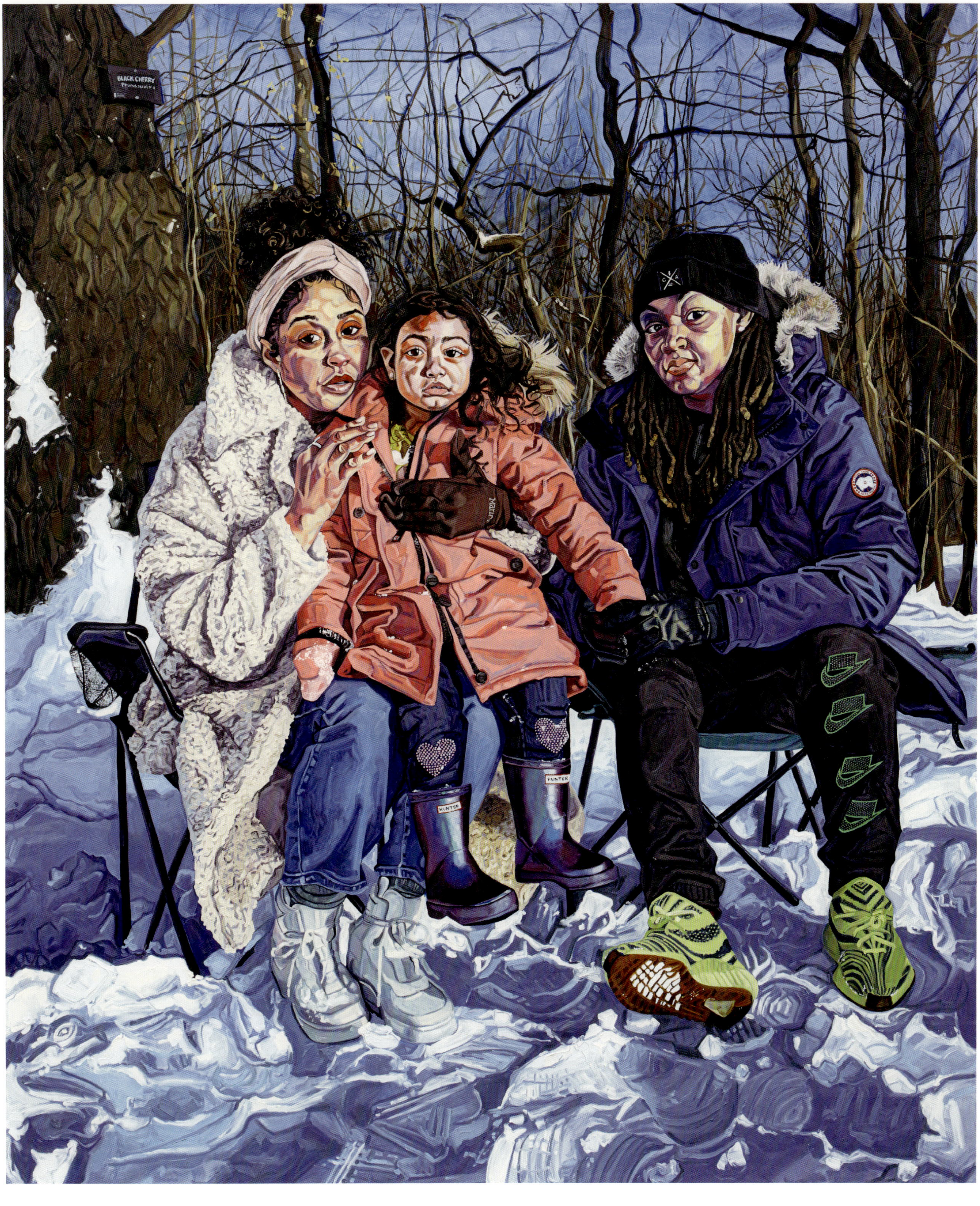
BLACK CHERRY
HUNTER
HUNTER

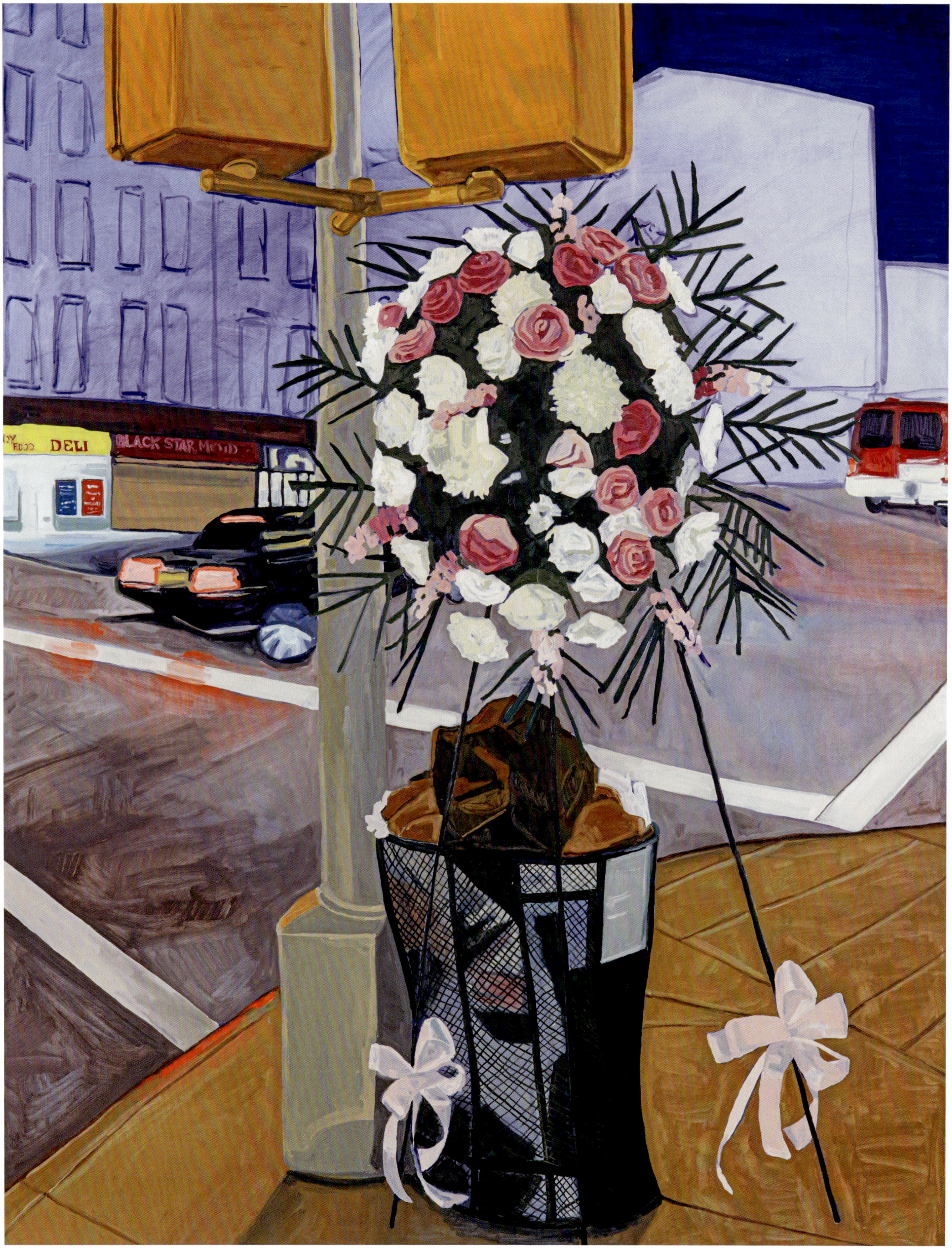
DELI
BLACK STAR

MEMORIAL, 2017
OIL ON CANVAS
183 X 142 CM

educating herself and renewing the plantings, finding a deep satisfaction in the immersive physicality of the work. And gradually she began to consider the possibility of centring the fruits of her labour in her compositions, so that both subject and painting would be generated by her own hands.

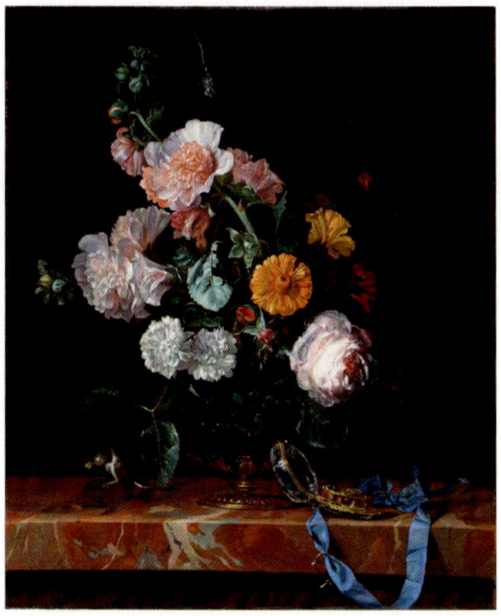

WILLEM VAN AELST
VANITAS FLOWER STILL LIFE, 1656—57
OIL ON CANVAS
56 X 46 CM

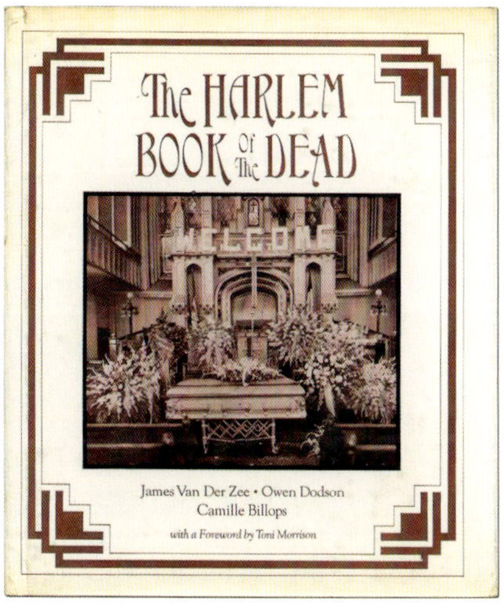

JAMES VAN DER ZEE
THE HARLEM BOOK OF THE DEAD, 1978
BOOK
28 X 22 CM

Casteel was initially hesitant to devote a significant portion of her creative attention to flowers – the placid preserve of hobbyists and domestic decor. But the excision of the human figure from Nasturtium marked a generative inflection point. It was quickly followed by Magnolia (2022) and In Bloom (2022): large-scale canvases in which botanical scenes become the armature for formal innovations and bravura chromatics that draw an almost otherworldly glamour from their earthly subjects. Other works from the same year return to the domestic setting of many of Casteel's portraits, but with the sitter replaced by a vase of flowers, as in Daffodil (2022) – a painting that overtly addresses the Flemish Golden Age tradition in which cut flowers are metaphoric of life's tragic brevity, beginning an inexorable decline as soon as they are plucked from the earth.

The consolatory role of flowers in rituals of remembrance and mourning had been broached by Casteel in an earlier painting, which at the time held a singular status in her oeuvre as a sort of monumental urban still-life.[5] Memorial (2017) depicts a large funeral wreath of pink and white blossoms surrounded by a spiky corona of greenery, held aloft by a stand decked with florid bows. The arrangement has been discarded next to an overflowing trashcan on the corner of Lenox Avenue and 128th Street, and made doubly strange by the glare of streetlamps and passing cars. This discordant tableau of resplendent living beauty shadowed by abjection and decay functions as a contemporary manifestation of the vanitas tradition, rendered on the grand scale of history painting. It also summons the ornate wreaths depicted on the cover of James Van Der Zee's The Harlem Book of the Dead (1978), the iconic volume documenting funerary rituals during the Harlem Renaissance that is entrenched in the neighbourhood's rich visual history. In a foreshadowing of the floral surrogacy of Nasturtium, Casteel has spoken

GRIEF/SPRING, 2024
OIL ON CANVAS
30 X 23 CM

of the disconcerting anthropomorphism of the sculptural arrangement in *Memorial*, noting how the precarious structure is 'intensely related to a human body' in both its upright scale and the implied absence of the deceased individual over which it stood sentinel.[6]

A quieter depiction of flowers as vessels of lament is found in a recent work titled *Grief/Spring* (2024), which Casteel painted on her return from the funeral of a young family member. In this small oil sketch, a handful of daffodils in a simple glass jar, rendered in rapid brushwork against a scumbled pale green, bow their heads away from the viewer. Daffodils are often figured as nature's sorrowful mourners in elegiac poetry; in Milton's *Lycidas*, for example, 'daffadillies fill their cups with tears'.[7] With piercing tenderness, Casteel takes forward the elegy's traditional expression of a grief that seems to permeate the whole world, to the extent that nature itself mourns the lost beloved.

But as the bifurcated title of *Grief/Spring* indicates, flowers are equally harbingers of rebirth. The blooms that animate Casteel's garden scenes are thrillingly and insistently alive, eliciting deep cultural connotations of the garden as prelapsarian paradise. This imagery of almost primordial abundance is vividly matched by the artist's stylistic brio, cohering into a lush alchemy of light, colour and organic form. An emergent interest in the compositional potential of plant life can be traced in certain passages of Casteel's earlier works, such as the sumptuous renderings of floral upholstery in *Jiréh* (2013) and *Serwaa and Amoakohene* (2019), or the exquisitely painted roses on the subway rider's shirt

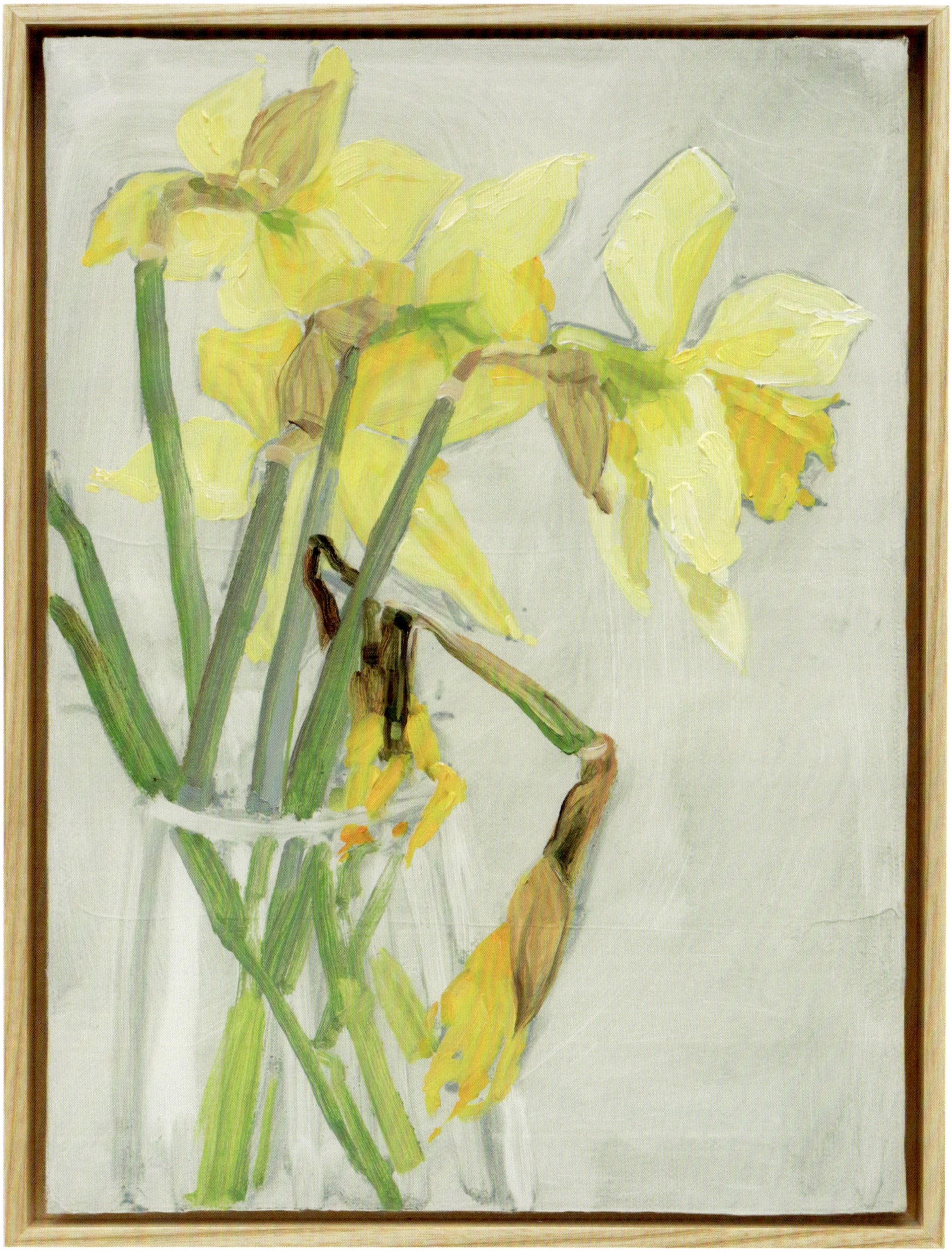

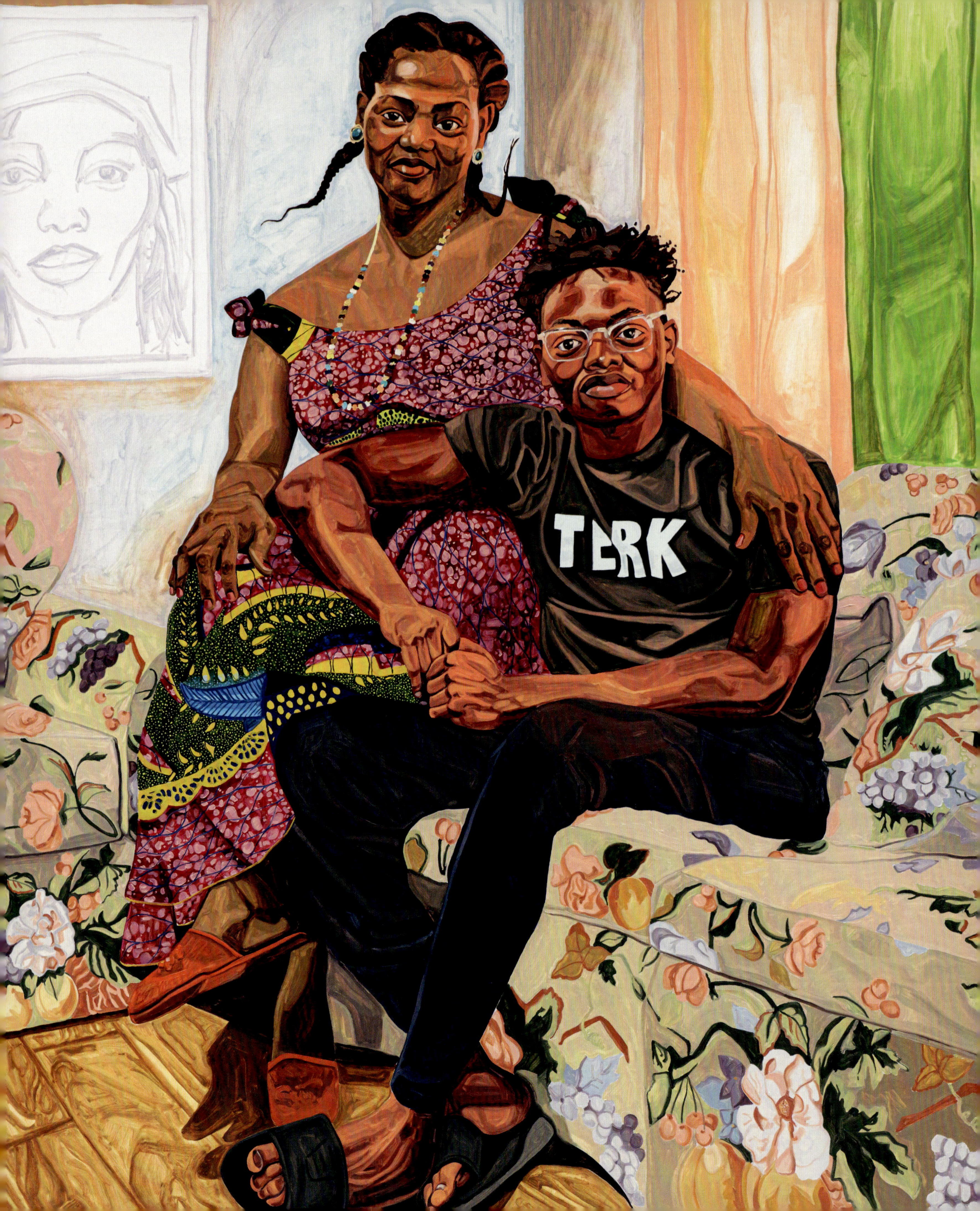
TERK

SERWAA AND AMOAKOHENE,
2019
OIL ON CANVAS
229 X 198 CM

in Bounty (2020) that beatify the tired commuter with their near-lifelike adornments. In the garden paintings of recent years, this formal affinity bursts into full realization, facilitating a creative latitude that the artist has referred to as a long-sought 'freedom' within the medium.[8] Indeed, it might be posited that in departing from the interpersonal dynamics of the portrait form, Casteel answers a question she posed in a conversation with Thelma Golden the year before she painted Nasturtium. Given that 'Being a black artist painting people of color is a nonnegotiable, unchangeable fact', she wondered, 'is there still room to just be a painter?'[9] Casteel has been candid about the pressures of the market fervour and often-reductive discourse that has swirled around Black figurative painting over the past decade. In expanding her practice to include imagery that operates outside the internalized responsibilities and externalized pressures of portraiture (or in the case of Nasturtium's designation as a self-portrait, remaking the genre on her own terms), she opened a fertile new arena for painterly experimentation.

Nasturtium's revelatory role within the arc of Casteel's career manifests in part from this removal of social context in favour of a broader interconnectedness with the natural world. The garden's association with the cultivated self provides an apt visual manifestation of interiority; instead of exchanging gazes with her subjects or with the viewer, Casteel turns inward and rescinds her bodily presence entirely. In doing so, she surfaces the fraught politics of visibility that have historically enmeshed the Black subject.[10] Sublimating her identifiable being within the contours of her own land – within the garden brought into being by her hands – she short-circuits the famous Du Boisian formulation of 'always looking at oneself through the eyes of others'.[11] Casteel's refusal to make herself conventionally visible is renewed in the 2022 painting Field Balm. The image is abruptly cropped to show only the artist's feet, as she stands in her garden wearing Croc sandals decorated with cartoonish emblems and a Black Lives Matter pin, her legs rendered in the same violet tones that undergird Nasturtium. 'It's another intersection between myself and the land', Casteel states. 'I'm literally grounding myself in my own point

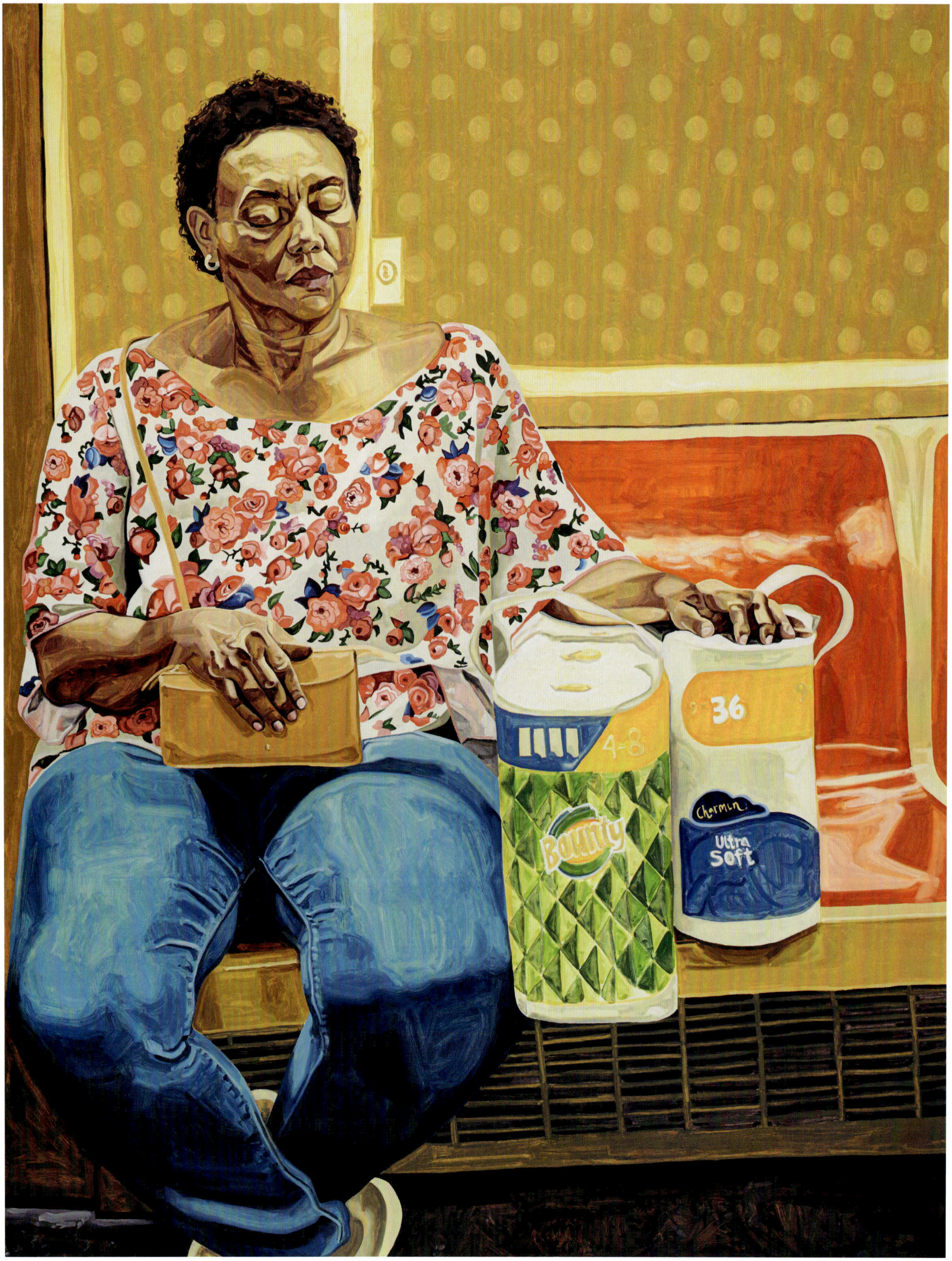
4-8
Bounty
36
Charmin
Ultra
Soft

right,
ROSE-COLORED GLASSES,
2018
OIL ON CANVAS
114 X 76 CM

opposite,
BOUNTY, 2020
OIL ON CANVAS
183 X 142 CM

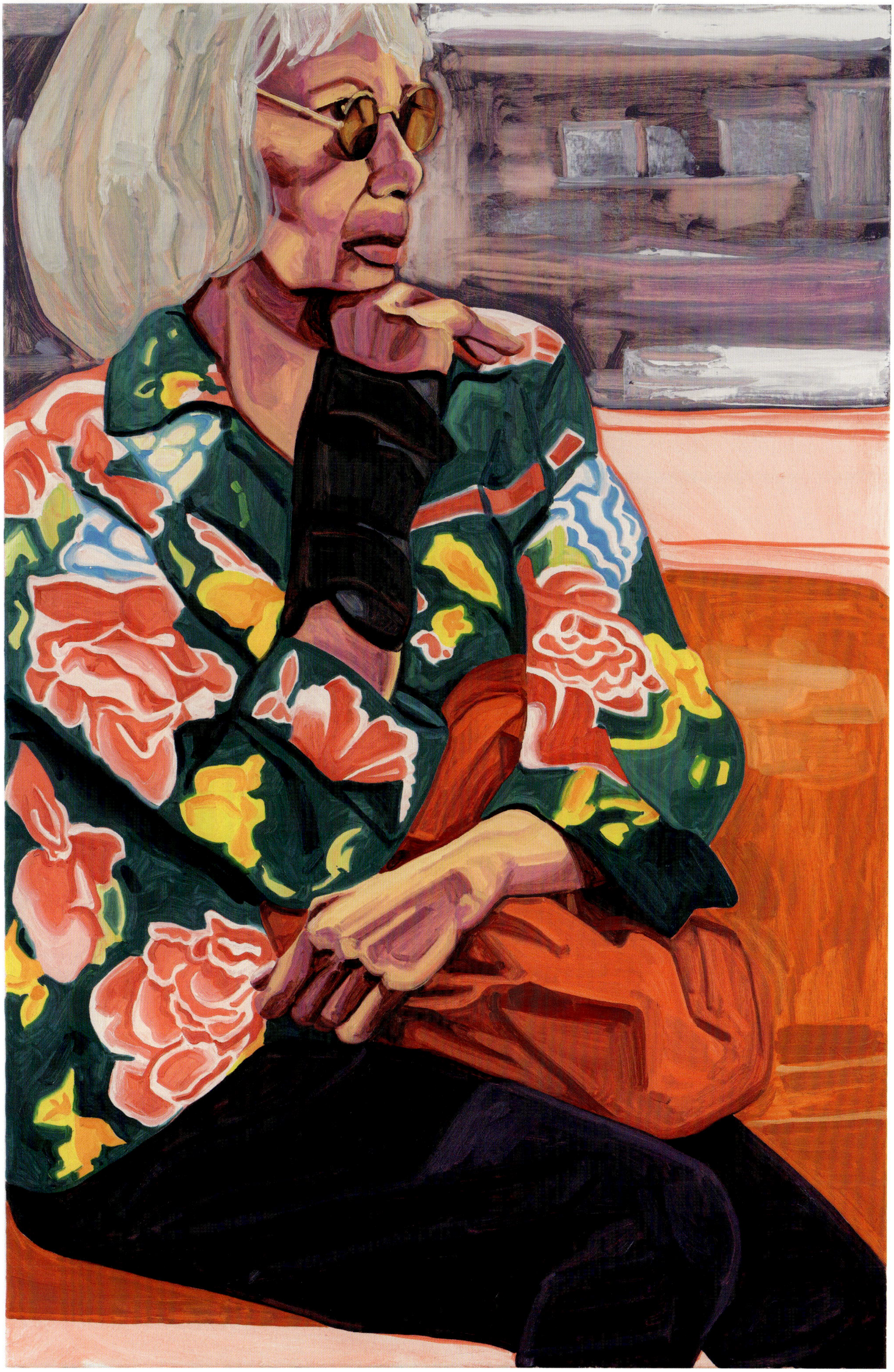

FIELD BALM, 2022
OIL ON CANVAS
91 X 76 CM

of view. There's both an absence and a presence within the frame.'[12] The work's title is derived from the diminutive groundcover flowers that seem to grow around the artist's shoes, but might equally refer to the salve found in this mode of occluded self-depiction.

During my recent visit, the studio was filled with canvases at various stages of completion on which Casteel was working simultaneously. On one wall, a cloud of small oil sketches that the artist executes en plein air in her garden documented a range of floral varieties, each one functioning as a highly distilled colour study. Nearby, a large painting sketched out the façade of Casteel's small clapboard house encircled by a wild growth of plants. Fluttering above the door was a depiction of David Hammons' African American Flag (1990). Hammons' work, which reimagines the United States flag in Pan-African red, black and green, adorned the façade of the Studio Museum in Harlem until its recent closure for rebuilding. Its presence in Casteel's scene reads as a joyful resolution of some of the tensions elicited by her recent moves – both literal and iconographic – in its infusion of Black history and Harlem lore into the rural landscape.

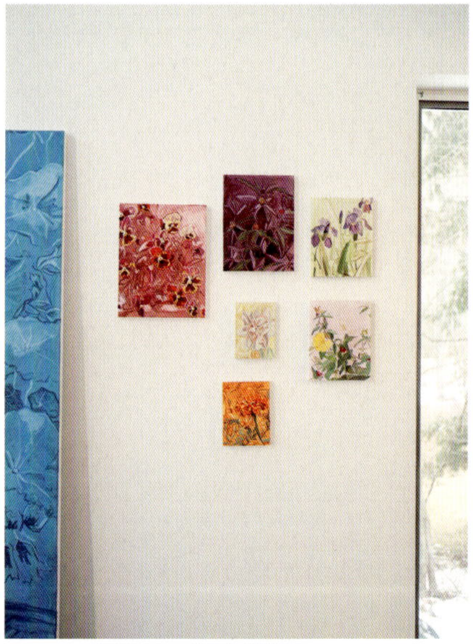

VIEW OF THE ARTIST'S STUDIO IN THE HUDSON VALLEY, NEW YORK, 2024

Of the works I saw in progress that day, all focused on garden scenes, flowers, or figures in a pastoral setting, suggesting the enduring agency of this imagery for the artist. The one exception was a portrait of Casteel's friend and Upstate neighbour Nina (p. 41), who was pictured in her home next to a stack of books, with reproductions of artworks (including, notably, floral still-life paintings) tacked to the wall. When I remarked on how the figure's skin was modelled in glorious yellows and pinks that endowed her with an intense radiance, the artist told me that this palette had been derived from an enormous dinner-plate dahlia from her garden that had sat on her painting cart at the time of the work's creation. 'It felt natural for me to transfer the sunset tones of the dahlia to the figure', noted Casteel. 'She is a flower too.'[13]

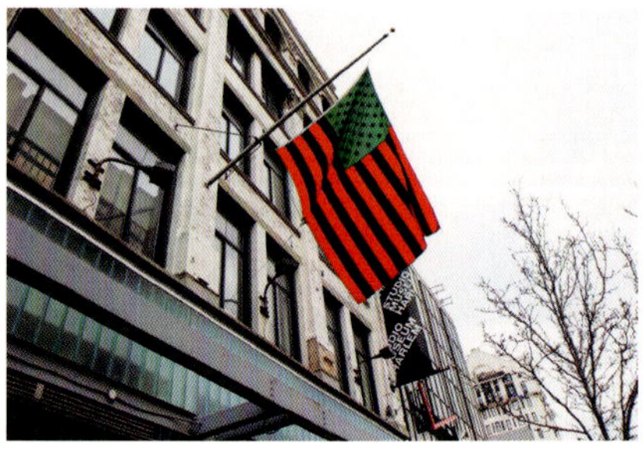

DAVID HAMMONS
AFRICAN AMERICAN FLAG, 1990
CANVAS AND GROMMETS
150 X 240 CM

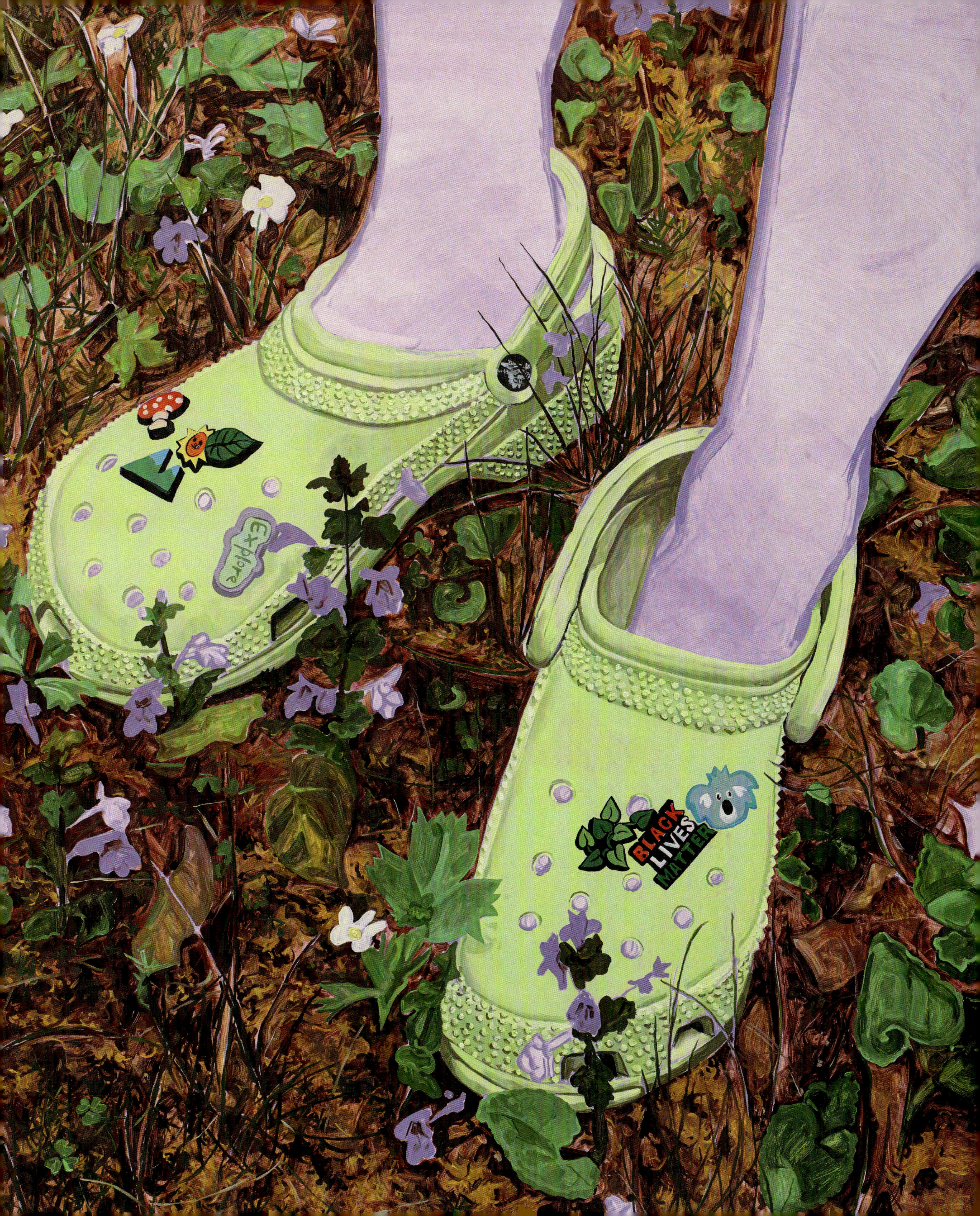
Explore
BLACK
LIVES
MATTER

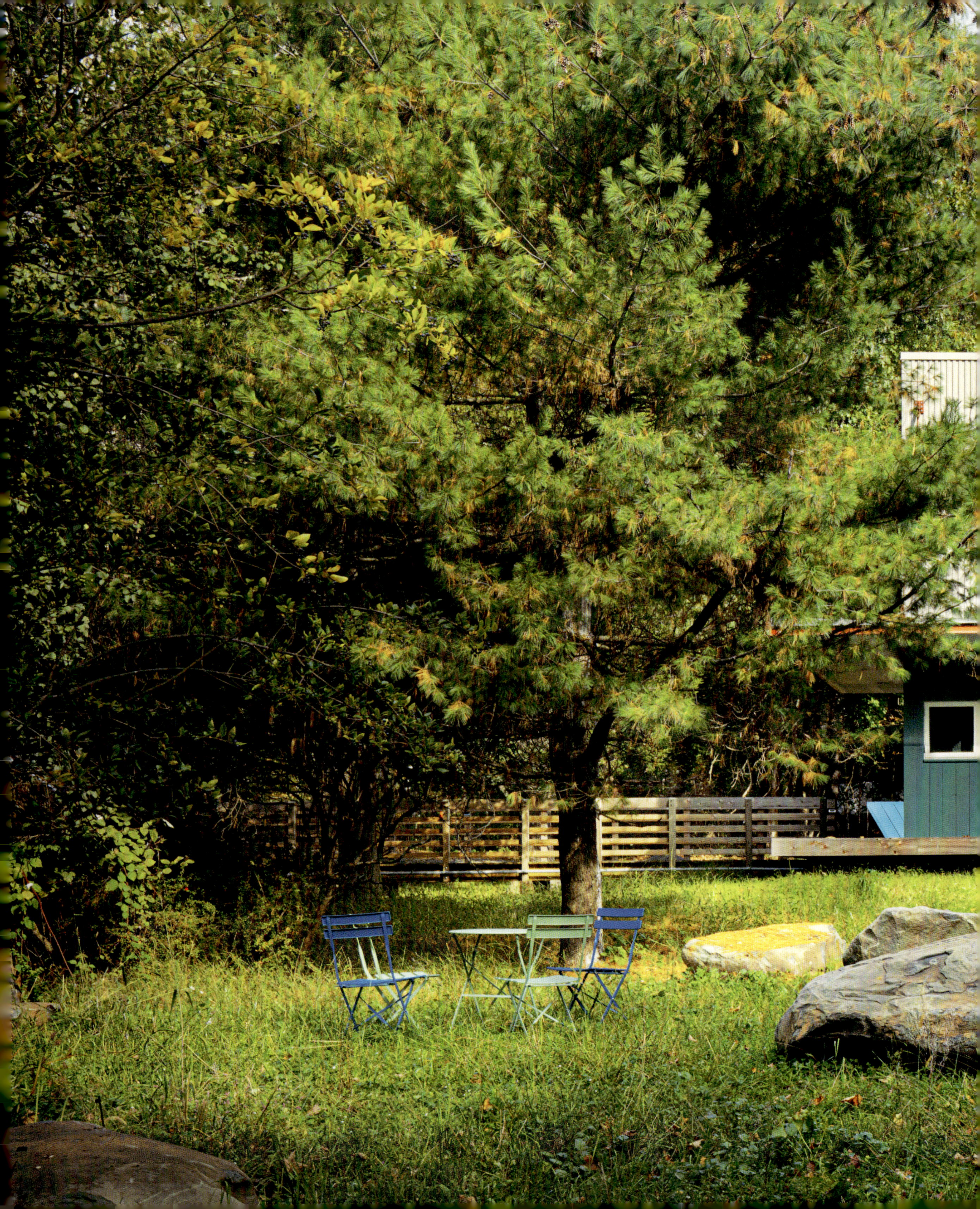

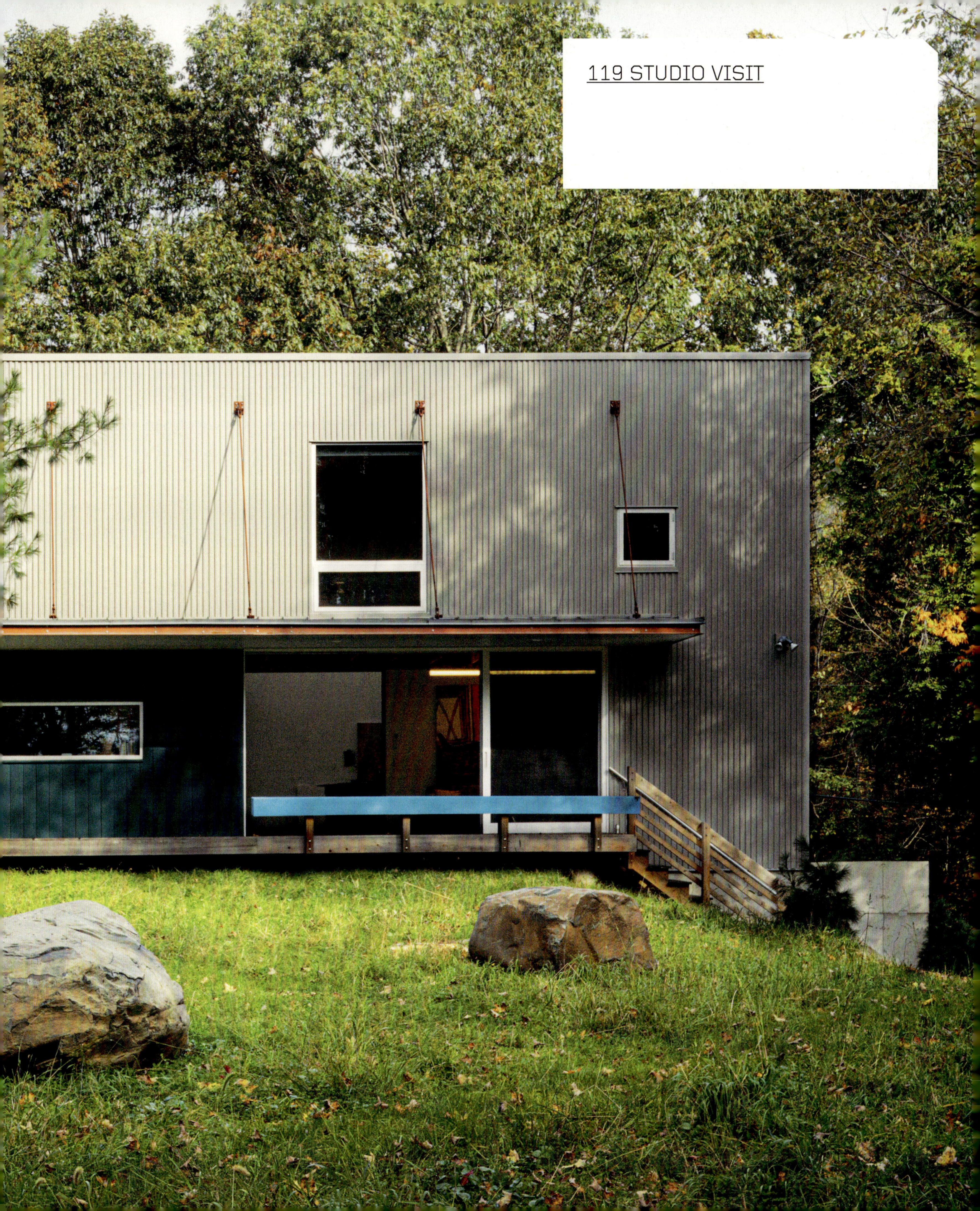

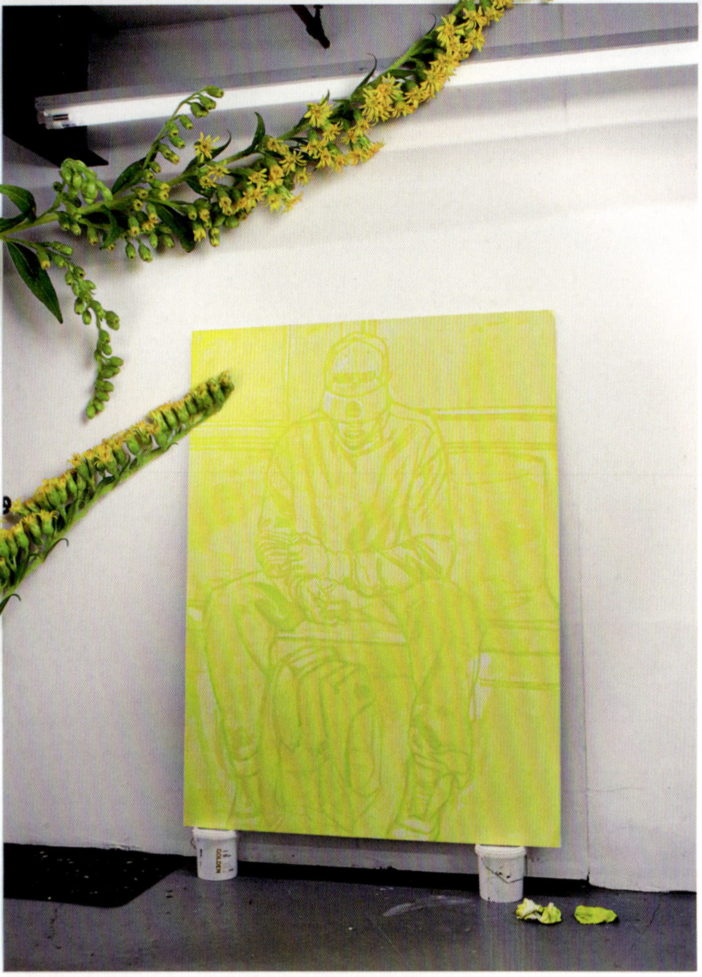

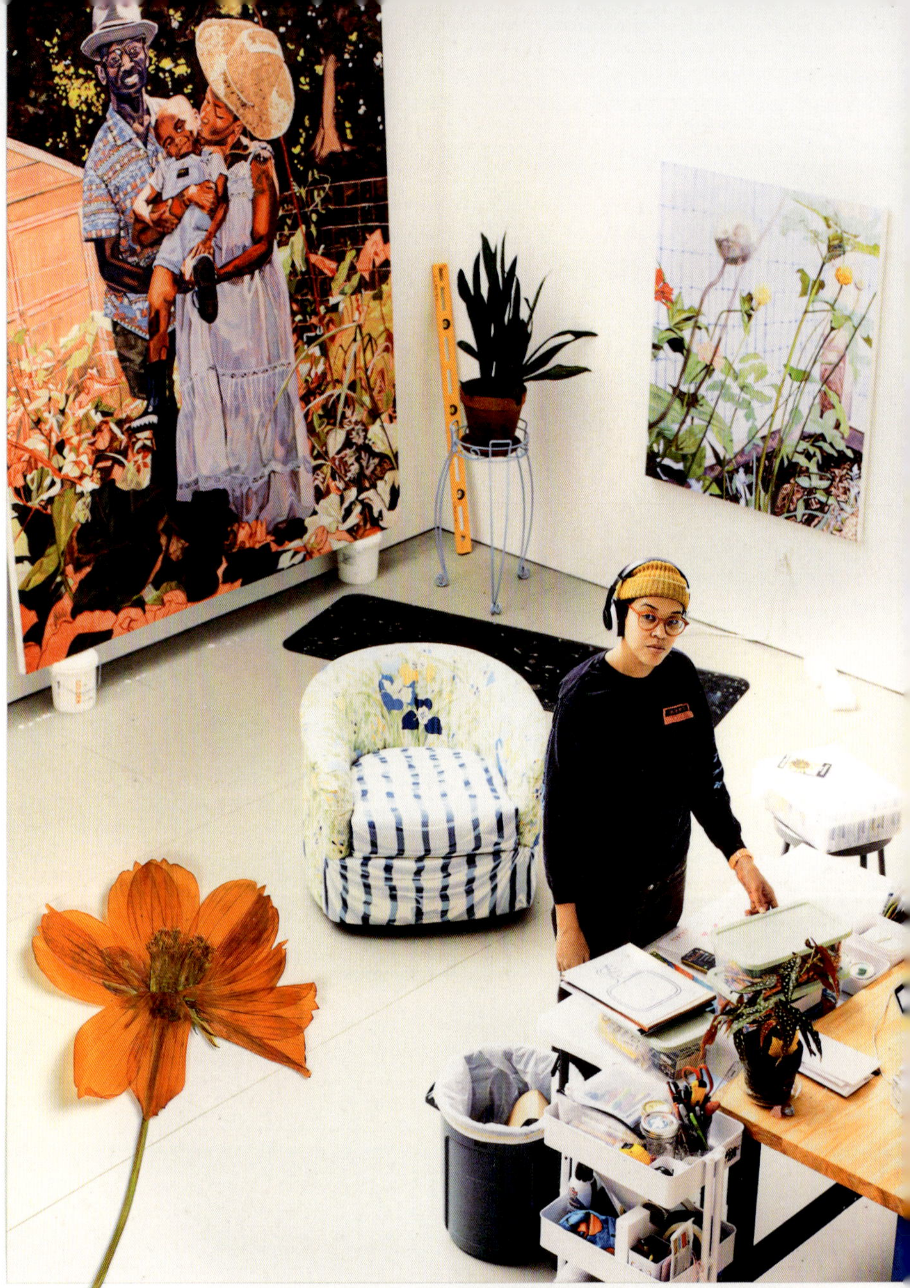

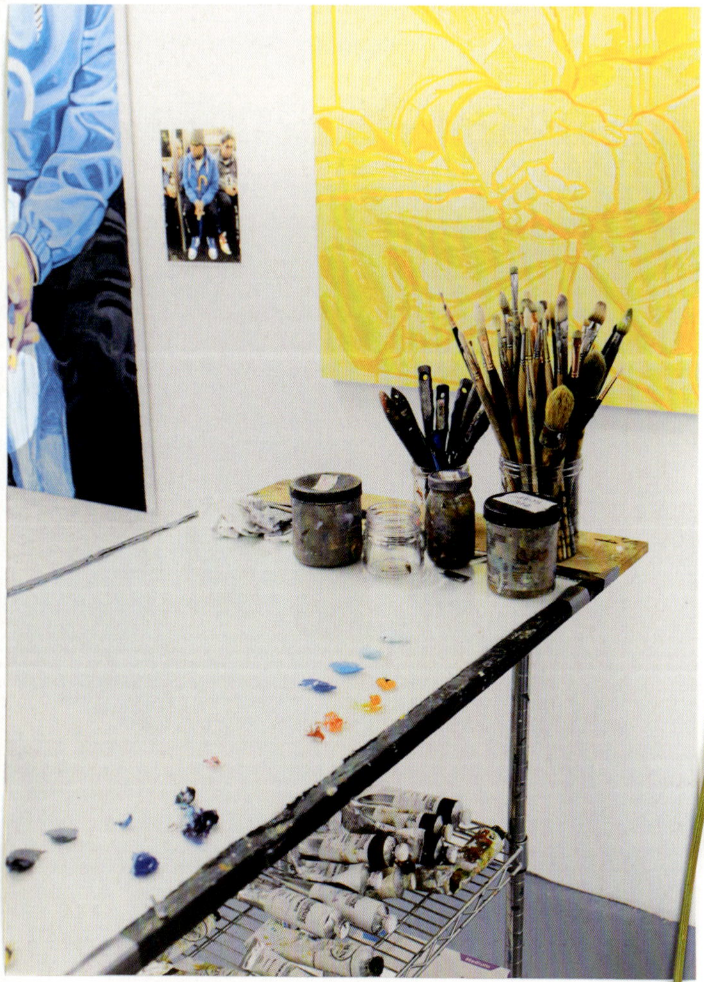

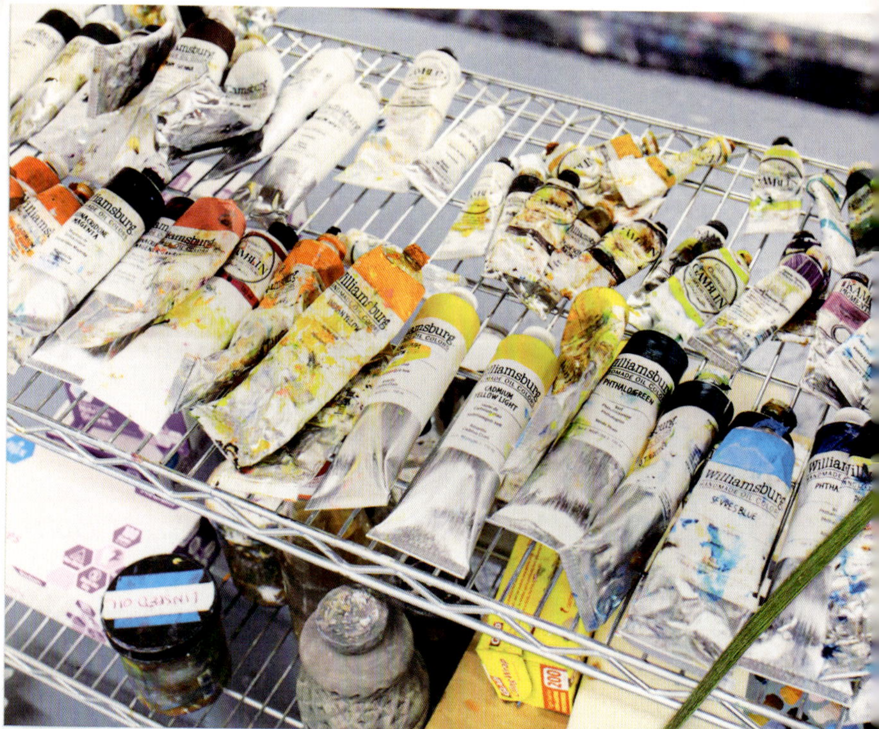
Williamsburg

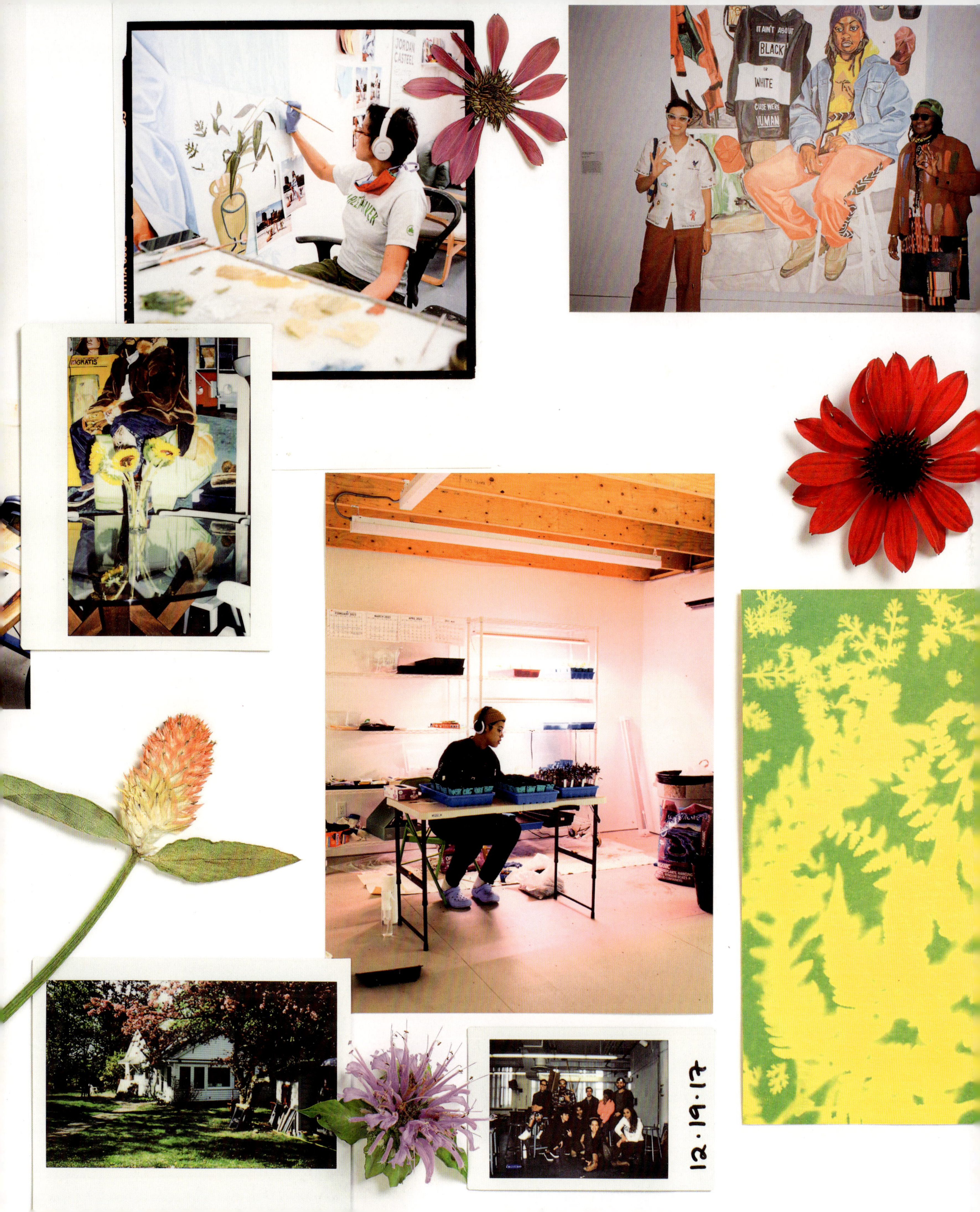
JORDAN
CASTEEL
IT AIN'T ABOUT
BLACK
WHITE
CUSE WERE
GRATIS
12·19·17

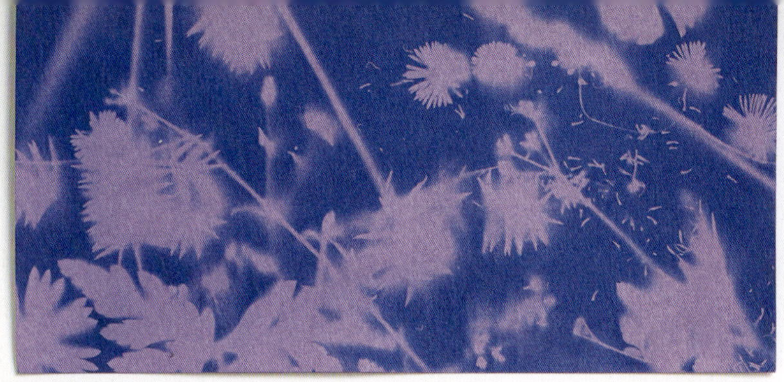

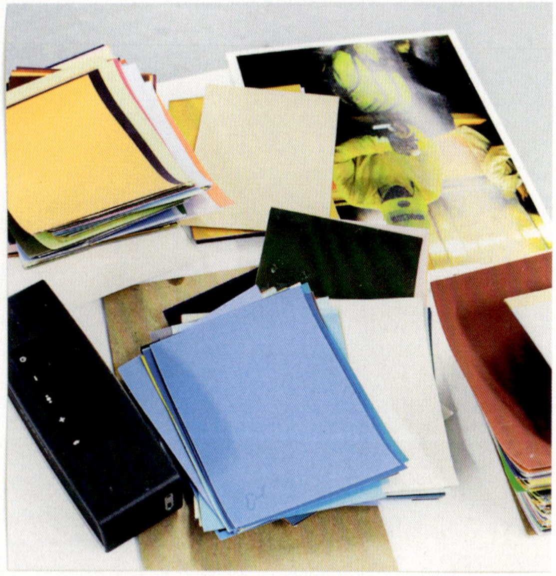

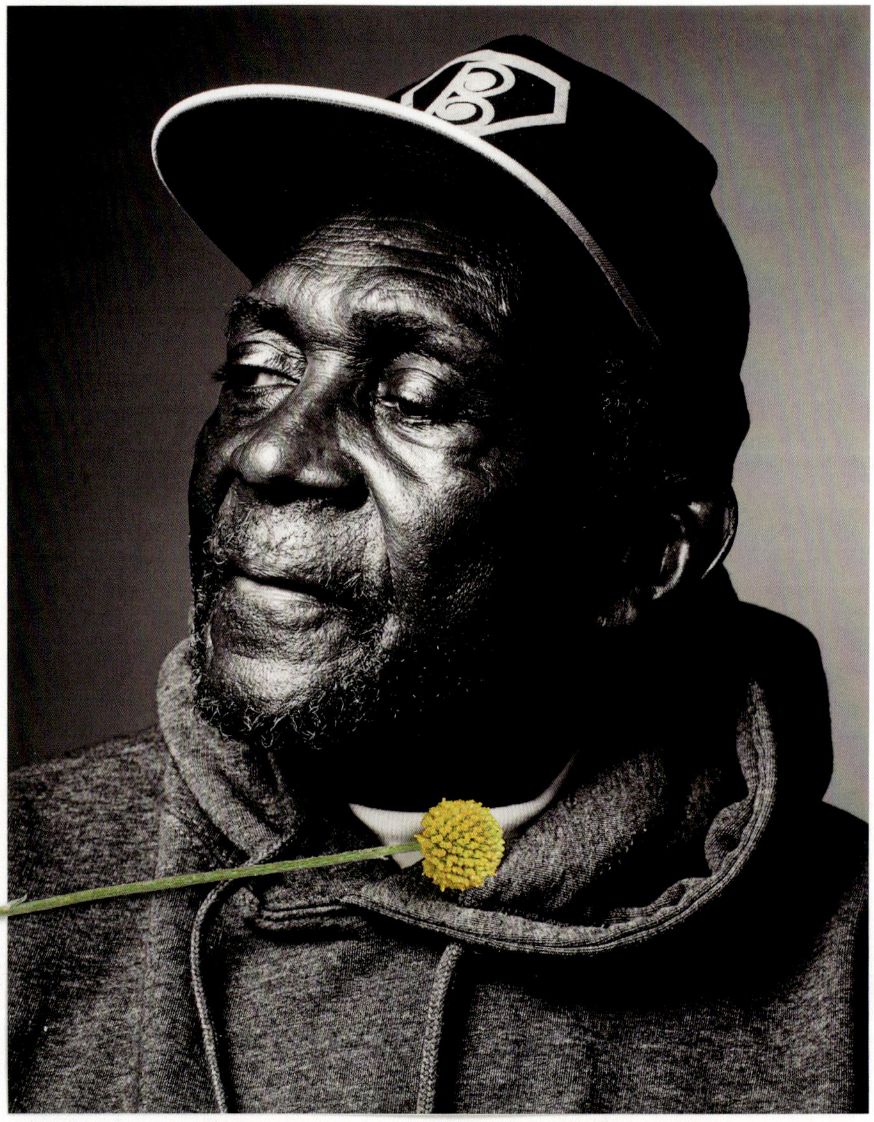

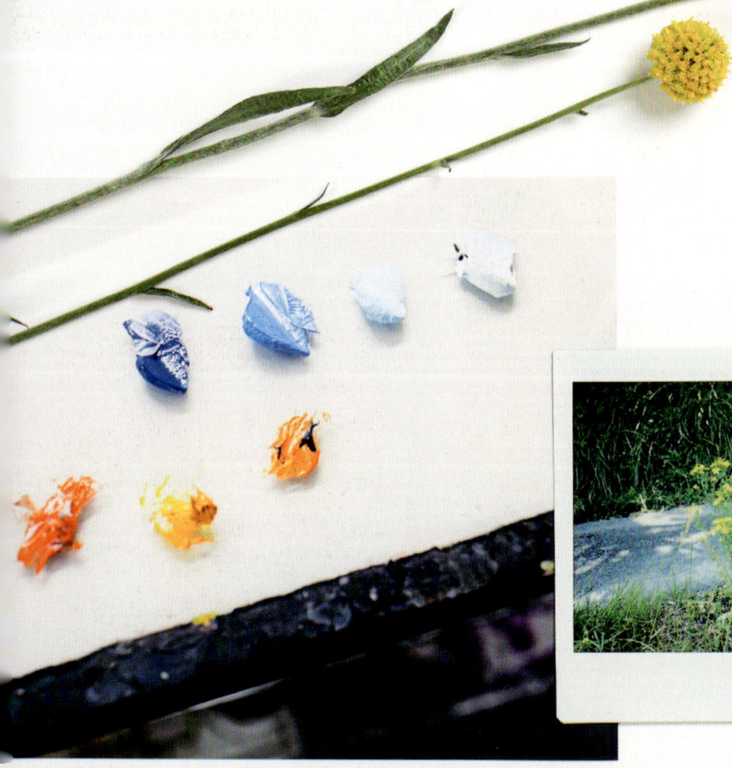

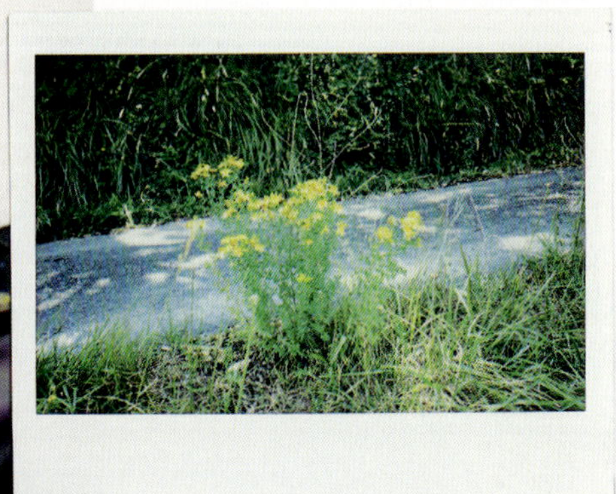

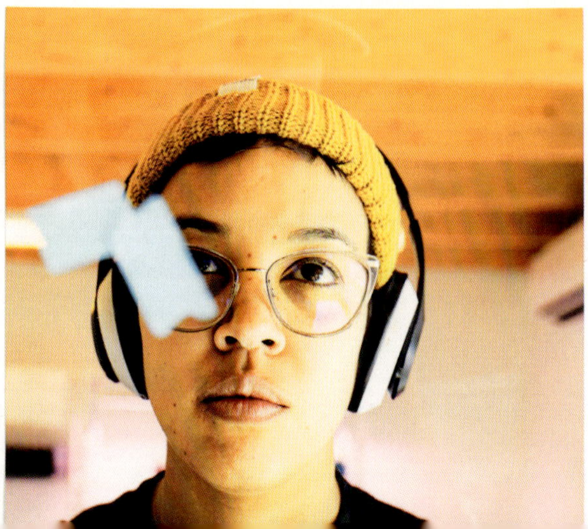

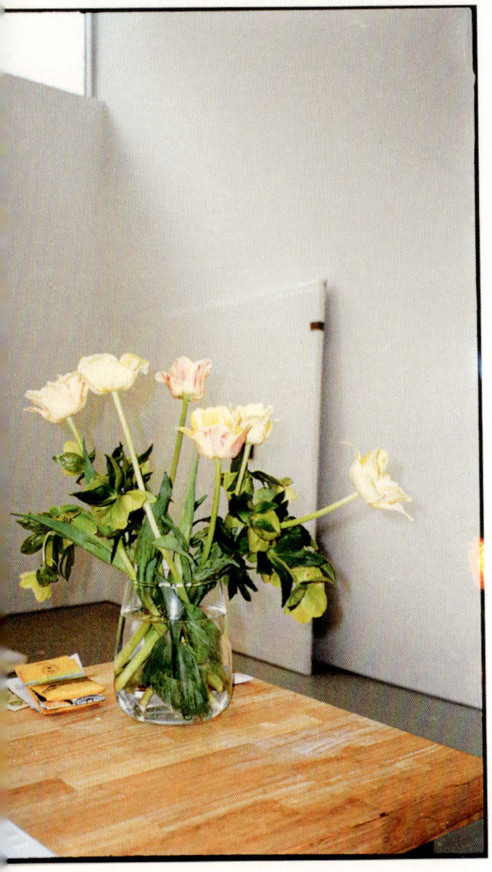

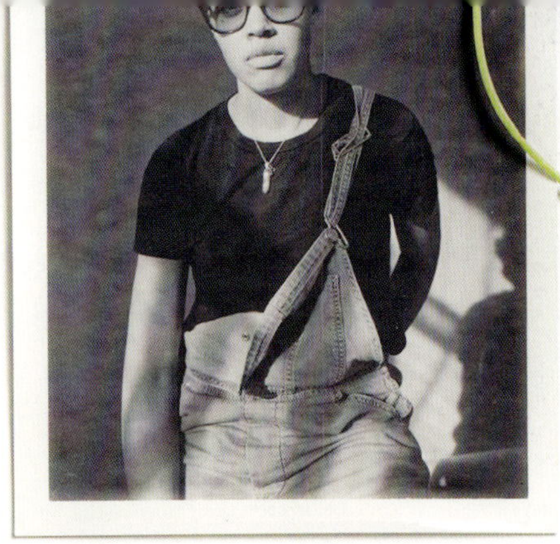

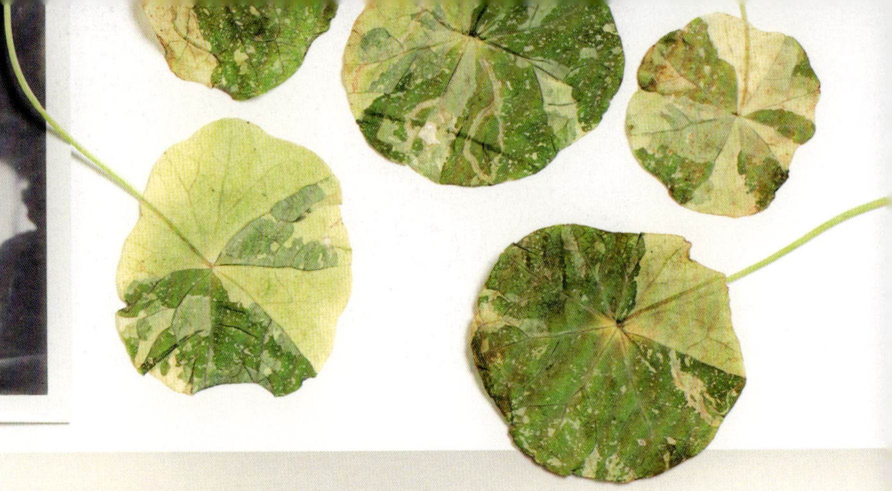

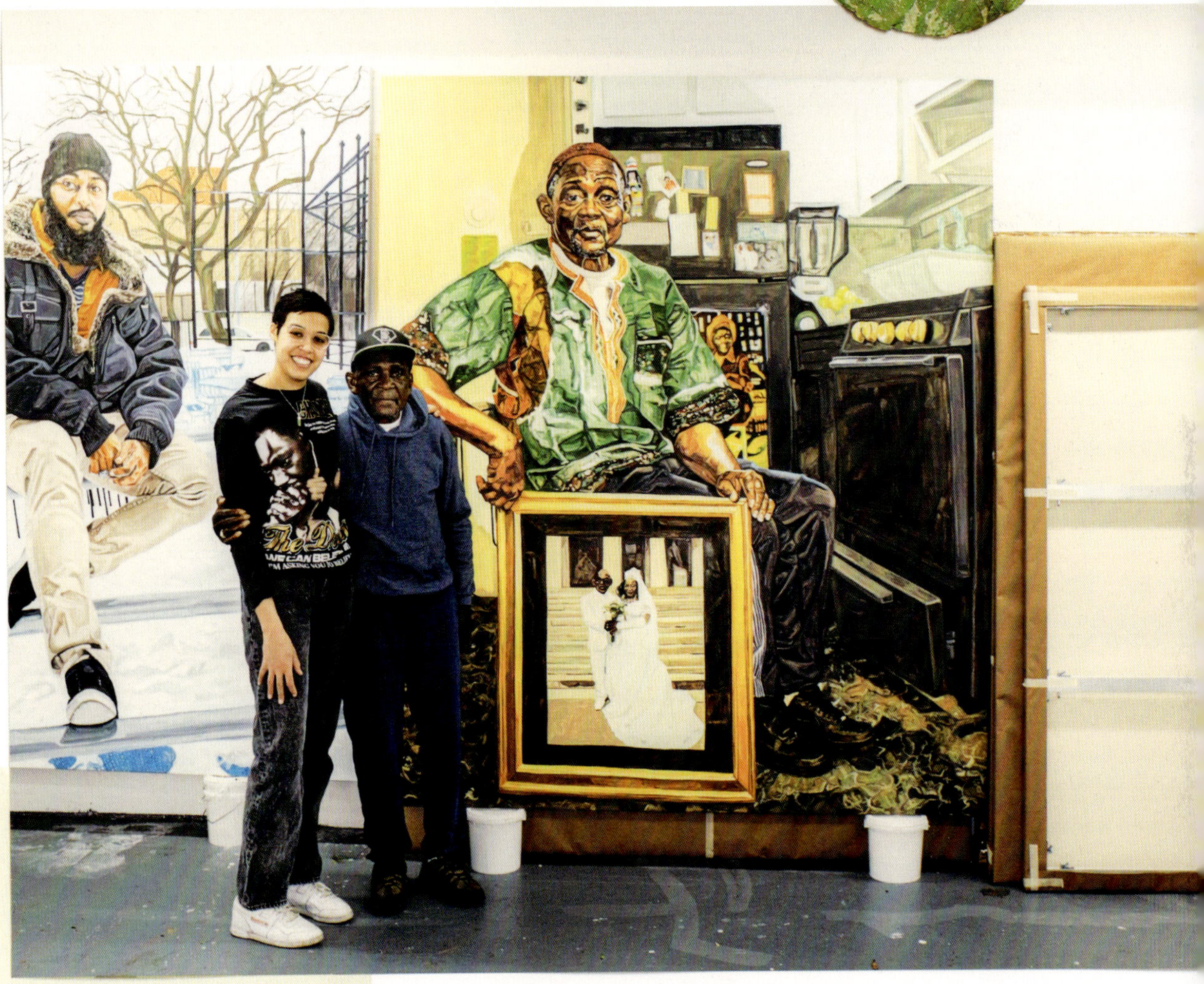

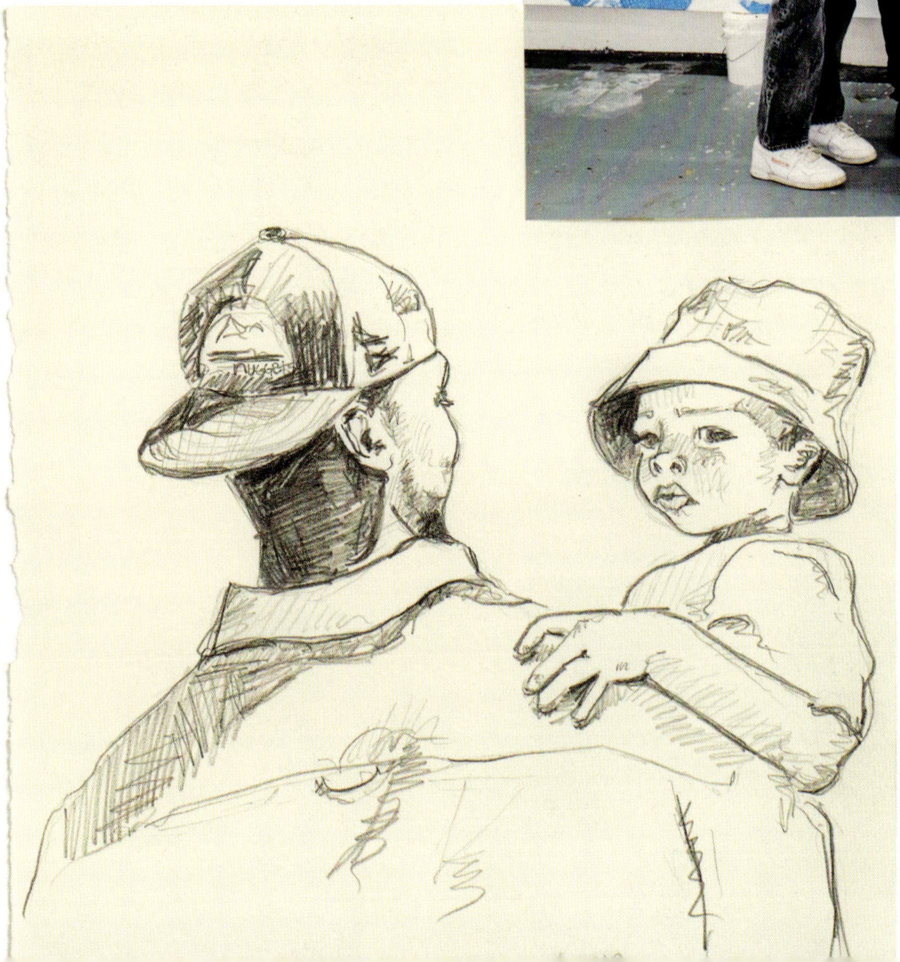

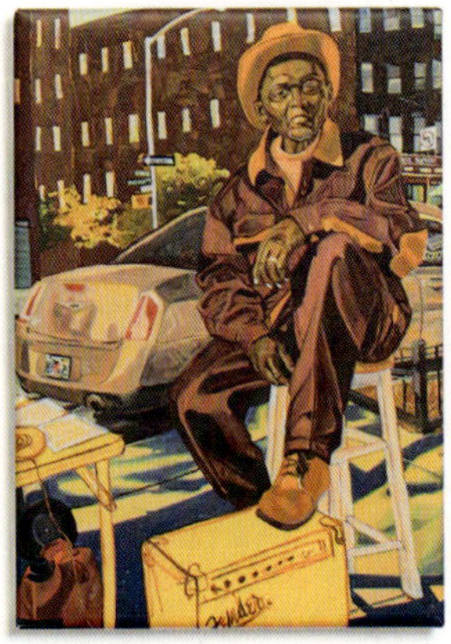

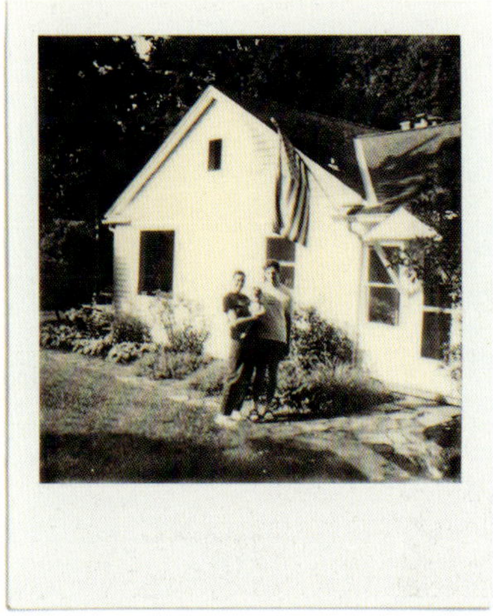

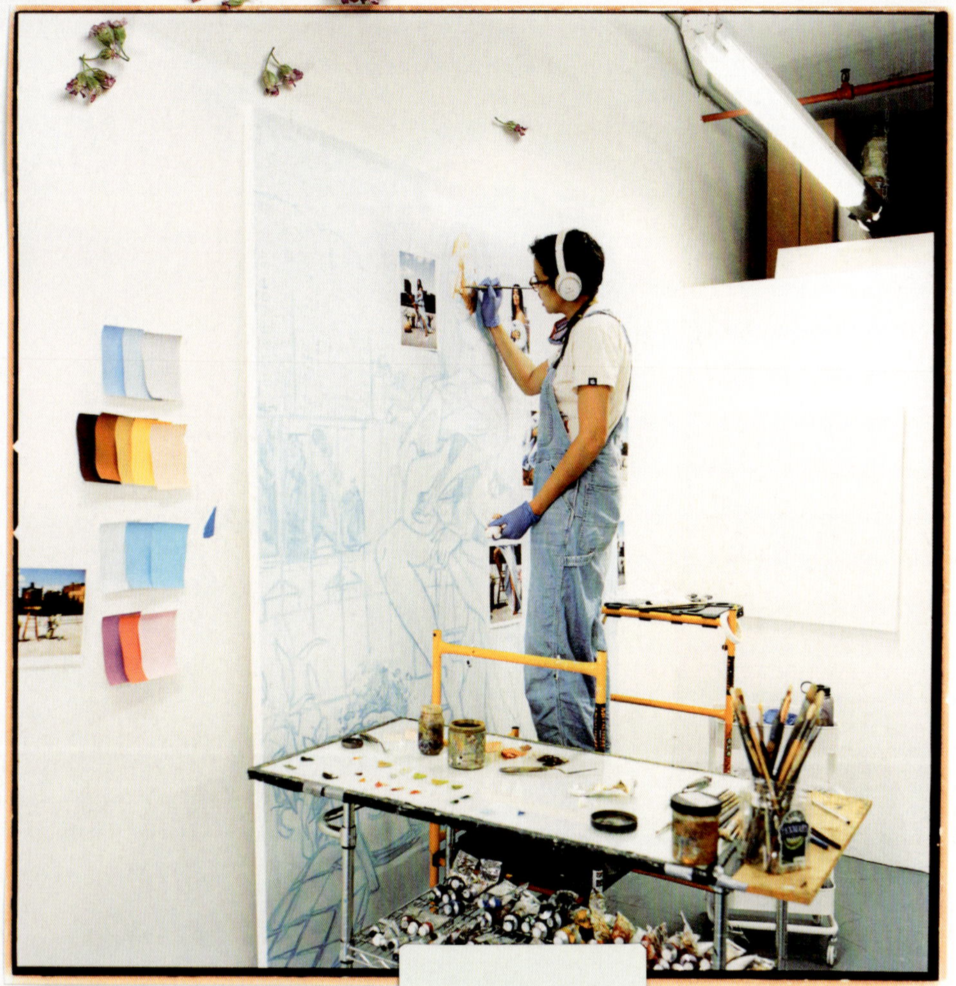

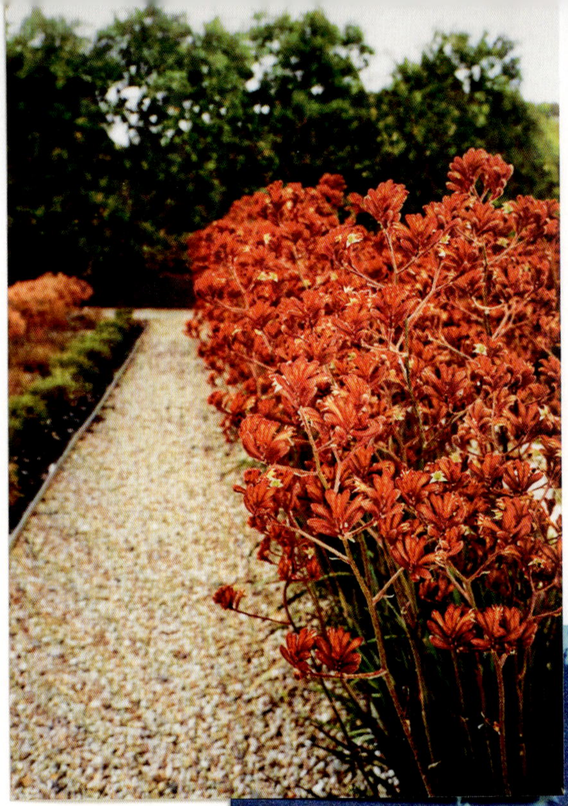

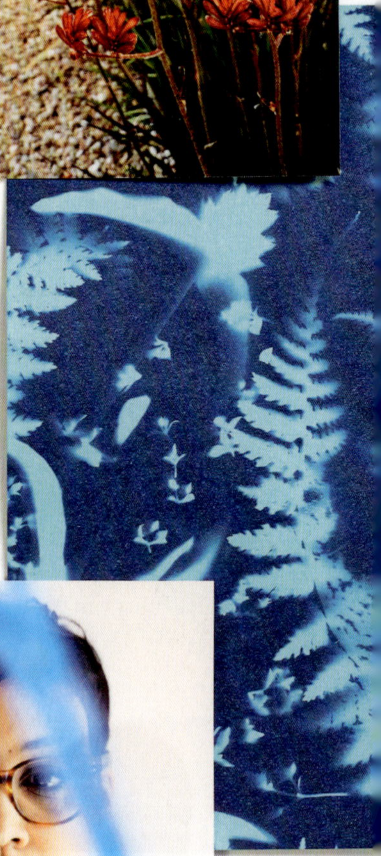

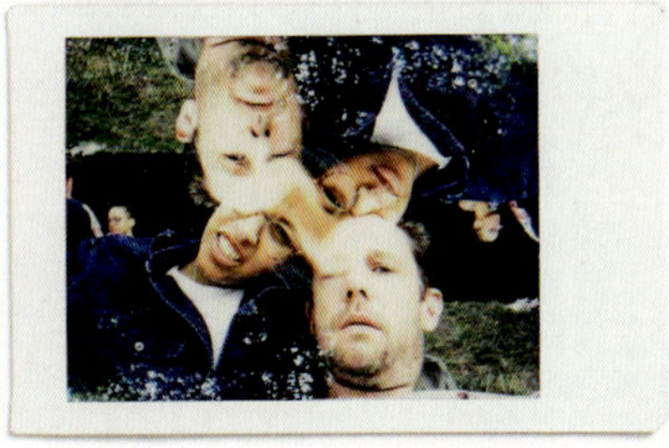

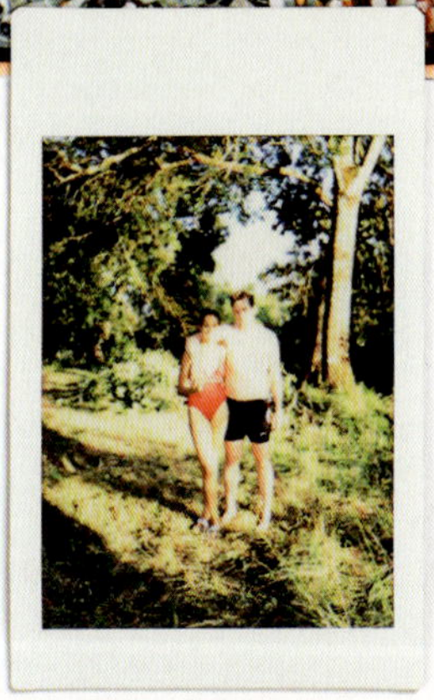

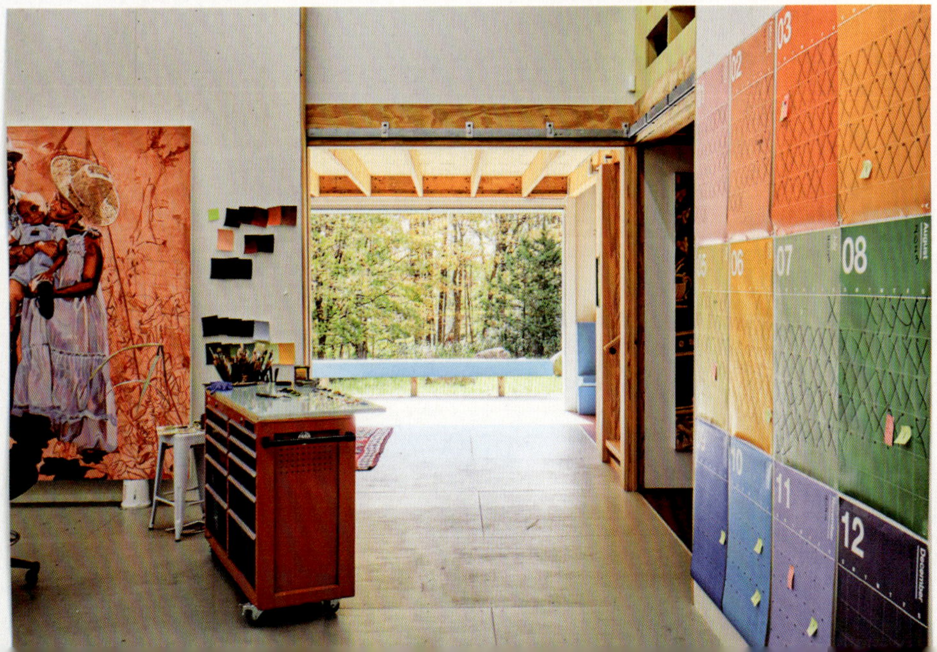
02
03
07
08
11
12

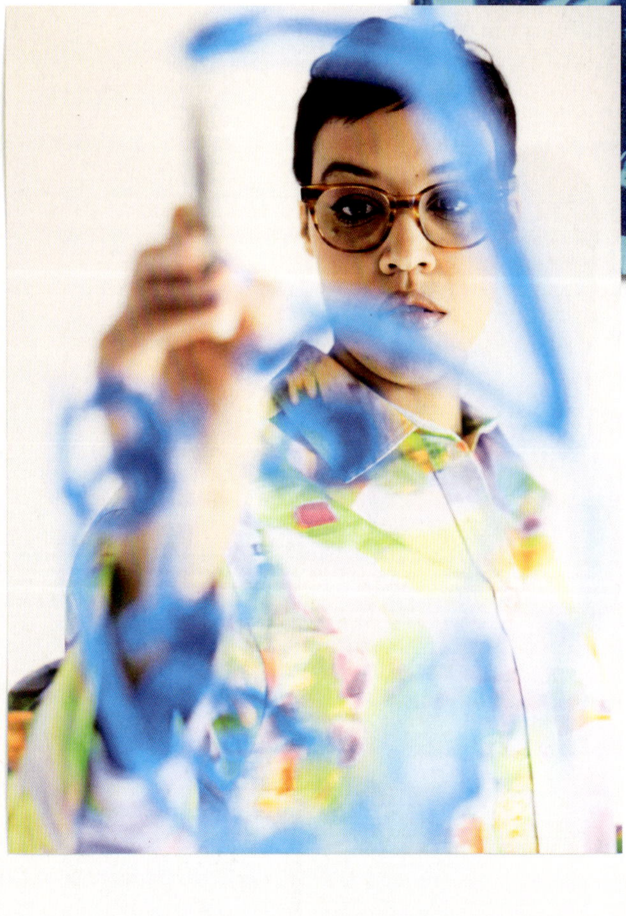

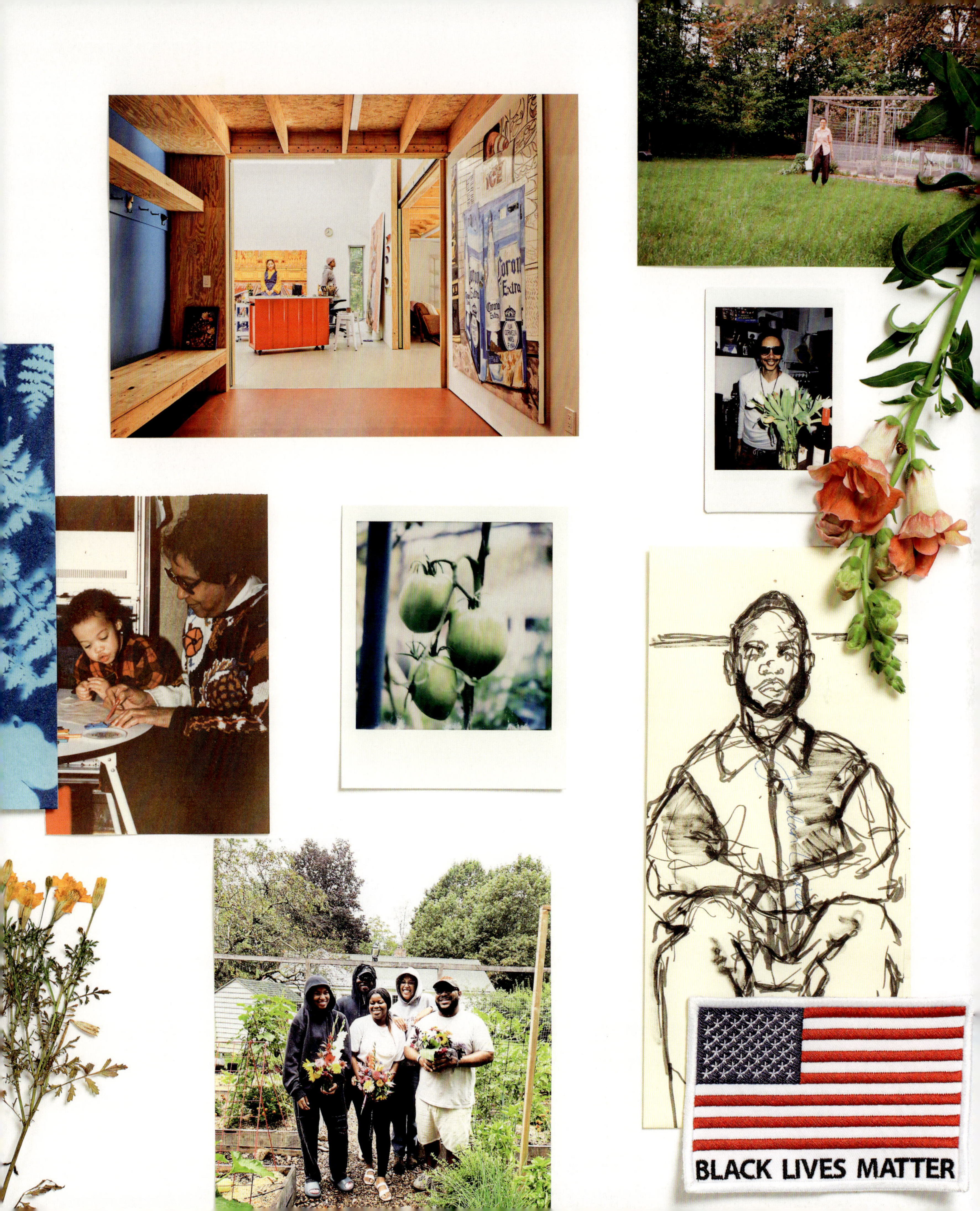
BLACK LIVES MATTER

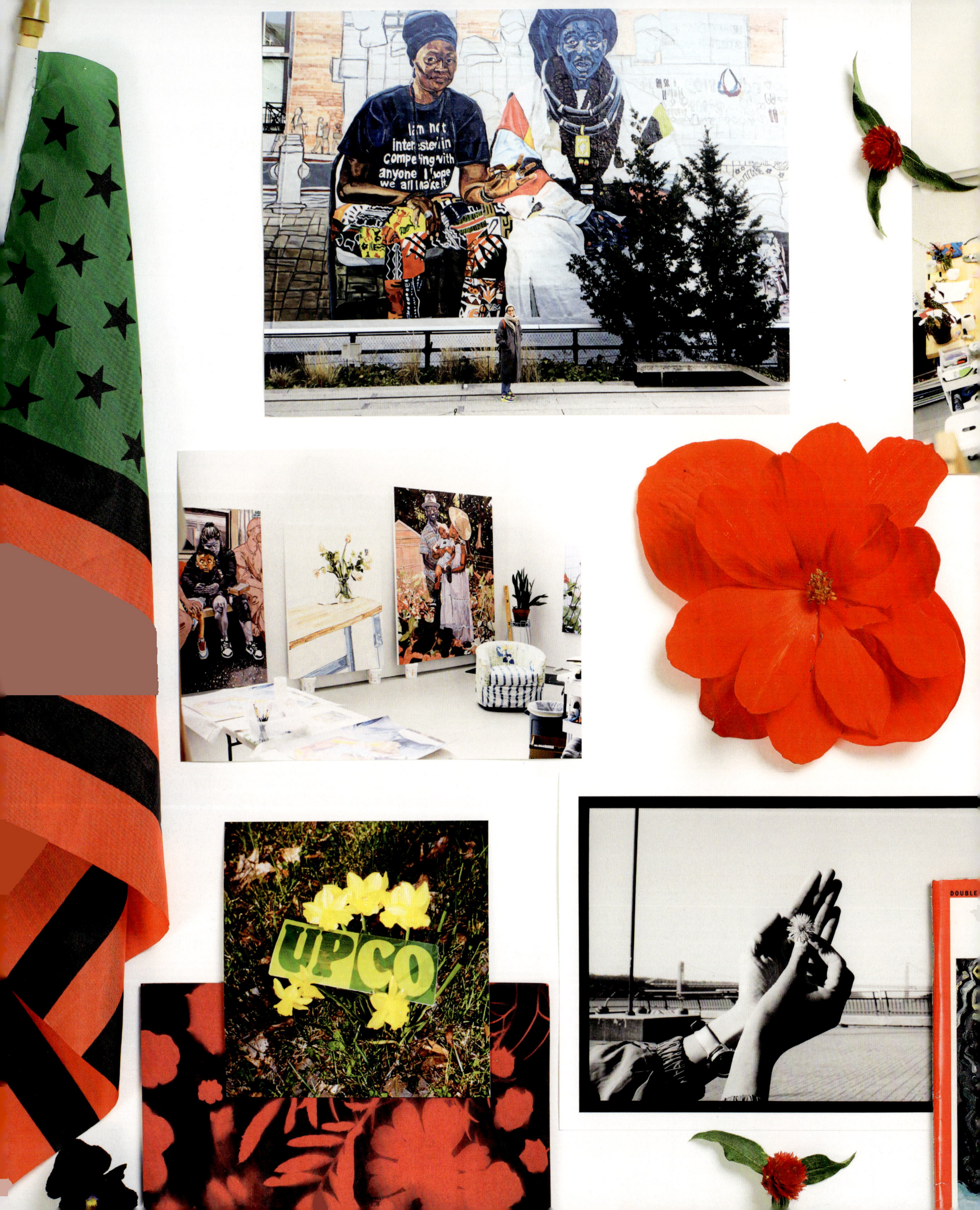
I am not
interested in
Competing with
anyone I hope
we all make it
UPCO
DOUBLE

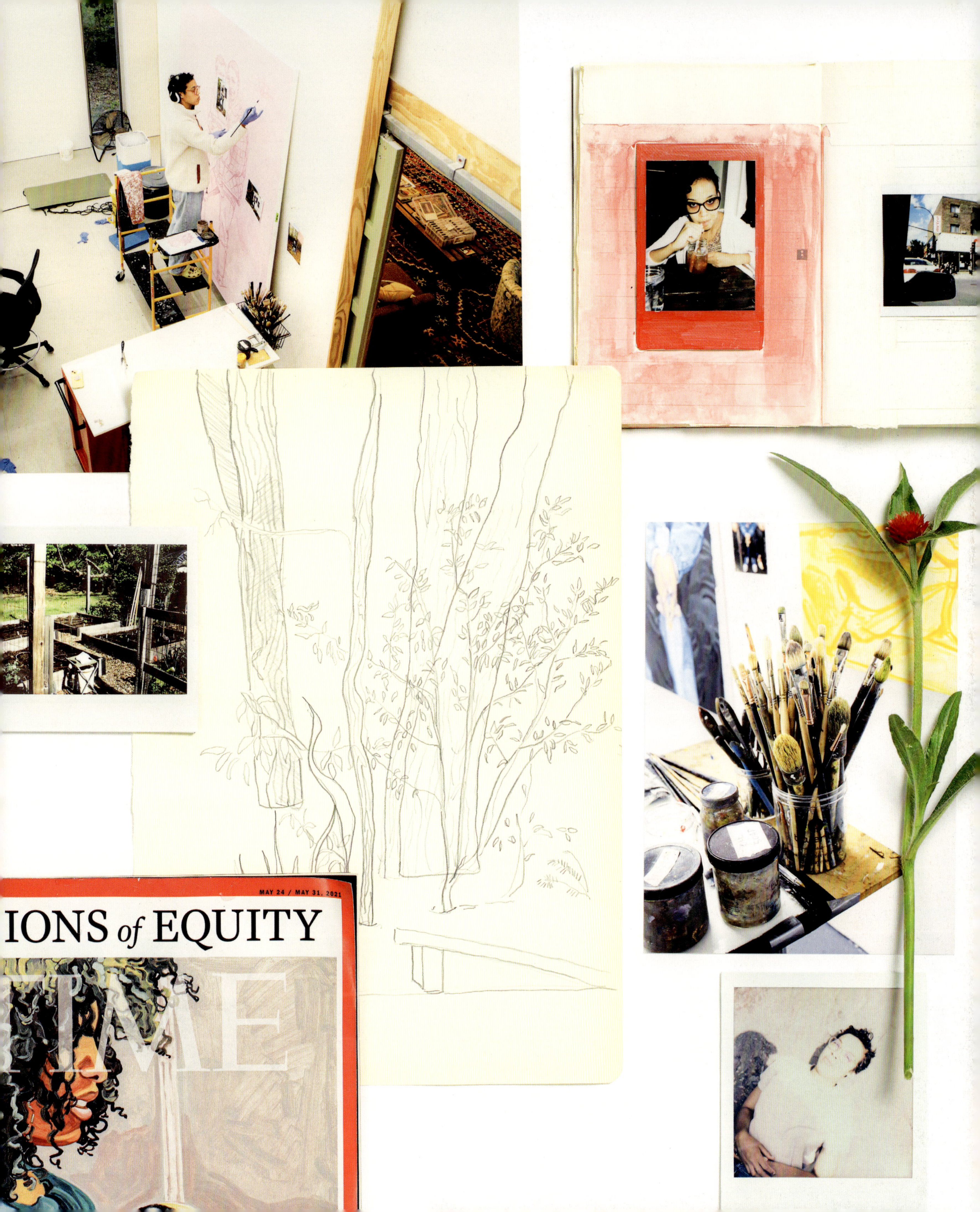
MAY 24 / MAY 31, 2021
IONS of EQUITY
IME

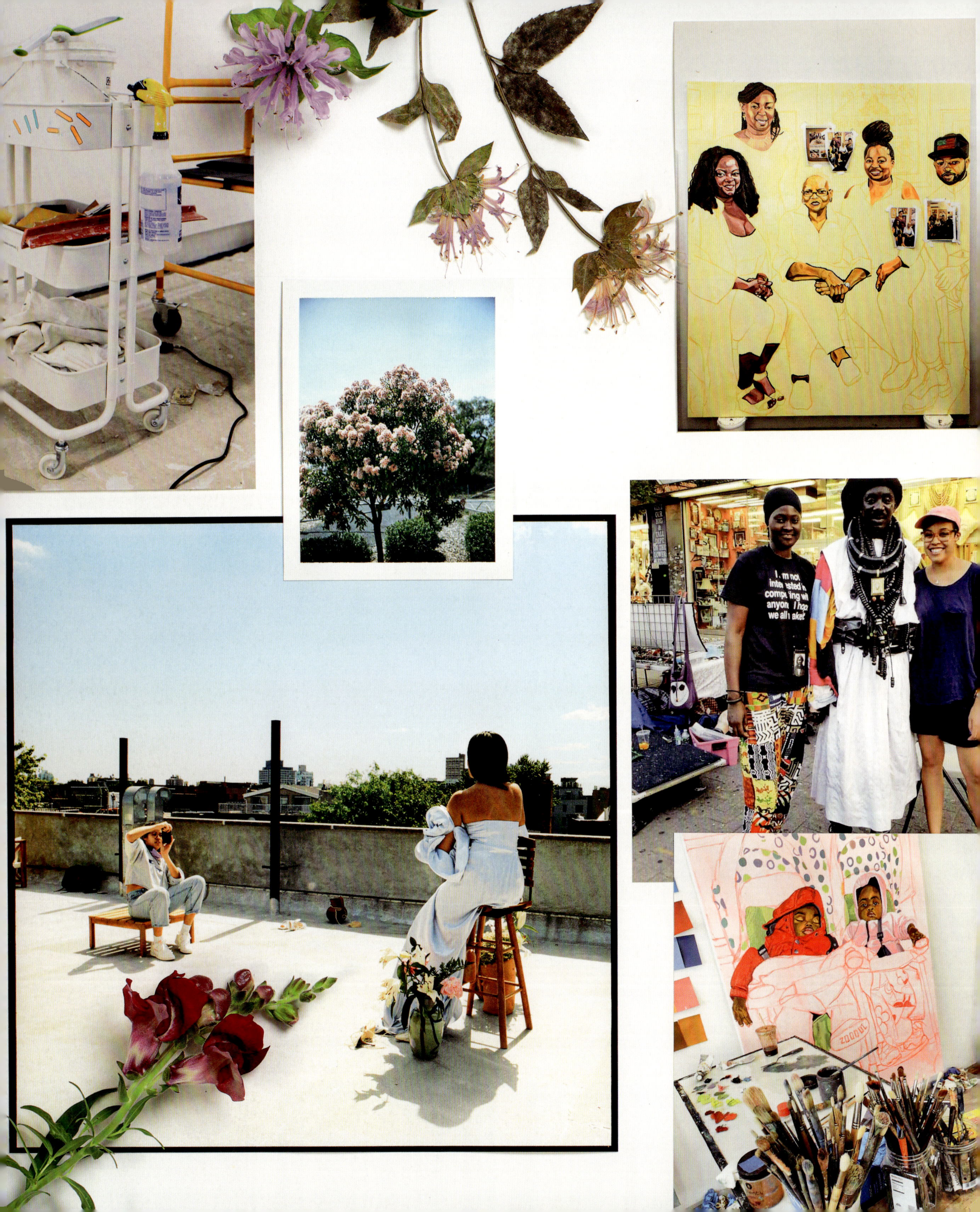

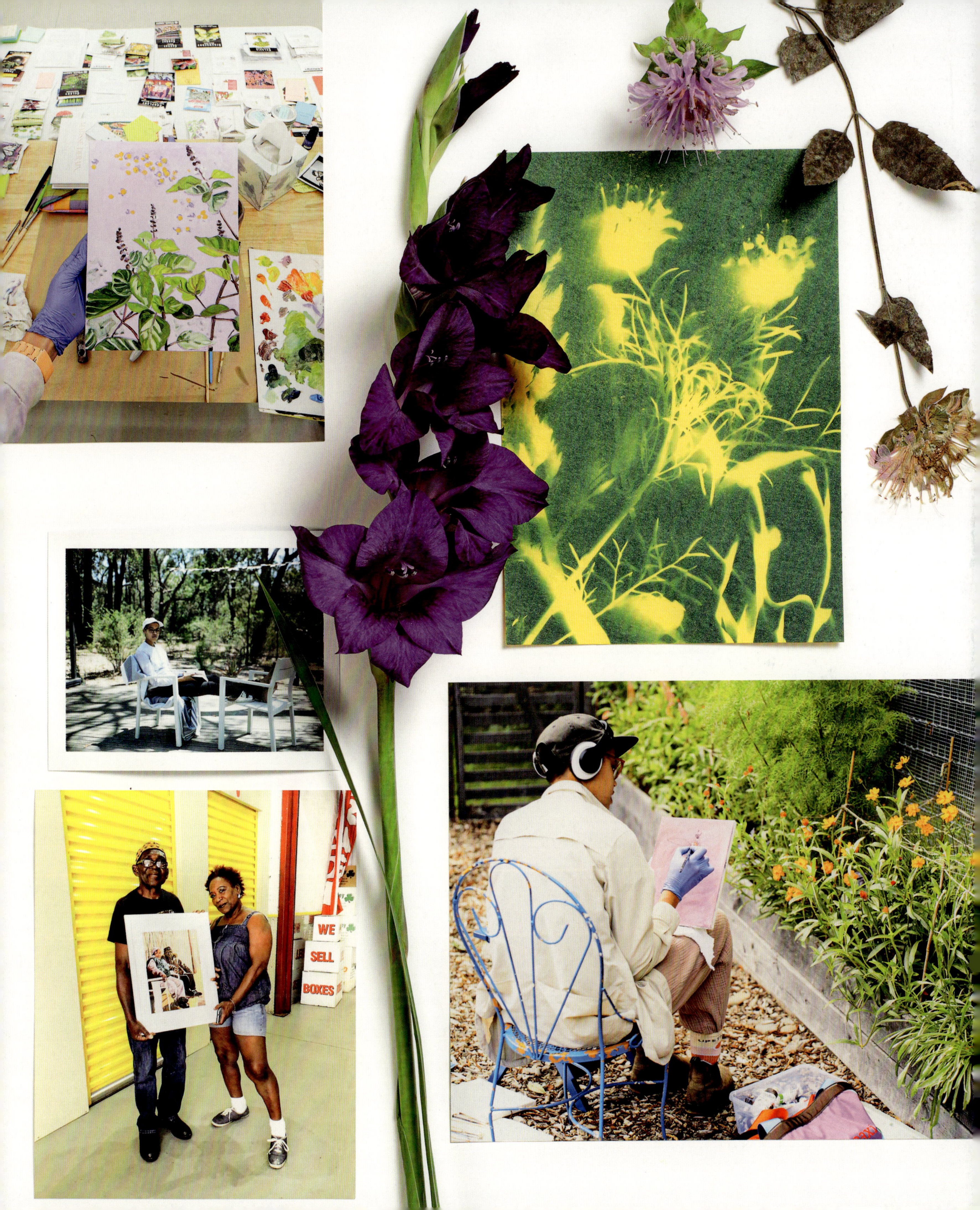
WE
SELL
BOXES

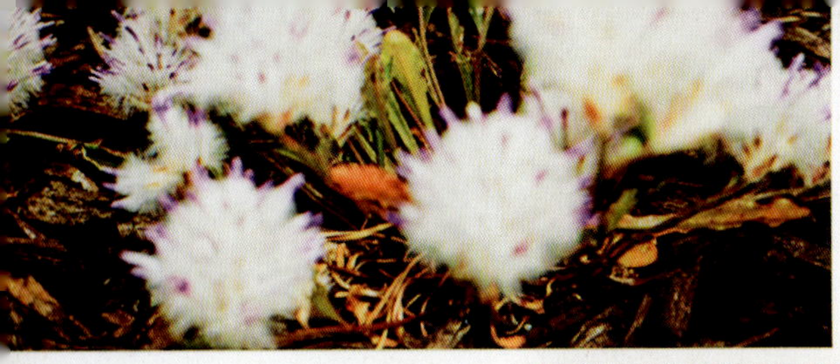

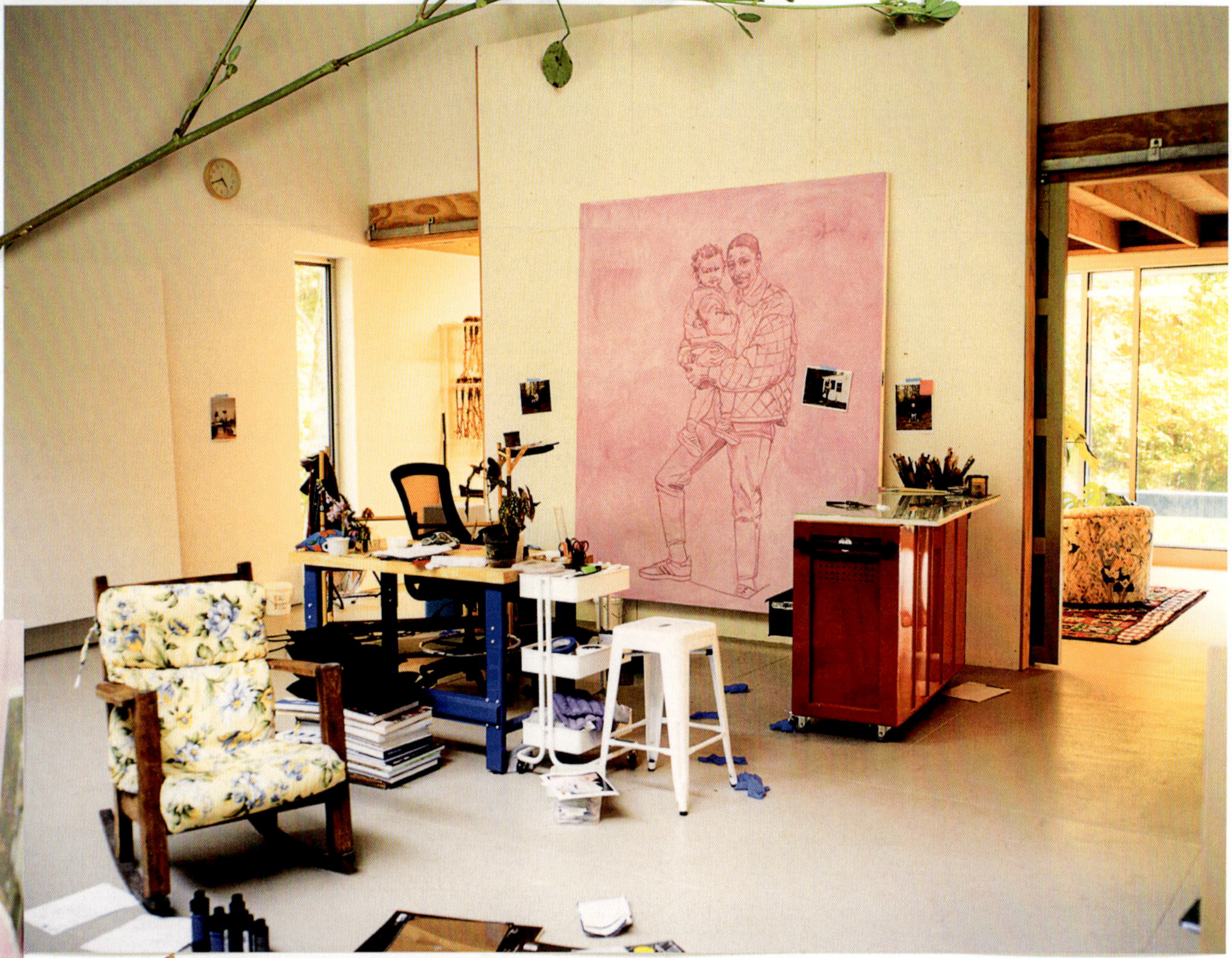

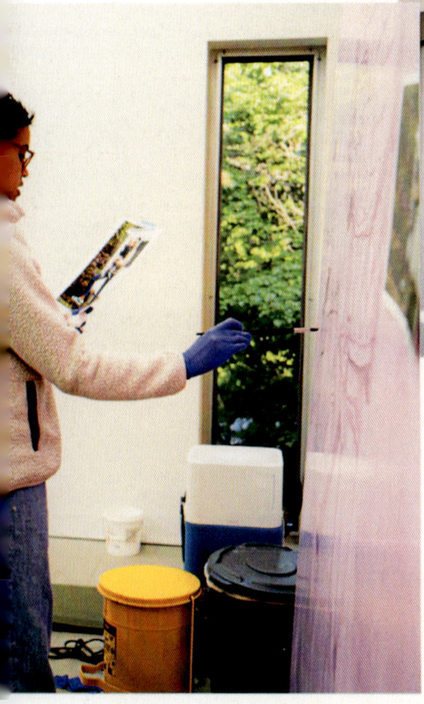

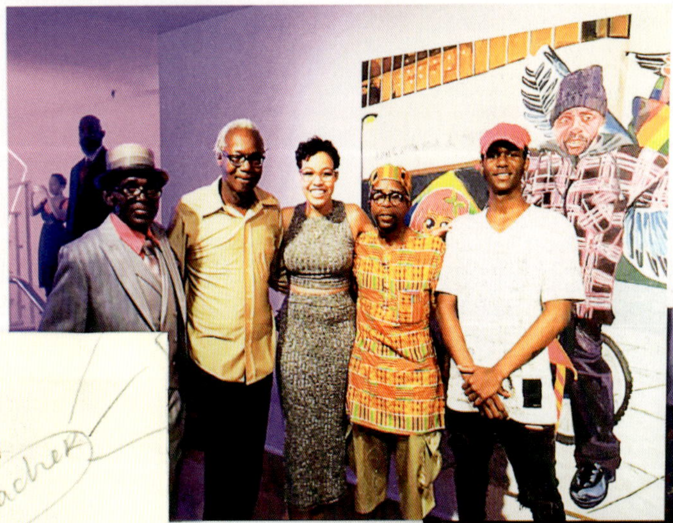

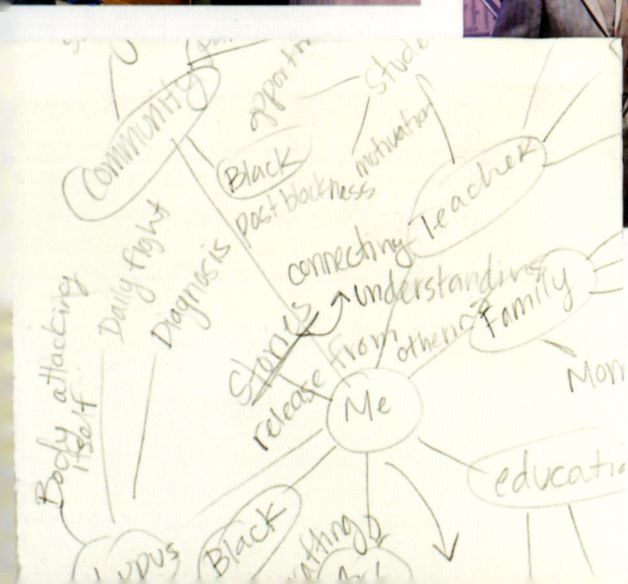
Community
Black
post blackness
motivation
Teacher
Diagnosis
Daily fight
connecting
understanding
Family
Body attacking itself
Stories
release from others
Me
educati
Lupus
Black

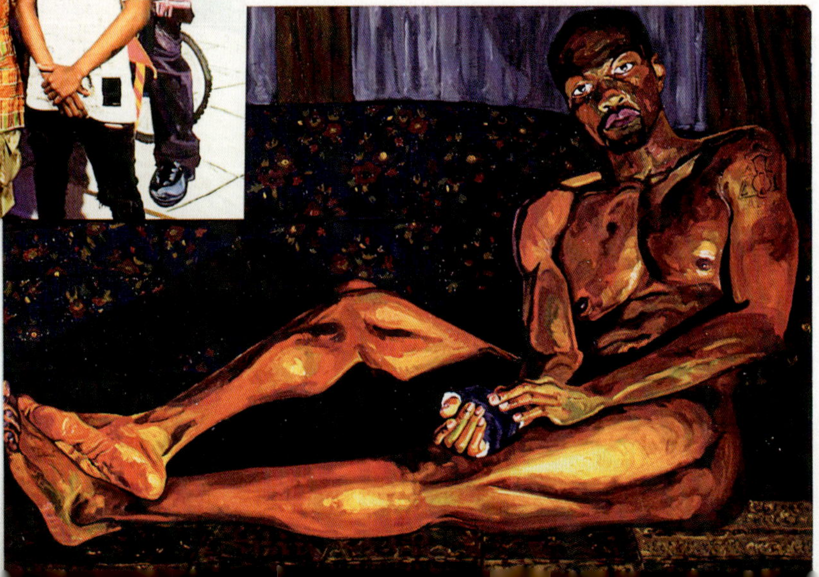

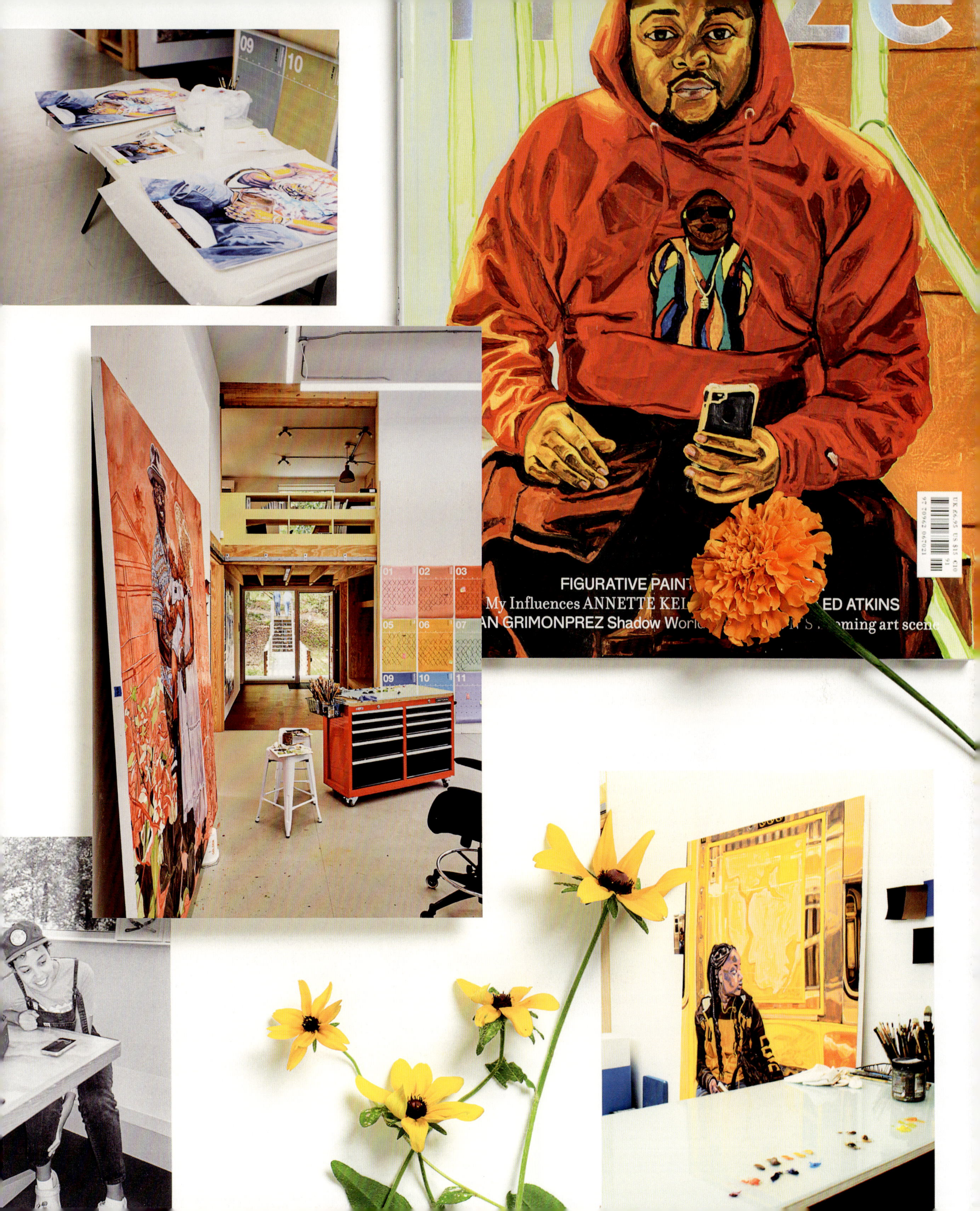

FIGURATIVE PAINT
My Influences ANNETTE KEL
ED ATKINS
AN GRIMONPREZ Shadow Worl
ming art scene

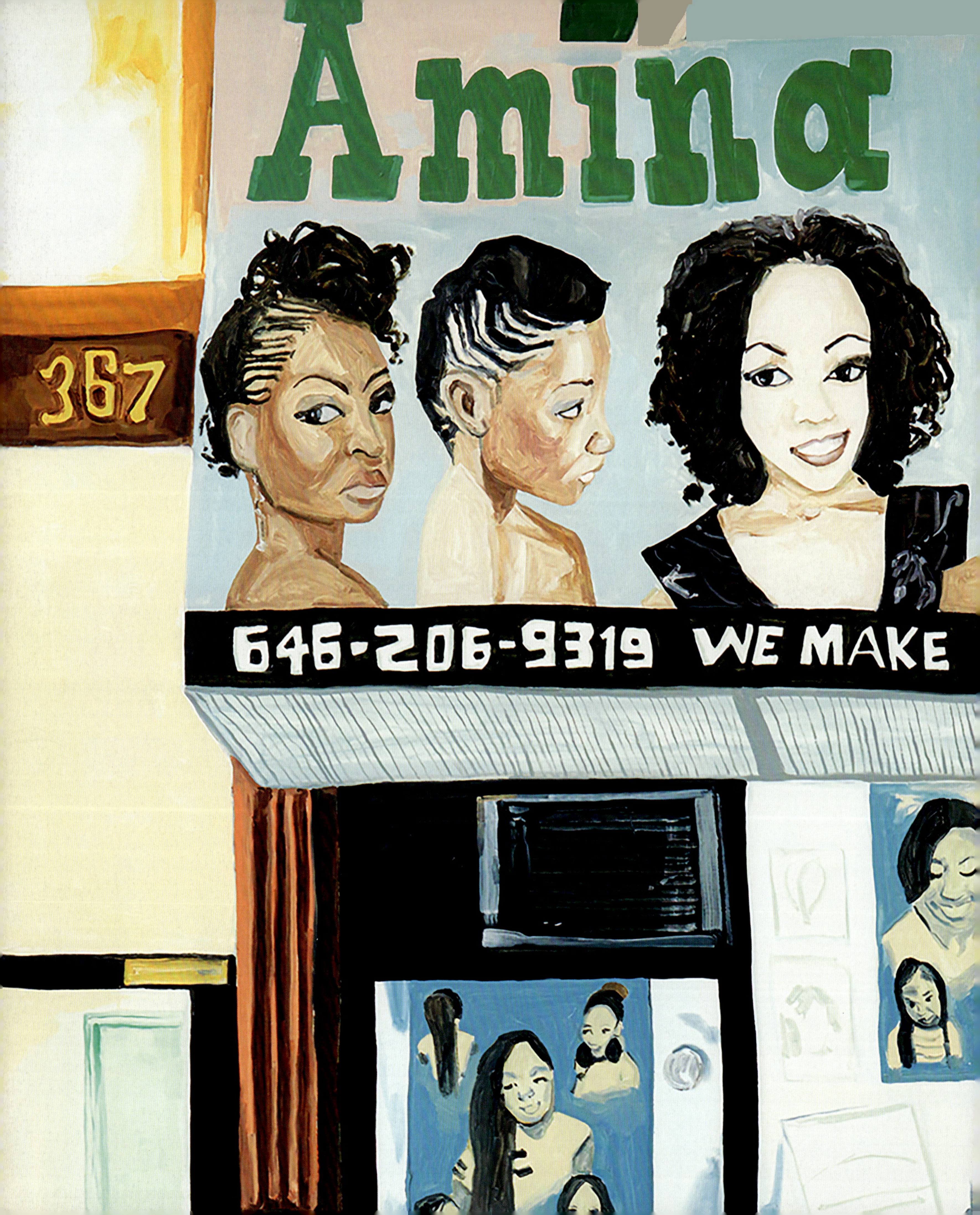
Amina
367
646-206-9319 WE MAKE

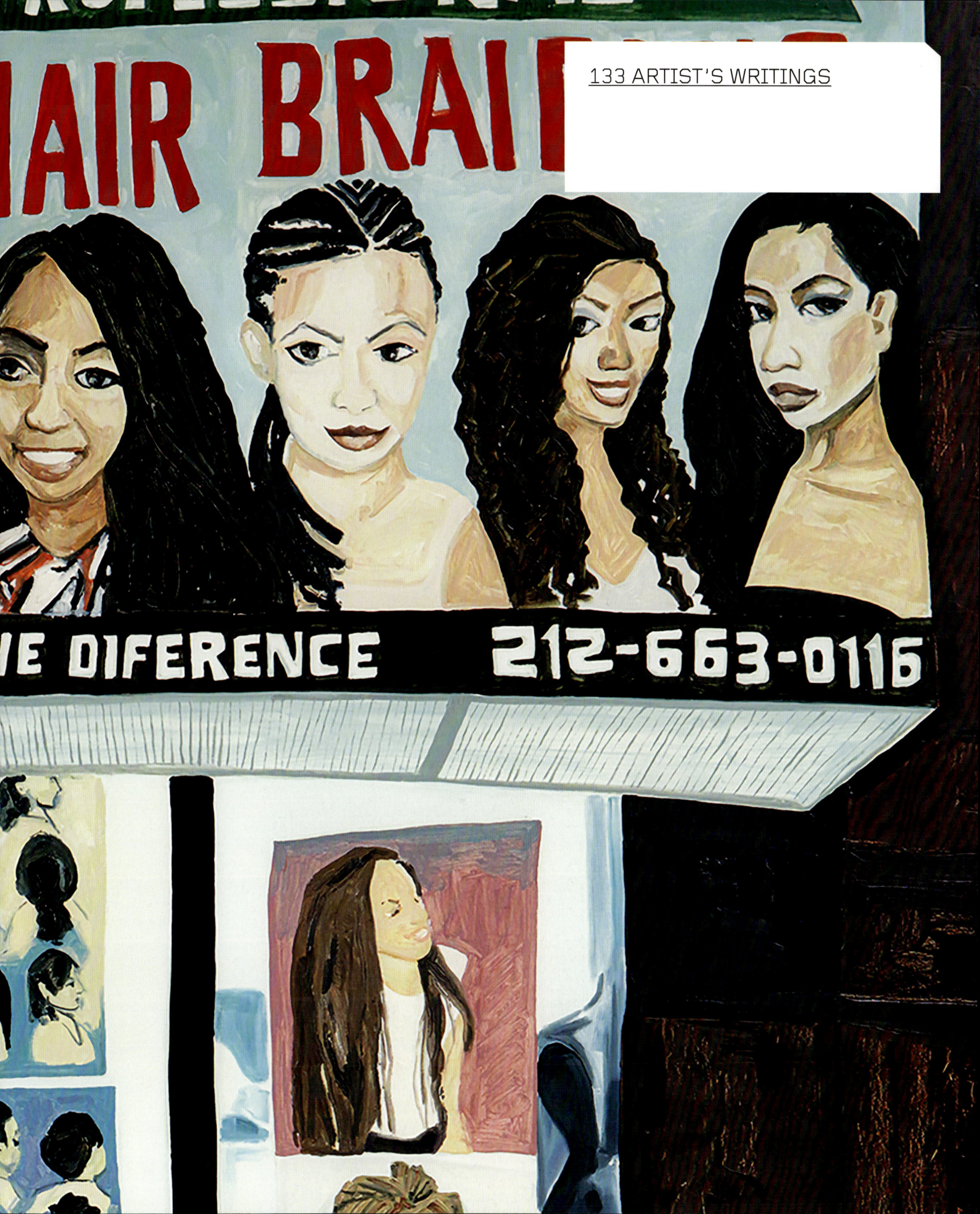
AIR BRAI
DIFERENCE
212-663-0116

Quote from Jordan Casteel in conversation with Lauren Haynes, Hill Art Foundation, 18 November 2024

right,
HARLEM PUBLIC, 2021
OIL ON CANVAS
239 X 203 CM

previous pages,
AMINA (DETAIL), 2017
OIL ON CANVAS
229 X 198 CM

During my second year in grad school, I was very focused on trying to paint the humanity of Black men. With that vision in mind, I painted my friend Cory who was wearing a "You Mad, Bro?" shirt while sitting on my mother's stoop in Denver. During a studio visit, the critic reacted, "What is this shirt trying to tell me? It just feels a bit in my face, you know?"

I thought, *this is a black man whose humanity I want you to observe*. The stubborn part of me said, *Okay, bet, if this is a distraction — I'll just get rid of his clothes.*

Looking back, that feedback was a catalyst for the "Visible Man" series. Nearly 10 years later, I'm interested in how our clothing and chosen accessories carry meaning — there's so much that comes out in the things we wear. There are subtle signals in the environments we occupy every day.

I really do enjoy the challenge and process of painting all of the text. I always write the text and then painstakingly outline it. For example, in *The Carolinas* (2022, p. 107), I wrote the HUNTER text in black paint first and then went around it carefully with my white paint. [The act of writing] becomes an opportunity for me to relish in a difficult thing. It becomes like meditation. Similarly, I think it's in the twins painting, (*Twins*, 2017) where they were wearing Jordans, and I mimicked the shapes of the letters before realizing what it said. And years later, another kid was wearing the same shoes and I actually saw that it said "Jordan".

There have been several moments like that, where I am not sure what I am writing while painting, but then realize after there's something unique about the text. In *Amina*, 2017 the signage says "WE MAKE THE DIFERENCE". "Difference" is spelled wrong, but I didn't realize that until the painting was on view and someone asked me about it. I went back to the reference image and sure enough, it is misspelled on the storefront.

There's something playful and intriguing about brands and a person's things—like a pair of Marmot gloves, someone's books, a brand of paper towels, a bodega sign. They mark a person's time and place, anchoring them in a specific moment.

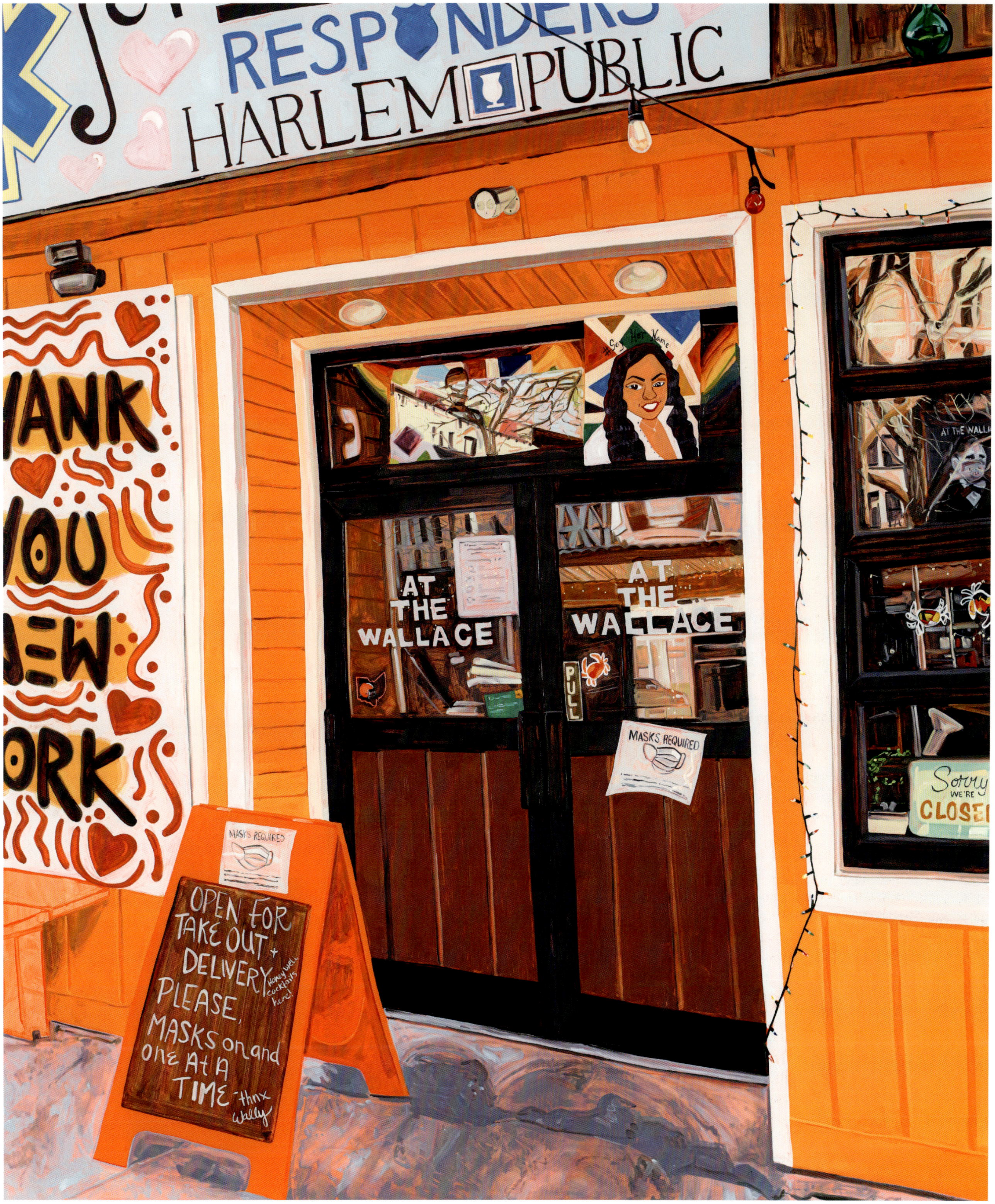
RESPONDERS
HARLEM PUBLIC
AT THE WALLACE
AT THE WALLACE
PULL
MASKS REQUIRED
MASKS REQUIRED
OPEN FOR TAKE OUT + DELIVERY
PLEASE, MASKS on and one At A TIME -thnx Wally
Sorry WE'RE

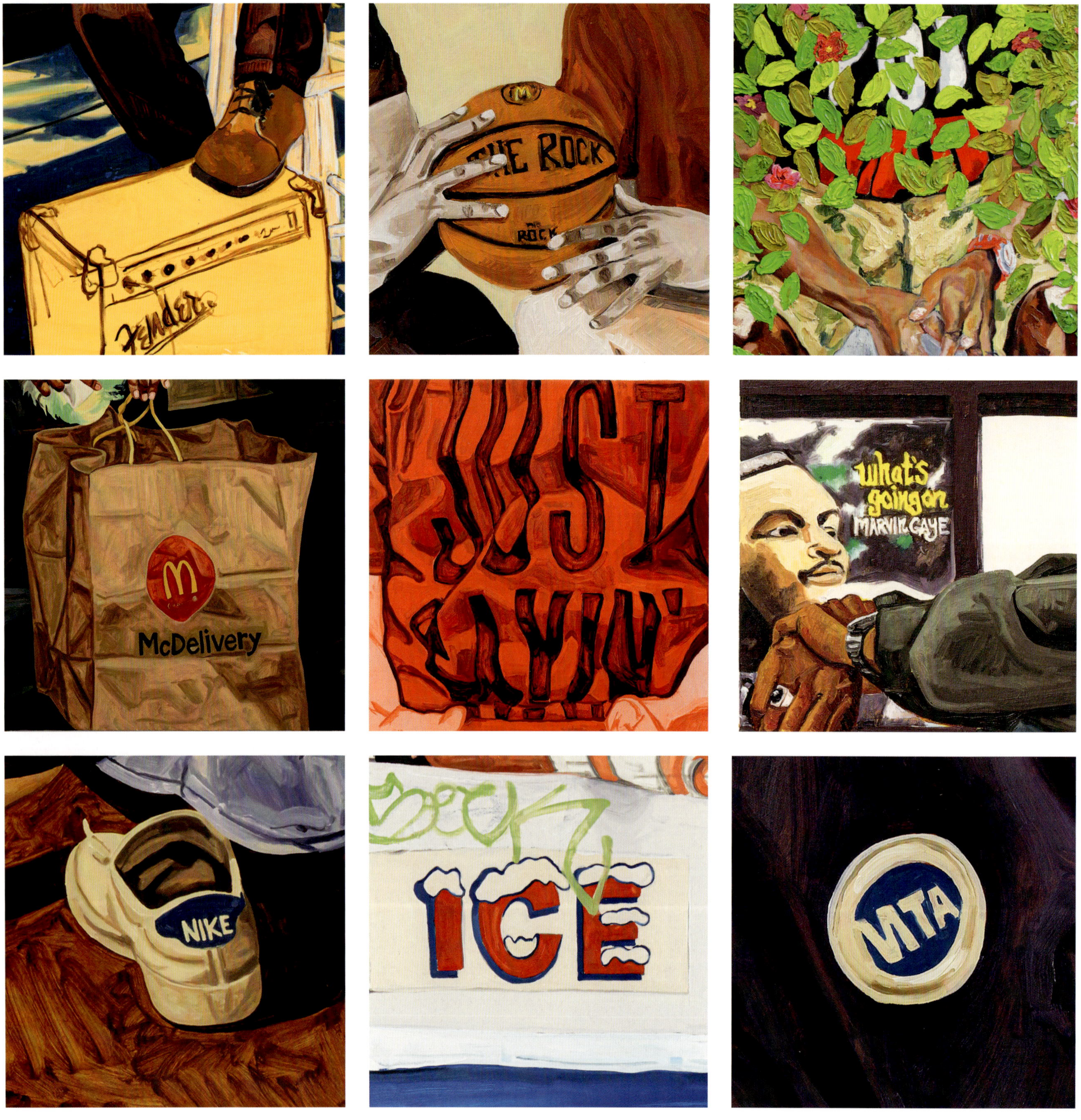
Fender
THE ROCK
ROCK
McDelivery
what's going on
MARVIN GAYE
NIKE
ICE
MTA

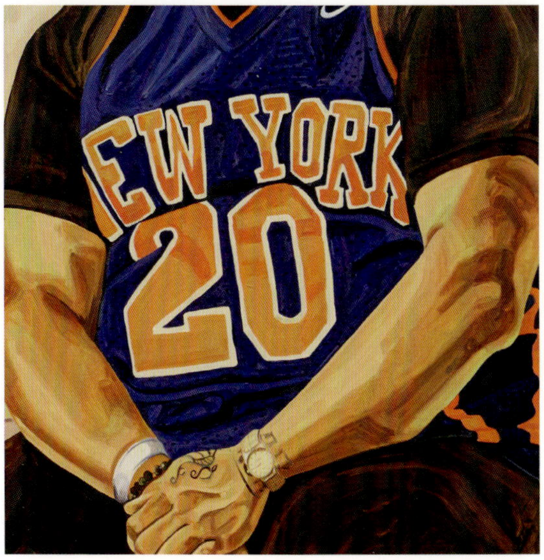
EW YORK
20

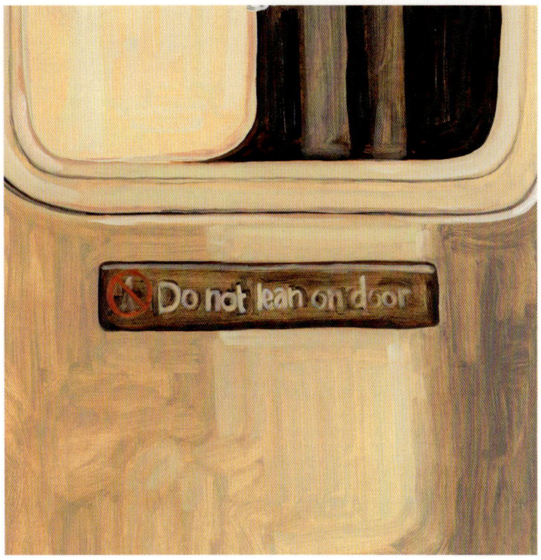
Do not lean on door

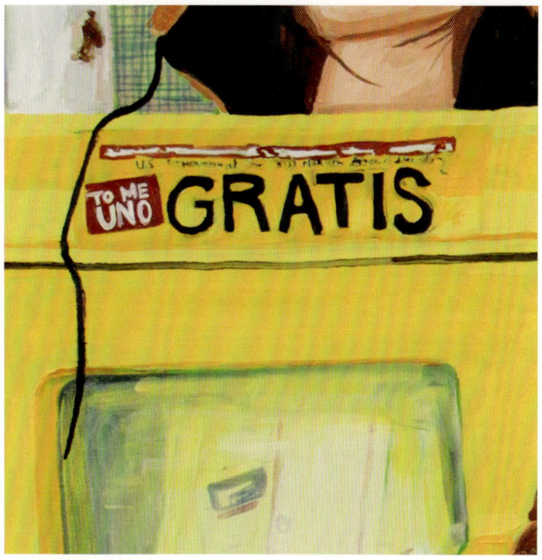
TO ME UNO
GRATIS

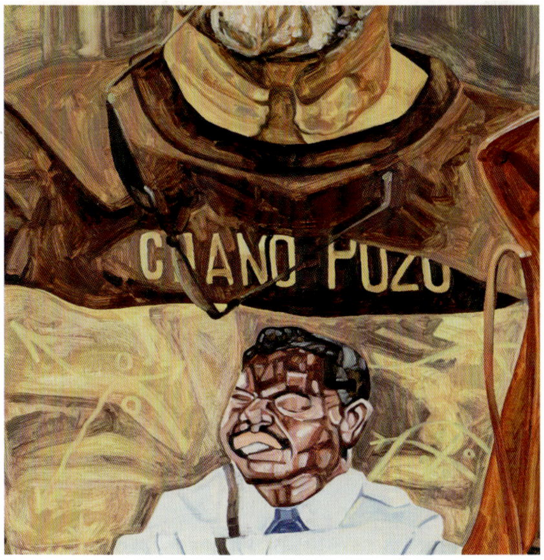

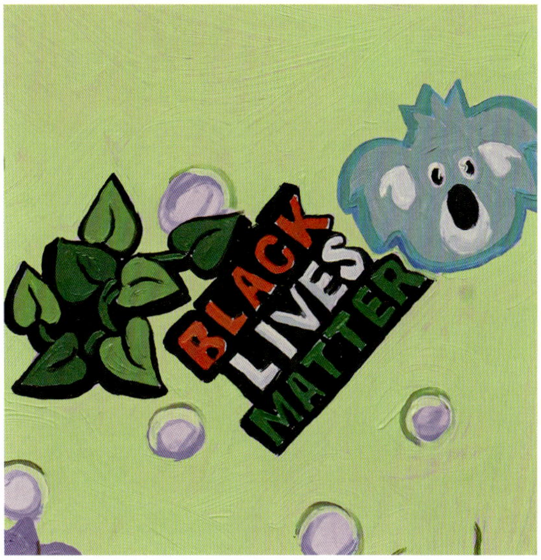
BLACK
LIVES
MATTER

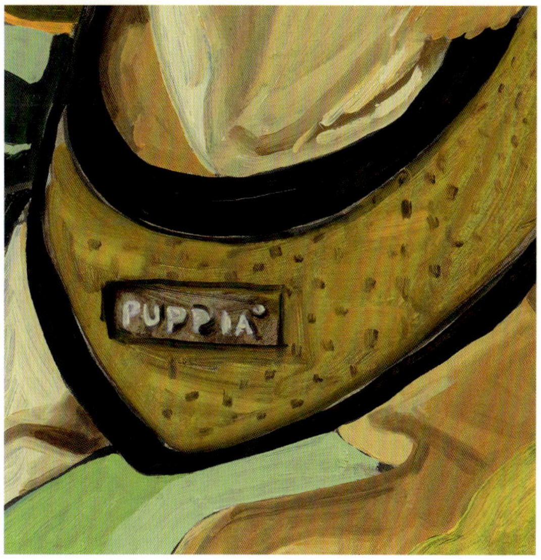
PUPPIA

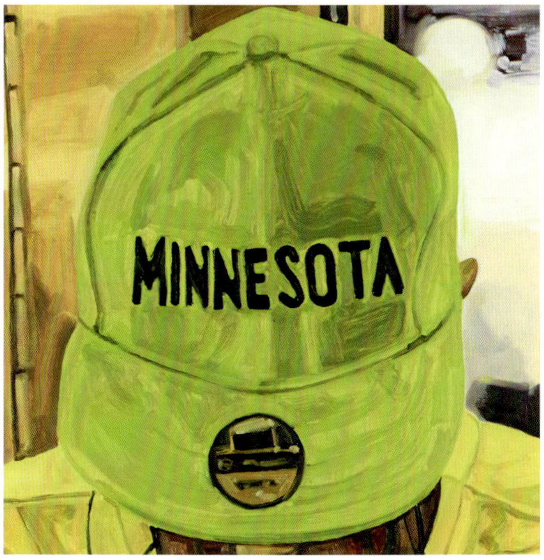
MINNESOTA

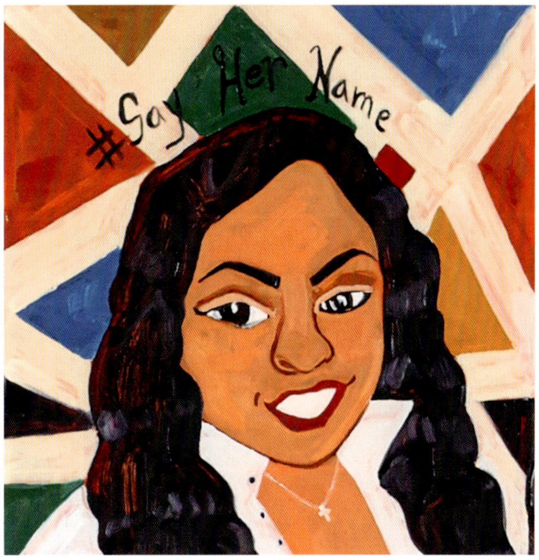
#Say Her Name

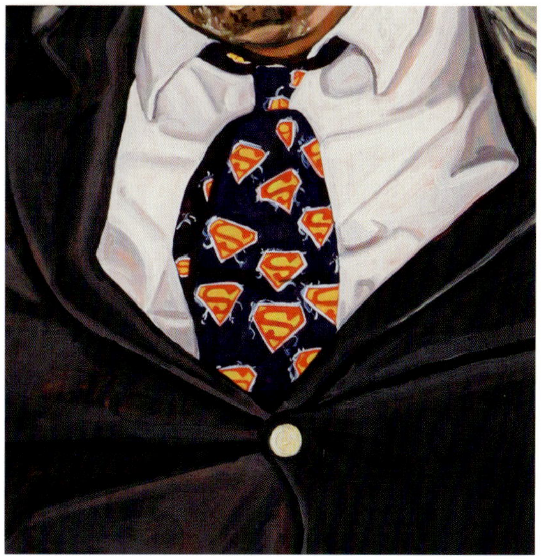

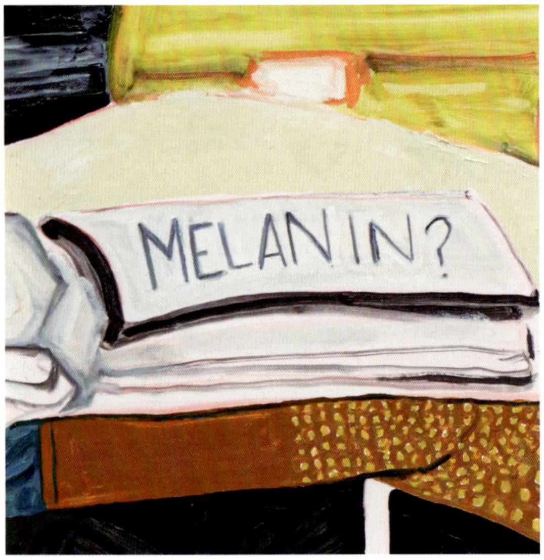
MELANIN?

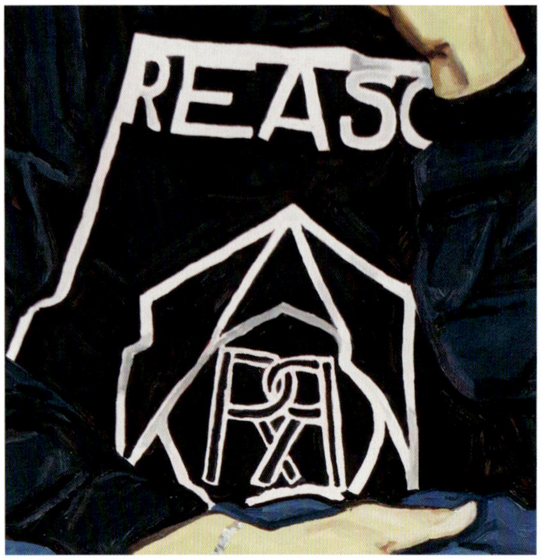
REASC

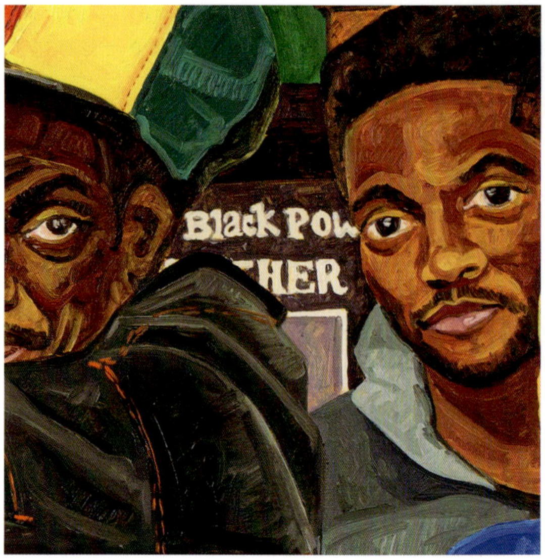
Black Pow

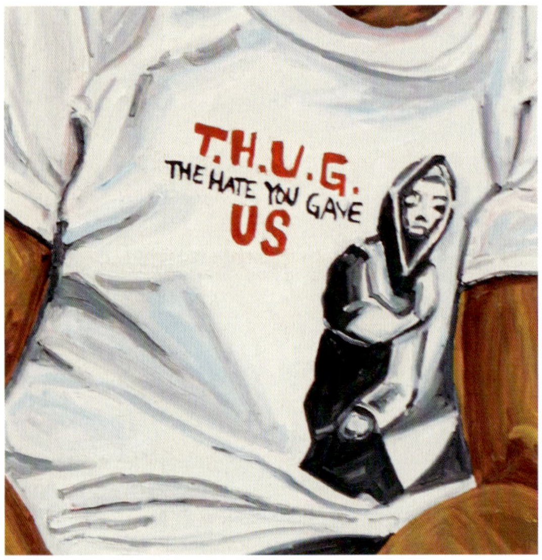
T.H.U.G.
THE HATE YOU GAVE
US

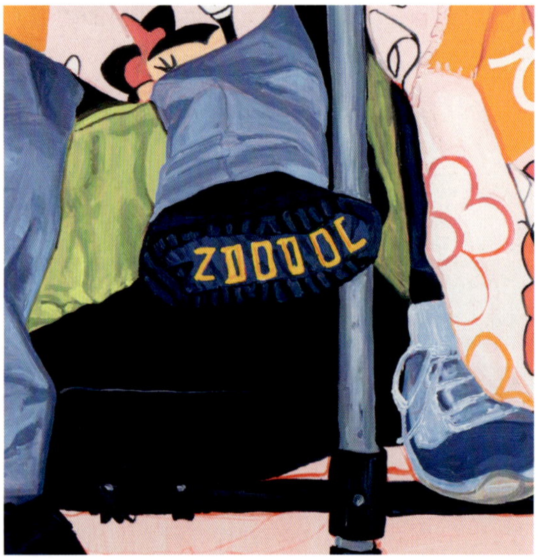

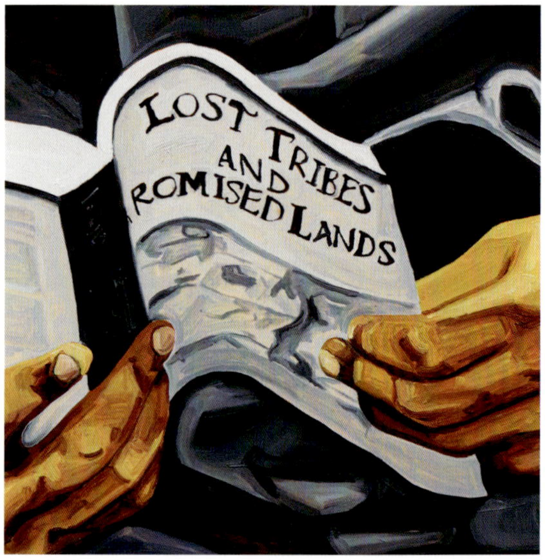
LOST TRIBES
AND
ROMISED LANDS

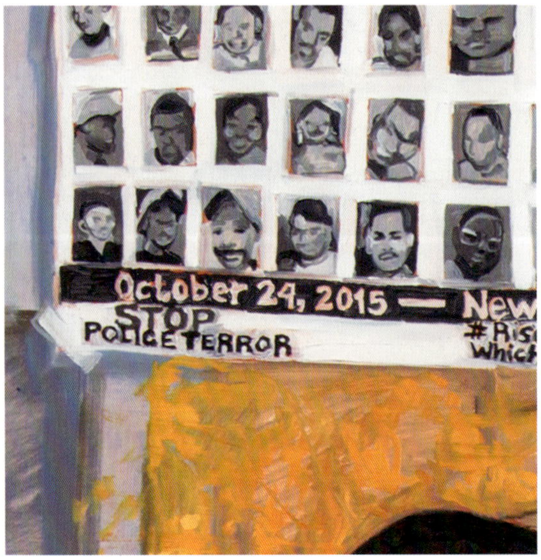
October 24, 2015 — New
STOP
POLICE TERROR

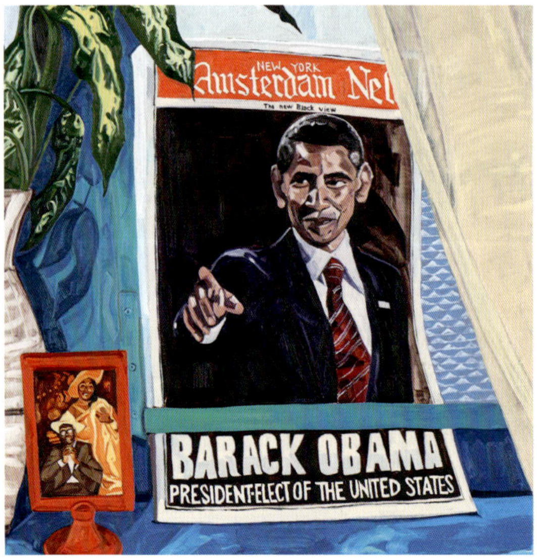
New York
Amsterdam Ne
BARACK OBAMA
PRESIDENT-ELECT OF THE UNITED STATES

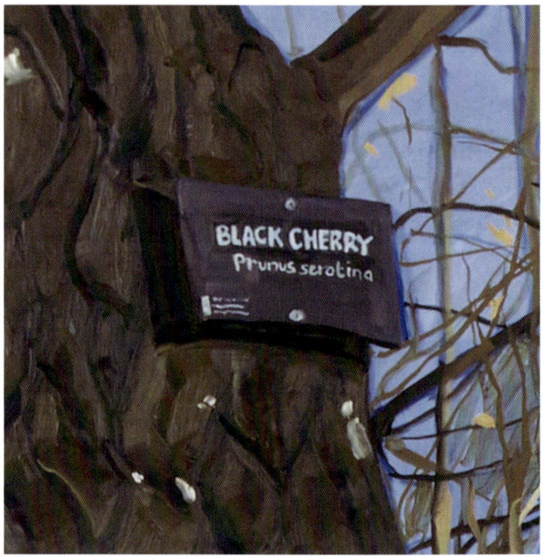
BLACK CHERRY
Prunus serotina

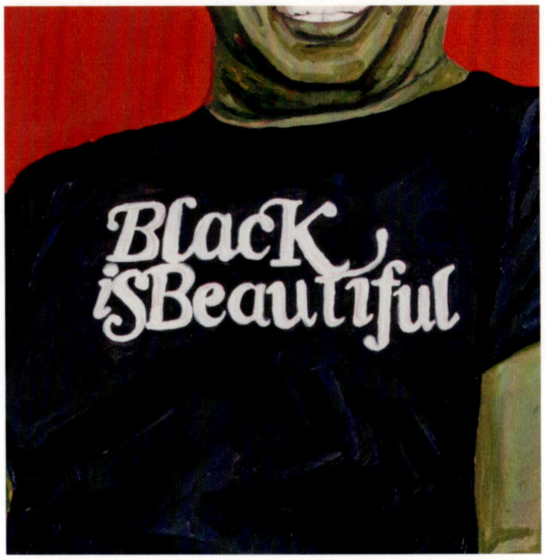
Black
isBeautiful

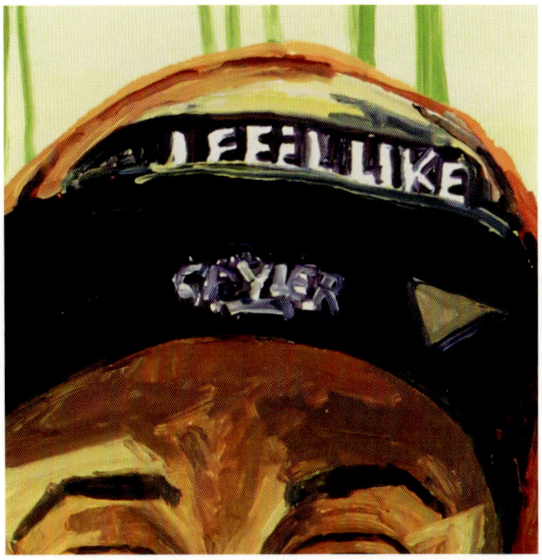

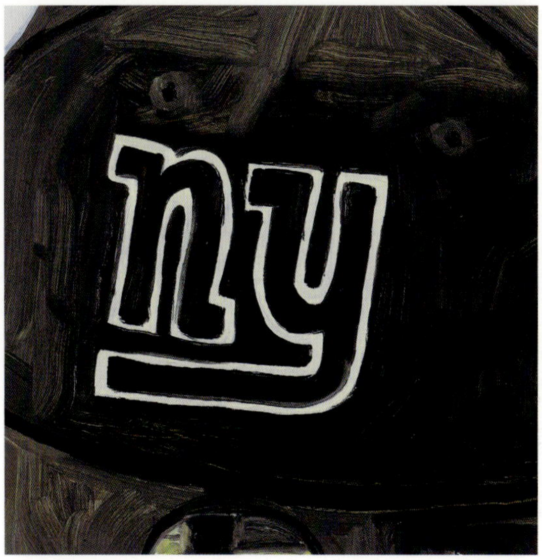
ny

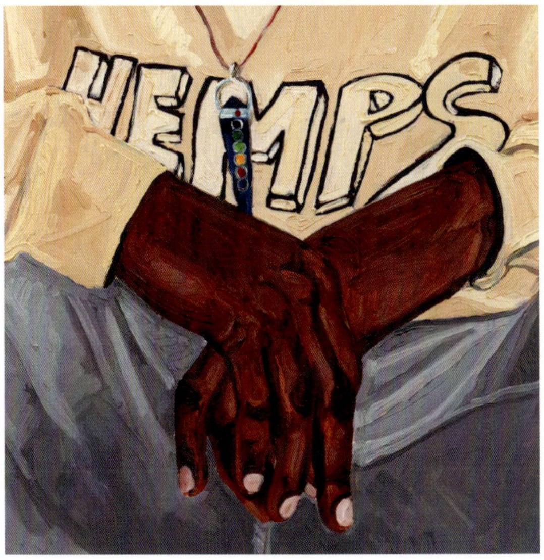
HEMPS

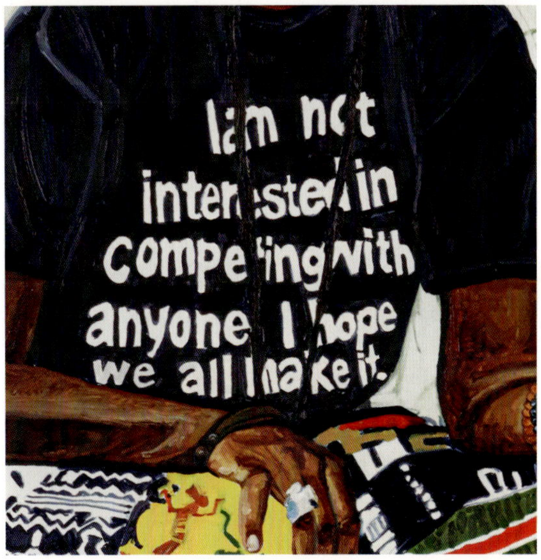
Iam not
interested in
competing with
anyone I hope
we all make it.

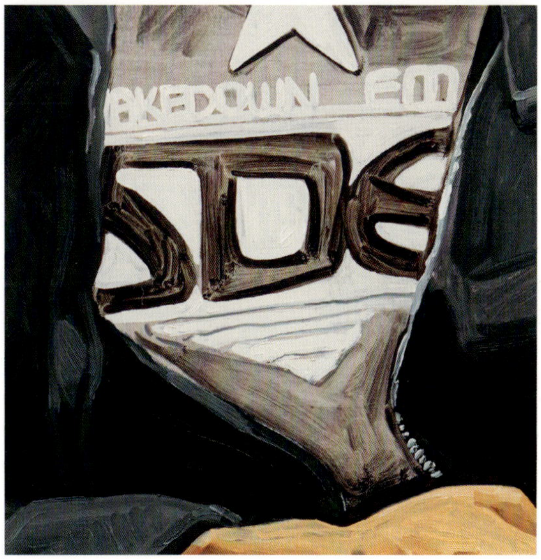

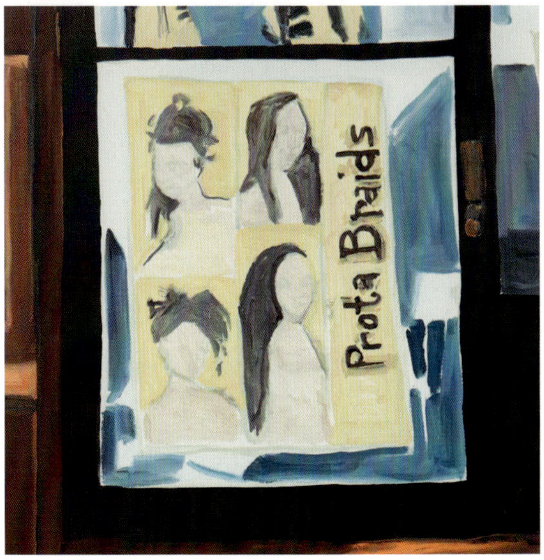
Prota Braids

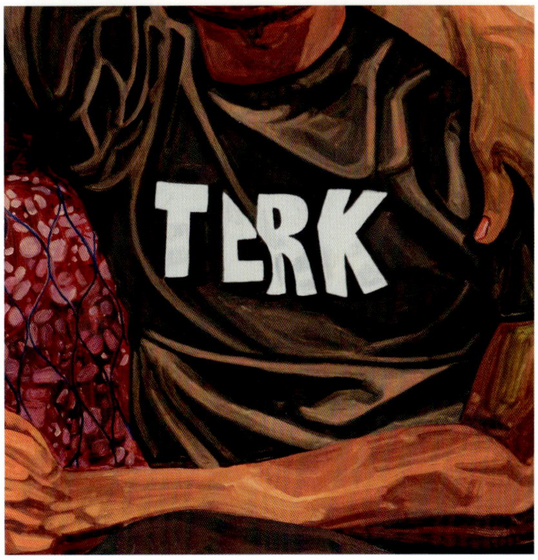
TERK

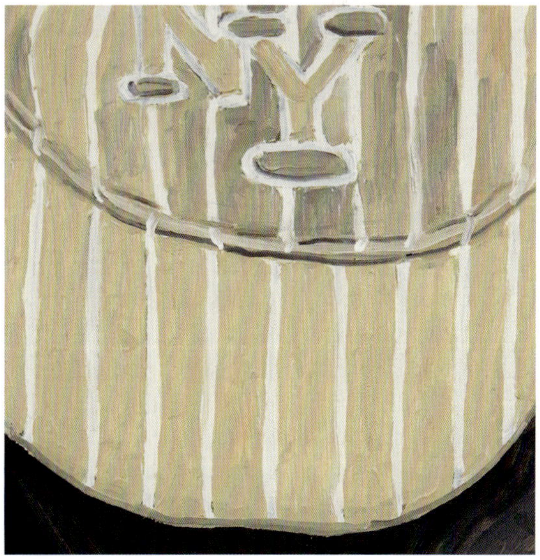
NY

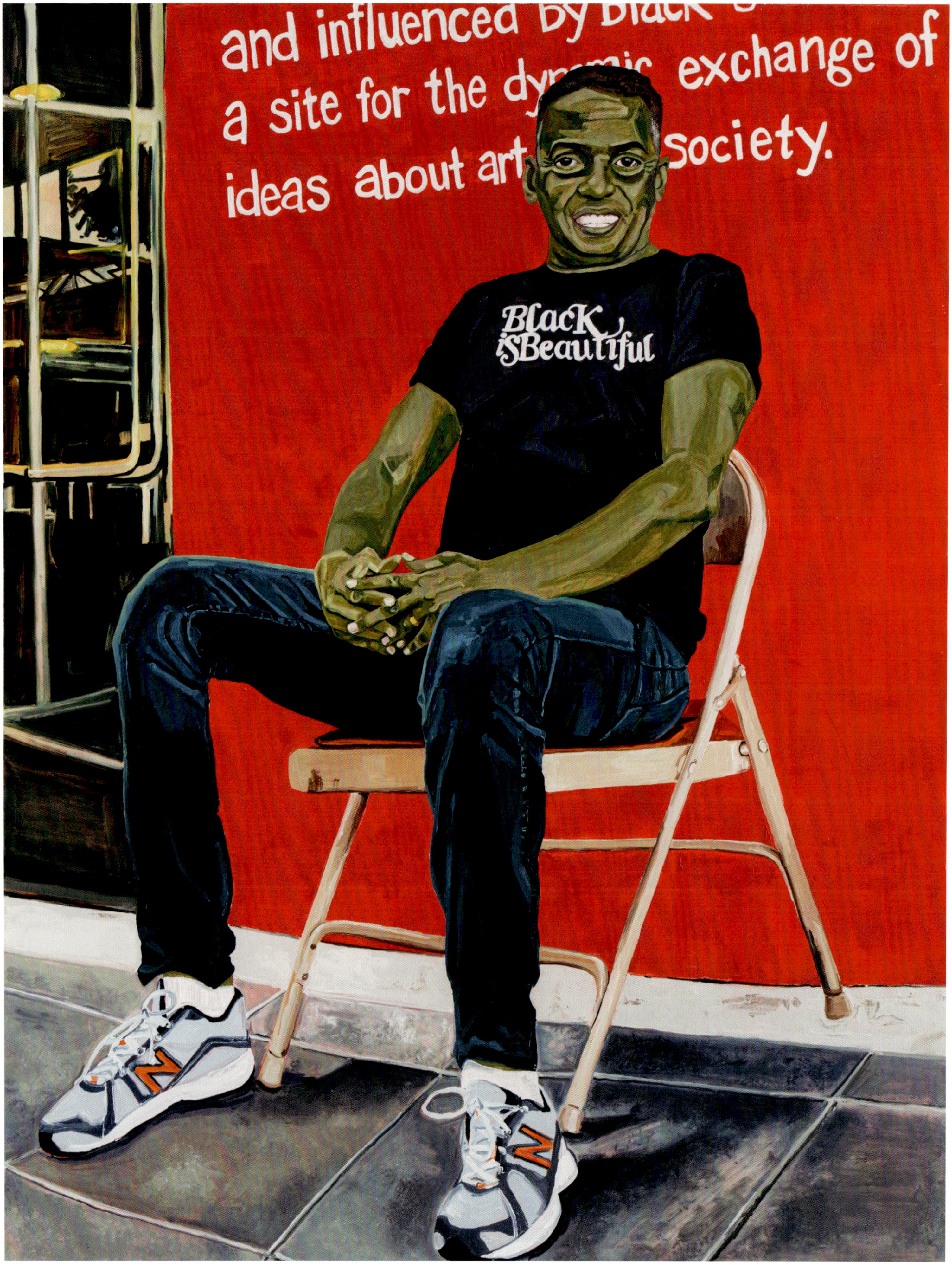
and influenced by Black
a site for the dy exchange of
ideas about art society.
Black is Beautiful

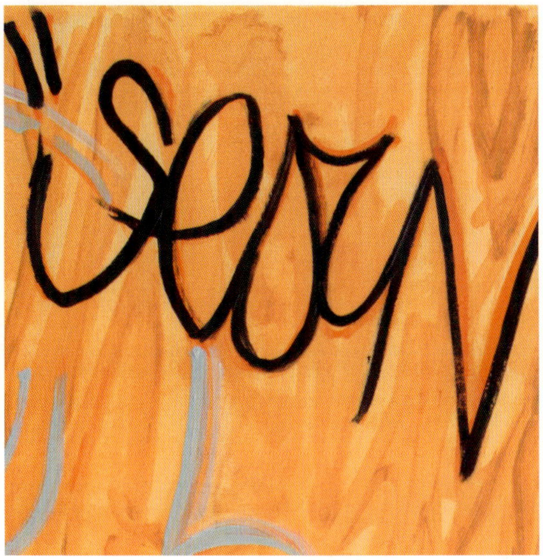

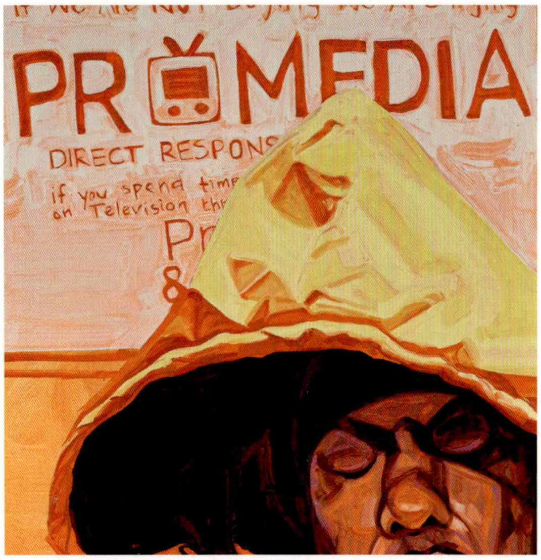

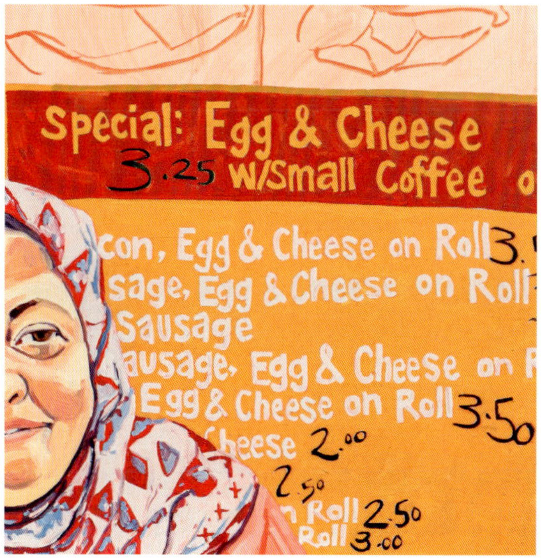

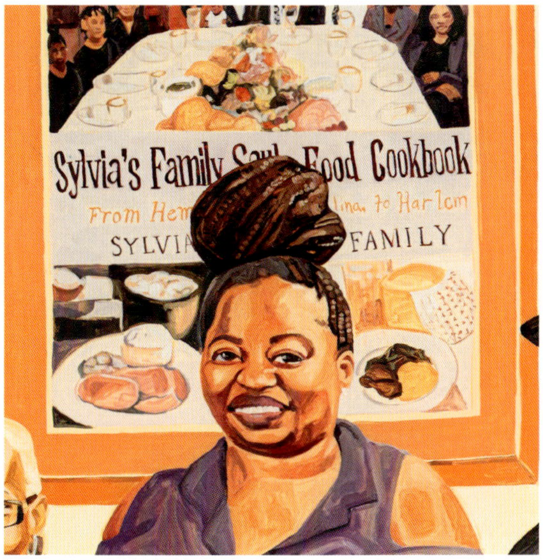

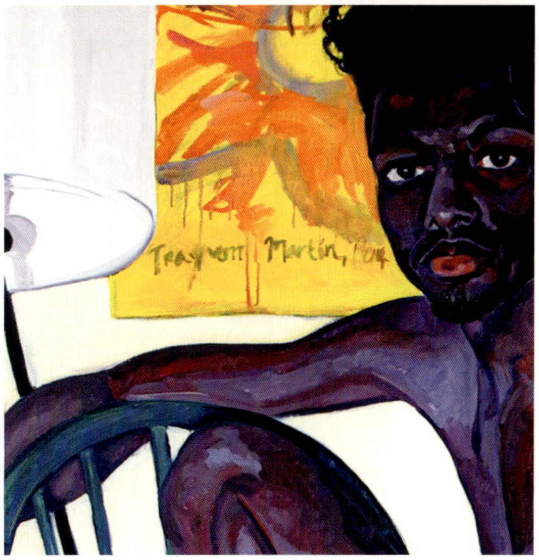

opposite,
TIMOTHY, 2017
OIL ON CANVAS
198 X 152 CM

next pages,
FALLOU, 2018
OIL ON CANVAS
229 X 198 CM

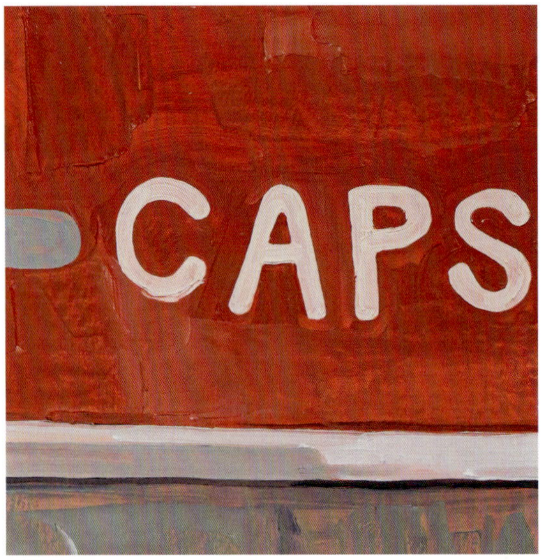
CAPS

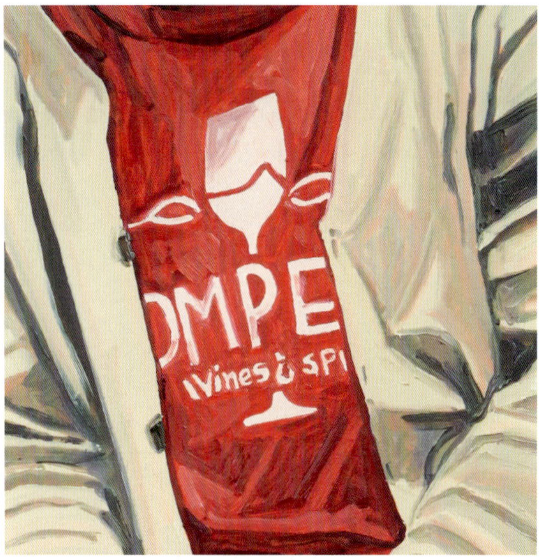
OMPE
Wines

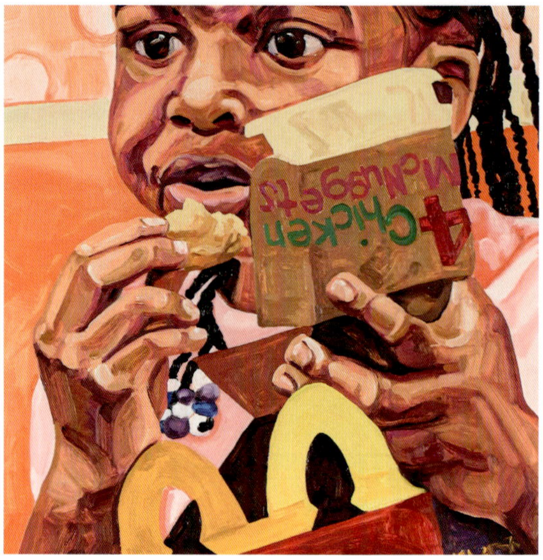
4 Chicken
McNuggets

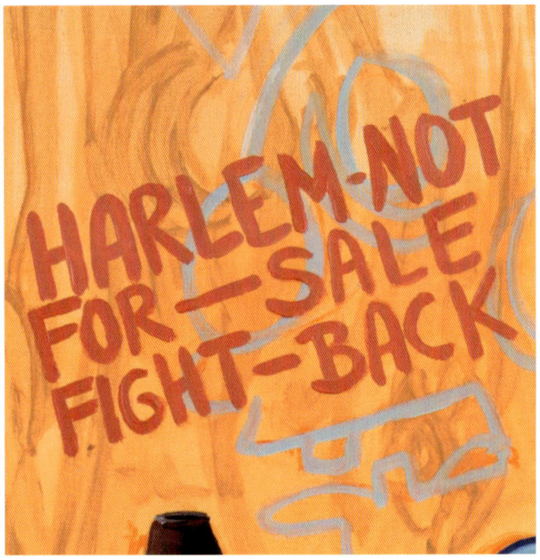
HARLEM-NOT
FOR—SALE
FIGHT-BACK

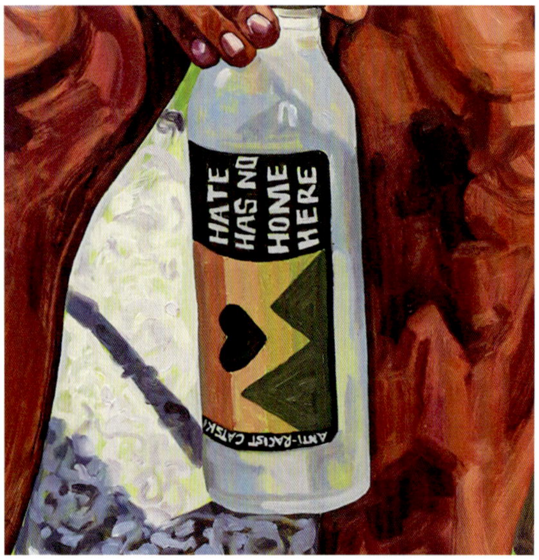
HATE
HAS NO
HOME
HERE

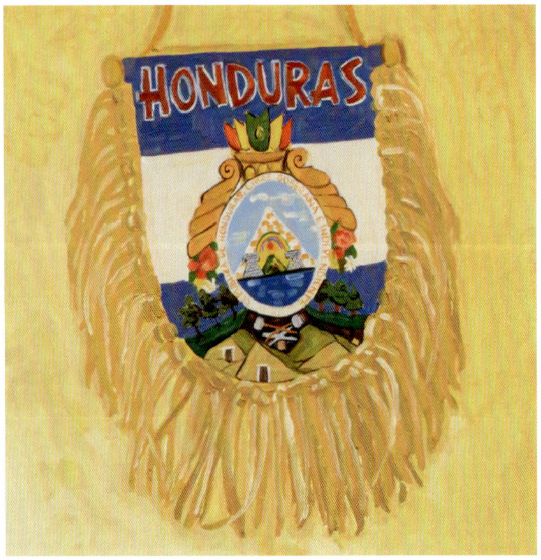
HONDURAS

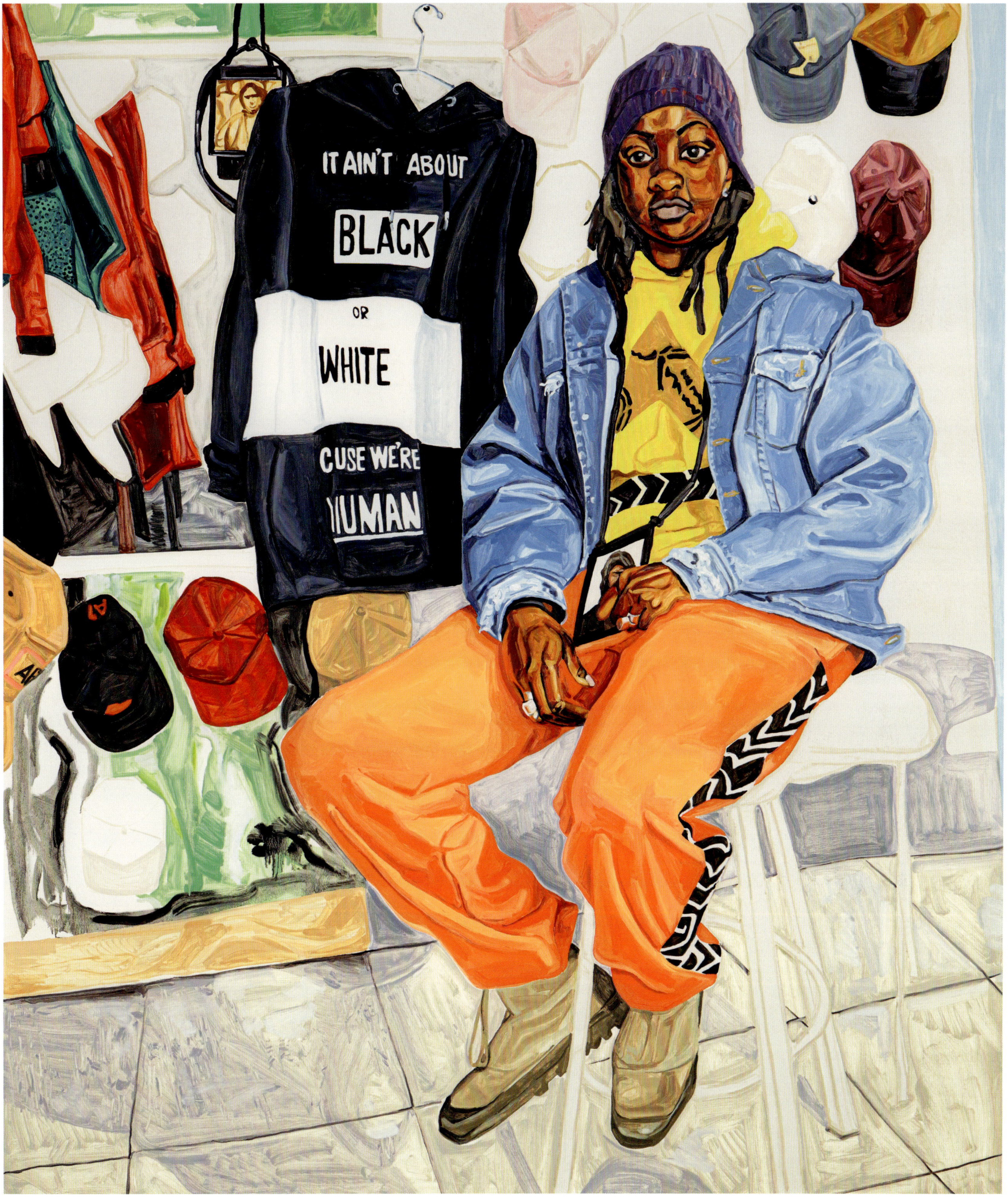
IT AIN'T ABOUT
BLACK
OR
WHITE
CUSE WE'RE
UMAN

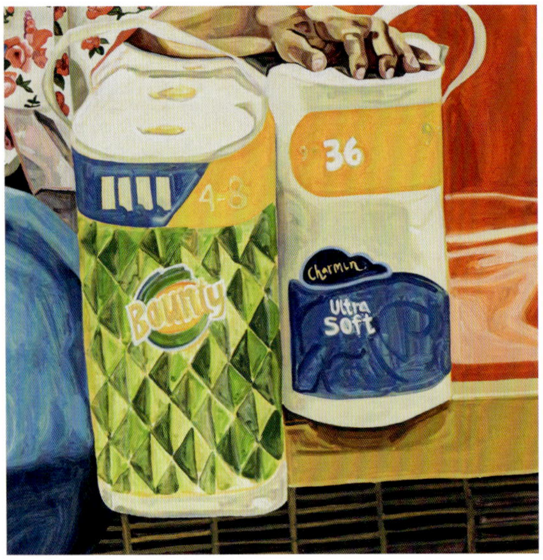
36
Bounty
Ultra Soft

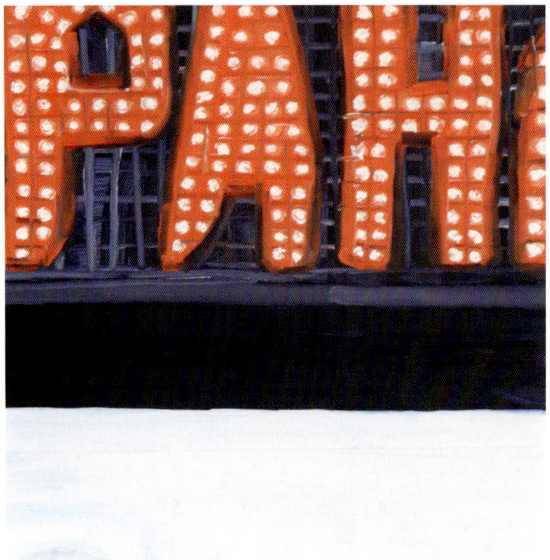

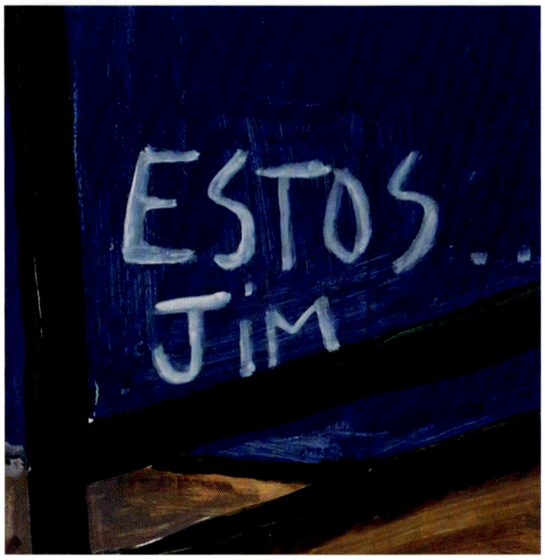
ESTOS..
JIM

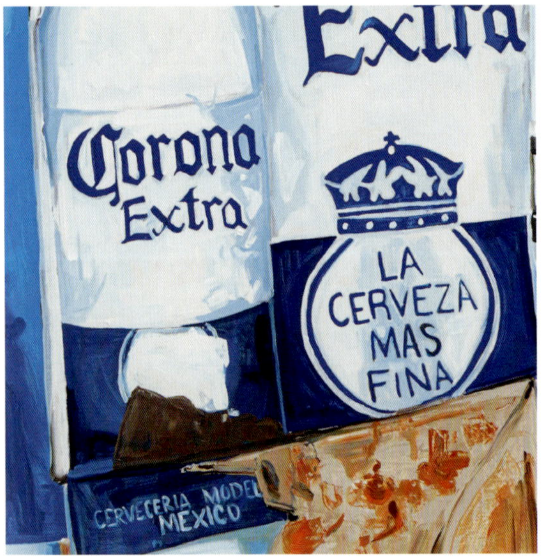
Extra
Corona Extra
LA CERVEZA MAS FINA
CERVECERIA MODEL
MEXICO

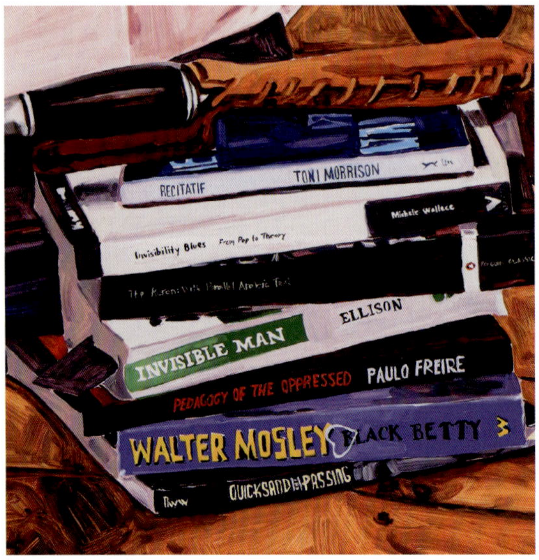
RECITATIF
TONI MORRISON
Michele Wallace
Invisibility Blues
ELLISON
INVISIBLE MAN
PEDAGOGY OF THE OPPRESSED
PAULO FREIRE
WALTER MOSLEY
BLACK BETTY
QUICKSAND AND PASSING

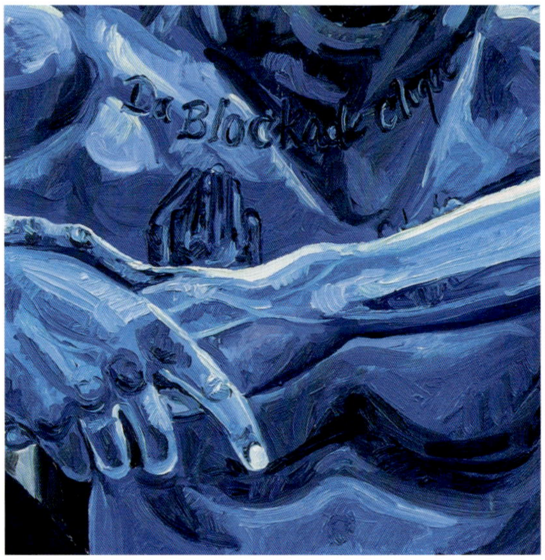

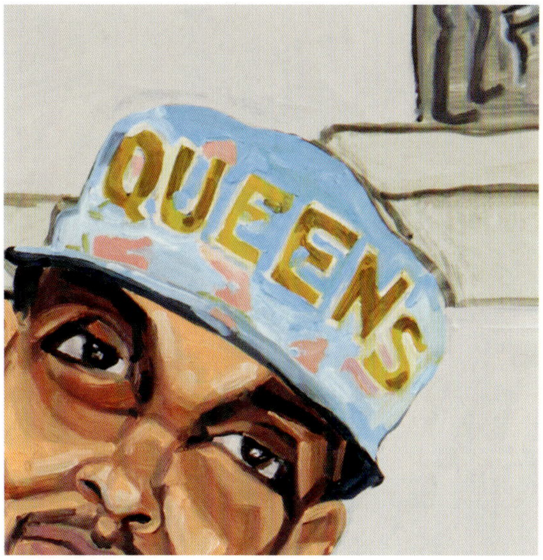
QUEENS

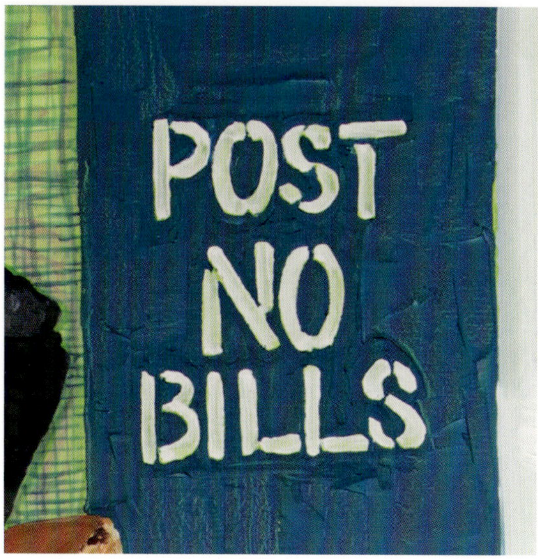
POST
NO
BILLS

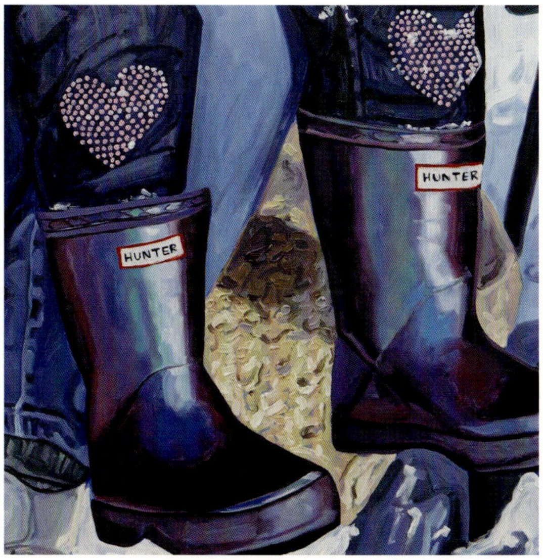
HUNTER
HUNTER

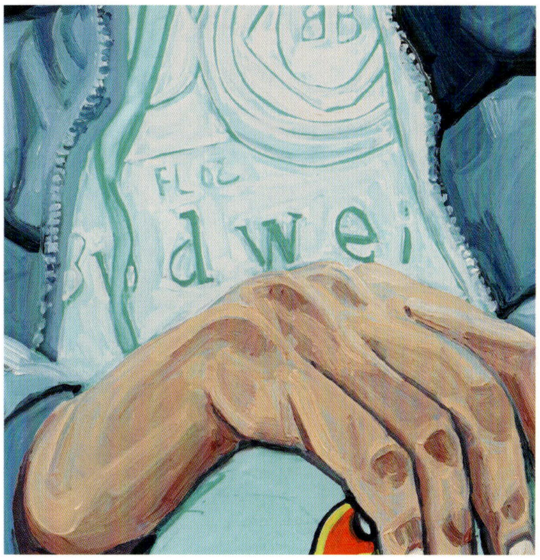

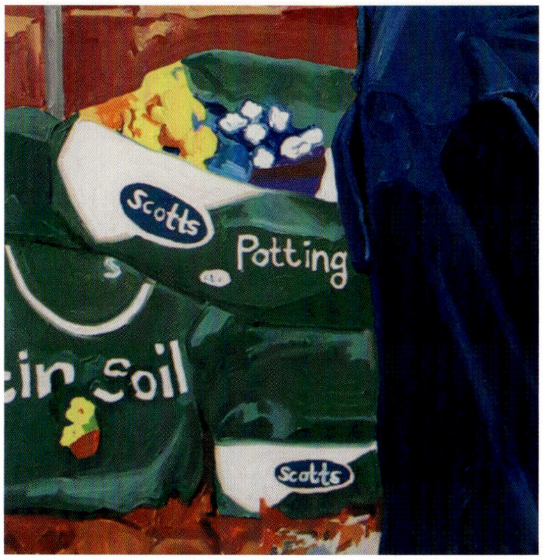
Scotts
Potting
Soil
Scotts

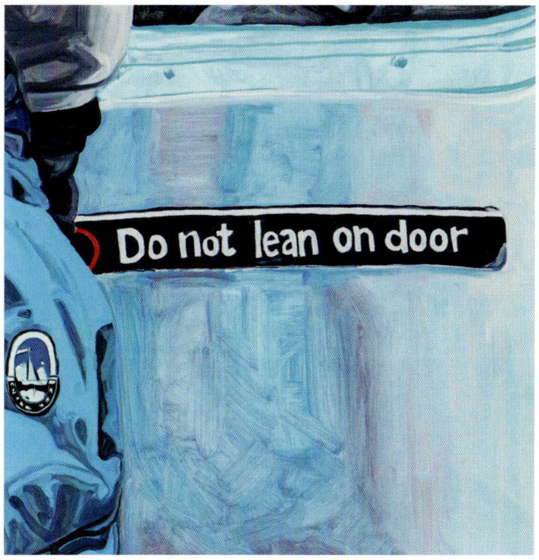
Do not lean on door

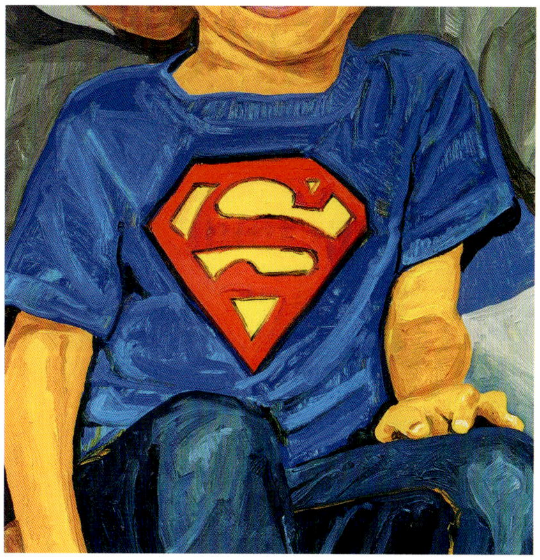

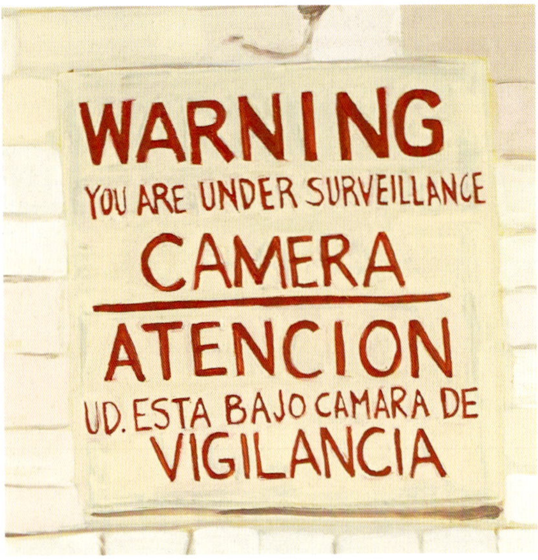
WARNING
YOU ARE UNDER SURVEILLANCE
CAMERA
ATENCION
UD. ESTA BAJO CAMARA DE
VIGILANCIA

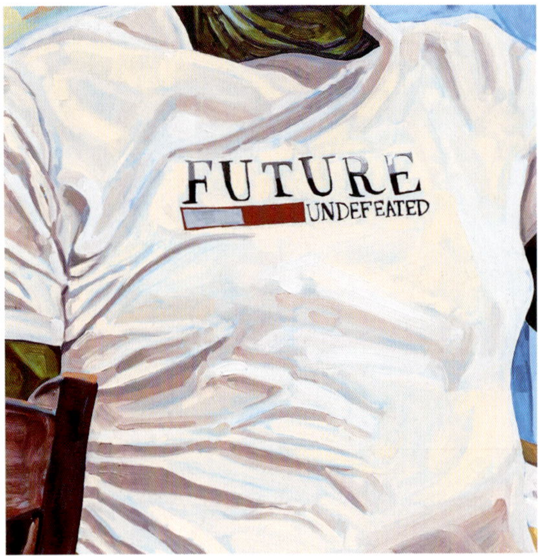
FUTURE
UNDEFEATED

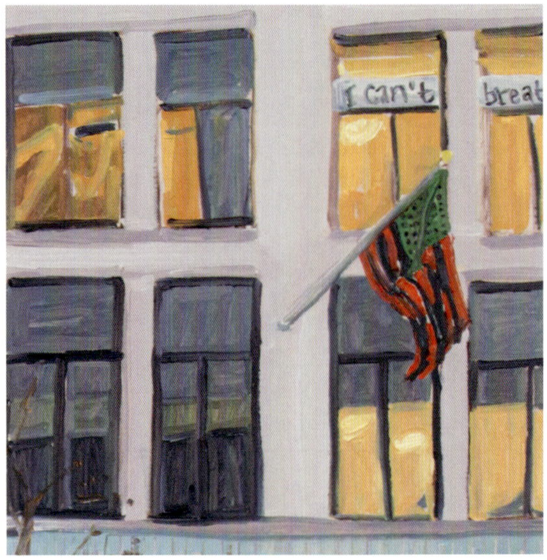
I can't
breat

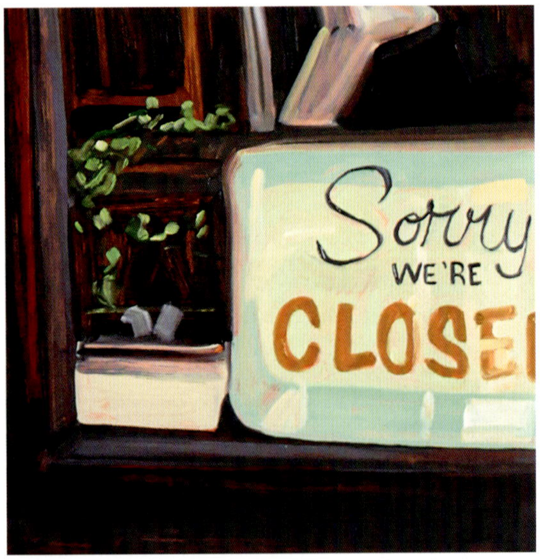
Sorry
WE'RE
CLOSE

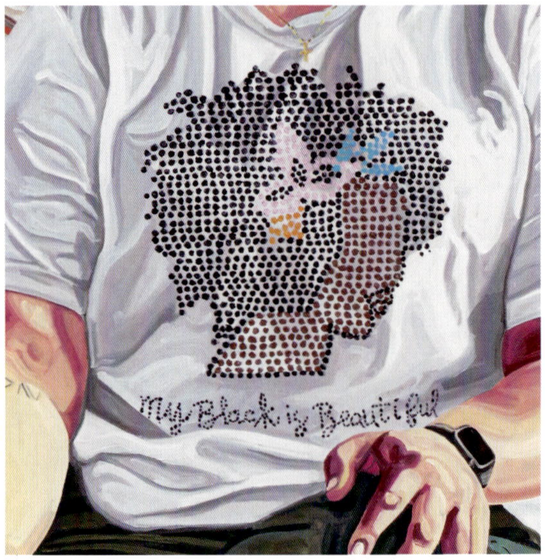
My Black is Beautiful

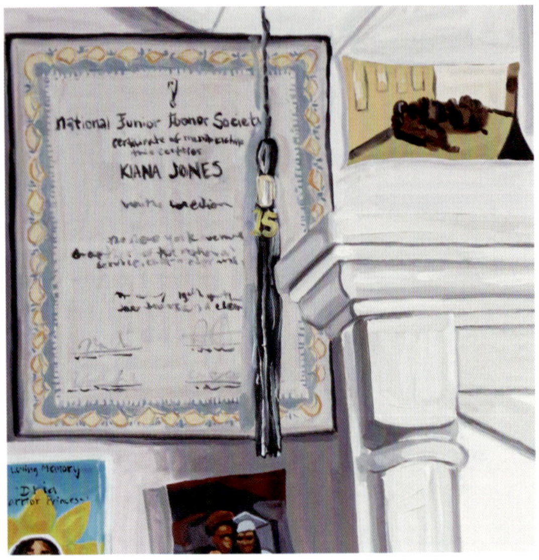
National Junior Honor Society
KIANA JONES

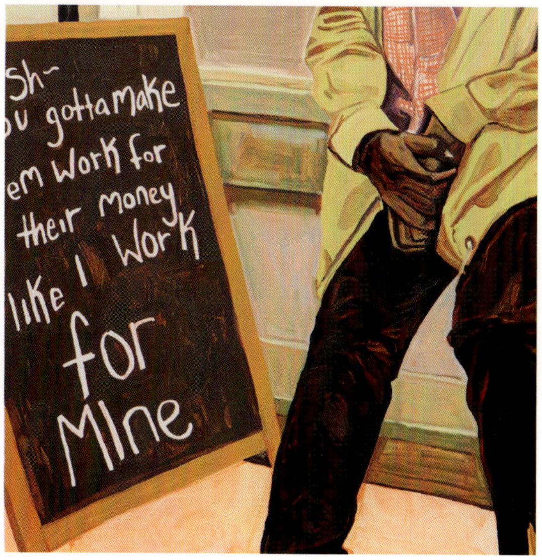
Sh-
u gotta make
em work for
their money
like I work
for
Mine

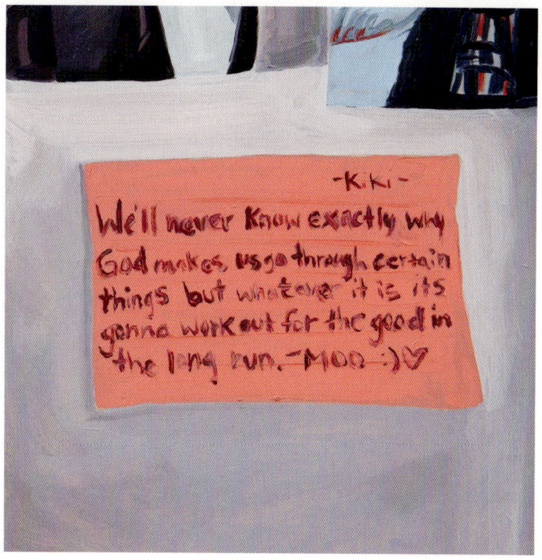
-Kiki-
We'll never know exactly why God makes us go through certain things but whatever it is its gonna work out for the good in the long run. -Moo-:)♥

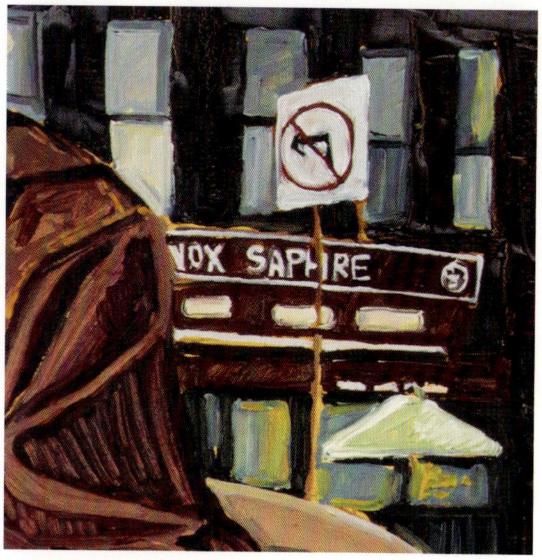
NOX SAPHIRE

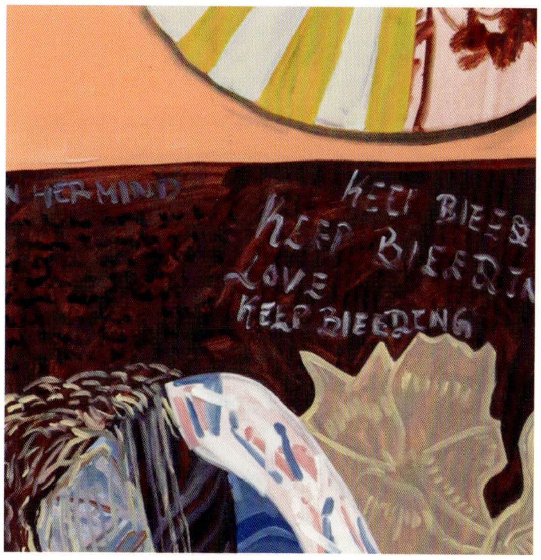
HER MIND
KEEP BLEEDING
LOVE
KEEP BLEEDING

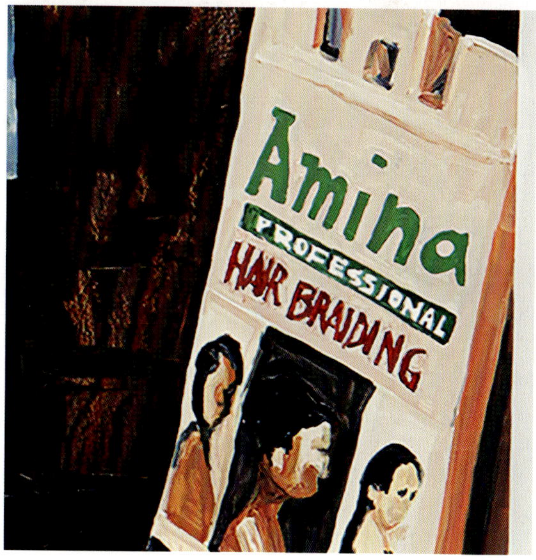
Amina
PROFESSIONAL
HAIR BRAIDING

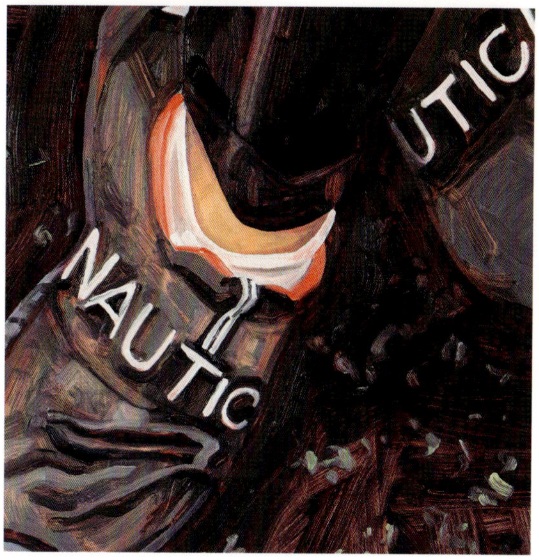
UTIC
NAUTIC

NOTES

INTERVIEW: PAGES 005–037

1 Thelma Golden, 'My Brother', in Thelma Golden, (ed.), *Black Male: Representations of Masculinity in Contemporary Art* (New York: Whitney Museum of American Art and Harry N. Abrams, 1994), 9.
2 Morgan Parker, 'Hottentot Venus', published in *The Paris Review*, no. 216, Spring 2016, 203.

SURVEY: PAGES 039–099

1 Toni Morrison, *The Source of Self-Regard: Selected Essays, Speeches, and Meditations* (New York: Knopf, 2019), 239.
2 Jordan Casteel in conversation with Massimiliano Gioni, 'Many are Called', in *Jordan Casteel: Within Reach* (New York: New Museum of Contemporary Art, 2020), 21.
3 Thelma Golden, *Freestyle* (New York: Studio Museum in Harlem, 2001), 15
4 Thelma Golden, as quoted in Greg Tate, *Flyboy 2* (Durham: Duke University Press, 2016), 230.
5 Kyle Macmillan, 'Art's New View: The 12 best Colorado artists 35 and under', *The Denver Post*, 22 May 2011.
6 Ibid.
7 Kaitlin Wylde, '7 Contemporary Artists Keeping Traditions Alive', *Nylon*, 6 March 2017. https://www.nylon.com/articles/contemporary-artists-classic-tradition#:~:text=I%20am%20a%20painter's%20 painter,painters%20who%20have%20come%20before.
8 Ralph Ellison, *Invisible Man* (New York: Random House, 1952), chapter 1.
9 Toni Morrison, as quoted in Hilton Als, 'Toni Morrison and the Ghosts in the House', *The New Yorker*, 19 October 2003. https://www.newyorker.com/magazine/2003/10/27/ghosts-in-the-house
10 bell hooks, *Black Looks: Race and Representation* (Boston: South End Press, 1992), 4.
11 Chloe Wayne, 'Jordan Casteel', https://nyc.moma.org/jordan-casteel-ab8c0fd26d9d, 12 April 2016.
12 Ibid.
13 Mansa Ra, wall text on the occasion of the exhibition 'Jordan Casteel: Returning the Gaze', Denver Art Museum, 2 February–18 August 2019.
14 Conversation with the author, 22 November 2024.
15 https://www.thehighline.org/blog/2020/05/28/art-in-times-of-crisis/
16 Roland Barthes, *The Death of Author*, published in *Aspen*, no. 5-6, 1967. The original French, 'La mort de l'auteur' was published in *Manteia*, no. 5, 1968.
17 Jordan Casteel in Elizabeth Fullerton, 'Jordan Casteel: There Is a Season', *Studio International*, 29 October 2021. https://www.studiointernational.com/jordan-casteel-there-is-a-season-review-massimo-de-carlo-gallery-london

FOCUS: PAGES 101–117

1 Jasmine Sanders, 'EJ Hill and Jordan Casteel Teach Us How to Paint', *Interview*, 23 March 2022, https://www.interviewmagazine.com/art/ej-hill-and-jordan-casteel-teach-us-how-to-paint, accessed 2 November 2024.
2 Conversation with the author, 20 October 2024.
3 Jordan Casteel, quoted in *Jordan Casteel: Within Reach* (New York: New Museum, 2020), 14.
4 Dawoud Bey, 'Seeing Eye to Eye', *Jordan Casteel: Within Reach*, p. 31.
5 It is notable that Casteel's one sustained engagement with the still-life genre while a graduate student was a series of paintings depicting her own prescription pill bottles – imagery that might be read as its own play on the *memento mori* trope.
6 Casteel interviewed for the Los Angeles Museum of Contemporary Art's 'Collecting the Contemporary' video series, https://www.youtube.com/watch?v=7PDpLt9LIpQ, accessed 18 November, 2024.
7 John Milton, 'Lycidas' (1637), https://www.poetryfoundation.org/poems/44733/lycidas, accessed 18 November 2024.
8 Conversation with the author, 20 October 2024.
9 Casteel quoted in 'A Harlem Family: Jordan Casteel in Conversation with Thelma Golden', *Jordan Casteel: Within Reach*, 41.
10 For a foundational discussion of the Black gaze in relation to a White-dominant gaze, see bell hooks, 'The Oppositional Gaze, Black Female Spectators', in *Black Looks: Race and Representation* (Boston: South End Press, 1992), 115–32; for an incisive examination of strategies of obfuscation by Black artists over the past fifty years, see Ashley James's introductory essay in *Going Dark: The Contemporary Figure at the Edge of Visibility* (New York: Guggenheim Museum, 2023), 16–35.
11 W. E. B. Du Bois, *The Souls of Black Folk* (1903; New York: Signet Classics, 2012), 9. See 'A Harlem Family: Jordan Casteel in Conversation with Thelma Golden', *Jordan Casteel: Within Reach*, 41, for Golden's invocation of Du Bois in relation to Casteel's practice in 2020.
12 Conversation with the author, 20 October 2024.
13 Ibid.

right,
PRETTY IN PINK, 2019
OIL ON CANVAS
114 X 76 CM

next pages, from left,
DEVAN, 2014
OIL ON CANVAS
188 X 137 CM

JONATHAN, 2014
OIL ON CANVAS
183 X 137 CM

JIRÉH, 2013
OIL ON CANVAS
183 X 132 CM

ELIJAH, 2014
OIL ON CANVAS
132 X 183 CM

NOELLE, 2019
OIL ON CANVAS
198 X 152 CM

BENYAM, 2018
OIL ON CANVAS
229 X 198 CM

INSTALLATION VIEW AT
THE NEW MUSEUM OF
CONTEMPORARY ART,
NEW YORK, 2020

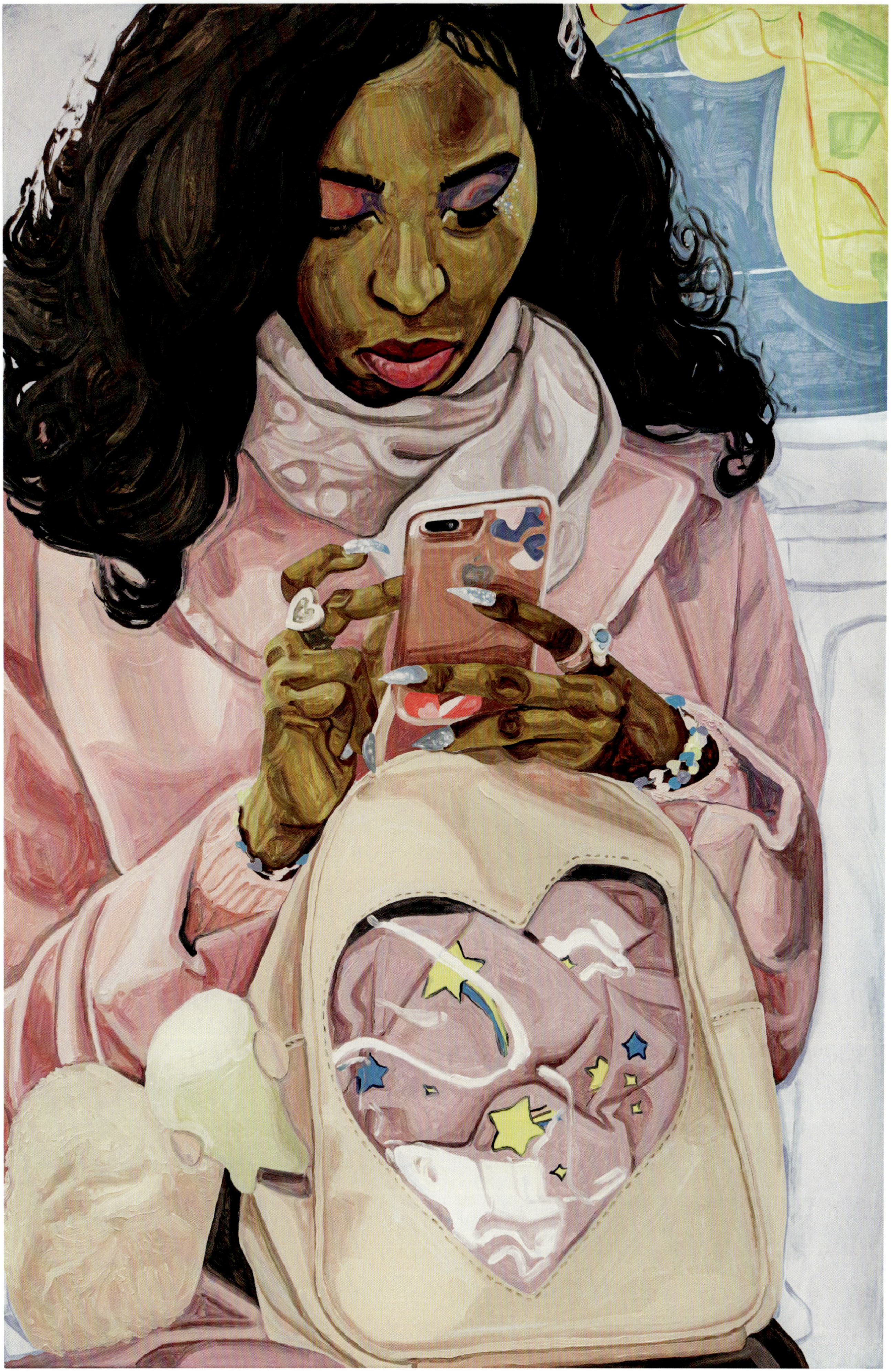

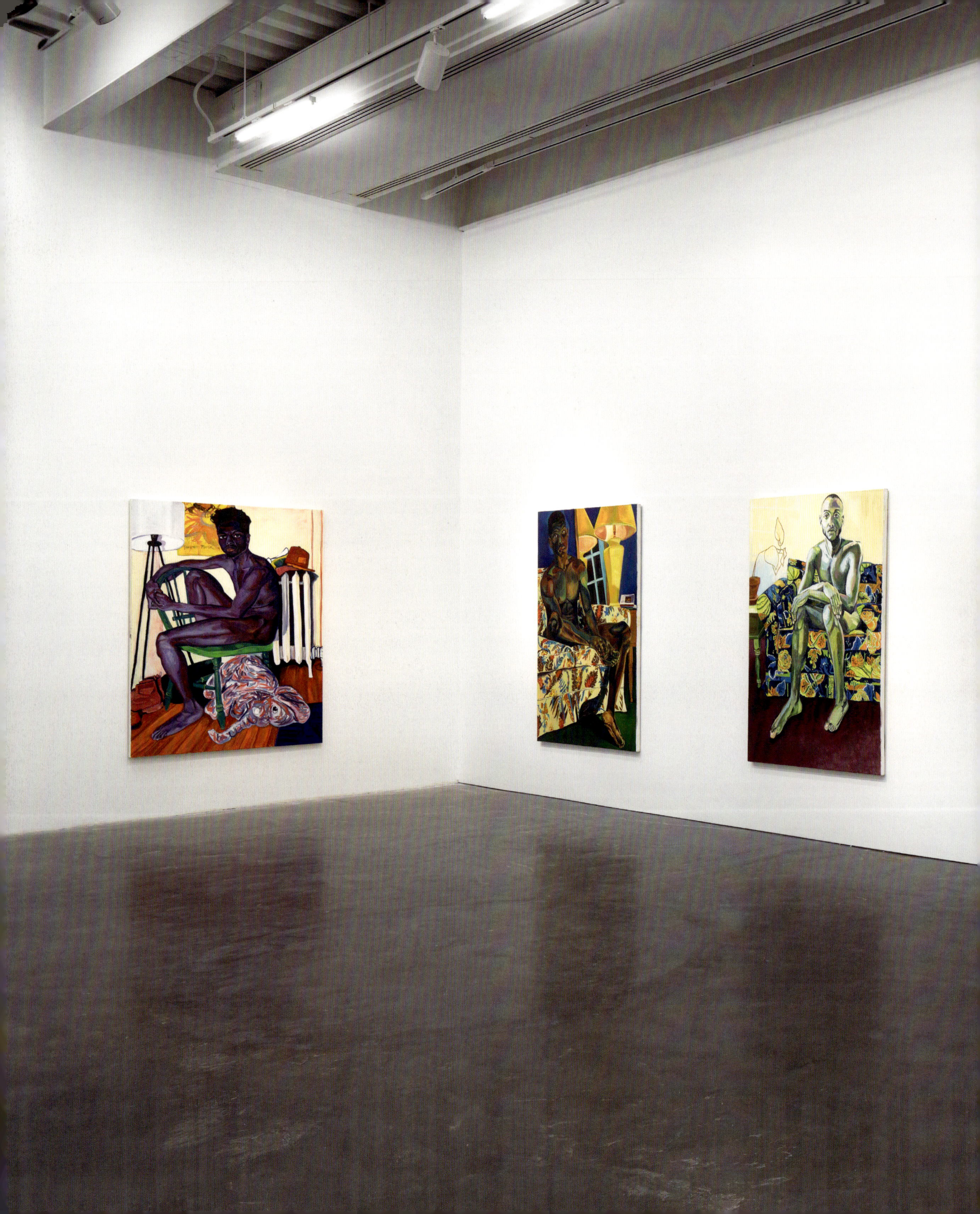

151 CHRONOLOGY

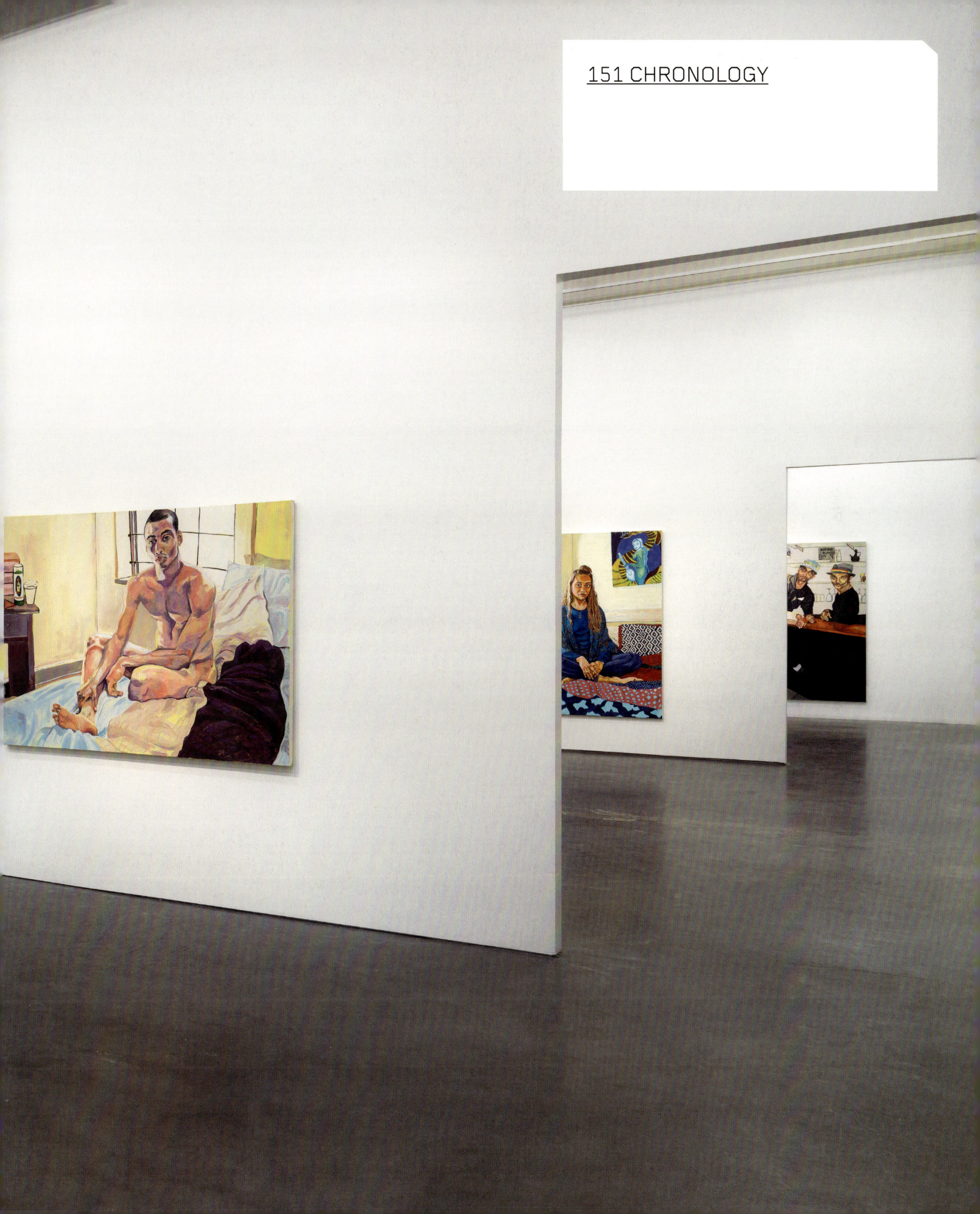

CHRONOLOGY: Jordan Casteel, born 1989 in Denver. Lives and works in New York.

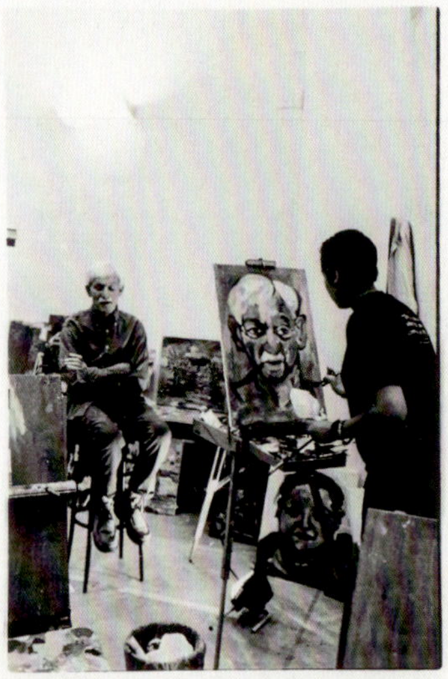

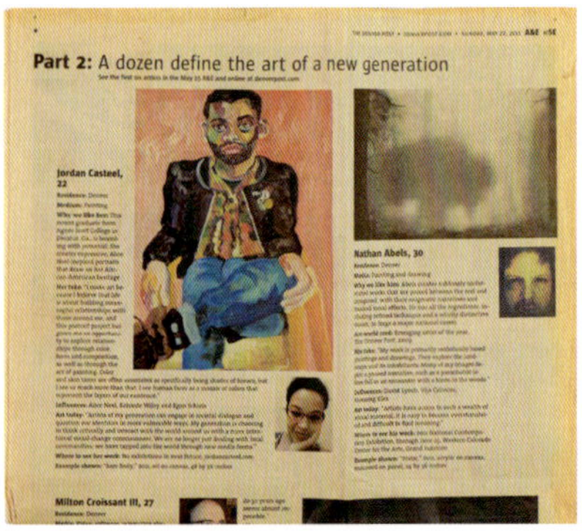

Part 2: A dozen define the art of a new generation

Jordan Casteel, 22

Nathan Abels, 30

Milton Croissant III, 27

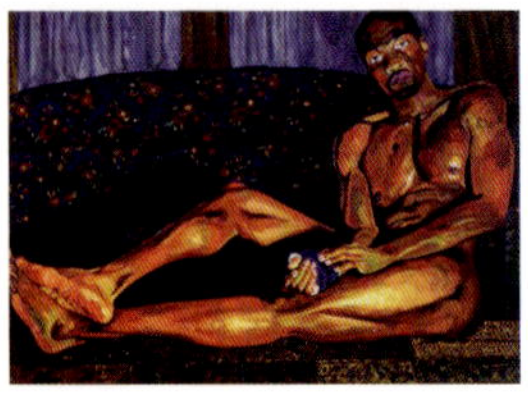

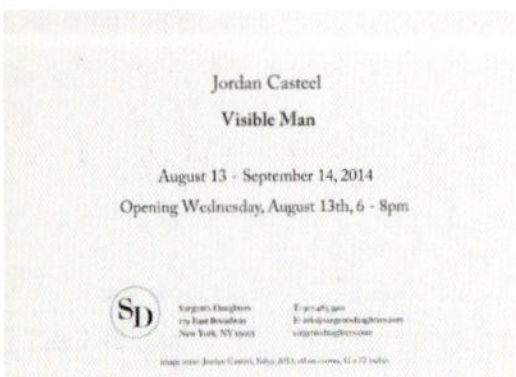

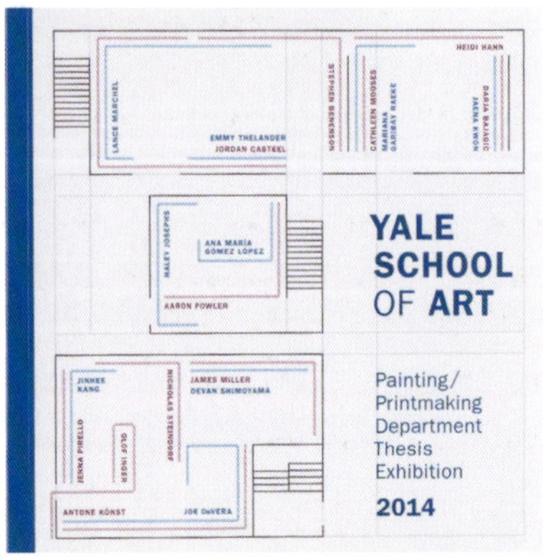

SELECTED EXHIBITIONS AND PROJECTS
2010–15

SELECTED ARTICLES AND INTERVIEWS
2010–15

2010

Attends the Lamar Dodd School of Art, University of Georgia, Cortona, Italy

2011

'Yasan: 100 Year of Women's Struggle Ceremony and Sword',
SELLARS PROJECT SPACE, Denver (group)

'Ciao: I Direttori',
TERMINUS 100, Atlanta (group)

'Collage Arts Colloquium',
DALTON ART GALLERY, AGNES SCOTT COLLEGE, Decatur, Georgia (group)

Obtains a B.A. at Agnes Scott College, Decatur, Georgia

2011 (articles)

MacMillan, Kyle, 'Art's New View', Denver Post, 22 May

2012

'First-Year Graduate Student Exhibition',
GREEN HALL GALLERY, YALE SCHOOL OF ART, New Haven, Connecticut (group)

'Celebrating the Culture of African-American Art: A Brookfield Invitational Exhibition',
REPUBLIC PLAZA, Denver (group)

2013

'For ED: Splendor in the Grass with Olympic Lad and Lass',
GREEN HALL GALLERY, YALE SCHOOL OF ART, New Haven, Connecticut (group)

'Second-Year Graduate Student Exhibition',
GREEN HALL GALLERY, YALE SCHOOL OF ART, New Haven, Connecticut (group)

2014

'Visible Man',
SARGENT'S DAUGHTERS, New York (solo)

'The Gaze',
THE STUDY, AISLING GALLERY, New Haven, Connecticut (solo)

'MFA Thesis Exhibition',
GREEN HALL GALLERY, YALE SCHOOL OF ART, New Haven, Connecticut (group)

'13 Artists',
24/6.106.353.V.1, YALE SCHOOL OF ART, New Haven, Connecticut (group)

Obtains a M.F.A. at Yale School of Art, Yale University, New Haven, Connecticut

2015

'Brothers',
SARGENT'S DAUGHTERS, New York (solo)

'Thats On Me',
PARIS BLUES, New York (group)

'Color II: Identity and Society',
THE GUND, KENYON COLLEGE, Ohio (group)

Attends the Studio Museum in Harlem, Artist-In-Residence, New York

2015 (articles)

Zevitas, Steven, 'Jordan Casteel', no. 116, New American Paintings, February–March

Fateman, Johanna, 'New York: Jordan Casteel', Artforum, October

Sargent, Antwaun, 'Making Black Men Visible – By Painting Them Together', Vice, October

Kirszenbaum, Martha, 'Blinds and Mirrors', Flash Art, no. 305, November–December

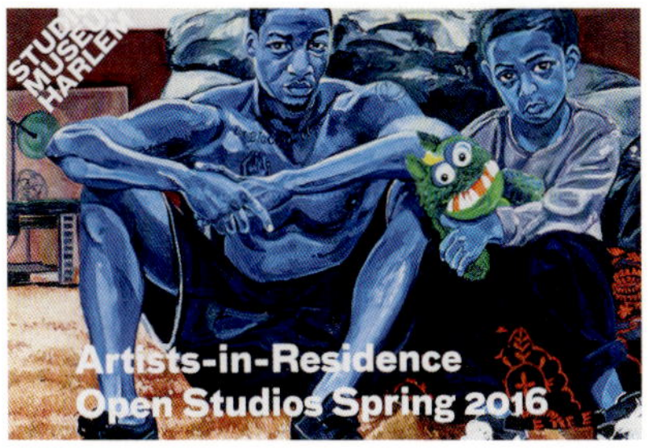

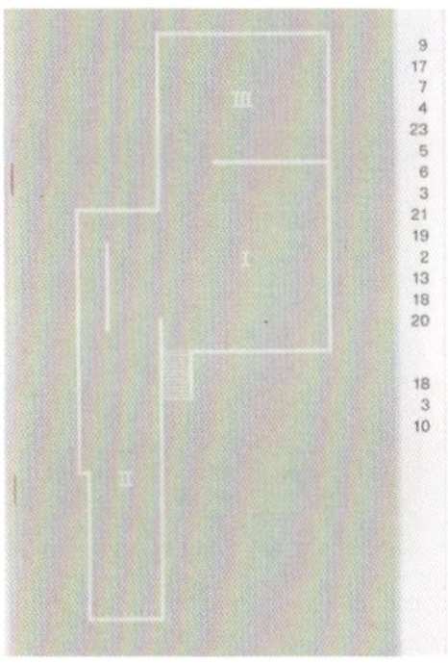

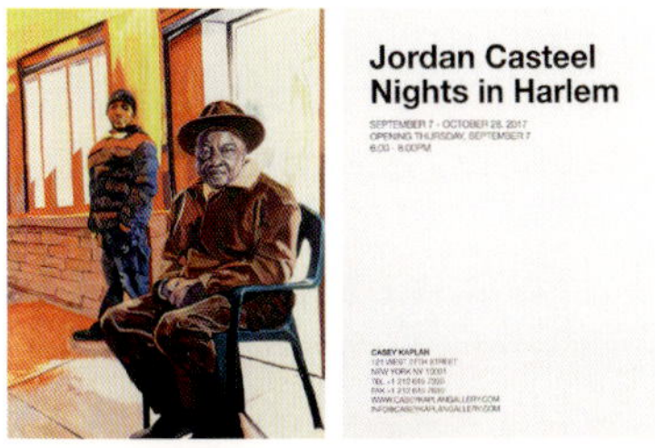

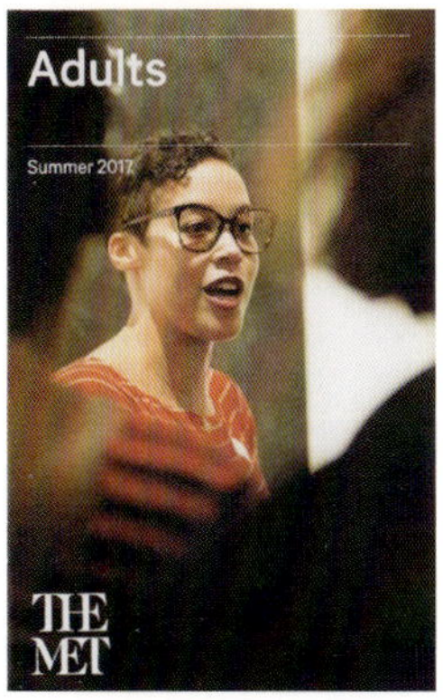

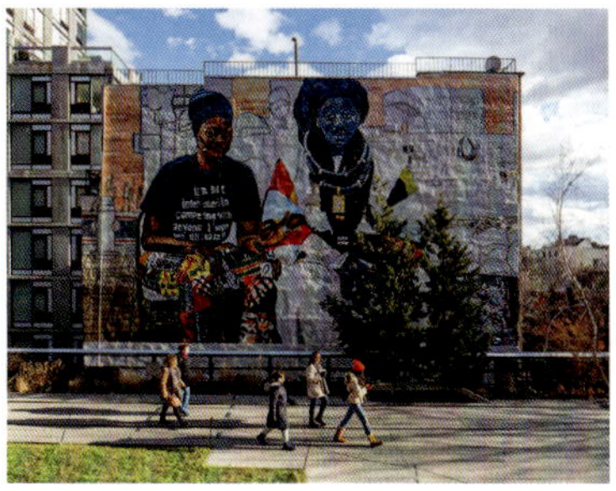

SELECTED EXHIBITIONS AND PROJECTS
2016–19

SELECTED ARTICLES AND INTERVIEWS
2016–19

2016

'Do You See Me?',
DIGGS GALLERY, WINSTON-SALEM STATE UNIVERSITY, Winston-Salem, North Carolina (group)

'Tenses: Artist in Residence 2015–16',
THE STUDIO MUSEUM IN HARLEM, New York (group)

'Intimisms',
JAMES COHAN, New York (group)

'Imitation of Life',
HOME, Manchester (group)

'Learning to See Color',
VICKI MYHREN GALLERY, UNIVERSITY OF DENVER SCHOOL OF ART (group)

2016

Cotter, Holland, 'What to See in New York Galleries This Week', The New York Times, 15 September

Smith, Roberta, 'What to see in New York Art Galleries This Week. "Intimisms"', The New York Times, 7 July

Kaack, Nicole, 'Conversation with Jordan Casteel', NYAQ, no. 6, November–February

Langmuir, Molly, '15 Women Artists Who Are Changing Their World – and Ours', Elle Magazine, December

---

2017

'Nights in Harlem',
CASEY KAPLAN, New York (solo)

'Jordan Casteel: Harlem Notes',
HARVEY B. GANTT CENTER, Charlotte, North Carolina (solo)

'The Half-Life of Love',
MASSACHUSETTS MUSEUM OF CONTEMPORARY ART (MASS MoCA), North Adams (group)

'Regarding the Figure',
THE STUDIO MUSEUM IN HARLEM, New York (group)

'Occupancies',
808 GALLERY, FAYE G. JO AND JAMES STONE GALLERY AND THE ANNEX, BOSTON UNIVERSITY (group)

'Group Show',
THE CANTOR ARTS CENTER, STANFORD UNIVERSITY, California (group)

2017

Wylde, Kaitlin, '7 Contemporary Artists Keeping Traditions Alive', NYLON, 6 March

Clinton, Leah, 'Jordan Casteel: On the Power of Art Right Now', Elle Magazine, 13 March

Herriman, Kat, 'Jordan Casteel', Interview Magazine, August

'Jordan Casteel', The New Yorker, September

D'Souza, Aruna, 'Painting in Black and White: Race and The New Figurative Art', VICE, September

Noor, Tausif, 'Jordan Casteel', Artforum, September

D'Arcy, David, 'In New Portraits, Jordan Casteel Makes Eye Contact With the Men of Harlem', NY Observer, 27 September

Crain, Jonathan, 'People Person', Barneys The Window, Fall

Geers, David, 'Acts of Recognition', Frieze, no. 191, October

---

2018

'One Day at a Time: Manny Farber and Termite Art',
MUSEUM OF CONTEMPORARY ART (MoCA), Los Angeles (group)

'Both, and',
STEVENSON, Cape Town (group)

2018

Petrovich, Dushko, 'The New Face of Portrait Painting', T: The New York Times Style Magazine, 12 February

Felsenthal, Julia, 'Jordan Casteel is Making You Look', Vogue, February

Wheeler, Andre-Naquian, 'Jordan Casteel's Harlem portraits shine a magical light on black experience', i-D Magazine, Spring

Danoghue, Katy, 'Jordan Casteel on What It's Like to Make People Really See Someone', Whitewall, 4 May

Knight, Christopher, 'Review: Helen Molesworth's final show at MOCA is the anti-celebrity show we need right now', Los Angeles Times, 19 October

Webb Evans, Tiana, 'Folks on Chairs: African-American Home Life as Seen Through the Lens of Art', Pin-Up, November

---

2019

'The Baayfalls',
THE HIGH LINE, New York (solo)

'The Practice of Freedom',
CASEY KAPLAN, New York (solo)

'Jordan Casteel: Returning the Gaze',
DENVER ART MUSEUM, toured to IRIS & B. GERALD CANTOR CENTER FOR VISUAL ARTS, STANFORD UNIVERSITY, Palo Alto, California (solo)

2019

Kazanjin, Dodie, 'In her First Solo Museum Show, Jordan Casteel's Humanizing Portraits Get Even Closer', Vogue, January

Smith, Mychal Denzel, 'Close-Up: Held Still', Artforum, February

Weathers, Chelsea, 'Jordan Casteel: Returning the Gaze at the Denver Art Museum', Artforum, April

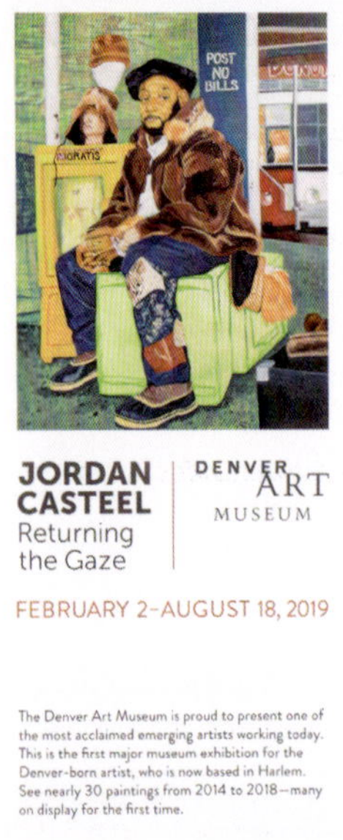

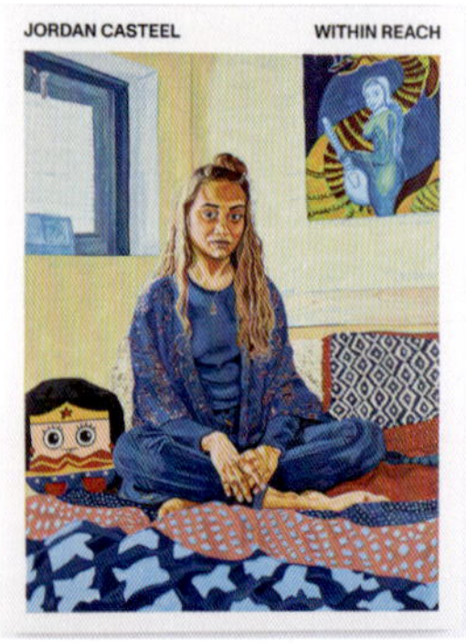

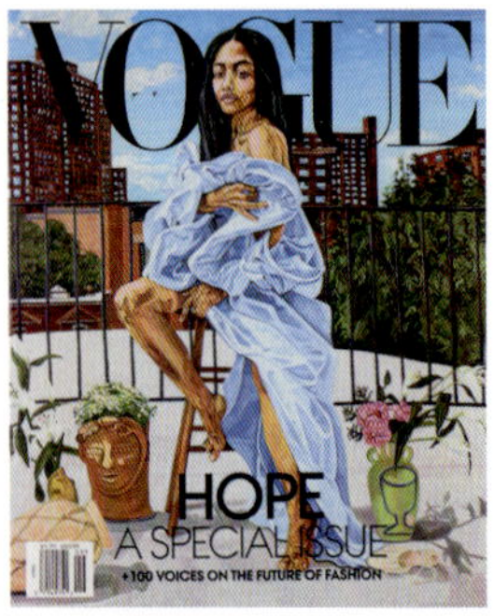

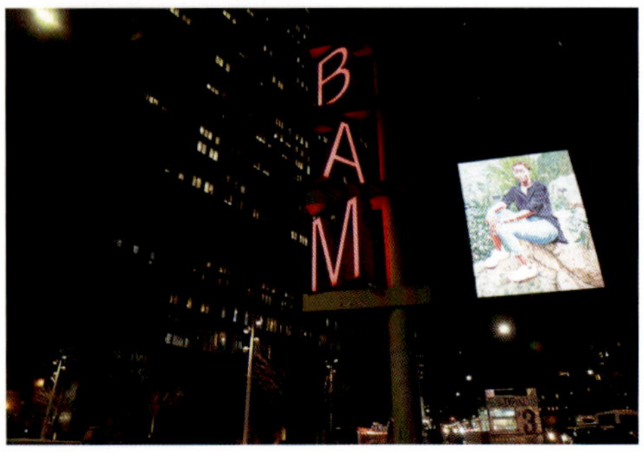

SELECTED EXHIBITIONS AND PROJECTS
2019–20

2019 (cont.)
'Every Day: Selections from the Collection',
BALTIMORE MUSEUM OF ART (group)

'Young, Gifted, and Black: The Lumpkin-Boccuzzi Family Collection',
OSILAS GALLERY, CONCORDIA COLLEGE, Bronxville, New York, toured to MANETTI SHREM MUSEUM OF ART, UNIVERSITY OF CALIFORNIA, Davis; LEHMAN COLLEGE, THE CITY UNIVERSITY OF NEW YORK (CUNY) (group)

'Side by Side: Selections from the Permanent Collection',
DALTON GALLERY, AGNES SCOTT COLLEGE, Decatur, Georgia (group)

'Punch',
JEFFREY DEITCH, Los Angeles (group)

'Harlem: In Situ',
ADDISON GALLERY OF AMERICAN ART, Massachusetts (group)

'Trance',
AÏSHTI FOUNDATION, Beirut (group)

'Black Refractions: Highlights from The Studio Museum in Harlem',
MUSEUM OF THE AFRICAN DIASPORA, San Francisco, toured to GIBBES MUSEUM OF ART, Charleston, South Carolina; KALAMAZOO INSTITUTE OF ARTS, Michigan; SMITH COLLEGE MUSEUM OF ART, Northampton, Massachusetts; FRYE ART MUSEUM, Seattle; UTAH MUSEUM OF FINE ARTS, Salt Lake City (group)

'She Persists: A Century of Women Artists in New York',
GRACIE MANSION, New York (group)

Delivered Agnes Scott College Commencement Speech, Decatur, Georgia, 11 May

SELECTED ARTICLES AND INTERVIEWS
2019–20

2019 (cont.)Sargent, Antwaun, 'Why an Alice Neel Painting Is Stuck in This Artist's Psyche', T: The New York Times Style Magazine, 28 May

Musiwa, Elaine, 'Swizz Beatz & Jordan Casteel, Hank Willis Thomas & Derrick Adams: A top collector and three trailblazing artists on breaking down barriers and recognizing the value of African American art', Departures Magazine, September

'Reimagining Color: Elevating the Ordinary', Scholastic, no. 2, October–November

2020
'Jordan Casteel: Within Reach',
NEW MUSEUM OF CONTEMPORARY ART, New York (solo)

'On Beauty',
SAN FRANCISCO MUSEUM OF MODERN ART (group)

'Never Done: 100 Years of Women in Politics and Beyond',
THE FRANCES YOUNG TANG TEACHING MUSEUM AND ART GALLERY, SKIDMORE COLLEGE, Saratoga Springs, New York (group)

2nd UPTOWN TRIENNIAL, New York (group)

'Art on the Grid',
PUBLIC ART FUND, New York (group)

'Tell Me Your Story',
KUNSTHAL KADE, Amersfoort, The Netherlands (group)

'Duro Olowu: Seeing Chicago',
MUSEUM OF CONTEMPORARY ART, Chicago (group)

2020
Obrist, Hans Ulrich, 'Jordan Casteel: Always a Maker', Muse Magazine, February

Lescaze, Zoë, 'Jordan Casteel Won't Let You Look Away', The New York Times, 14 February

Packard, Cassie, 'Reciprocating Gaze: Jordan Casteel Interviewed by Cassie Packard', Bomb, April

Wolpow, Nina, 'ArtSeen, Jordan Casteel: Within Reach', The Brooklyn Rail, April

Miss Rosen, 'Celebrating our essential humanity in the paintings of Jordan Casteel', Document Journal, 15 April

Steinhauer, Jillian, 'Portraits That More Than Meet The Eye', The New York Times, 29 April

Belcove, Julie, 'From the Leonardo at the Louvre to the Rise of Jordan Casteel: The Best of the Art World', Robb Report, 16 June

Lee, Yaniya, 'Inside 'Young Gifted And Black': A Project Celebrating The Great Black Artists Of Our Time', Vogue UK, August

Kazanjian, Dodie, 'The Making of Vogue's September 2020 Covers', Vogue, August

Fateman, Johanna, 'Goings on About Town: Jordan Casteel', The New Yorker, September

Wetzler, Rachel, 'Real Work: The Work of Realist Art', Art in America, September

Libbey, Harrington, 'New York's Reopened Museums: Where to Go and What to See', The New York Times, 10 September

SELECTED EXHIBITIONS AND PROJECTS
2021–23

SELECTED ARTICLES AND INTERVIEWS
2021–23

2021

'There is a Season',
MASSIMO DE CARLO, London (solo)

'Rituals of Resilience',
MINNEAPOLIS INSTITUTE OF ART (group)

'Bodywork: Discomfort and Existence',
MASSIMO DE CARLO, Milan (group)

'Let Freedom Ring',
BROOKLYN ACADEMY OF MUSIC, New York (group)

'The Human Body',
HILL ART FOUNDATION, New York (group)

'A Face Like Mine',
THE MATTATUCK MUSEUM, Waterbury, Connecticut (group)

'And I will wear you in my heart of heart',
THE FLAG ART FOUNDATION, New York (group)

'Knowledge of the Past Is the Key to the Future',
THE METROPOLITAN MUSEUM OF ART, New York (group)

'Crystal Bridges: The First Decade',
CRYSTAL BRIDGES MUSEUM OF AMERICAN ART, Bentonville, Arkansas (group)

'New Time: Art and Feminisms in the 21st Century',
BERKELEY ART MUSEUM, UNIVERSITY OF CALIFORNIA (group)

'Multiple Voices/Multiple Stories',
ROLLINS MUSEUM OF ART, Winter Park, Florida (group)

'The Nancy and Sean Cotton Collection',
DETROIT INSTITUTE OF ARTS (group)

'Permanent Collection 2021',
PEREZ ART MUSEUM MIAMI (PAMM), Miami (group)

'Black American Portraits',
LOS ANGELES COUNTY MUSEUM OF ART (LACMA), toured to SPELMAN COLLEGE OF FINE ART, Atlanta; MEMPHIS BROOKS MUSEUM OF ART (group)

Wins a MacArthur Foundation Fellowship Award

2021

Tillet, Ufeffby Salamishah, 'How the Studio Museum in Harlem Transformed the Art World Forever', Harper's Bazaar, 26 February

Williams, Victor, 'Meet The Artist Who Created God Bless the Child, Featured on Time's Cover', Time Magazine, 13 May

Greenberger, Alex, 'Artists Jordan Casteel and Daniel Lind Ramos, Historian Nicole Fleetwood Win MacArthur Fellowships', ARTnews, September

Hussein, Nimco, 'Jordan Casteel Finds Beauty in the Fleeting Commonplace', Frieze, no. 224, November–December

Ogunnaike, Lola, 'Living The Dream', Architectural Digest, December

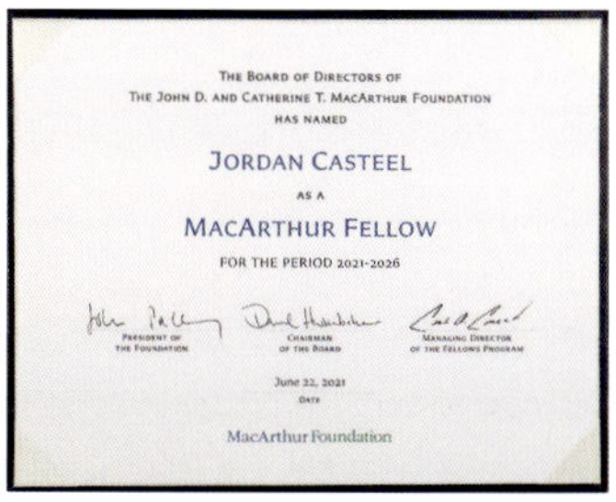
THE BOARD OF DIRECTORS OF
THE JOHN D. AND CATHERINE T. MACARTHUR FOUNDATION
HAS NAMED
JORDAN CASTEEL
AS A
MACARTHUR FELLOW
FOR THE PERIOD 2021-2026
PRESIDENT OF THE FOUNDATION
CHAIRMAN OF THE BOARD
MANAGING DIRECTOR OF THE FELLOWS PROGRAM
June 22, 2021
DATE
MacArthur Foundation

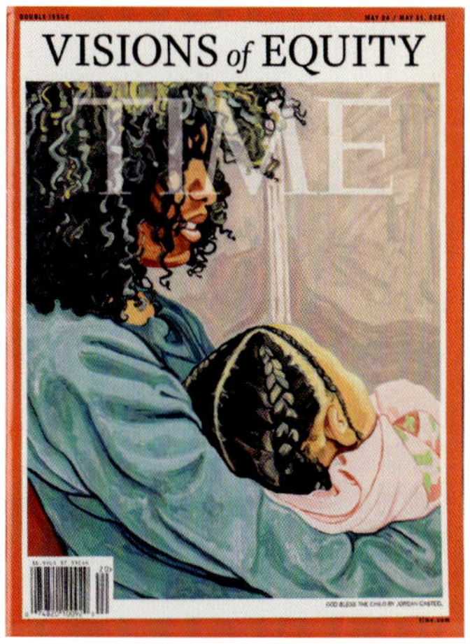

2022

'In bloom',
CASEY KAPLAN, New York (solo)

'Women Painting Women',
THE MODERN, Fort Worth, Texas (group)

'To Begin Again, Artists and Childhood',
INSTITUTE OF CONTEMPORARY ART, Boston (group)

'Dark Light, Realism in the Age of Post Truth. Selections Salamè Collection',
AÏSHTI FOUNDATION, Jal El Dib, Lebanon (group)

'Fashioning America: Grit to Glamour',
CRYSTAL BRIDGES MUSEUM OF ART, Bentonville, Arkansas (group)

2022

Gay, Roxanne, 'Where Artist Jordan Casteel Sees Herself Going', The Cut, February

Garcia, Sandra E., 'Jordan Casteel Artist: Thinking In Her Studio', T: The New York Times Style Magazine, 21 April

Berman, Judy, 'Jordan Casteel: 33. Vibrant painter', Time Magazine 100 Next, 10 October

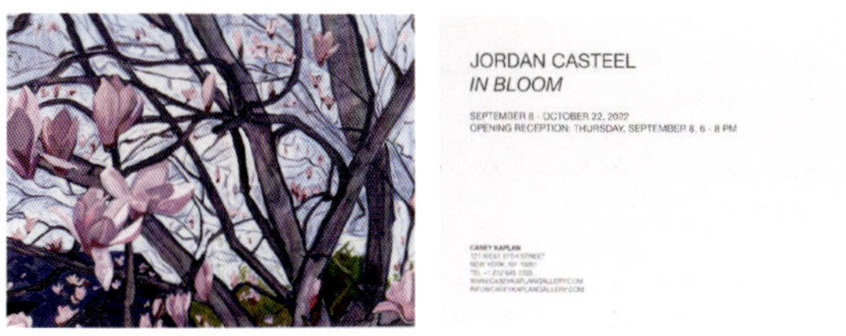

2023

'Jordan Casteel: Recent Landscapes',
CASEY KAPLAN, New York (solo)

2023

'Six Questions to Jordan Casteel', Aperture, no. 250

Patterson, Sara Elise, 'Jordan Casteel: The Acclaimed Painter of People — and Now Plants', Kinfolk, no. 48, Summer

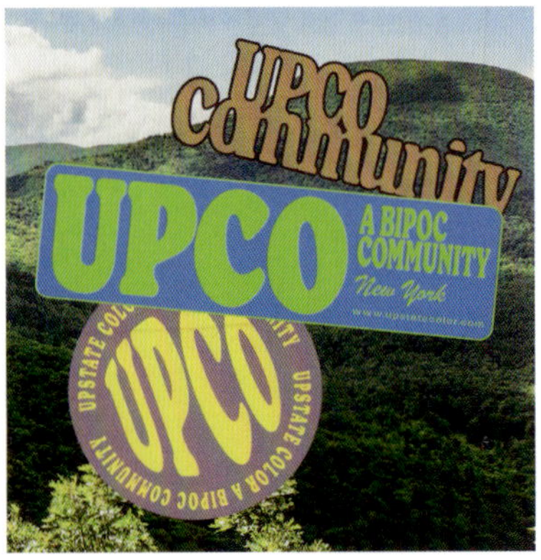

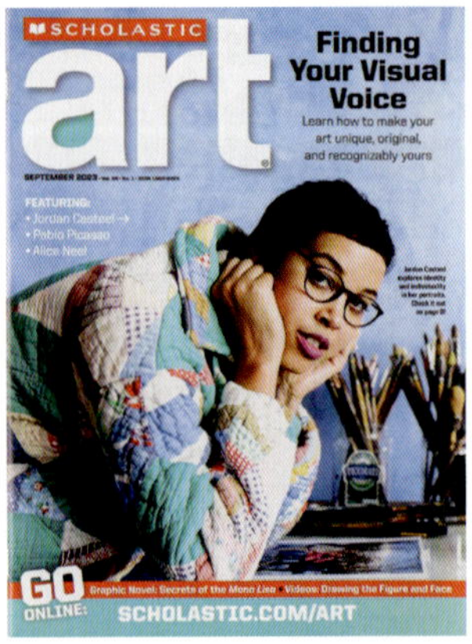

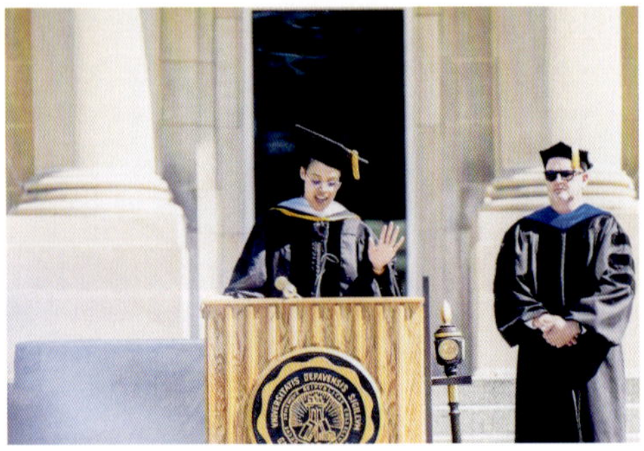

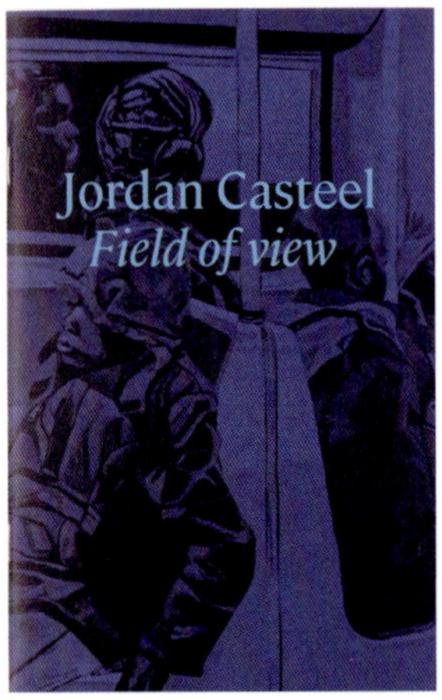

SELECTED EXHIBITIONS AND PROJECTS
2022–25

SELECTED ARTICLES AND INTERVIEWS
2022–25

2023 (cont.)

'In Our Eyes: Women's, Nonbinary, and Transgender Perspectives from the Collection',
ROLLINS MUSEUM OF ART, Orlando, Florida (group)

'Long Story Short',
MUSEUM OF CONTEMPORARY ART (MoCA), Los Angeles (group)

'In New York, Thinking of You',
THE FLAG ART FOUNDATION, New York (group)

'Fashioning America: Grit to Glamour',
NEW ORLEANS MUSEUM OF ART (group)

'The Culture: Hip Hop and Contemporary Art in the 21st Century',
BALTIMORE MUSEUM OF ART, toured to SAINT LOUIS ART MUSEUM; SCHIRN KUNSTHALLE, Frankfurt; CINCINNATI ART MUSEUM, Ohio; ART GALLERY OF ONTARIO, Toronto (group)

'Kindred Worlds: The Priscila and Alvin Hudgins Collection',
HUDSON RIVER MUSEUM, New York (group)

'Framing the Female Gaze: Women Artists and the New Historicism',
LEHMAN COLLEGE ART GALLERY, New York (group)

Receives a DePauw University Honorary Degree, Greencastle, Indiana

Elected to Board of Trustees of the Metropolitan Museum of Art, New York

2023 (cont.)

'Q&A with Jordan Casteel: This Painter tells Scholastic Art how and why she makes portraits', Scholastic Art, September

---

2024

'Jordan Casteel: Field of view',
HILL ART FOUNDATION, New York (solo)

'A New Subjectivity 1979/2024',
PARRISH ART MUSEUM, Water Mill, New York (group)

'Day for Night: New American Realism',
GALLERIE NAZIONALI BARBERINI CORSINI, Rome (group)

'Giants: Art from the Dean Collection of Swizz Beatz and Alicia Keys',
BROOKLYN MUSEUM, New York, toured to THE HIGH MUSEUM, Atlanta; MINNEAPOLIS INSTITUTE OF ART (group)

'The Time is Always Now: Artists Reframe the Black Figure',
NATIONAL PORTRAIT GALLERY, London, toured to THE BOX, Plymouth, England, PHILADELPHIA MUSEUM OF ART; NORTH CAROLINA MUSEUM OF ART, Raleigh (group)

'Ancestral: Afro-Americas (United States and Brazil)',
MUSEU DE ARTE BRASILEIRA, São Paulo (group)

Wins the John Koch Award, American Academy of Arts and Letters, New York

2024

Lee, Shannon, 'The group forging a community of color upstate', Times Union, 22 February

Fortini, Amanda, 'Is There Something Radical About Painting Flowers?', T: The New York Times Style Magazine, 28 February

Sporn, Stephanie, 'Artist Jordan Casteel's "Best Show Yet" Pairs Her Richly Patterned Paintings with Batsheva Hay's Mad Cap Furniture', Vogue, September

Fequiere, Roxanne, 'The T List: Six things we recommend this week', T: The New York Times Style Magazine, 11 September

Wetzler, Rachel, 'Beauty Treatment', Artforum, December

2025

'Jordan Casteel: A Presentation of Work',
THADDAEUS ROPAC, London (solo)

CASEY KAPLAN, New York (solo)

BIBLIOGRAPHY

MONOGRAPHS AND ARTIST'S BOOKS

Hart, Rebecca R., Isolde Brielmaier, Greg Tate and Elizabeth Alexander, Jordan Casteel: Returning the Gaze, Denver Art Museum, 2019

Gioni, Massimiliano, Amanda Hunt, Dawoud Bey, Thelma Golden, Lauren Haynes and Lisa Phillips, Jordan Casteel: Within Reach, New Museum of Contemporary Art, New York, 2020

Haynes, Lauren, and J. Tomilson Hill, Jordan Casteel: Field of View, Hill Art Foundation, New York, 2024

EXHIBITION CATALOGUES AND SURVEYS

Deitch, Jeffrey, Aria Dean, Alison M. Gingeras and Johanna Fateman, Unrealism: New Figurative Painting, Rizzoli Electa, New York, 2019

Erickson, Ruth, To Begin Again: Artists and Childhood, Distributed Art Publishers, New York, 2023

Eshun, Ekow, Bernardine Evaristo, Esi Edugyan and Dorothy Price The Time is Always Now: Artists Reframe the Black Figure, National Portrait Gallery, London, 2024

Gingeras, Alison M., Elizabeth Fullerton, et al, Great Women Painters, Phaidon, London, 2022

Gioni, Massimiliano, Dark Light: Realism in the Age of Post-Truths. Selections from the Tony and Elham Salamé Collection–Aïshti Foundation, Aïshti Foundation, Beirut, and Skira, Milan, 2023

Gioni, Massimiliano, and Flaminia Gennari Santori, Day for Night: New American Realism, Gallerie Nazionali Barberini Corsini, Rome, and Skira, Milan, 2024

Godfrey, Mark, and Katy Siegel, Making Their Mark: Art by Women in the Shah Garg Collection, Gregory R. Miller & Co. and the Shah Garg Collection, New York, 2023

Golden, Thelma, Connie Choi, Kellie Jones, Pauline Willis, Eliza A. Butler, Akili Tommasino, Taylor Aldridge, Larry Ossei Mensah, Daniela Fifi et al, Black Refractions: Highlights from The Studio Museum in Harlem, Rizzoli, New York, 2019

Karnes, Andrea, Women Painting Women, DelMonico Books, New York, and Modern Art Museum of Fort Worth, Texas, 2022

Kim, Christine, Black American Portraits, Distributed Art Publishers, New York, 2023

Jansen, Charlotte, et al, Prime: Art's Next Generation, Phaidon, London, 2022

Martin, Courtney J., Mary Schmidt Campbell, Chris Bedford, Joost Boosland, Mark Bradford, Mark, Alexis Clark, Nicholas Cullinan, Mark Godfrey, Norman L. Kleeblatt and Katy Siegel, Four Generations: The Joyner/Giuffrida Collection of Abstract Art, Gregory R. Miller & Co., New York, 2019

Molesworth, Helen, Gregg Bordowitz (eds), Glenn Ligon, Sue Schardt and Jason Simon, One Day at a Time: Manny Farber and Termite Art, Museum of Contemporary Art, Los Angeles, 2019

Naeem, Asma (ed.), Gamynne Guillotte, Hannah Klemm and Andréa Purnell, The Culture: Hip Hop & Contemporary Art in the 21st Century, Gregory R. Miller & Co., New York, 2023

Pasternak, Anne, Kimberli Gant and Indira A. Abiskaroon, Giants: Art from the Dean Collection of Swizz Beatz and Alicia Keys, Brooklyn Museum and Phaidon, New York, 2024

Perrée, Rob, Tell Me Your Story, Kunsthal KAdE, Amersfoort, The Netherlands, 2000

Sanghvi, Minita, and Rachel Seligman, Never Done: 100 Years of Women in Politics and Beyond, Frances Tang Teaching Museum, Skidmore College, Saratoga Springs, New York, 2020

Sargent, Antwaun, Graham C. Boettcher, Jessica Bell Brown, Connie H. Choi, Anthony Graham, Lauren Haynes, Jamillah James, Thomas J. Lax, Hallie Ringle, Adeze Wilford, Gordon Dearborn Wilkins, Matt Wycoff, Bernard Lumpkin and Thelma Golden, Young, Gifted, and Black: The Lumpkin-Boccuzzi Family Collection, Distributed Art Publishers and Lehman College at City University of New York, 2020

Schwarz, Gabrielle, et al, Great Women Artists, Phaidon, London, 2019

SELECTED PUBLIC COLLECTIONS

ALFOND COLLECTION OF CONTEMPORARY ART, CORNELL FINE ARTS MUSEUM, Rollins College, Winter Park, Florida

THE ART INSTITUTE OF CHICAGO

CRYSTAL BRIDGES MUSEUM OF AMERICAN ART, Bentonville, Arkansas

DENVER ART MUSEUM

THE FORD FOUNDATION, New York

LOS ANGELES COUNTY MUSEUM OF ART

NASHER MUSEUM OF ART AT DUKE UNIVERSITY, Durham, North Carolina

MEMPHIS BROOKS MUSEUM OF ART

THE METROPOLITAN MUSEUM OF ART, NEW YORK

MINNEAPOLIS INSTITUTE OF ART

MUSEUM OF CONTEMPORARY ART, Los Angeles

MUSEUM OF MODERN ART, New York

PÉREZ ART MUSEUM, Miami

SAN FRANCISCO MUSEUM OF MODERN ART

SOLOMON R. GUGGENHEIM MUSEUM, New York

IRIS & B. GERALD CANTOR CENTER FOR VISUAL ARTS AT STANFORD UNIVERSITY, California

THE STUDIO MUSEUM IN HARLEM, New York

WHITNEY MUSEUM OF AMERICAN ART, New York

ILLUSTRATED WORKS

COMPARATIVE IMAGES

PHAIDON PRESS LTD.
2 COOPERAGE YARD
LONDON E15 2QR

PHAIDON PRESS INC.
111 BROADWAY
NEW YORK, NY 10006

PHAIDON SARL
55, RUE TRAVERSIÈRE
75012 PARIS

PHAIDON.COM

First published 2025

ISBN:
978-1-83866-881-5
Signed Edition:
978-1-83729-117-5

A CIP catalogue record of this book is available from the British Library and the Library of Congress.

Commissioning Editor
Michele Robecchi

Production Controller
Gary Hayes

Design
Melanie Mues, Mues Design, London

Layout
Cantina, London

Printed in China

PUBLISHER'S ACKNOWLEDGEMENTS

Special thanks to Jennifer Hoffman-Williamson at Jordan Casteel Studio, New York; Casey Kaplan, Veronica Levitt and Kaytlin Nodine at Casey Kaplan, New York; Caitlin Arnell Argles, James Brown, Clive Burroughs, Jude Grover, David Hammons, Batsheva Hay, Claudette Johnson, Melissa Larner, Kerry James Marshall, Bridget McCarthy, Violeta Mitrova, João Mota, Michelle Pamisa, Mansa Ra, Tracey Smith, Hans Stofregen, Andie Trainer, Elaine Ward, Jonathan Whale.

We would also like to thank the following institutions: Solomon R. Guggenheim Museum, New York/Gift, Mr. and Mrs. Gus and Judith Leiber, 1988; Smithsonian American Art Museum/Purchase through the Julia D. Strong Endowment and the Smithsonian Institution Collections Acquisition Program/Gift of Mr. and Mrs. Alfred T. Morris, Jr. Washington, DC; Baltimore Museum of Art/The Cone Collection, formed by Dr. Claribel Cone and Miss Etta Cone of Baltimore, Maryland/Pearlstone Family Fund/The Andy Warhol Foundation for the Visual Arts, Pittsburgh/Art Fund established with exchange funds from gifts of Dr. and Mrs. Edgar F. Berman, Equitable Bank, N.A., Geoffrey Gates, Sandra O. Moose, National Endowment for the Arts, Lawrence Rubin, Philip M. Stern, and Alan J. Zakon/Baltimore Museum of Art, Gift of the Childe Hassam Fund of The American Academy of Arts and Letters, New York; Whitney Museum of American Art, New York/with funds from the Photography Committee/Yale Art Gallery/Janet and Simeon Braguin Fund, New Haven, CT; Museum of Contemporary Art, Chicago/Katherine S. Schamberg; The Museum of Modern Art, New York; The Studio Museum in Harlem, New York/Hudgins Family; Morgan & Morgan, Dobbs Ferry, New York; The North Carolina Museum of Art, Raleigh/Purchased with funds from the State of North Carolina; Artists Rights Society (ARS), New York; DACS (Design and Artists Copyright Society), London.

Photographers: Dan Bradica, Jordan Casteel, John Gruen, Dario Lasagni, Adam Reich, David Schulze, Todd-White Art, Jason Wyche.

ARTIST'S ACKNOWLEDGEMENTS

I am appreciative of everyone who contributed time, thought and passion to help bring this project to life. That includes Keith Fox, who helped shepherd it forward from the beginning, and the support of Phaidon: Michele Robecchi and Gary Hayes.

My gratitude extends to those who helped lay the foundation on which I am able to show up as the artist I am today: David Schulze, Casey Kaplan, Veronica Levitt, Kaytlin Nodine, Jennifer Hoffman-Williamson, Thaddaeus Ropac, Anaïs Ferrier, Sarah Rustin, Thelma Golden, Darren Walker, Elizabeth Alexander, Sarah Lewis, Sheena Wagstaff, Lauren Haynes, Amanda Hunt, Robert Storr, Max Hollein, Sam Messer, Nell Ruby, Anne Beidler, Priscilla Jeffery, Isolde Breilmaier, Lauren Y. Casteel, Marcia Cantarella, Alexandria Okon, Wayde McIntosh, EJ Hill, Amy Sherald, Toyin Ojih Odutola, Genevieve Gaignard, Darrell Anderson, Dawoud Bey, Sargent's Daughters, Amit Saxena, Timothy Stockton, James Boyd, the late Yvonne Boyd, Greg Tate and Margaret B. Young.

It is through taking risks and exploration of self – new experiences and environments – that I have found my voice. 18 years coming of age in Denver; four years learning with women at Agnes Scott College; one semester oil painting in Cortona, Italy with the University of Georgia; two years of inspiration and dedication at Yale School of Art; a year as a resident at The Studio Museum in Harlem and five years as a professor at Rutgers University – Newark. Harlem was the first place in New York I could call home. Now the Hudson Valley and Upstate Color ground me all over again.

Last but definitely not least – to every person who returned my 'hello', welcoming me and my painting practice into their lives, thank you. I am because of you. I have learned to see myself most fully through the knowing of you. Thank you for trusting me, moving with faith, and reminding us all of the beauty that exists when you choose to see deeply.

CONTEMPORARY ARTISTS:

Contemporary Artists is a series of authoritative and extensively illustrated studies of today's most important artists. Each title offers a comprehensive survey of an individual artist's work and a range of art writing contributed by an international spectrum of authors, all leading figures in their fields, from art history and criticism to philosophy, cultural theory and fiction. Each study provides incisive analysis and multiple perspectives on contemporary art and its inspiration. These are essential source books for everyone concerned with art today.

MARINA ABRAMOVIĆ KLAUS BIESENBACH, KRISTINE STILES, CHRISSIE ILES VITO ACCONCI FRAZER WARD, MARK C. TAYLOR, JENNIFER BLOOMER AI WEIWEI HANS ULRICH OBRIST, KAREN SMITH, BERNARD FIBICHER DOUG AITKEN DANIEL BIRNBAUM, AMANDA SHARP, JÖRG HEISER PAWEŁ ALTHAMER ADAM SZYMCZYK, ROMAN KURZMEYER, SUZANNE COTTER FRANCIS ALŸS CUAUHTÉMOC MEDINA, RUSSELL FERGUSON, JEAN FISHER, MICHAEL TAUSSIG UTA BARTH PAMELA M. LEE, MATTHEW HIGGS, JEREMY GILBERT-ROLFE CHRISTIAN BOLTANSKI DIDIER SEMIN, TAMAR GARB, DONALD KUSPIT MONICA BONVICINI ALEXANDER ALBERRO, JANET KRAYNAK, JULIANE REBENTISCH LOUISE BOURGEOIS PAULO HERKENHOFF (WITH THYRZA GOODEVE), ROBERT STORR, ALLAN SCHWARTZMAN MARK BRADFORD ANITA HILL, SEBASTIAN SMEE, CONNIE BUTLER CECILY BROWN COURTNEY J. MARTIN, JASON ROSENFELD, FRANCINE PROSE CAI GUO-QIANG DANA FRIIS-HANSEN, OCTAVIO ZAYA, TAKASHI SERIZAWA JORDAN CASTEEL LEGACY RUSSELL, ASMA NAEEM, KATHERINE BRINSON MAURIZIO CATTELAN NANCY SPECTOR, FRANCESCO BONAMI, BARBARA VANDERLINDEN, MASSIMILIANO GIONI VIJA CELMINS ROBERT GOBER, LANE RELYEA, BRIONY FER NIGEL COOKE DARIAN LEADER, TONY GODFREY, MARIE DARRIEUSSECQ RICHARD DEACON PIER LUIGI TAZZI, JON THOMPSON, PETER SCHJELDAHL, PENELOPE CURTIS TACITA DEAN JEAN-CHRISTOPHE ROYOUX, MARINA WARNER, GERMAINE GREER MARK DION LISA GRAZIOSE CORRIN, MIWON KWON, NORMAN BRYSON PETER DOIG ADRIAN SEARLE, KITTY SCOTT, CATHERINE GRENIER STAN DOUGLAS SCOTT WATSON, DIANA THATER, CAROL J. CLOVER MARLENE DUMAS DOMINIC VAN DEN BOOGERD, BARBARA BLOOM, MARIUCCIA CASADIO, ILARIA BONACOSSA JIMMIE DURHAM LAURA MULVEY, DIRK SNAUWAERT, MARK ALICE DURANT, KATE NESIN OLAFUR ELIASSON MADELEINE GRYNSZTEJN, DANIEL BIRNBAUM, MICHAEL SPEAKS ELMGREEN & DRAGSET LINDA YABLONSKY, MARTIN HERBERT, CONNIE BUTLER, JASON SCHMIDT CERITH WYN EVANS HANS ULRICH OBRIST, NANCY SPECTOR, DANIEL BIRNBAUM PETER FISCHLI AND DAVID WEISS ROBERT FLECK, BEATE SÖNTGEN, ARTHUR C. DANTO TOM FRIEDMAN DENNIS COOPER, BRUCE HAINLEY, ADRIAN SEARLE THEASTER GATES CAROL BECKER, LISA YUN LEE, ACHIM BORCHARDT-HUME ISA GENZKEN ALEX FARQUHARSON, DIEDRICH DIEDERICHSEN, SABINE BREITWIESER ANTONY GORMLEY ERNST GOMBRICH, JOHN HUTCHINSON, LELA B. NJATIN, W. J. T. MITCHELL DAN GRAHAM BIRGIT PELZER, MARK FRANCIS, BEATRIZ COLOMINA PAUL GRAHAM ANDREW WILSON, GILLIAN WEARING, CAROL SQUIERS SHILPA GUPTA ALEXANDRA MUNROE, NAV HAQ, ELVIRA DYANGANI OSE HANS HAACKE WALTER GRASSKAMP, MOLLY NESBIT, JON BIRD MONA HATOUM GUY BRETT, MICHAEL ARCHER, CATHERINE DE ZEGHER, NANCY SPECTOR SHARON HAYES JULIA BRYAN-WILSON, JEANNINE TANG, LANKA TATTERSALL THOMAS HIRSCHHORN BENJAMIN H. D. BUCHLOH, ALISON M. GINGERAS, CARLOS BASUALDO JIM HODGES JANE M SAKS, ROBERT HOBBS, JULIE AULT JENNY HOLZER DAVID JOSELIT, JOAN SIMON, RENATA SALECL RONI HORN LOUISE NERI, LYNNE COOKE, THIERRY DE DUVE CAMERON JAMIE PHILIPPE VERGNE, RALPH RUGOFF, ELENA FILIPOVIC CHRIS JOHANSON CORRINA PEIPON, BOB NICKAS, JULIE DEAMER RASHID JOHNSON CLAUDIA RANKINE, SAMPADA ARANKE, AKILI TOMMASINO ILYA KABAKOV BORIS GROYS, DAVID A. ROSS, IWONA BLAZWICK ALEX KATZ ROBERT STORR, CARTER RATCLIFF, IWONA BLAZWICK, BARRY SCHWABSKY ON KAWARA 'TRIBUTE', JONATHAN WATKINS, RENÉ DENIZOT KAWS DAN NADEL, THOMAS CROW, CLARE LILLEY, JASON SCHMIDT MIKE KELLEY ISABELLE GRAW, JOHN C. WELCHMAN, ANTHONY VIDLER MARY KELLY MARGARET IVERSEN, DOUGLAS CRIMP, HOMI K. BHABHA WILLIAM KENTRIDGE CAROLYN CHRISTOV-BAKARGIEV, DAN CAMERON, J. M. COETZEE JANNIS KOUNELLIS 'TRIBUTE', PHILIP LARRATT-SMITH, RUDI FUCHS YAYOI KUSAMA AKIRA TATEHATA, LAURA HOPTMAN, UDO KULTERMANN, CHATERINE TAFT CHRISTIAN MARCLAY JENNIFER GONZALEZ, KIM GORDON, MATTHEW HIGGS KERRY JAMES MARSHALL CHARLES GAINES, GREG TATE, LAURENCE RASSEL PAUL McCARTHY KRISTINE STILES, RALPH RUGOFF, MASSIMILIANO GIONI, ROBERT STORR CILDO MEIRELES PAULO HERKENHOFF, GERARDO MOSQUERA, DAN CAMERON WILLIAM MONK ISABELLE GRAW, TERRY R. MYERS, ÀNGELS MIRALDA WANGECHI MUTU ADRIENNE EDWARDS, COURTNEY J. MARTIN, KELLIE JONES, CHIKA OKEKE-AGULU YOKO ONO LAURIE ANDERSON, ERIKO OSAKA, THIERRY RASPAIL LUCY ORTA ROBERTO PINTO, NICOLAS BOURRIAUD, MAIA DAMIANOVIC JEAN-MICHEL OTHONIEL GAY GASSMANN, CATHERINE GRENIER, ROBERT STORR TREVOR PAGLEN LAUREN CORNELL, JULIA BRYAN-WILSON, OMAR KHOLEIF JORGE PARDO CHRISTINE VÉGH, LANE RELYEA, CHRIS KRAUS NICOLAS PARTY STÉPHANE AQUIN, STEFAN BANZ, ALI SUBOTNICK, MELISSA HYDE ADAM PENDLETON ALEC MAPES-FRANCES, ADRIENNE EDWARDS, ANDRÉA PICARD RAYMOND PETTIBON DENNIS COOPER, ROBERT STORR, ULRICH LOOCK RICHARD PRINCE ROSETTA BROOKS, JEFF RIAN, LUC SANTE NEO RAUCH INGRID MÖSSINGER, RALPH KEUNING, DAVID SALLE LILI REYNAUD-DEWAR ÉLISABETH LEBOVICI, DIEDRICH DIEDERICHSEN, MONIKA SZEWCZYK PIPILOTTI RIST HANS ULRICH OBRIST, PEGGY PHELAN, ELIZABETH BRONFEN UGO RONDINONE LAURA HOPTMAN, ERIK VERHAGEN, NICHOLAS BAUME, JASON SCHMIDT DAAN ROOSEGAARDE NICO DASWANI, FUMIO NANJO, CAROL BECKER STERLING RUBY KATE FOWLE, FRANKLIN SIRMANS, JESSICA MORGAN ANRI SALA HANS ULRICH OBRIST, MARK GODFREY, LIAM GILLICK DORIS SALCEDO NANCY PRINCENTHAL, CARLOS BASUALDO, ANDREAS HUYSSEN WILHELM SASNAL ANDRZEJ PRZYWARA, DOMINIC EICHLER, JÖRG HEISER THOMAS SCHÜTTE JULIAN HEYNEN, JAMES LINGWOOD, ANGELA VETTESE DANA SCHUTZ HAMZA WALKER, DAN NADEL, LYNNE TILLMAN STEPHEN SHORE MICHAEL FRIED, CHRISTY LANGE, JOEL STERNFELD ROMAN SIGNER PAULA VAN DEN BOSCH, GERHARD MACK, JEREMY MILLAR LORNA SIMPSON KELLIE JONES, THELMA GOLDEN, CHRISSIE ILES, NAOMI BECKWITH NANCY SPERO JON BIRD, JO ANNA ISAAK, SYLVÈRE LOTRINGER SIMON STARLING FRANCESCO MANACORDA, DIETER ROELSTRAETE, JANET HARBORD FRANK STELLA ANDRIANNA CAMPBELL, KATE NESIN, LUCAS BLALOCK, TERRY RICHARDSON JESSICA STOCKHOLDER BARRY SCHWABSKY, LYNNE TILLMAN, LYNNE COOKE, GERMANO CELANT SARAH SZE OKWUI ENWEZOR, BENJAMIN H. D. BUCHLOH, LAURA HOPTMAN WOLFGANG TILLMANS PETER HALLEY, JAN VERWOERT, MIDORI MATSUI, JOHANNA BURTON LUC TUYMANS ULRICH LOOCK, JUAN VICENTE ALIAGA, NANCY SPECTOR, HANS RUDOLF REUST BERNAR VENET FLORENCE DERIEUX, BARRY SCHWABSKY, CLAIRE LILLEY ADRIÁN VILLAR-ROJAS HANS ULRICH OBRIST, CAROLYN CHRISTOV-BAKARGIEV, EUNGIE JOO JEFF WALL THIERRY DE DUVE, ARIELLE PÉLENC, BORIS GROYS, JEAN-FRANÇOIS CHEVRIER, MARK LEWIS GILLIAN WEARING RUSSELL FERGUSON, DONNA DE SALVO, JOHN SLYCE LAWRENCE WEINER BENJAMIN H. D. BUCHLOH, ALEXANDER ALBERRO AND ALICE ZIMMERMAN, DAVID BATCHELOR FRANZ WEST ROBERT FLECK, BICE CURIGER, NEAL BENEZRA JONAS WOOD MARK GROTJAHN, HELEN MOLESWORTH, IAN ALTEVEER YIN XIUZHEN HOU HANRU, WU HUNG, STEPHANIE ROSENTHAL LISA YUSKAVAGE ARIEL LEVY, BARRY SCHWABSKY, LENA DUNHAM, JASON SCHMIDT ZHANG HUAN ROSELEE GOLDBERG, YILMAZ DZIEWOR, ROBERT STORR